The Commonwealth of Massachusetts
Department of the State Treasurer
State House
Boston, Mass. 02133

Shannon P. O'Brien
Treasurer and Receiver General

Dear Public Employee,

Congratulations! You have taken an important step toward taking control of your financial future by enrolling in the Commonwealth's 457 Deferred Compensation Plan. Ours is a nationally recognized retirement plan that offers participants a fully diversified array of investment options and services that can, in appropriate combinations, meet the varied investment needs of all our public employees.

Your participation means that you are taking advantage of one of the very best supplemental retirement plans in the country. Over the course of my term as Treasurer, we've made important upgrades to administration services and investment options in your Deferred Compensation Plan so that it now provides the high-quality investment and educational resources you need to construct a diversified portfolio. Along with a suitable long-term investing strategy, the Plan now offers, at remarkably low cost, all the tools you need to succeed.

Please accept *Let's Talk Money* with my compliments. I hope you will find it an invaluable resource in managing your personal finances, including your retirement savings. Written in a style we can all understand, *Let's Talk Money* is filled with hundreds of money management tips and easy-to-use worksheets to help you get organized. Nationally recognized authors Dee Lee and David Caruso have done a terrific job bringing it all together. I know you will enjoy *Let's Talk Money*—my own copy is well-worn and full of margin notes!

Your financial life is a work in progress. You have taken an important step toward a secure retirement by enrolling in the Deferred Compensation Plan, and I hope you continue to take action in other areas of your financial life. I encourage you to use your Plan wisely to prepare for a comfortable retirement.

Good luck!

Warm regards,

Shannon P. O'Brien
State Treasurer

Let's Talk Money

Your Complete Personal Finance Guide

Dee Lee
David Caruso

2002 Updated Edition

Chandler House Press
Worcester, Massachusetts

Let's Talk Money
Your Complete Personal Finance Guide, Updated 2002 Edition

Copyright © 2002 by John A. Woods, CWL Publishing Enterprises

This is a *CWL Publishing Enterprises Book*, developed and produced for Chandler House Press by CWL Publishing Enterprises, John A. Woods, President, www.cwlpub.com.

Retail price: $19.95

ISBN 1-886284-40-7
Library of Congress Catalog Card Number 98-89745
Special Edition
ABCDEFGHIJK

Published by
Chandler House Press
335 Chandler Street
Worcester, MA 01602 USA

Cover Design
Beck Designs

Chandler House Press books are available at special discounts for bulk purchases. For more information about how to arrange such purchases, please contact Chandler House Press, 335 Chandler Street, Worcester, MA 01602, or call (800) 642-6657, or fax (508) 756-9425, or find us on the World Wide Web at www.chandlerhousepress.com.

Disclaimer: The opinions expressed herein are solely those of the authors and are based on the authors' personal experiences. They are not intended to be the norm for all investors. Reasonable care has been taken in the preparation of the text to ensure its clarity and accuracy. The book is sold with the understanding that the author and the publisher are not engaged in rendering legal or accounting services. Laws vary from state to state, and readers with specific financial questions should seek the services of a professional advisor. The authors and publisher specifically disclaim any liability, loss, or risk, personal or otherwise, which is incurred as a consequence, directly or indirectly, of the use and application of any of the contents of this book.

Contents

Preface

The two of us sat in a restaurant in Boston several years ago locked in a heated discussion about writing a book. There were so many things we wanted our readers to know and we wanted the information to be easy to digest. We wanted a book that people would use as a resource. We wanted a book that could walk someone through the entire process of financial planning and not intimidate anybody, a book that covered most of the important financial information that a person would use in a lifetime.

We understand that most people have little or no time for extra reading, so we wrote the book to help readers attack one financial problem at a time, if they so chose. The book should be read from cover to cover, but many of you might not have the time to do that. So we used a modular style. If you want to get out of debt and set up a spending plan, you read the first section of the book. Then, when you've done that and you now have dollars to invest, you move on to the sections on setting goals or investing.

We believe that financial planning can be broken down into six simple steps.

✔ **What have you got?**

> Doing a net worth statement
> Figuring out where you spend your money
> Getting out of debt

✔ **What do you want from life?**

> What are your life goals—home, car, education, retirement?

✔ **How do you invest to achieve your goals?**

> Learn what it takes to be an intelligent investor.

✔ **What are the right investments for your goals?**

> Do you use stocks, mutual funds, or bonds?

✔ **What obstacles will you encounter along the way?**

> Find out why taxes and inflation are your mortal enemies.

✔ **How do you protect your assets?**

> What's out there to protect what you have achieved?
> What kind of insurance do you need?
> How fancy does your estate planning need to be?
> Where can you find professional help if you can't go it alone?

Our mission statement for our professional lives as well as for this book is to educate and motivate people so they can afford their dreams. The hardest thing for us to do is to motivate someone not only to buy this book, but also to read it, to understand it, and to put the lessons learned into practice.

We believe that the financial planning process is simple, but not easy. It's not easy because you have to be motivated; you need that persistent kick in the butt that pushes you to keep at it. But the things you need to do to make a better life for yourself are truly simple. And we will show you just how simple.

We would like you to think of our book as a blueprint for financial success and a tool kit showing you how to construct that success. The blueprint is your plan for the house of your dreams. It helps you decide how big the job will need to be, who's going to do what, and what resources you need to pay for it. You need a blueprint before you begin. The tool kit is the technical stuff that helps you build your dream house. Then, after you build the place, the odds are pretty good that you'll need to maintain it and improve it over time. If you can't do it on your own, we'll help you find someone who's qualified to lend a hand.

We've tried to intersperse good, solid financial information with a bit of motivation and humor that will get you from setting goals to learning how to protect your assets. Obviously, no one book can answer all your financial questions as thoroughly as you might need, but this book will be a good resource to start you in the right direction.

We've discovered over the years that for the most part investment decisions are going to be led by *emotions*, not by *intellect*. We are emotional beings, so most of us make up our minds based on our emotions and then we use our intellects to rationalize that we're right. You've got to understand and harness your emotions if you're going to achieve your financial goals.

We would like to wish you luck with your endeavor to bring order to your financial world and we hope we can be a part of your success.

Warm regards,
Dee Lee and Dave Caruso

Acknowledgments

A book like this is definitely a collaborative effort, and there are several people who have brought their skills and dedication to its completion. First we want to thank Dick Staron, publisher at Chandler House Press for getting behind this project. John Woods of CWL Publishing Enterprises was the book's champion from the start and was responsible for the its development and production. Bob Magnan also of CWL did a terrific job as editor. Dale Mann conceived and drew the wonderful cartoons that help bring the book's concepts to life. Jennifer Goguen, production manager at Chandler House Press was responsible for the final product you now hold in your hands. Thanks to all of them.

We also want to thank Jim Flewelling for his diligent research and insight to get the book completed. Doug Lee and Doris Huxley helped create many of the charts and worksheets you'll see through out the book. And a very special thank you to our families, friends, and staff for putting up with us as we waged the war of words to get this finished product out the door.

This book could not have been written without the support of our spouses and children, who had to endure the birth of this book. Dee's husband, Doug, who was always willing to create another graph or chart late at night. Her children, Jennifer and Bryan, who were often asked just to listen to something that had been written or were willing for her to share their stories throughout the book. David's wife, Diane, who did double duty with the kids while Daddy was busy writing, always had time to read a section and make a comment. And the kids, Alex and Laura, who gave up a lot of play time with Daddy this past year.

Now, *let's talk money!*

What Have You Got?

Part One is the first step in your financial planning process. We have some worksheets that you'll need to spend some time with so that you can get a handle on your finances. Figuring out your net worth will give you an essential starting point. What do you own and what do you owe?

Then we take a look at your cash flow. How much money are you earning? Are you living paycheck to paycheck? Or worse—does the money run out before the month does? We'll help you set up a spending plan so you can begin to save and invest.

Then we'll tackle the black hole of finances, debt. You know if you are over your head in debt and it's usually credit cards that got you there. We'll offer some practical tips to help you move from the red ink to the black ink and get your budget on track. We said this was the starting point, so we'll even attempt to help you organize your stuff. We can't promise superior results here, since you will be the one deciding what to keep and what to toss. But we'll make the decisions easy by providing you with a list of what to keep and even where to store it.

Chapter 1 | What'cha Got?

Taking Inventory

Think of your financial life as just one big bucket. What's in the bucket at any point in time is your *net worth*, the inventory of all the stuff that is yours. You pour your income, paychecks, interest, and dividends into this bucket. You also accumulate all of your other stuff in this bucket. Coming out of a faucet at the bottom of your bucket are your expenses. You decide how much you're going to spend and you can open or close that faucet. But there are two pinholes in your bucket you can't stop up easily—taxes and inflation. Your money leaks out of these holes all of the time. (We'll tell you more about these holes in Chapters 23 and 24.) We call what goes into your bucket and comes out of your bucket your *cash flow*. But what's in your bucket at any given time we call your *net worth*.

> *Money is better than poverty, if only for financial reasons.*
> —*Woody Allen*

Don't confuse your *income* with your *net worth*. Lots of people make oodles of money but aren't wealthy. Why? Because they spend every dime they make. You may have a lot coming into your bucket, but if most of it flows right out again you're not building your net worth. You're just spending what you make, mostly on stuff that becomes less valuable the minute you take it out of the store because it *depreciates*.

What you want to do is fill up your bucket with things that are going to become *more* valuable over time, such as investments, and not *less* valuable. You want things that *appreciate* in value, that add to what you've got in your bucket rather than taking away from it.

But we're getting a little ahead of ourselves. Before we talk about adding more to your bucket, let's find out what's already in it. As we mentioned just above, what's in that bucket is your net worth. But we need a way to figure out just what that is. A net worth statement is a snapshot, a financial picture of where you are financially on the day you sit down and prepare it.

Figuring out your net worth is the *starting point* for all financial planning. So that's why figuring out what's in your bucket is Chapter 1—just in case you wondered. We've included a net worth worksheet at the end of this chapter. We've broken out the categories, so that if you're coupled (when we think of coupled, the picture of two connected train cars comes to mind), there are three columns for you to fill in—for yourself, for your spouse, and joint. We did this because it will be useful to have things broken down like this when we talk about estate planning in Chapter 26.

Assets

The stuff in your bucket is your *assets*. Assets are *good*. For most of us, our two biggest assets are our homes and retirement investments.

Your home and other personal assets such as cars, furniture, jewelry, collectibles (yes, you can put in your Beanie Babies), snowmobiles, boats, and so on are what we call *lifestyle assets*. They're expressions of how you live, things you can enjoy and use now. Although you can sell these assets if necessary, their financial value and possibility of appreciating are not the major reasons you own them.

The next category of stuff is what we call *invested assets*. These assets hopefully are appreciating in value and helping you increase your net worth continuously over time. Some examples of these assets would be investments in mutual funds, stocks, and bonds or your retirement plans, such as 401(k) plans, 403(b) plans, and 457 plans. These assets are important to you because they will provide the money to help you reach your future goals.

> Rich or poor, it's nice to have money.
> —*Fred Theil*

We also have something on the worksheet called *cash equivalents*. These are assets that are in very safe types of investments and easy for you to turn into cash in case of an emergency. They include your checking account, saving accounts, certificates of deposit, money market accounts, and savings bonds.

Your invested assets, your lifestyle assets, and your cash equivalents are all assets. But because they serve different purposes, it's useful to tally them separately in developing a net worth statement. You may be living high on the hog today, but will you have enough to live well tomorrow? Calculating your net worth is the first step in answering that question.

Let's take a look at how to do it. It's not crucial that your figures be exact, but your estimates should be reasonable. Most people tend to overvalue their stuff. Remember that the 10-year-old furniture is just old furniture—not antiques. What would you get for that stuff if you had a giant estate sale? Use those numbers to fill out the net worth worksheet. With a car, use the wholesale Blue Book value. (Find that on the Web at **www.kelleybluebook.com**.) If you own your home, use the amount you could get if you sold the property today. If you've recently refinanced or taken out a home equity line of credit, use that value. If all else fails, use the assessed value on your tax bill, though that's usually lower than the actual value. The values of your invested assets are easier to find. Go get your most recent account statements and use those numbers. Or, if you have access to the Internet, you can probably call up today's value for the stocks and mutual funds.

Liabilities

Oh, yeah, one more thing. When you're figuring out your net worth, you also have to remember to put down what you owe others—that's what accountants call *liabilities*. Liabilities include money you owe for current bills or money you've borrowed, such as a mortgage, a car loan, a school loan, or credit cards. So fill in on the worksheet what you own and what you owe.

Net Worth

Now, you're ready to calculate your net worth. Just subtract what you owe from what you own. Voilà! Your net worth appears on the bottom line.

> I been rich and I been poor. Rich is better.
> —Sophie Tucker

If anybody were to ask you at this precise moment what you're worth, this would be the figure. But in terms of your future, it's not just your net worth that matters. You also need to look at the types of assets and liabilities that give you that bottom-line figure.

Lifestyle Assets or Investment Assets

Let's look at the kinds of assets you've been accumulating in your bucket. If you're under 30, you're likely accumulating lifestyle assets. People under 30 generally leave their parents' home and set out on their own, and they start out with what we call "old American." This is the stuff that no one wants anymore but still has some life left in it. Gradually, they begin to purchase new clothes, furniture, stereo equipment, and cars. They often forgo putting money into invested assets because they think they have plenty of time to do that—and besides, they're having too much fun spending what they earn.

If you're under 40, you're probably still in the accumulation mode, but now you may be looking at bigger things, such as a home, a vacation house, a second car—and kids. People in this stage of life have begun to think about saving for retirement and educating those little people who have now moved in and taken over the household. But it's so expensive to pay for child care and insurance and on and on … that folks at this stage of life often put off saving and investing for the future. They believe they still have plenty of time before the kids go to college or move out. And retirement, well, that's at least 20 years away.

If you're under 50, you may be dealing with educating those kids as well as (finally) beginning to seriously think about accumulating retirement assets. But there are so many other things to spend that paycheck on. Stuff has begun to wear out, so you may be in the replacement stage. You need new furniture, new appliances, and maybe even a new roof. If you're in a second marriage, you may be starting the accumulation stage all over again. Who can save?

Then we reach the under-60s—and it's time to begin to hyperventilate. People at this point realize they don't have much time left. Their invested assets may look OK on paper—as long as they don't plan on retiring until they're at least 70.

If you see yourself in any of these scenarios, you just had your wake-up call. Accumulating stuff can be fun, but that stuff will not provide the kid with a college education or provide you another source of income in retirement. So review your net worth worksheet and see what you actually own and owe. If it's all or mostly lifestyle assets, you need to begin accumulating invested assets. And the younger you start, the less you'll need to save, for you have time on your side. So our advice right here would be to *stop buying the toys and start buying the mutual funds.* (We'll tell you more about how to do that in Chapter 15.)

A quick lesson here on collectibles. Beanies Babies were once all the rage. They were cute and adorable everyone loved them. Many people thought they were the way to instant wealth. Then the bubble burst. Collectibles are fads, what is in vogue right now. For them to be worth anything you have to find a buyer who is willing to pay you the price you think they're worth. A word here on dealers, remember they want to resell whatever they buy, so they will not pay full value for your Beanie. They need to mark it up to make a profit. That said, have fun collecting Beanies, and if the kid wants to play with them, buy 2 of everything, one for your collection and one for the kid. But what you really need to be collecting are *mutual funds.*

Bad Debt or Good Debt?

The liabilities on the net worth worksheet are the skeletons in your closet. Before we check them out, let's talk here about good debt versus *bad* debt.

Yes, there's such a thing as *good* debt! It's the debt you take on when you purchase something like your home or car, something for which you'd otherwise have to save for years. With the average price of homes over $150,000, it would take most families many years to accumulate that much in savings to purchase one outright. So you take on debt to purchase a home or a car or to finance an education. This is good debt. A home provides us with shelter. A car provides us with the transportation that most of us need to get to work so that we can earn a living to support our families. An education is an investment in yourself or your kids. So good debt helps us provide for the needs of our families.

> Money used to talk. Then it whispered. Now it just sneaks off.

Bad debt, on the other hand, is the debt we accumulate with our credit cards. It's usually used to purchase items that we consume, such as dinners in restaurants, or items that depreciate very quickly, such as sneakers. If you have a negative net worth, it's usually because you're financing your lifestyle with credit cards rather than your paycheck. (We'll talk more about credit card debt and the help you might need to get rid of it in Chapter 3.)

A negative net worth can also indicate that a piece of property that you bought and financed has actually gone down in value. It's what's called an up-side-down mortgage. For example you may have purchased a condo at $100,000 with a $90,000 mortgage. The real estate market crumbles, and your condo loses 25%. The value of your condo is now $75,000, but the mortgage is still close to $90,000.

We called liabilities "skeletons." That's because what you owe can come out of the closet to haunt you. In a perfect financial world, you would have a net worth with no liabilities listed. But we're realistic and know that, until we reach retirement, most of us will still be filling in numbers under the liabilities category. We just want you to have *good* debt listed there and not *bad* debt.

Take a look at your debt and you can quickly assess how you're doing. Debt follows you around wherever you go. Potential landlords and potential employers both have access to your credit history, and you could lose out on the perfect apartment or be turned down for the perfect job because of too much debt. You want to get rid of the bad debt on your net worth worksheet so you can put your energies into building up your net worth. Bad debt is expensive. You can get a house mortgage for around 7%; credit cards can charge you as much as 25%.

The American economy is built on the fact that Americans like to accumulate stuff. Now we don't want to mess up the economy, but you have a choice here—you can either buy stuff or invest. We vote for the investments. But if you're going to buy stuff, at least pay cash for it.

Why Bother to Figure Out Your Net Worth?

Have you ever gotten one of those magazine solicitations in the mail and found this little envelope that says, "Open me only if you don't take us up on our fabulous subscription offer"? Well, here's our offer. If we haven't gotten you to fill out the net worth worksheet yet, this is our last-ditch effort.

Knowing your net worth is important! Here's why. It lays the foundation for what we're going to do in the rest of this book and, more important, for your financial plan. We like to think of your net worth as a scorecard: we should all want our net worth to increase over time. Figuring out your net worth for the first time is the hardest. After that, it's just a matter of updating it periodically, usually once a year.

If you're coupled, we strongly suggest that the two of you do this exercise together, for several reasons. First, in a partnership both partners should fully understand their finances; working on this together is a good start. Second, you will serve as a system of checks and balances for each other, so you do not inflate the value of your possessions. Third, you're less likely to forget something with both of you working on it. Our experience over the years has been that it's easy to leave things out, such as the savings bonds that are sitting in the desk drawer.

Once you've completed your net worth worksheet, you'll have a very good idea about what you own, what it's worth, what you owe, and how much you're worth.

To reiterate, here are the reasons for preparing a net worth statement:

✔ It helps you to figure out *what you've got*.
✔ It helps you figure out *who actually owns your stuff*.
✔ It helps you figure out *where it is*.
✔ It establishes a starting point for *insurance planning*.
✔ It establishes a starting point for *estate planning*.
✔ It establishes a starting point for *investment planning*.
✔ It helps you *check your financial progress* every year.

Now for the worksheets.

Net Worth   Date:_____

Assets (what you own)

Cash or Equivalents	Self	Spouse	Total
Cash	_____	_____	_____
Checking Accounts	_____	_____	_____
Savings Accounts	_____	_____	_____
Money Market Fund	_____	_____	_____
Certificates of Deposit (CDs)	_____	_____	_____
Savings Bonds/Treasuries	_____	_____	_____
Life Insurance (Cash Value)	_____	_____	_____
Total Cash Equivalents	_____	_____	_____

Invested Assets

Retirement Assets

	Self	Spouse	Total
IRA Accounts	_____	_____	_____
Pension/Profit Sharing	_____	_____	_____
401(k), 403(b), 457 Plans	_____	_____	_____
Keogh Accounts	_____	_____	_____
Annuities (surrender value)	_____	_____	_____
Other	_____	_____	_____

Investments

	Self	Spouse	Total
Stocks	_____	_____	_____
Bonds	_____	_____	_____
Mutual Funds	_____	_____	_____
Government Securities	_____	_____	_____
Royalties	_____	_____	_____
Rental Property	_____	_____	_____
Business Equity	_____	_____	_____
Receivables (money owed you)	_____	_____	_____
Limited Partnerships	_____	_____	_____
Patents, Copyrights	_____	_____	_____
Trusts	_____	_____	_____
Other	_____	_____	_____
Total Invested Assets	$_____	$_____	$_____

Lifestyle Assets	Self	Spouse	Total
Personal Property			
Home	_____	_____	_____
Vacation Home	_____	_____	_____
Automobiles	_____	_____	_____
Household Furnishings	_____	_____	_____
Clothes and Jewelry	_____	_____	_____
Antiques, Collectibles	_____	_____	_____
Boats, RVs, etc.	_____	_____	_____
Other	_____	_____	_____
Total Lifestyle Assets	_____	_____	_____
Total Assets	$ _____	$ _____	$ _____

Liabilities (what you owe)

Debts	Self	Spouse	Total
Medical/Dental	_____	_____	_____
Taxes Owed	_____	_____	_____
Educational Loans	_____	_____	_____
Alimony	_____	_____	_____
Child Support	_____	_____	_____
Mortgage	_____	_____	_____
Business Loans	_____	_____	_____
Personal Loans	_____	_____	_____
Pledges	_____	_____	_____
Contracts	_____	_____	_____
Property Taxes Owed	_____	_____	_____
Mortgage on Rental Property	_____	_____	_____
Home Equity Loans	_____	_____	_____
Credit Card Debt	_____	_____	_____
Other	_____	_____	_____
Total Liabilities	$ _____	$ _____	$ _____
Total Assets	$ _____	$ _____	$ _____
Minus Total Liabilities	$ _____	$ _____	$ _____
Net Worth	$ _____	$ _____	$ _____

Chapter 2

Where Does Your Money Go?

Cash Flow

Most people don't have a clue as to where their money goes each month. What comes in seems to just go out—and maybe even a bit more.

The first step is to find out where it goes. If net worth is what's in your bucket, then the income you're pouring in helps fill the bucket. And you control the flow of spending. Your income, on the other hand, is a little hard to control because your job pays only so much. There are ways you could make more money, including getting a better job or robbing a bank, but doing a "Bonnie and Clyde" doesn't really work in the long run. No benefits and definitely no retirement plan.

In Chapter 1, we told you that it was important to look at your net worth to understand where you stand financially, for both the long term and the short term. The most important number to use for your short-term perspective is your *cash flow*. That, as you remember from Chapter 1, is the amount of money coming into your bucket compared

with the amount going out. If you've got more money incoming than outgoing, that's good. And if it's 10% or more, that's even better. On the other hand, if there's more money going out than coming in, that's bad. It's important to understand how and where you spend your money. It's only from your cash flow that you're going to accumulate enough money to save and invest.

To help you figure out your cash flow, we've included a worksheet at the end of this chapter. Take the time to complete this worksheet; it's definitely worth doing. You'll then know where and how you spend your money.

We often buy things to make up for losses in our lives. Understanding your spending habits and taking control of them are important to your financial well-being. And if you're within 15 years of retirement, understanding your cash flow will give you a good idea how much income it will take to maintain your present lifestyle in retirement.

Whether you use a computer program such as Quicken or the old-fashioned pencil-and-paper method, you have to find out where the money goes before you can manage it. Remember how we advised you, if you are coupled, to do your net worth worksheet together? Well, you need to do this one together also. Here are the ground rules: no expense is right or wrong, it just is—especially if it's your partner's. And no bickering. Decide what can be eliminated only after you have compiled all of your numbers.

There's some work involved here and accuracy counts (but not neatness!). Guessing at the numbers won't work here. If you're off by $100 a month on what you really spend, that oversight equals $1,200 over the year. Think about this: if you can invest $100 a month over 20 years and if we assume an after-tax return of 8%, that sum could amount to as much as $60,000. So, as you can see, $100 a month is really a big deal.

Your cash flow begins with the total amount of money you have coming in regularly, such as your paycheck, dividends, interest, and child support. If you're just starting out, the only thing you may have coming in regularly is your paycheck.

From this total income, you then subtract your expenses. These will be more difficult to identify. Ideally, you'd like an accurate record of every expense your household has incurred for the last 12 months. But most of us don't keep records that complete, so you'll have to do some digging. Most people can't come up with all of their expenses in a single session. You may need to spend a month or so keeping track of your expenses.

And in figuring your expenses, don't forget things such as vacations, holidays, birthdays, home repairs, car repairs, real estate taxes, and insurance premiums. Don't forget tax payments you owed when you filed your federal, state, and local tax returns. Now add up all those expenses. Then subtract your expenses total from your income total. That's your cash flow.

If you're spending less than you earn, you've got a positive cash flow. This means you have income left over each month. What should you do with it? We suggest saving it and investing it. In later chapters we'll help you do so.

On the other hand, if you don't find much left over at the end of the month, figure your expenses again and take careful note of where you're spending your money. Maybe there are some items you could cut out or just spend less on.

If you're just breaking even and not saving at least 5% of your income, then you need to spend the time finding ways to save more. You probably need to think about the word *budget*. Uh-oh. It's a little like flossing: it takes time, but the results are definitely worth the effort. Think about what changes you could make to spend less and save more. For example, saving $25 a week can reap you big rewards over time.

Negative Cash Flow

If the number at the bottom of your worksheet is negative, you're spending more than you're earning. Not good! In this situation, you have no choice: you need to set up a budget and become disciplined about following it.

A negative cash flow means you're using debt, usually credit card debt, to pay for expenses that your income doesn't cover. Sure, it's common to charge almost everything—big purchases and little. And it's so easy to forget how much you've charged until you get your monthly statement. Then, the bank makes it so convenient for you to just pay the minimum amount, so the debt starts to add up.

A negative cash flow is a clear sign that you have financial problems. Only the government seems to get away with borrowing more and more to pay expenses. The secret: the government has a printing press that prints money. If you tried the same strategy, you'd be off on a government vacation for a few years, where your plastic would be useless. You'd stop depending on credit cards, but that approach seems a bit extreme!

If your cash flow is negative, the first step in remedying this is to reduce your expenses so your money lasts, at least from paycheck to paycheck. Refuse to spend more than you earn. Your cash flow worksheet will tell you where you're spending the money. Your *fixed* expenses, such as rent or mortgage payments and car payments, are things that you can't change in the short term. Your *discretionary* expenses, however, you can change, usually immediately—and that's where you need to focus your initial efforts. Sure, you still have to eat, but you can

Sound advice: Spend less than you earn.

decide how much you spend on your food. Instead of stopping after work and picking up dinner, plan to cook at home more often. The same is true for entertainment, clothes, contributions, gifts, and toys (whether for the kids or for you). Many of these expenses you can reduce or even eliminate. Getting to a positive cash flow is going to take some work—and only you can do it. Check out Chapter 3 for more help with debt control.

Go away from your worksheet for a while, and then come back to take an objective look at it. What changes do you need to make so that you have money left over each month to save and invest? We're not going to tell you what to cut, since everyone perceives what's important differently. But if this is all the money you having coming in, how do you keep it all from slipping away? Only you can do that—and it won't be easy if you and your family have gotten used to a standard of living subsidized by credit cards. It may mean radical, probably painful behavior changes. But if you want to ever achieve your financial goals you'll have to build up discretionary funds to invest. (And, as we have mentioned before, robbing a bank is not a good career move.)

Your Cash Stash a.k.a. Emergency Fund

Everyone needs a *cash stash*. This is savings you set aside for an emergency, a rainy day fund. Grandma had it right when she stashed a little bit away in the cookie jar each week. But we're not talking about just a one-day storm here. Your emergency fund is for a rainy day of biblical proportions, when it rains so long and so hard that the floodwaters start to rise. It may come in the form of a natural disaster such as a hurricane or a mudslide or if the roof falls in. Or it could be a job loss or an illness that keeps

> Establish an emergency fund and you'll be surprised how quickly an emergency develops.

you out of work for a long time. It may also be helping out one of your kids or a parent with a financial crisis. This is how you plan for those things you can't really plan for—you keep a cash stash handy.

In the financial planning industry, the rule of thumb is that you should have three to six months of living expenses set aside in an emergency fund. But no rule of thumb can cover all situations. How much you need depends on a handful of factors: your basic living expenses, your family situation, the stability of your household income, your health insurance, your disability insurance, and your homeowner's insurance.

We'd like you to be prepared for any emergency that may come your way. And we're conservative here, for our years of experience have taught us that most people go through a crisis situation when they need emergency cash. How much cash do you need? Our recommendations are as follows:

✔ Bare minimum for anyone:　*3 months*

✔ Children and two steady incomes　*3-6 months*

✔ Children and one steady income　*4-6 months*

✔ Children and no steady income　*6-9 months*

People who earn most of their money on sales commissions, such as realtors or small business owners, may not have a regular paycheck. You need to have an extra cushion here, even if you're single with no children. If you feel uncertain about your job status, a rather common feeling these days, you may want to increase the amount in your cash stash. Some people tell us they'll use their credit card or a home equity line of credit if they have an emergency. Be careful here: if you're out of work or your home has been damaged, it's hard to open a home equity line of credit. If you're retired and have a regular pension and Social Security, a cash stash in the sugar bowl will do just fine for you. But don't let the kids know it's there!

> Money is not the root of all evil—no money is.
> —Mark Twain

Your emergency fund is just that—money to be used for emergencies. When income drops or stops coming in, you'll need this money to keep paying your mortgage and buying groceries. It's not mad money, a vacation fund, or a Christmas Club. It's your family's first line of defense when something major goes wrong. Keep it separate from your regular spending money accounts. This means it shouldn't be in your regular checking account where you can write a check on it easily. You do want access to it in case of emergency, but you're better off putting it in a money market mutual fund where it can earn maximum interest and still be available. Put three months' worth of living expenses here and let it grow.

Now many of you will be complaining that you don't want your money just sitting in an account not earning much. Well, if you want to take some risk you can put it a balanced mutual fund or a short-term CD. But you want it available if you need it, so it's got to be *liquid*— financial jargon meaning that you can easily turn it into cash.

What if you don't have three months' worth of living expenses stashed away? No excuses now. Take a look at your cash flow. Where can you make a difference? What can you cut out or cut back on to be able to save more money? Can you put in some overtime? Can you take on a part-time job? When the next raise comes along, plan to save it—and the first savings goal should be your cash stash.

Pay Yourself First

Are you living from paycheck to paycheck? You get it; you spend it, right? The current thinking in financial planning circles is that when you get paid you should make out a check to yourself and deposit it into your savings account. Yeah, sure, and pigs fly! That sounds good, but it's the rare individual who can do this. Why? Because we always have other uses for our money. So you need someone who can do it for you.

> *I have enough money to last me the rest of my life, unless, I buy something.*
> *—Jackie Mason*

The financial industry has figured out ways to help you—automatic savings or investment plans. You can set up plans through work or directly with your bank or a mutual fund company to have money go automatically from your checking account into savings each month. What you don't have, you won't miss—and you can't spend.

Check your benefits department at work to see what plans are offered. It may be in the form of a simple savings account or even a savings bond program, to buy EE bonds. But you need to do something to get started. Saving through work is the ideal way to fund your cash stash.

Your bank will also be willing to help you set up your checking account so that a fixed amount transfers into your savings account each month. This may be a good beginning, but it's not a strategy that will pay you very much interest. But it's a way to start. You could get the bank to transfer the money into a bank money market account, if there's one available. Then, once you reach your cash stash goal of three months of living expenses, stop the transfers and begin to concentrate on your retirement plan savings or saving for other goals.

Many mutual fund companies will let you open an account without making the minimum deposit required if you set up an automatic investment plan. The mutual fund company will debit a specified amount from your checking account each month. Many companies have minimums of $100 or more, but there are still some around that you can get into for $50 a month or less. This is a user-friendly way to start investing for your future.

Let's do a "what if?" here. Let's say that you're saving for your kid's education. You use an automatic investment plan and set aside $100 a month for 18 years. You choose a growth mutual fund that invests in large company stocks that has had an average after-tax return of 9%. In 18 years you would have accumulated $54,000 to help defray college expenses. The key with any savings plan is to be consistent. And having money automatically deducted from your account makes it almost—we did say *almost* here—painless.

The following mutual fund families have systematic investment plans available for a minimum investment of $50/month:

Aim 800-347-1919

Franklin Templeton 800-342-5236

Heartland* 800-432-7856

Invesco* 800-525-8085

Strong Balanced Fund* 800-368-1030

T. Rowe Price Associates* 800-638-5660

*No-load mutual funds available (funds for which you don't have pay a fee to purchase shares).

These mutual fund families have systematic investment plans available for a minimum investment of $25/month:

Evergreen Funds 800-343-2898

Oppenheimer 800-525-7048

Van Kampen American Capital 800-421-5666

Spend Less and Save More

The simplest advice we can give you here is always spend less than you earn. If you follow this advice, you'll always have money left over at the end of the month to save and invest. This is how many millionaires got their start. You need something left over each month—not just once in a while but every month—to make this work. How do you start to save? Where do you start?

Let's take a look at your cash flow and start with the discretionary expenses. These are usually expenses where we have choices. What kind of life insurance do we purchase? Do we learn to groom our dogs ourselves? Take a look at each of your *discretionary* expenses and see whether you can eliminate an expense here or cut back there.

Then survey the *basic* expenses. What can you do here to lower an expense? For example, you might refinance your mortgage, set the temperature on your thermostat lower in the winter and higher in the summer, and so on. And we should mention that this involves changing your old habits and adopting new ones. If you are coupled, please tackle this problem together. Also we suggest that you keep track of your savings and tally up the amount each month and for the year. You may be pleasantly surprised. But whatever you save should be in your savings account and not spent on things you could probably do without. In figuring how to cut expenses and save more, here are some things we know work.

Coupons. Here's an idea that may encourage you to use coupons. If you have children, offer them half of the savings for clipping and using the coupons when shopping with you. At 28, Dee's son still clips and uses coupons because as a boy he got half of whatever the family saved, which shows this can be a good life lesson as well. Try shopping only weekly; there are too many temptations otherwise. Coupons abound for things other than groceries, such as car maintenance, pizzas, cleaners, dog grooming, and so on. For services you're already using, you can save 10% or more on what you spend.

Electricity and Heat. Turning lights off and turning the heat down at night does save money. Make it someone's job to do this or get an automatic thermostat. You may soon be able to shop for different electricity suppliers because of deregulation in the industry.

Takeout and Restaurants. Take the time to cook at home. You can make an "Egg McMuffin" far cheaper at home. When cooking, double or triple the recipe so there are plenty of leftovers that you can just heat up when you get home from work. Americans spend close to 50% of their food dollars on takeout and restaurants. Pack your lunch unless you're eating in a company-subsidized cafeteria.

Cars. Pump your own gas and change your oil every 3,000 miles. Buy a gallon of windshield fluid and keep your reservoir filled so you don't have to stop at a service station for a fill-up. It's hard to do much more of the maintenance on new cars yourself, since they're full of computer chips.

Water Use. Turn down the temperature of your water heater: 125 degrees is hot enough, and it's safer, especially with kids around. Use cold water to wash clothes, take shorter showers, and don't leave water running while brushing teeth. Keep track of rainfall so that you don't over-water your lawn in the summer. Repair leaky faucets immediately.

Insurance. On older cars you may want to drop the collision rider. If you're handy around the house, you may want to raise the deductible on your homeowner's insurance. Are you purchasing insurance you don't need? Children do not need life insurance! Term life insurance is cheaper than cash value insurance such as whole life. Also comparison shop when purchasing insurance.

Telephone. Do you need all of the fancy services offered? Do you need two lines and a cellular? Writing has definitely gone out of fashion, but letters give someone something to hold onto and reread. Try using e-mail if you own a home computer: it's a great way to stay connected to your family for the cost of a local call.

Clothing. Do you shop because you need something? Or is shopping now recreational for you? The malls are filled with adolescents and families spending an afternoon or an evening shopping. Discipline yourself to shop the sales and specials. Use discount stores and even church rummage sales for kids' clothes. Ski swaps are a great place to outfit kids for skiing. If your kids can't live without designer jeans or sneakers, make them pay for half from their savings accounts; we're sure they'll take better care of them if they've paid for them. When kids are old enough to work, make them responsible for purchasing their own clothes.

Cleaners. Does everything need to go to the cleaners? Can you iron your clothes once a week while watching *ER*? Use coupons. If you're taking your shirts or blouses in weekly for laundering, shop around for the best price. Dee's son now does his own shirts, once he figured out how much he would be spending on laundering shirts for work—about $12,000 over a 40-year span. Dee showed him that, if he invested the monthly savings of $20 in a growth mutual fund, with an 8% after-tax return he would have $70,000 in his shirt account by retirement. That was enough to change his habits; he now irons his shirts while watching ESPN.

Hobbies. Some hobbies are very expensive; choose something to do that costs little and gives you exercise at the same time, like walking or biking—as long as you don't go out and purchase the latest fashions to wear.

Pets. Pets can be expensive, especially dogs that need grooming every month. Learn to do it yourself or, when choosing a pet, consider what it will cost for upkeep. Check with your vet about what animal food to purchase. Animals don't know if they are getting a gourmet treat or a plain old dog biscuit. You should be able to find coupons for pet grooming and pet food in your local newspaper as well as at the vet's office.

Gifts. Gift giving can get out of hand. Everyone wants that wonderful "Hallmark" feeling at Christmas, but it's a feeling that many people are still paying for into April. We often use gifts to make up for not spending time with someone. Here are some holiday shopping tips.

✔ *Create a spending plan.* How much can you reasonably afford to spend on the holidays? Be realistic here. Many of us want a holiday with our homes all lit up, a beautifully decorated tree laden with ornaments, with piles of presents all perfectly wrapped with matching bows and ribbons. TV commercials show us what our homes should look like—perfect! And perfect is expensive! When making out a spending plan, start with the gifts, but don't forget the cards, postage, decorations, wrappings, dinners, entertaining, travel, and any clothes you may purchase for the occasion. It adds up very quickly. What are you willing to scrimp on? Maybe you send cards only to friends and family far away. Maybe you scale down your entertaining, shop the discount stores, eliminate some people from your gift list. However you decide to save, once you've made the decision, don't allow guilt to cause you to backslide.

✔ *Make out a list.* Do not go *looking*; go *shopping*. Know what you want for each person and how much you're willing to spend, and then put it on the list so you're not tempted to overspend.

✔ *Shop early.* Shop early in the season. You'll find better selections. Also, if you delay, you're more likely to do impulse shopping because you're desperate. Don't take the kids, relatives, or friends shopping with you. Put on comfortable shoes and go for it. You'll be much more efficient.

✔ *Leave the credit cards at home.* It's tough to do, but remember: this is the "new you." Pay with cash or by check. This way you'll be sure to stick to your spending plan. And if you do use your credit card—they are convenient—stick to that plan so you can pay the entire credit card bill in January.

✔ *Keep track of what you spend.* Take your list with you; then, when you've made a purchase, check it off. Keep a running tally of how much you're spending. This helps prevent overspending, because you'll know exactly how much you've spent.

Here are some other ideas that have worked for families we've interviewed:

✔ If you have a large family, draw names out of a hat at Thanksgiving. So rather than buying lots of presents for your family, you buy only one for each member. Using this method, you can afford nicer gifts and still spend less.

✔ Instead of individual gifts, consider buying a family gift, such as a membership or tickets to the aquarium with a book on the ocean, a popcorn maker with a gift subscription to the local video store, or a gourmet magazine subscription with a few jars of special herbs. Pool money among family members to buy a large gift for grandma, like a microwave.

✔ Give the gift of time. You don't have to give it during the holidays. Give a certificate to the recipient telling what he or she will receive at a future date. When Dee's kids were in college, she promised them a homemade goody a month, so she was able to bake for them when the whirlwind of the holidays had quieted down. Give your elderly neighbor trips to the grocery store, religious services, or the library. It doesn't take you much extra time if you're already going. Think about the true meaning of the holidays. Bringing family and friends together is truly the best part of the holidays.

Cash Flow		
Income	**Monthly**	**Annually**
Salary	_____	_____
Salary/Spouse	_____	_____
Self-Employed Income	_____	_____
Social Security	_____	_____
Social Security/Spouse	_____	_____
Pension	_____	_____
Pension/Spouse	_____	_____
Rental Income	_____	_____
Alimony Received	_____	_____
Child Support Received	_____	_____
Dividends	_____	_____
Interest–Taxable	_____	_____
Interest–Tax-Exempt	_____	_____
Capital Gains	_____	_____
Other	_____	_____
Other	_____	_____
Total Income	$ _____	$ _____

Expenses	Monthly	Annually
Basic Expenses		
Mortgage	_____	_____
Rent	_____	_____
Real Estate Taxes	_____	_____
Utilities	_____	_____
Telephone	_____	_____
Other Household Expenses	_____	_____
Homeowner's Insurance	_____	_____
Food	_____	_____
Clothing	_____	_____
Health Care	_____	_____
Medical Insurance	_____	_____
Automobile Expenses	_____	_____
Automobile Insurance	_____	_____
Transportation	_____	_____
Alimony	_____	_____
Child Support	_____	_____
Work-Related Expenses	_____	_____
Child Care	_____	_____
Loan Payments	_____	_____
Credit Card Payments	_____	_____
Taxes		
Federal	_____	_____
State	_____	_____
Social Security	_____	_____
Medicare	_____	_____
Total Basic Expenses	$ _____	$ _____

Expenses	Monthly	Annually
Discretionary Expenses		
Life Insurance	_____	_____
Disability Insurance	_____	_____
Education Costs	_____	_____
Pets	_____	_____
Cleaning Expenses	_____	_____
Dining Out (include take-out)	_____	_____
Contributions	_____	_____
Vacations	_____	_____
Entertainment	_____	_____
Memberships/Dues	_____	_____
Subscriptions	_____	_____
Hobbies	_____	_____
Gifts	_____	_____
Personal Care	_____	_____
Home Repairs	_____	_____
Miscellaneous	_____	_____
Other	_____	_____
Savings		
Pension Plans	_____	_____
Investments	_____	_____
Other	_____	_____
Total Discretionary Expenses	$ _____	$ _____
+ Total Basic Expenses	$ _____	$ _____
= Total Expenses	$ _____	$ _____

Chapter 3 | In a Big Hole

Plastic Money

Now we're going to talk about credit and debt—and getting out of debt. If you have a positive net worth, you can skip most of this chapter. Just read this first section on credit cards and then check out the last section on getting a look at your credit history.

We Americans love our credit cards and carry more credit cards in our wallets than pictures of our loved ones. There are over 1 billion credit cards out there right now, just waiting to be used. Did you know that credit cards didn't exist in 1959? In the olden days (before the '60s), people either paid cash for something or used a store charge card. According to CardTrak, Americans racked up close to $1.3 trillion worth of credit card charges in 2000, if you count Visa and MasterCard debit cards and all American Express cards. Any way you look at it, it's a lot of money—and a lot of debt for some of us.

When you apply for a credit card, you're actually applying for a short-term loan. When you charge something today and you don't pay for it until next month or months later, the bank has loaned you money to cover your purchases. The bank that issues you your card pays the retailer for your purchase and charges the retailer a 3% to 4% service charge to do so. If you don't pay the bill the following month, the bank also charges you a fee, the interest rate to carry you on its books. So credit cards are a very profitable source of revenue for banks, since the interest rates can run from the teaser rate of 4% up to as much as 25%.

Card issuers are very happy with the increased use of credit cards. They make money on credit cards—sometimes lots of money. For example, Sears made more profit on its credit card operation than on its merchandise! (It said so on page 17 of the Annual Report.) But consumers are getting smarter: 42% of all cardholders now pay off their balances each month.

> *Credit is what keeps you from knowing how far past broke you are.*

So let's talk about which credit card is best for you. We hope that you're one of those consumers who pay off their balance each month. If so, look for a card that carries no annual fee. If you're a good and loyal customer, you can ask your card issuer to cancel your annual fee, stating that you don't want to change cards but will do so if necessary. If you carry a balance from month to month, then look for a card with a low interest rate. You can find lists of credit cards with no fee or low rates in either *Money* or *Kiplinger's Personal Finance* magazines.

Now that even dentists and grocery stores are accepting credit cards, card usage has increased. Consumers are using reward cards to make many of their purchases, so they get rewarded with everything from frequent flyer miles to CDs. The most popular for years have been the airline cards that give customers miles for every dollar they spend. But the more sophisticated the cardholders, the more demanding they've become, so card issuers are looking for all kinds of ways to get you to use their cards. You can get airline rebates, travel rebates, automobile rebates, cash back, gasoline rebates, and even entertainment rebates. You can use your GM MasterCard to earn up $2,500 toward the purchase or lease of any GM truck or car or your Amoco Visa to get a 3% rebate on gas.

Smart consumers can use a credit card to their advantage. Check out **www.cardtrak.com** or **www.bankrate.com** for more updated information on rebate cards. Both of these Web sites also provide good general information on credit.

Debit Cards

Debit cards are a distant relative of credit cards. When you use a debit card, the bank subtracts money from your account, usually a checking account. Debit cards come in different formats:

✔ ATM (Automatic Teller Machine) card
✔ Check card, also known as a *debit card*

ATM cards are the most popular, since they allow you to access your account at banking machines across the world to get cash for a price. Many bank customers never see the lobby of their banks anymore, because they use ATMs for all of their transactions. An ATM is the magical money machine that can leave you clueless in terms of where your cash goes. ATMs are a great convenience, but only if you use them properly. If you ask a child of four or five, "Where does money come from?" he or she may answer, "The ATM machine." Children have no concept that you must first earn the money that you put into the bank so that you can withdraw it when you need to buy something.

Has this ever happened to you? You go to an ATM and take out $100. Then it just seems to disappear from your wallet. You wonder where it went. This could be the black hole in your cash flow calculations, if you don't know how much cash you withdrew from your ATM or how you spent it. A good exercise would be to keep track of what you purchase with your ATM withdrawals.

Banks can't seem to generate a great deal of interest in check cards, because the money you spend is yours—it comes right out of your checking account. You're not borrowing it from the bank. A check card is used like a credit card to purchase goods and services, with the bank collecting a fee from the merchant. Recently banks have begun to send out check cards when ATM cards expire. If your ATM card has a Visa or MasterCard logo on it, it's now also a check/debit card card.

A debit card offers two major advantages to you:

✔ You don't have to carry around a lot of cash.

✔ You can't use it unless you have enough money in your account to cover the cost of your purchase.

If you have overdraft protection on your account, you may still be able to use that check card. But guess what? The overdraft protection kicks in with an interest charge, usually 19%. Good for the bank, but not good for you.

Debit cards have a down side compared with credit cards. You lose the "float" on your money, that time lag that allows you to charge something and not get the bill until the next month. Also, you may not have the same rights with a debit card as you have with a credit card when there's an error in billing or a duplicate billing. There are ways to handle these problems, but it may not be quite as simple as with a credit card. Fortunately, many states are passing laws to address this situation.

Re-establishing Your Credit

When you use your credit card, it means you are receiving an *unsecured* loan. This means the bank has no collateral in case you default on that loan. When you take out a mortgage or a car loan, the bank can always repossess the house or car if you default. In other words, these are *secured* loans.

Some consumers have fallen into such regular and undisciplined use of their credit cards that their debt has grown so high they can't pay it. Such consumers may have to declare bankruptcy. Other consumers get way behind in their payments and end up with a very poor credit history. When they need to re-establish their credit, these people will

likely have to get a *secured* credit card. And these are not easy to get.

To get a secured card, you must find a bank that's willing to take a risk with you, and then you set up an account by depositing money, perhaps $200 to $500. The bank will then issue you a credit card for the amount you've deposited. If you're late in making a payment or miss a payment, the bank will use the money in your account to cover the payment. Consumers can usually apply for an unsecured credit card within 12 to 18 months after re-establishing their credit.

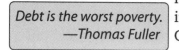
Debt is the worst poverty.
—*Thomas Fuller*

Credit Card Companies Want Your Business

Credit card companies send out over 2 billion pre-approved offers to consumers every year. Why? Because, as we've said before, it's a very profitable business. And here's how it works!

If you have a $2,000 balance on your credit card with an 18% interest rate and pay only the minimum each month of 2%, it will take you 30 years to pay off the debt. And the total interest costs will be close to $5,000. That's why your mailbox is stuffed with mail from these guys.

Do you want to stop those annoying credit card offers? Until recently there's been no way to stop them. Now, under a revision of the Fair Credit Reporting Act in 1998, credit agencies are required to set up a toll-free number that consumers can call to have their names taken off those pre-approved offers list. But the call will close your credit file to the banks for only two years. If you want to permanently stop all pre-approved offers, you need to request a form and send it back to the reporting agency. Here are the numbers for the three major reporting agencies: Experian 800-353-0809, Equifax 800-556-4711, and Trans Union 800-680-7293. (Note: These are not numbers for checking your credit history, but dedicated numbers for stopping the junk mail offers from littering your mailbox.)

Get Control of Your Debt

You know if you're in debt. You didn't need to fill out the net worth worksheets to know that and you certainly didn't need us to tell you that. But, after filling out the forms, you now know exactly how bad it is. And we hope you now know that you need to do something about it. Many Americans are in debt; it seems to be a way of life so we can have the stuff we want. We put a little money down and then borrow to pay off the rest. But if we lose our jobs or experience some other major life event, we can end up facing insurmountable debt. We fall behind on mortgage payments, we get hit with large medical bills, or we run up huge credit card debt.

> *If you think nobody cares you are alive, just miss a couple car or mortgage payments.*

Once a person gets into a hole of debt like this, it's very difficult to climb out. Unfortunately, many people jump into this hole willingly. They use their credit cards to subsidize a life style they can't afford and then they go into debt. If you're one of these people, go back to Chapter 2 and see where the money goes each month. Try to understand what you're doing. If you want to change your situation, you're going to need help.

More on Credit Cards and Debt

Credit cards are easy to get—too easy, in our opinion. They're a wonderful convenience: you can use them to purchase almost anything, almost anywhere. Today close to 60% of cardholders carry a balance from month to month. And when credit cards are abused, the balances grow larger and larger, until consumers are not able to make even the minimum payment each month. Personal bankruptcy filings have increased 43% since 1992. Job loss was the No. 2 reason for filing bankruptcy. The No. 1 reason was being overextended, not having nearly enough income to pay the bills.

Are you having problems with debt? Let's look at some of the warning signs.

✔ Your cards are maxed out.

✔ You're barely making minimum payments.

✔ You're missing minimum payments.

✔ You don't know how much you owe.

✔ You can't name all of your creditors.

✔ You regularly fill out applications for new cards.

✔ Credit has been denied.

✔ You use more than 20% of your income to pay off installment debt.

✔ You hide bills from family members.

✔ Creditors are beginning to call.

Are any of those warning signs familiar? If so, you need to take charge of the situation. Before you can begin to work on your goals for savings and retirement and learn about investing, you need to crawl out of the hole of debt. Things may appear to be out of control, but you can turn the situation around. Help is available.

How to Pay Off Your Debt

Before anyone suggests the "B" word, *bankruptcy*, we suggest that you try to pay off your debt on your own. Bankruptcy is a constitutional right governed by state and federal law, and it may very well be the only way out of the hole you've dug. Bankruptcy is intended to help individuals caught in severe financial circumstances beyond their control, such as the loss of a job, a severe illness, or a natural calamity. These individuals can petition the bankruptcy court to reduce or even eliminate their debts. But if your debt has grown out of an abuse of credit cards, you have an obligation to repay the people and the institutions that trusted you.

Getting Out of Debt

So where do you start? You need to get out a pad and pencil and make a list of your creditors. How much do you owe each of them? What is the interest rate each is charging you? Have you been late or missed payments? These days, late or missed payments can mean extra charges of $15 to $30 per month, in addition to interest charges. If things have gotten that bad, you need to contact your creditors and let them know about your situation. Most will want to work with you to figure out a repayment plan. If your debt is mostly from credit cards, you may try requesting a lower interest rate from the issuers.

If your credit history is not messed up, you may be able to fix the debt problem yourself before it gets out of control. The answer may be in the mail or just a phone call away.

We know that credit card companies want your business and they send you pre-approved applications with low teaser rates that are good sometimes for as long as six months to a year. Grab the first one that comes and transfer your debt. If the credit line isn't high enough to accommodate all of your debt, ask the company to raise it. A lower interest rate will make all the difference in the world. If you take up the offer of a new card, look for hidden fees such as a transfer fee and read the fine print. When does the interest rate rise? Does it rise for new purchases? And what is the charge for late payments? Remember: this is a legal contract with the credit card company. And here's a word of caution: *the big print giveth and the little print taketh right back*. If you get one of these cards, don't pay just the minimum amount each month; tighten your belt and pay off as much as you can.

If you can't use the above method of consolidation and you're carrying a balance on several cards, pay off the card with the highest rate first, then tackle the next highest, and so on. You have three successive goals here: first, to reduce the interest load; second, to pay off all of your debt; and third, to be able to pay the credit card bills in full each month.

You may need look to other resources for borrowing. If you own your home, you may be able to refinance or take out a home equity line of credit. The interest rates are much lower than for credit cards and the interest is deductible on your taxes. A last resort may be your 401(k) or 403(b) plan at work. Does it allow borrowing? Using your retirement plan money to pay off consumer debt is definitely not good fiscal policy. But it might be the only avenue open to you. However you go about it, pay off your debts.

> *If you want to keep out of debt, you must* earn *more than you* yearn.

There's No Easy Way Out

Beware of offers to help you consolidate your debts. Primarily they're TV ads during the evening news that promise to help you with your debts. These offers are usually from finance companies that charge very high interest rates and spread the loan payments out over many years, so you don't feel much pain.

But think about this scenario for a moment. You went on vacation and charged it all on your credit card. You did some fun things, saw interesting sights, ate great food, and brought home a T-shirt. It's just a fond memory now, except for the T-shirt, which quickly shrank and faded, so you're now using it to wax the car. Then along comes this finance company that helps you consolidate your debts and extends your payments out over 20 years. So what happens now? You'll be paying for that vacation for 20 years—and paying for it many times over. Was it worth it? Of course not! You don't want to take on *long-term debt* to pay for *short-term pleasures*.

And watch out for the company that will offer you a 125% home equity loan. That may look like a great deal, but you're putting perhaps your largest asset, your home, at risk for that vacation or some other short-term pleasure. As George Bush would say, "Not prudent!"

Another piece of advice: while you're struggling to pay off this debt, don't start buying more stuff. If you realize that you don't know how to

use credit cards safely, you may need to perform some plastic surgery. It's easy: get out the scissors and cut up those cards. Cancel all but one and then leave that one at home unless you're traveling. Canceling means that you must write to the companies and inform them you're canceling. Just cutting up the card won't do it.

You don't need to carry a wallet full of cards. Make

two key decisions: that you'll purchase something only if you really need it and that you'll carry around only cash or your checkbook.

Now here's something that may help, especially if you feel out of control with impulse shopping. We've tried this with clients, so we know it works.

Take your credit card and put it in a bowl of water. That's right—water! Now stick it in the freezer. Uh-huh—the freezer. After a few hours your credit card is an icicle. Now if you want to use it, you need to take the time to defrost it. That should take a while, maybe enough time so that the impulse to buy those shoes will have passed. A note of caution here: don't use the microwave to defrost your cold card. The microwaves will ruin the back of the card and melt it, rendering it useless. Then again, maybe that's not a bad thing.

Outside Help

OK, so what if you just can't make the above suggestions work? There's help out there. Contact the National Foundation for Consumer Credit (NFCC). This is a network of 1,450 nonprofit community organizations that provide consumer credit education, budget and debt counseling, and debt repayment programs for families and individuals. Many NFCC members are locally managed nonprofit agencies operating under the name Consumer Credit Counseling Service (CCCS). Call NFCC at 800-388-2227 or visit the Web site at **www.nfcc.org**. CCCS may be able to do things for you that you cannot do for yourself, such as negotiating with the credit card companies to lower or even stop the interest on your debt. The counselors can help establish a spending plan, determine your financial options, re-establish credit, and arrange a debt management plan. NFCC is a nonprofit organization and can provide services at no cost or at a fee on a sliding scale, so no one is ever turned away.

Another source for help may be the Debt Counselors of America (DCA), at 800-680-DEBT. DCA is a nonprofit Internet-based counseling service that uses Certified Financial Planners. DCA helps consumers with debt, credit, and money problems through its Web site, **www.dca.org**, primarily by providing articles that you can purchase and by hosting chat rooms where you can get answers to your questions.

Getting a Look at Your Credit History

It's important to get a look at your credit history before a potential creditor does. Why? You want to be sure the information on your report is correct. Imagine finding your dream home and applying for a mortgage and being turned down. By the time you do straighten out the mess, your dream house has been sold to someone else. You're not a happy camper. So if you're considering making a major purchase such as a home, car, or life insurance, looking for a new job, or even finding a new apartment, check your credit history beforehand. Even potential employers can get a look at your credit history if you give them permission—and if you don't give them permission you probably won't get the job anyway. However, only people with legitimate business needs can get a copy of your report, so you don't have to worry about your in-laws getting their hands on it.

According to Consumer Union, 48% of consumer credit reports are inaccurate. And other studies have shown similar results. Many errors on reports were serious enough to keep consumers from obtaining a loan or a credit card.

As we mentioned earlier in this chapter, there are three major credit-reporting agencies: Experian, Equifax, and Trans Union. They don't share information, so if you're checking your report, you'll need to check with all three agencies. If you've been denied credit within 60 days, you can get a free credit report; the very most you'll have to pay is $8 a report. If there are inaccuracies on your report or you find listings of credit cards you've cancelled, you have the right to have your report repaired in a timely manner. Write to the reporting agency and get it straightened out. Figure 3-1 gives you a form letter you can use to do this.

Here are the addresses of the major credit reporting agencies:

Experian (formerly TRW)
National Consumer Assistance Center
P.O. Box 949
Allen, TX 75013-0949
Phone: 888-397-3742
www.experian.com

Equifax
Information Service Center
P.O. Box 740241
Atlanta, GA 30374-0241
Phone: 800-685-1111
www.equifax.com

Trans-Union
Consumer Disclosure Center
P.O. Box 390
Springfield, PA 19064-0390
Phone: 800-888-4213
www.tuc.com

Date:

Credit Reporting Agency
Address

Dear Sir or Madam:

I hereby request my credit report.
Name:_____
Telephone Number:_____
Street Address:_____
City, State ZIP:_____
Social Security Number:_____
Date of birth:_____
Current address:_____Lived here as of:_____
Previous address:_____Lived here as of:_____
Spouse's Name:_____

As proof of my identification and current residence, I have enclosed a
copy of (enclose a copy of one of the following: your driver's license,
a recent utility bill or a recent credit card bill).

Thank you very much for your kind attention to this matter.

Sincerely,

Signature

Name

FIGURE 3-1. A LETTER YOU CAN USE TO GET A COPY OF YOUR CREDIT REPORT

Cost: $8 in all states except: Maine, $3; Connecticut, $5; Massachusetts, Maryland, Vermont, Georgia, Colorado, and New Jersey, the firstcopy is free.

We've checked our own credit histories, so we know you'll find errors on your report. Take the following situation as just one example of what happens all too often.

Dee has adult children and some of their credit histories were mixed in with hers. Her daughter Jennifer applied for a Stafford loan when she entered graduate school; she was turned down because of too much outstanding debt. Jennifer knew she didn't owe anyone anything and had even paid off her undergraduate loans before applying for graduate school. So she checked her credit history and she found credit cards from her college years, many of them store credit cards. She can remember vividly one Christmas when she didn't have a lot of money to spend and she found a wonderful offer: if she opened a store credit account, she would get a great discount on top of the sale price. So she took advantage of that opportunity, then never used the cards again. Unfortunately, she never cancelled them. So her credit history showed these various open lines of credit. She had to write to each of the creditors to cancel the cards and request that they send this information onto the reporting agencies. It took the whole first semester of graduate school to straighten out the mess.

So the moral of the story is to check your credit history *before* you need a loan. (Bonus moral: cancel credit cards that you're not using.)

When you check into your credit history, beware of the "fix-it firms." These companies claim to be able to repair your credit history. You don't need them. They cannot erase your bad credit and create a new identity for you. If your report contains incorrect information, you can correct it yourself. Credit repair companies by law are required to give you a copy of the booklet "Consumer Credit File Rights Under State and Federal Law" before you sign a contract, and they cannot ask you to pay up front.

If your credit report contains negative information that's accurate, you can't remove it. But it doesn't stay on forever. Federal law regulates how long accurate negative information can remain on your credit report. All negative information drops off your credit report after seven years, except for Chapter 7 bankruptcy filings, which stay on your report for 10 years.

Remember, it's a federal crime to make false statements on a loan or credit application—and that includes putting down an incorrect Social Security number. Don't mess with the feds.

How Debt Hurts You: Bankruptcy

In Chapter 1 we talked about good debt and bad debt. But too much of any kind of debt can be a problem. Debt hurts you in many ways. It encumbers your ability to advance in your profession or buy a home. And it can also destroy personal relationships, taint reputations, and mess up families. Talk with some homeless families and they'll show you the extreme consequences of debt.

Bankruptcy and You

"Bankruptcy" is a scary word for bank and credit card companies. Filing for bankruptcy may absolve you of your debts or allow you to get on a payment schedule to repay them, but it does not wipe the slate clean. Bankruptcy filings are listed on your credit report for up to 10 years. And it may very well be the reason a landlord won't rent to you or the bank won't give you a mortgage. A bankruptcy filing tends to frighten creditors away. Also it probably won't solve your problems: most taxes, child support, and alimony survive bankruptcy, so you'll still be responsible for making these payments.

A record 1.25 million individuals filed for bankruptcy in 2000. Bankruptcy has become an epidemic. The credit card issuers want some changes in the bankruptcy laws. There is proposed legislation in Washington to modify the laws. So if you're considering filing for bankruptcy, be sure you get updated information.

As mentioned earlier in this chapter, the bankruptcy laws were intended to help individuals who were in severe financial circumstances that they had not caused. The right to file for bankruptcy is regulated by federal law and is handled in federal court. We will cover only the two types of bankruptcy available for individuals—Chapters 7 and 13. These rules can be found, as you might suspect, in chapters 7 and 13 of the bankruptcy code.

Chapter 7 is often referred to as "straight bankruptcy" or "liquidation." The court appoints a trustee to collect and sell (liquidate) all property that is not exempted and pay creditors at least part of the debts owed. In Chapter 7 bankruptcy, very little property is exempt. Even your home and your car can be sold if they are mortgaged.

Chapter 13 bankruptcy permits a debtor to keep his or her home and other real property even in the face of foreclosure. Under the provisions of a Chapter 13 bankruptcy, debtors must reorganize their debts and pay them over an extended time period. This type of bankruptcy filing is best for the individual who has a steady income.

If you're considering bankruptcy, you can go it alone and learn how to file yourself. But we would recommend getting some professional help. If you can't afford an attorney, look to resources that may be free or provided on a sliding scale through legal aid services. Check with Consumer Credit Counseling Services or Debt Counselors of America to find out what's available to you where you live. Or call your local bar association and ask for a referral. You'll want an attorney who specializes in bankruptcy work. Filing for bankruptcy should only be a last resort, for truly desperate situations, since it will have a lasting effect on your financial well-being.

Credit Card Debt Resources

Here are some places to get tips on dealing with too much debt or to get basic information about credit cards:

Consumer Credit Counseling Services is a nationwide, nonprofit organization that charges what you can afford. To find an office near you, call 800-388-2227 or visit the Web site at **www.nfcc.org**.

myvesta.org provides informational materials, counseling, and referrals. Call 800-680-3328 or visit the Web site at **www.myvesta.org**.

The National Center for Financial Education publishes *The Do-It-Yourself Credit File Correction Guide*. To order, send a $10 check to NCFE, P.O. Box 34070, San Diego, CA 92163-4070. Add $3 for first-class mail. You can also visit the Web site at **www.ncfe.org** or call 888-462-2227.

Debt Counselors of America is a nonprofit organization that assists families and individuals with credit and debt management. Visit their Web site at **www.dca.org** or call 800-680-3328

Chapter 4

Get a Handle on the Paper Shuffle

Organize Your Stuff

Have you ever walked into a room and stood there wondering why you were there? It happens to all of us. And the busier we become, the more our rooms and our brains are cluttered with stuff—so much stuff in fact that we lose track of some of it. Does that sound like you?

This chapter is about organizing your stuff. Why in a financial book should there be a chapter devoted to the proverbial paper shuffle? Well, from experience we know that, if we can help you get your stuff organized, it will be easier for you to do your financial planning. And if something should happen to you, it will be easier for your family to locate the important stuff they may need.

> Order is Heav'n's first law.
> —Alexander Pope

If you've done your net worth statement, you have a good grasp on the kind of stuff you own, but do you know where the papers are for all of that stuff?

You may be the type of person we refer to as "Shoebox Sally." Everything goes into a shoebox (or some similar container), which then goes into the closet, and eventually ends up in the attic or basement. In that box you put your canceled checks, your receipts, and even your pension plan statements. But when you need to find something, it may take you hours, even days to locate it—if you're able to locate it at all. Besides the shoebox filing system, we know that you use the kitchen drawers, the area behind the toaster, and the top of the refrigerator as well.

The Manual Filing System

There's a better way. Don't just do this for yourself; do it for the people who may eventually have to go through your stuff to find something.

Go to one of those giant office supplies stores, like Staples or Office Depot. You'll find everything you need there to help you get organized. Our preference would be a filing cabinet. They come in all sizes and all colors, so you can decorate an area of your home as "your office." But filing cabinets take up space. So if you don't have enough space for a filing cabinet, think smaller. You can use those plastic crates that stack. They create a nice lightweight filing system that's easy to move around. You can keep your crates in a closet and haul them out when you need them. Don't forget to pick up some folders and labels while you're at the store.

> *A place for everything and everything in its place.*

That should about do it for the filing system. Now you just need to find some time to start sorting through the stuff you've accumulated over the years.

Using a Computer to Organize

Computers can also help you get organized. If you're using a program like Quicken to handle your checking account, you can also use the program to keep track of all of your holdings in mutual funds and stocks (your "portfolio"). And if you subscribe to an online service, you can update your portfolio holdings daily or evenly hourly if you want. By the way, we don't recommend that. You can easily become neurotic and consume vast quantities of Maalox if you get into updating your portfolio hourly.

Just one word of caution: back up your files on disk. It's a good idea to keep a paper copy as well. This is especially important if you are coupled and only one of you is computer-literate. A sad story but true: Dee was called into a situation to help a 40-year-old widow re-create lists of her stock and mutual fund holdings, for her recently deceased husband had kept everything on his computer at work—password-protected. It took over six months to re-create a paper trail.

The Important Stuff

So you've dragged out of the attic all of those shoeboxes and you're now wondering where to begin? We've listed below the papers that we think are important to keep and how long to keep them. We've come to the conclusion that people are either pack rats who save everything or tossers who keep nothing longer than a month. You need to be somewhere in between, knowing what to keep and what to toss.

Master File

Set up a master file that contains lists of all of your assets and all of your important documents (wills, trusts, durable power of attorney, medical directives, and passports). List all of your advisors and their updated addresses and phone numbers. Do the same for insurance policies, credit cards, investment, and bank accounts. At the end of this chapter is a worksheet that will help you organize your lists. It's a one-page document locator, so at a glance you will know what you have filed and where.

Taxes. Maintain a separate file for each calendar year for your personal tax data: records of income, transactions such as property sales, itemized deductions, etc. IRAs or pension contributions should be noted in this file as well as having a folder of their own. Keep copies of Form 1099s, as well as any documentation of your deductions, such as cancelled checks.

Banking. When reconciling bank statements (and you should be doing this monthly), transfer any canceled checks needed for tax documentation to the current year's files. Keep all checks that relate to the house, e.g., new roof. You'll need these when you sell your home, to help establish its cost basis. File these in your real estate file. Keep all other checks for one year. Retain check ledger and bank statements for at least seven years.

Stocks, Bonds, and Mutual Funds. It's best to maintain a file for each account and a folder for each holding. Keep all cost information relating to investments, so you can determine your cost basis when you sell them, to determine whether you had a profit or a loss. Keep copies of all 1099s—the form sent to you by the fund indicating capital gains and dividends paid during the year. You'll need all those old 1099s to determine the cost basis for your mutual funds.

Insurance Policies. You want separate folders for each type of insurance you have. Keep the most recent policy in your current file, along with any endorsements or addendum. Also keep old policies that provide liability protection, such as your homeowner's policy, for at least three years, just in case you should find yourself facing a lawsuit. Records of pending and paid health insurance claims should be kept in a separate file labeled "medical insurance payments."

Credit Cards. Retain the loan agreements and any new information the card issuer may send out with your monthly statement. Retain purchase slips and billing statements for at least one year. Staple all pertinent charge slips to the warranties so if you have to return an item you can find the paperwork. Maintain a list of all card numbers and the phone numbers to call in the event a card is lost or, worse, stolen.

Real Estate Documents. Closing papers, settlement sheets, deeds, and titles should be maintained in a separate file for each property. Keep copies only. The originals should be in a safety deposit box or fireproof safe. Keep in this file any documents, such as canceled checks or receipts, for work that increases the cost basis of your real estate.

Ownership Papers. Purchase records, receipts, and other items pertaining to ownership of cars, boats, or other large equipment or appliances should be maintained in separate files, with the warranties and instruction books. If something goes wrong, you know where to look.

Employment Records. Keep information relating to employee benefits, employee contracts, and copies of W-2s. Keep the W-2s until you are able to reconcile them with Social Security benefit statements.

Tax Returns. Keep copies of your tax returns for at least seven years. The IRS in most instances has three years to audit a return, unless they suspect fraud, in which case there's no time limit.

Warranties/Service Contracts/Instruction Booklets. File warranties and service contracts along with the receipts, in case you have to return an item or have it serviced. Maintain a file for instruction booklets, which you should update as you purchase new items.

Personal Data. Originals of personal records such as birth certificates, marriage certificates, adoption papers, military service documents, and divorce decrees should be stored in a safety deposit box or a fireproof safe. Original wills and trusts are best kept in another safe place, such as your lawyer's safe. This is because safety deposit boxes are often sealed upon death. Keep copies of wills, trusts, original durable powers of attorney, and medical directives in a safe but accessible place in your home.

Monthly Bills. Monthly phone, electricity, fuel oil, gas, and grocery bills can be filed in a house or maintenance file or individually. Keep for one year and then discard. You can keep lists of your annual expenses for comparison purposes.

Pensions and IRAs. Set up a permanent file for each retirement plan. File all annual statements showing contributions, distributions, and any rollovers. If you file IRS Form 8606, which is for a non-deductible IRA, keep copies in this file as well.

Miscellaneous. Now that so many people own video cameras, video-tape your home and its contents, to create a permanent record of all of your valuables. This will be helpful in the case of a robbery or a fire. Store the video in a safety deposit box or a fireproof safe. If you don't have a video of your home and its contents, keep a list of your belongings in a safe place and take pictures of your possessions. We know how tedious it can be to draw up a list but, as you've probably now discovered, you own a lot of stuff and you need to take steps to protect it.

What and Where

The worksheet we promised is on the next page. It will make life simpler—and we promise it will save you lots of time when you need to find an important document. But even more significant is that, if something should happen to you, others will be able to find those documents. Organizing your stuff will give you a sense of accomplishment. But what's more important is that it will be a gift to your family.

We also recommend that, as you get on in age, you hold annual family meetings to let everyone know where your stuff is located. No, not where the car keys are, but where you keep your files. Tell them if you've changed or added advisors in the last year and give them updated lists.

After completing the worksheet, make a copy for your files and then also give a copy to your attorney, a family member, or a trusted friend for safekeeping.

Location of Important Documents

For _____

Social Security No. _____

Spouse _____

Social Security No. _____

My valuable papers and assets are stored in these locations:

(A) Residence   Where _____

(B) Safe Deposit Box Bank _____   **Address** _____

(C) Lawyer's Office Address _____

(D) _____

(E) _____

(F) _____

Mark letter of location of each item on the blank line

___My Will (original)
___My Will (copy)
___Powers of Attorney
___Health Care Proxy
___My Burial Instructions
___Cemetery Plot Deed
___Spouse's Will (original)
___Spouse's Will (copy)
___Spouse's Power of
   Attorney
___Spouse's Health Care
   Proxy
___Spouse's Burial
   Instructions
___Document Appointing
   Children's Guardian
___Handwritten List of
   Special Requests
___Safe Combination,
   Business
___Safe Combination,
   Home
___Trust Agreements
___Life Insurance, Group
___Life Insurance, Individual
___Other Death Benefits
___Property and Casualty
   Insurance

___Health Insurance Policy
___Car Insurance Policy
___Homeowner's Insurance
   Policy
___Employment Contracts
___Partnership Agreements
___List of Checking and
   Savings Accounts
___Bank Statements,
   Cancelled Checks
___List of Credit Cards
___Certificates of Deposit
___Checkbooks
___Savings Passbook
___Record of Investments
___Securities
___Brokerage Account
   Records
___Stock Certificates
___Mutual Fund Shares
___Bonds
___Other Securities
___Corporate Retirement
   Plans
___Keough or IRA Plan
___Annuity Contracts
___Stock Option Plan
___Computer Password

___Stock Purchase Plan
___Profit-Sharing Plan
___Income and Gift Tax
   Returns
___Title and Deeds to Real
   Estate and Land
___Title Insurance
___Mortgage Agreement
___Rental Property Records
___Notes and Other Loan
   Agreement
___List of Stored Valuable
   Possessions
___Auto Ownership Records
___Boat Ownership Records
___Birth Certificate
___Citizenship Papers
___My Adoption Papers
___Military Discharge Papers
___Marriage Certificate
___Children's Birth Certificates
___Children's Adoption Papers
___Divorce/Separation Records
___Names and Addresses of
   Relatives and Friends
___List of Advisors
___Listing of Professional
   Memberships

Part Two

What Do You Want from Life?

W e all have goals. And most of our goals involve finances in some way, shape, or form. There's no getting around it: we need dollars to help us achieve our objectives in life. In this section, we'll highlight the four goals that matter to most Americans.

We'll help you decide if you want to buy a house. And if you do, we'll help you get from circling the ads in Sunday's paper to moving in.

Then, when you and the bank own a house with a garage, you want a car to park in the garage. We know just where to get one.

Now that you have the American dream—a house with a car in the garage and two kids to fill those spare bedrooms—you decide you want to educate those kids so they'll eventually move out. Hey, we understand: we want our kids to be educated and independent, too!

So how do you come up with the bucks to pay for what may be the largest single purchase of your earning career, college education for the kids? We can help here. (No, we strongly discourage robbing banks!) We'll give you some guidance on investing and what the real cost will be for your children to improve their minds and develop their earning potential. And buried in this section is some good solid advice on teaching your kids about money.

The biggest goal for all of us is retirement. We need to plan as if we will live to become centenarians. But some of us may be looking at retiring at 50, which would give us 50 years in that stage of our life called retirement. So how do you plan to pay for it? And can you be sure that your money will last as long as you do? This is the place to get the information.

Chapter 5

Owning the American Dream:
A House with a Car in the Garage

Buy or Rent?

S o you want the American dream, a home of your own with a car in the garage? At the end of this chapter, we'll help you put the car in the garage. But if you're currently renting, buying a home right now may not be the best move for you. There are pros and cons to this issue, especially if you're single and under 35.

If you've started a house search, you may have found that realtors tell you that if you rent you're just throwing money down the drain. We're here to tell you that may not be the case. We've also heard of well-meaning friends and relatives saying the same thing to those who

rent. If you're single, these are the same people who are wondering if you're ever going to get coupled and may even be pestering you about that. It's that commitment thing that keeps cropping up. Buying a house is definitely not as permanent as getting married, but it's still a big commitment.

The Disadvantages of Home Ownership

There are lots of issues to consider if you're thinking of buying a home. Are you ready for the commitment of home ownership? Maintaining a home takes time and money. Unless your new home is a condo with only a window box for flowers, there's outside maintenance you must do regularly. You can't just pick up and go on a two-week vacation without hiring someone to mow the lawn. Maybe you even need someone to water the flowers and check for newspapers. If you live in the north, it snows, right? So who shovels or plows the driveway and walks for you? Do you get up an hour earlier the morning of a snowstorm to get the driveway cleared so you can get to work? Do you hire someone to do it for you? Are you getting our drift here? A home is a responsibility—a big one.

We've been talking about the *time* commitment. So what about the *money* part? You'll need a mower to cut the grass and hoses to water it so it grows faster and thicker. Shovels, rakes, and snow blowers may start to show up on your Christmas wish list. What about the inside of your new digs? More rooms to clean and more windows to wash. And when you move from a three-room apartment to a seven-room house, you're likely to need more furniture. And appliances—you may need a refrigerator, a washer, and a dryer.

In the movie *The Money Pit*, Tom Hanks and Shelley Long bought a charming fixer-upper they found in the country, only to be quickly overwhelmed by the maintenance and repair it required. If you're thinking of buying a house, rent the video for a good laugh. Obviously the film exaggerated the problems of owning a home, but homeowners know that any house will have problems on a smaller scale.

The Wall Street Journal ran an article entitled "Every House Is a Money Pit" in September 1998. The conclusion: over a 30-year period a homeowner will spend three or four times the purchase cost of the home for maintenance and repairs. While that might be a slight exaggeration, over a 30-year period you'll probably replace your carpets two or three times, put on a new roof, paint the exterior of your home at least four times, and replace all of your appliances at least once.

Besides time and cost, there are other reasons you may not be ready to purchase a home. If you think you'll be living in an area for only three years or less, you probably won't have time to break even on your closing costs. In other words, when you sell, you'll likely lose money on the deal. And you certainly shouldn't be entertaining the idea of home ownership if you are in rocky marital situation; a house would only add to the turmoil. When renting, you're freer to take a new job and the move is easier and less costly. Finally, your money will probably earn a better rate of return if invested in the stock market rather than in the down payment on a house.

Now our intent here is not to discourage you from owning a house and enjoying your version of the American dream. But the next time your Uncle Ed says you're throwing money down the drain, you'll have some facts to throw back at him.

The Advantages of Home Ownership

So let's flip the coin over and discuss some of the advantages of home ownership.

Nowhere else in the world does the government help you with your purchase. Only in the U.S. do you a get a deduction for mortgage interest and property taxes paid. Long ago the government wanted to stimulate the building industry and the economy, so politicians came up with these tax breaks. And they've worked. Over 67% of U.S.

households own their homes—although most of them share that house with a bank.

There have been times when members of Congress have wondered about the wisdom of their predecessors, but this is a tax deduction that's ingrained in our system. So you'll get this deduction if you own a home. But remember: if you're in the 28% tax bracket, the deduction amounts to just 28¢ for every dollar you pay out.

> *A man's home is his castle or so it seems when he has to pay taxes on it.*

Then, when you sell your home, the government gives you another break. Changes in the tax law now allow you to shelter from capital gains up to $250,000 if you're single and $500,000 if you're married filing jointly. (You'll learn more about that in Chapter 24.)

Another plus to home ownership is more space. Those seven rooms are now easily filled with a boisterous growing family and overflowing with stuff. You may also be lucky enough to be living in an area where the real estate prices are appreciating more than just at the rate of inflation. And when you speak with your elders, they'll tell you it's a blessing to start retirement living in a home that's paid for.

Buy or Rent?

So, should you look into buying or should you continue to rent? The decision involves dollars and cents as well as common sense. You've got to consider your lifestyle and your needs as well as the costs of owning a home. Studies have shown that to reach a break-even point you must stay in a home for at least four years and that to start pulling ahead, to start getting some appreciation, you need to stay with it for 10 years.

Buying a House

OK, you've made the decision and you're ready to start hunting for the right house. Before you start circling ads in the Sunday paper, you need to do some homework. You need to figure out what you can afford.

How much cash do you have for a down payment? Normally 20% is the accepted down payment, but you can get into programs now with as little as 3% down. How low will they go? That's about as low as we've seen with conventional financing, though some VA loans are available to qualified veterans with nothing down. The more money you have for a down payment, the more house you'll be able to buy. So sometimes waiting and adding to your savings is the way to go.

How much can you afford to pay each month? Take a look at your cash flow and your current housing expenses. If there's no extra income floating around, then what you see is what you've got to spend. Now for the math part. There's a formula that lenders use when loaning money to a potential homeowner. Your total housing costs (mortgage payments, insurance, and taxes) should not exceed 28% of your gross income. There's more. Housing costs plus all of your other debt (credit cards, school loans, and auto loans) should not exceed 36% of your gross income. So do some calculations. Add up all of your current annual debt payments. Then divide that figure by your annual income. The answer is the percentage of your income you're using to repay debt. If it's more than 8%, you're probably better off paying down your consumer debt before taking on the burden of a mortgage.

If you don't want to do the math yourself, you can speak with a potential lender or real estate broker to help you figure out if you would qualify for a mortgage. Pre-qualification is usually free, so stay away from any professional who wants to charge you for this service. Pre-qualification is not a guarantee of getting a loan; after all, the lender or broker is just trying to figure out what you can afford.

If you get this far, check your credit history before you go to the next step, which is getting a pre-approval. When you're looking to be pre-approved, you'll fill out a loan application. The lender will want your credit history. Then a loan underwriter will review all of this. That's the normal process, but you can find mortgage companies that offer faster service. You can even find companies that will pre-qualify you via the Internet.

If you're very serious about buying a house, we suggest you get pre-approved for a mortgage. This will show sellers that you're serious and, if there's more than one offer on the table, you will have an advantage because you know and they know you can get the money to make the purchase.

OK. Back to the Sunday papers and the open houses. Decide how far you want to live from your work and, if you have children, check out the school system. The better the school system, the more expensive the town or city is likely to be. Do you want to live in the city, the suburbs, or the country? Are you looking for amenities such as a shopping center, movie theatres, and sports facilities? Check out the area.

Often, the easiest way to do that is online. In our research, we've found that there are more than 35,000 Web sites related to real estate, so we're not even going to try to list them here.

The old-fashioned way of house hunting is still good. Head to a realtor's office and start looking for houses. Check out the town by spending some time there. See what special events might be going on, such as a Christmas fair. Talk to the people coming out of the post office or at the coffee shop. Ask about doctors and the nearest hospital. If you have kids you'll want to know where the hospital is, for by the time most kids make it to adulthood they have had at least one trip to the ER. Where are the churches or synagogues? Get a local newspaper and find out a little about local politics and what's considered important enough to make the front page.

What Kind of House?

Next, what kind of home do you want to purchase? A single-family home or a condominium? (We cover multifamily homes in Chapter 18.) How large do you need? How large do you want? Do you have animals or want to get some?

If you've already decided you want to live in the city, you may be limited in your search, for there may not be a lot of single-family homes available. You may find yourself looking at condos—and not by choice.

Condos may have a market in cities where land is at a premium and for individuals who may want a place of their own but don't want to deal with the lawn or other maintenance. They may be a good choice for people who are retired and want to winter in the South and summer in the North. Condos are often used as a first-time home purchase, but more often than not people end up losing money on them. You just might want to wait until you have enough money for a down payment on a house.

If you're considering a condo, there are a few things you should keep in mind. Buildings that are mostly tenant-occupied can be a problem because owners living offsite are not as interested in maintenance as they would be if they lived in the building. Next, there are condo fees. These have a way of creeping up, often faster than inflation, so check to see what kind of reserve fund the condominium association has accrued before you buy into the building. You want to be sure that if a new roof is needed there's money already there to cover it.

But if you have a choice, buying a single-family home is still the best deal around. It has better resale value and is easier to sell if you need to move it in a hurry. Plus, you've got options with a single-family dwelling: you can expand it, add a swimming pool, or turn the garage into a recreation room.

Before we move on to mortgages, a word of caution about size. It's not prudent to buy the biggest house. Longstanding advice about buying more house than you need can come around and bite you in the butt. If your home is consuming all of your cash flow, you may not be able to afford to do other things, such as invest in your 401(k). You've heard the stories about people being house poor. Homes are really not meant to be investments; they are people shelters and not tax shelters. Home ownership generates pride and a sense of accomplishment. Remember, when you look at the net worth statement, that a house is a use asset (you live in it) for most of its existence. Can it be an investment? Well, all of us need a place to live, so if you sell your home and make a profit, you may not have to pay much in taxes, but you'll probably need those dollars to put another roof over your head.

Mortgages, Down Payments, and PMI

Where do you find a mortgage? Today you may be able to get one on the Internet or at the supermarket. That's right: banks are going out to find people like you. Banks and mortgage companies no longer hold onto your mortgage; they sell them to get money to help finance another house. So grab the yellow pages, head to your local banks, or get on the Internet to find a mortgage.

But banks and mortgage companies are not the only ones offering loans. The Federal Housing Administration (FHA), which is an arm of the Department of Housing and Urban Development (HUD), operates several mortgage programs with low down payments. Buyers may be able to qualify for a mortgage with a down payment of 5% or less of the cost of the home. FHA loans are available from most of the lenders that offer conventional mortgages. The FHA guarantees participating lenders against loss from default on their loans. Check out your state or local housing agency for help with programs that are specific to your state. The Veterans Administration (VA) provides home financing, sometimes with no down payment, for qualifying veterans and also guarantees loss from default on these loans.

Let's just take a quick look at the key players in the secondary mortgage market. Most of you have heard of Fannie Mae. Well, believe us, she's not going to invite you to her place any time soon, but she may help you find a place of your own. Fannie Mae is derived from the acronym FNMA, which stands for the Federal National Mortgage Association. Freddie Mac is FHLMC, the Federal Home Loan Mortgage Corporation. Fannie and Freddie are quasi-governmental agencies that serve as intermediaries between Wall Street and the mortgage lenders. They are former government agencies that have been converted into for-profit government-sponsored enterprises (GSE).

Now there's also Ginnie Mae, a cousin of Freddie and Fannie. Ginnie is GNMA, the Government National Mortgage Association. Ginnie Mae works between Wall Street and the FHA and VA loan programs.

GNMA, FHLMC, and FNMA buy mortgages from lenders, package the mortgages as securities, and sell the securities to investors, thus ensuring a constant supply of fresh money for home mortgages. (If you're interested in investing, check out Chapter 16 to find out how to buy these repackaged mortgages.)

Now you know where to look for mortgages. What kind of mortgage do you want? Well, that depends.

The conventional mortgage is a 30-year fixed-rate mortgage, which means payments for 30 years at a set interest rate. Interest rates have been very low, so a 30-year mortgage has become quite popular. You can also get a 15-year or 20-year mortgage: you can pay off your mortgage sooner and usually at a lower interest rate. Let's suppose that you want to borrow $150,000. If you get a 30-year fixed mortgage at 7%, your monthly payment will be $1,000 and you'll pay $209,000 in interest to borrow that $150,000. If you get a 15-year fixed mortgage at 6.75%, your monthly payment will be $1,327 and you'll pay $89,000 in interest to borrow the $150,000. You'll save $120,000 over the life of the mortgage and own the home 15 years earlier—if you can afford to pay $327 more a month.

Our advice here would be, if you're buying your first home, to take the 30-year fixed rate and pay it off as if it were a 15- or 20-year mortgage. This gives you the cushion of the lower payments and still allows you to lower your interest costs. But make sure that your mortgage will allow prepayment without penalties. If paying extra each month is a hardship, then stick to the original 30-year payment schedule. Also, do it yourself! There are companies selling services that will help you prepay your mortgage with biweekly payment plans. What they offer you can do yourself, by making two extra principal payments a year.

> A man builds a fine house and now ... he has to furnish, watch, show it, and keep it in repair the rest of his days.
> —Emerson

Also available are adjustable-rate mortgages (ARMs), which are less costly in the beginning. The most common have a low rate the first year and then get recalculated each year, using an index of government bond rates. ARMs are usually not popular when 30-year fixed rates are low. No one wants to take a chance that his or her mortgage rate will go up from year to year. There are some ARMs that maintain a fixed rate for a number of years—three, five, seven, or 10—and then adjust annually. These might be useful if you think you'll be moving in less than 10 years.

So how much have you saved for the down payment? Putting down 20% makes the most fiscal sense, but many people don't want to wait the time it takes to accumulate a large down payment. There are FHA loans that allow you to get in for as little as 3%. But a word of caution here. Everything costs more than you anticipated, especially when it comes to owning a home. Getting in for a very small down payment may end up costing you more. If you can't afford the monthly payments, you could lose the house.

There's another cost associated with down payments under 20%—private mortgage insurance (PMI). The lender requires that you have insurance to protect them in case you default on the loan. Buying such insurance through the lender is convenient but it could be costly. See if you can get the insurance on your own. Here's why. Once you have 20% equity in your home, you should be able to cancel the insurance. That's not easy if you buy it through your lender. And in some cases the lender may ask that you bear the cost of an appraisal to prove that you have 20% of equity in your home. For new home purchases, lenders must alert the homeowner when his or her equity reaches 20%, to allow the homeowner to cancel the insurance. But lenders do not have to include the appreciation of your home; they can use just your payment schedule to calculate the 20% equity. With average policy costs of $700 annually, it's worth your time and energy to stay on top of this.

There's one more source for help when purchasing a home: your retirement plan. You can tap into a regular IRA without incurring an early withdrawal penalty of 10% if you use the money to buy your first home. The lifetime limit is $10,000 to build or buy a first home that will be your principal residence. If you hold the new Roth IRA for at least five years, you can withdraw money from your account free of income taxes if you use it to buy your first home ($10,000 limit). (We'll discuss IRAs in more detail in Chapter 19.)

Mortgage Math

So how much does all of this really cost? It will cost a lot more than you initially figure, so be sure you don't use all of your money for the down payment. When you want to get pre-approved, there may be an application fee of up to $250. Then there will be a charge for the credit history report, normally around $50. A documentation preparation fee of around $175 is now charged by about 65% of the lenders. That's just for starters. Oh, did we tell you that each lender you approach will charge these same fees if you show up wanting a mortgage?

You are now ready to make a commitment and you want a mortgage. Well, the lender may ask you to pay *points* on the mortgage in return for a lower interest rate. Points are prepaid interest on your mortgage, charged up front. Each point is 1% of the loan amount. One point on a $100,000 mortgage is $1,000. Points are tax-deductible and payment is expected upon closing. If you're not planning to hold the mortgage forever, using points may not work in your favor. You're going to need to figure that out or get your friendly lender to help. Also, if you need a jumbo loan (more than $275,000), you'll more than likely be paying a higher interest rate.

Now what if you want to compare mortgages? You'll need to use the *annual percentage rate* (APR). The APR is not foolproof, but it gives you the real rate for the interest, points, and other costs associated with a mortgage over the life span of the mortgage. So you can compare apples with apples. Of course, if you hold a 30-year mortgage for only 10 years, the actual APR will be higher. But APR is the only tool available when shopping for loans.

Closing Costs

Finally, we get to closing costs. If you make it to this point, just show up with a blank check and enough money in your account to cover the following expenses. First, there's a *title search*: someone checks the title records to be sure that you're buying the house from the legal owners and there are no liens on the house. That could cost as much as $700. Next, we have *title insurance*, which will protect you if the title search was incorrect and you lose your interest in the property. The lender will want to have the property appraised, inspected, and surveyed. Who's going to pay for that? Guess! So add that to the list. You'll also need to pay the attorney. The new deed and mortgage have to be recorded at the courthouse, so there's another expense on your list. Have we mentioned *escrow fees*? You may need to pay some costs up front and the lender will hold onto them until they are due, such as taxes.

There are many other fees that lenders often tack on, so you need to be alert. Washington is trying to do something about this, especially as there were 5.2 million sales of existing homes and 1.6 million sales of new construction in 2000. Congress is considering overhauling the laws that govern the mortgage process, to make it easier for the consumer. But for right now just keeping asking, "How much?" and "Why?" Do some research and comparison shop. Buying a home is one of the largest purchases you'll ever undertake. It's worth doing it right.

Refinancing

Refinancing a mortgage has gotten to be a science. The old rule of thumb was that if you were planning to stay in your home at least another four years and interest rates had dropped by at least two percentage points it was a good idea to refinance. Today anything goes. If you can get a no-point, no-closing-cost refinancing and the difference is only 0.05%, it's probably worth the paperwork and effort on your part. But if you start paying all of the closing costs again and the lender wants up-front points, you'd better stick with the old rule of thumb. But you need to do some homework here. And there are plenty of software and online programs to help you decide which is best for you.

Let's look at the reasons you may want to refinance:

✔ To reduce the rate on your current mortgage

✔ To switch from an ARM to a fixed-rate mortgage

✔ To consolidate debts

✔ To consolidate mortgages

✔ To reduce a 30-year mortgage to a 15-year mortgage

Home Buying Resources

We'll end our discussion of homes with a few resources that we'd recommend.

Books

The Banker's Secret by Marc Eisenson

10 Steps to Home Ownership: A Workbook for First-Time Buyers by Ilyce R. Glink, Web site: **www.thinkglink.com**

Starting Out: The Complete Home Buyer's Guide by Dian Davis Hymer

The Complete Idiot's Guide to Buying and Selling a Home by Shelley O'Hara

Web Sites

Quicken offers a money Web site with lots of good information: **www.quicken.com**

HSH Associates Financial Publishers has consumer information: **www.hsh.com**

BankRate Monitor offers educational material: **www.bankrate.com**

All three sites have up-to-date mortgage rates as well as worksheets with built-in calculators to help you figure out such things as what size mortgage you can afford or whether you should refinance. Some have links to help you get pre-approved. Check out your local bank or mortgage company online as well.

Putting a Car in the Garage

Buying a car probably ranks about No. 3 when it comes to major purchases, right after home buying and a college education for your kids. That is, unless you lump together all of the cars you'll ever buy. Think about this: we keep our cars an average of five years, so if we start buying officially at age 20 and stop at age 85, we will have owned 13 cars. And the prices keep going up, so if your very first car cost $8,000 and prices rise at an annual average of 3%, your last car will cost over $55,000, even if you don't upgrade. So over a lifetime of driving you will have spent $348,000 buying cars. That's a bundle of money any way you look at it. So it's a good idea to do a little research before buying a car.

The best way to buy is buy *used*. As soon as you drive a new car off the lot, it's used and has begun to depreciate in value. There are some very good deals on used cars, especially now that so many cars are

being leased. When these cars come on the market in bunches, the dealers may need to move them off the lot quickly. Many of them have partial coverage under the new car warranty.

But it may not pay to buy used if the vehicle you're thinking about depreciates very little in value. If it's a hot car, such as one of the sport utility vehicles, it may not be a lot cheaper to buy used. Check out the Blue Book value and arm yourself with information before you start your search. A word of caution here: start car shopping before you need to replace the vehicle you're driving now. It's a lot easier to be smart about buying a car if you're not driving from dealer to dealer in a clunker that may die at any moment.

> *Every now and then you see a car so old that it's actually paid for!*

So maybe you want a new car, but you don't know whether to buy or to lease. Most people don't fully understand the difference. Many just see that they can drive more car if they lease rather than buy. Leasing offers lower monthly costs, but in the long run it could end up costing you more if you decide to purchase your leased vehicle at the end of the lease.

Here's how leasing works. You're renting a car from a third party, the leasing company. The lease is based on the price the leasing company must pay for the car and the lease interest rate. There are other variables, such as the vehicle you choose, the depreciation schedule for that car, your up-front down payment, state taxes, and your driving habits. Confused? Most people are. So much so, in fact, that the Federal Reserve Board has published a guide, *Keys to Vehicle Leasing*. The Federal Reserve has also set rules for what dealers and lessors must tell customers. That's right: the Fed is in charge here. The regs may not have much teeth, but at least it's a start. To get your copy, call the Fed at 202-452-3244 or download it from www.bog.frb.fed.us.

Let's take a look at the differences between leasing and buying:

Advantages of Leasing

✔ The down payment is low.
✔ The monthly payments are low.
✔ You can drive more car than you could afford to buy.

✔ The tax rules favor leasing over borrowing if you use your car for business.

✔ You can purchase the car when the lease ends.

Disadvantages of Leasing

✔ The mileage limits can increase the cost of driving by 25¢ a mile.

✔ Wear and tear charges can add up to be expensive.

✔ You're locked into a three-year lease term and it's expensive to terminate early.

✔ There's no trade-in to help with the next lease or a purchase.

Just an aside from the authors: Dee owns her Volvo and Dave leases his Jeep.

Should you lease or buy? It's up to you, but get all of the facts before you commit, because once you sign a lease it can be costly to change your mind. A book that might be helpful is *Leasing Lessons for Smart Shoppers* by Mark Eskeldson. Here are three helpful Web sites:

✔ **www.leasesource.com** offers sample contracts and a lease vs. buy calculator.

✔ **www.edmunds.com** has car-buying information and prices.

✔ **www.kbb.com** has information on the wholesale and retail values of used cars.

Chapter 6 | Paying for Education

The More You Learn, the More You'll Earn

Your greatest financial asset is your ability to produce an income. The best investment you can make is in yourself. College graduates on average earn almost 60% more than high school graduates, and workers with a master's degree earn 100% more than high school graduates. Over time the wealth gap widens. The more money you earn, the more you'll have to save and invest and the more you can contribute to your retirement plan.

Many companies in the technology, service, and information sectors will hire *only* workers with a college degree. These jobs require higher math, language, reasoning, and communication skills. Only 10% of the population *is currently* working in manufacturing. And those jobs are very different from those in manufacturing only 10 or 20 years ago.

Your objective here should be to create choices and opportunities that will allow you some control over your job situation. Continuing education is the best and perhaps the only way you'll be able to compete in the job market. Information becomes obsolete very quickly today. The odds are that you'll have an average of eight jobs in your lifetime; if you're in a high tech field, it may be many times that. It's *your* responsibility to keep your career moving ahead.

Don't rely on your employer or the government, though both your employer and the government can often help you in several ways. Your employer may make available workshops or classes you can take. Find out what's available and sign up. If your company provides educational benefits in the form of tuition assistance, use the benefits to get a degree or upgrade your job skills. If your employer doesn't offer benefits or training seminars, take courses on your own. The federal and state governments not only provide subsidized educational opportunities for everyone, but often help pay for them as well. Look into education loans, grants, and even scholarships to help cover expenses.

The Taxpayer Relief Act of 1997 made some strides in helping taxpayers pay for education and the recent Economic Growth and Tax Relief Reconciliation Act of 2001 went even further to help. Effective in 2002 it helps with everything from private kindergarten to graduate studies. The newest tax law change will allow an employee to exclude from income any employer-provided education assistance both on the graduate level and the under graduate level.

The Hope Education Credit, a tax credit of up to $1,500 for qualified tuition and fees paid during the year on behalf of a student. It is 100% of the first $1,000 paid and 50% for the next $1,000 paid. It is available only for the first two years of a student's post-secondary education. The Lifetime Learning Credit is a credit of up to 20% of qualified tuition and fees paid during the taxable year on behalf of a student. Unlike the Hope credit, this credit may be claimed for an unlimited number of taxable years. There are income limits associated with both credits. To qualify, your adjusted gross income must be under $100,000 if you file a joint return or under $50,000 if you file single.

For 2001 you can not claim one of these credits if you have also used EE Bonds, an Education IRA or a distribution from a 529 plan to pay college expenses. The rules change for 2002 though. These credits can be claimed as long as the money from the other sources are not used for the same qualified education expenses for which the credit is claimed.

As many as 45% of college students are *over age 25*, so college isn't just for 18- to 22-year-olds today. Aim for a certificate or degree at the next level in your chosen area. If you want to change careers, you may need to go back to school for the basics. If you have a master's degree, you're probably better off for job purposes in most fields if you get another master's degree rather than a Ph.D.

In exploring opportunities to further your education, check out these types of schools:

✔ Vocational/technical schools

✔ Community colleges

✔ State and private colleges and universities

✔ Distance learning

This last category is a fast-growing group of online educational institutions, at least half of which are affiliated with campus-centered schools. About 55% of the colleges in the U.S. now offer some type of distance learning programs. You can get a college, graduate, or professional degree without leaving home. There are over 1 million students currently enrolled in such programs. A good resource is *The Best Distance Learning Graduate Schools: Earning Your Degree Without Leaving Home* by Vicky Phillips and Cindy Yager. Also check out **www.petersons.com/dlearn**.

Do some research to locate the kinds of programs you want. A good place to start is at the local library or get on the Web and start to browse. Even the smallest community college has its own Web page and provides access to its faculty members via e-mail. You can enhance your career opportunities by leveraging your experience and skills through continuing education.

> *Whenever you are asked if you can do a job, tell 'em, "Certainly, I can!"— then get busy and find out how to do it.*
> —Theodore Roosevelt

Remember that, to employers, you are what you know, and today's skills are becoming outdated very quickly. In almost every field, technology at some level will be part of the required skill set. Machinists need to know how to program software and operate computers. Truck drivers travel with their laptops. Shipping clerks keep track of inventory. Elementary school cafeteria workers know exactly how many pizzas to make for Friday's lunch. Take whatever opportunities arise. If your company is offering a computer class, be the first to sign up. Don't fall behind—or you'll be left behind.

Our best advice: always plan as if you're going to be downsized (politically correct jargon for "terminated") next week. Keep your resume up to date. Make notes about special projects you've worked on and place them in your personal job file. Networking is extremely important if you're downsized, so also keep your database up to date. A few years ago we would have said keep your Rolodex up to date, but the times they are changing. Many of the jobs that will be available in the 21st century aren't even on our radar screen today.

College for Your Kids: How Much Is It Going to Cost?

A friend of ours has triplets and having triplets you might expect the parents to have lots of war stories. Well, when the boys were born, more than one friend asked if the new parents knew how much it would cost to send three kids to college. Even with both mom and dad working and some financial aid, it's going to cost a bundle.

So if you can still hold your bundle of joy in your arms, now is the best time to start saving for college. That gives you 18 years or more to accumulate the small fortune you'll need. The best time to start is when they're still in diapers. According to the College Board, the average costs for an entering freshman in the fall of 1999-2000 school year was $23,651 for a private college and a public was $10,909. These numbers included tuition, some fees, room and board, and transportation.

We've added a modest inflation factor of four percent to those numbers because the College Board found that college costs increased not much more than 4% recently. Doing this, we came up with the average four-year cost to be $104,915 for a private college education and $46,509 for a public college education. So you can get a general idea of what it will cost to send those triplets to college in 18 years.

College costs have increased faster than the rate of inflation over the years, so using four percent is conservative. In the '80s college

Year	Inflation Rate = 4%		Inflation Rate = 6%	
	Private	**Public**	**Private**	**Public**
2000	104,915	46,509	108,989	50,562
2001	109,112	48,369	115,529	53,598
2002	113,476	50,304	122,460	56,811
2003	118,015	52,316	129,808	60,220
2004	122,736	54,409	137,596	63,833
2005	127,645	56,585	145,852	67,663
2006	132,751	58,848	154,603	71,723
2007	138,061	61,202	163,879	76,027
2008	143,584	63,651	173,712	80,588
2009	149,327	66,197	184,135	85,423
2010	155,300	68,844	195,183	90,549
2011	161,512	71,598	206,894	95,982
2012	167,973	74,462	219,308	101,741
2013	174,692	77,441	232,456	107,845
2014	181,679	80,538	246,414	114,316
2015	188,946	83,760	261,199	121,175
2016	196,504	87,110	276,871	128,445
2017	204,364	90,595	293,483	136,152
2018	212,539	94,218	311,092	144,321
2019	221,041	97,987	329,758	152,980
2020	229,882	101,907	349,543	162,159
2021	239,077	105,983	370,516	171,889
2022	248,641	110,222	392,747	182,202
2023	258,586	114,631	416,311	193,134
2024	268,930	119,216	441,290	204,722
2025	$279,687	$123,985	$467,768	$217,006

FIGURE 6-1. PROJECTED COLLEGE COSTS AT 4% AND 6% INFLATION RATES

inflation was at double digits. For comparison Figure 6-1 shows projected college costs through 2025 at both 4% and 6% inflation. You can see what a big difference it makes. A word of caution here: these are average numbers. And if you want your kid to go to Harvard, it's going to cost you a lot more.

From Dee's experience we've learned that these costs are just the beginning of what we'll call the "college experience." If you have a kid who is one or two years away from entering college, we need to tell you about all of the other things you'll be paying for. To estimate costs, we added up tuition, fees, room and board, and modest transportation costs.

What no one tells you about are the other expenses. Say junior just got into your alma mater, and it's clear across the country. You're proud, but have you thought about what it'll cost to fly that kid home three or four times a year? And what if he wants a car to make it easier on you so you don't have to drive to pick him up?

Then there's the dorm room. It will need some additional furniture, perhaps a refrigerator to feel like home. Of course, they'll need music, lamps, maybe a TV, a telephone, and an answering machine, so you can leave messages and ask them if they're OK. Then there's wall decorations, maybe an area rug, curtains, bedding-from experience we can tell you if the school requires extra long single sheets, nothing else will fit those mattresses. Did we mention clothes? The in-style may be the grungy look, but the prices are anything but grungy. Did we mention the computer the school just may require? We think you're getting the picture here.

And there's more. Entertainment—who pays for the concerts that appear regularly on college campuses, the new CDs, spring break trips, and the nightly food run for pizza? Then they have to have such things as shaving cream, razors, make-up, shampoo, toothpaste, and deodorant. And that telephone bill is really a biggie. Can't start college without your own cell phone! Your freshman just left his girlfriend back home, and he wants to call her every night—not you but her. Who's going to pay for that?

It's a good idea to sit down with your student and have a money talk before he or she heads off to college. And if you have a freshman consider yourself lucky because you won't have to undo any bad habits from years already spent in college. Discuss who's going to be responsible for each expense. Have your student earmark summer earnings to pay for some of these extra costs.

Mission Impossible: How to Pay for College

OK. We know you're numb: it's sticker shock! But keep in mind our friend with the triplets—there's always someone worse off than you. Now do you feel better? We've got some advice to help you feel even better.

There are ways you can save and invest for education expenses. Perhaps when you looked at Figure 6-1 you thought, "I'll never be able to save it all." Well, guess what? Most parents can't save enough to cover all of the costs. So how do you pay for it, short of robbing a bank each semester? And remember what we said about Bonnie and Clyde in Chapter 2? They got caught robbing banks.

Start saving as soon as you can. Putting away even small amounts each month adds up. Go back to Chapter 2 and check out those mutual fund families that let you invest for $50 or less. The more time you have before your kid starts school, the more risk you can take with the investments.

If you have five years or more, choose a growth mutual fund, even an index fund will work here. Check out Chapter 15 for more help. If you have under four years, look to a balanced mutual fund that invests in stocks and bonds. Keep in mind that you actually have almost an eight-year time horizon before you make the final payment for your kid's education. If the kid is a junior in high school and you have not begun to save, put the money into a money market account or a short-term CD. You want to be sure the money is available to make that first tuition payment in two years.

We have included two new ways to save for college using qualified state savings plan (529 plans) and the Education IRA. Check out chapter 14 to learn more about using EE Bonds for college education expenses.

529 Plans and Prepaid State Tuition Plans

Every state has some sort of a prepaid state tuition plans available and these plans have been around for a while. They allow you to lock in tuition costs at current levels. Some are good, some are OK, some not worth it, and most have restrictions that the child must be state resident to enter the program and must attend school in-state. If the child goes somewhere else or doesn't use the money, the returns are quite meager. All of these plans are run by the offices of the individual state treasurers.

In 1997 Congress sweetened the deal a bit, passing a law that allows assets in state-run college savings plans to grow tax-deferred until the child starts college, and then to be taxed at the child's tax rate. These plans are sometimes referred to as 529 Investment Plans. So many states began to set up enhanced programs that allowed the participants choices. They stopped restricting residency rules as well as the use of in-state schools exclusively. And the savings choices no longer were just state bonds but now mutual funds managed by financial institutions such as Fidelity or TIAA-CREFF. The earnings on these investments compounded tax-deferred until the kiddo began to use them for college expenses and then were taxed at the child's rate.

Now that was a pretty a sweet deal. Well Congress just made it sweeter!

Starting in 2002 the earnings on the 529 plans withdrawn to pay for college expenses, tuition, room & board, book, supplies and fees (you're still on the hook for the kid's phone bill!) are not subject to a federal income tax. Not bad! If you invested in one of the private pre-paid tuition programs sponsored by a post secondary institution or a consortium of schools the tax free exemption goes into effective in 2004. Nonqualified withdrawals are subject to income tax as well as penalties. The IRS slaps on a 10% penalty and the state may also include a penalty as well. The old regs would allow you to use the money for more than one child in a family if it had not been consumed by the first child. The new regs expand the definition of family to include cousins.

We love these plans! There is no income limit as to who can contribute to the plan for the child and there are plans out there that allow contributions as small as $15 per month. Also many plans allow up $250,000 to be contributed over time or at once on behalf of the child. You can take advantage of a special gifting rule (check out chapter 26) with these plans and gift up to $50,000 and if your spouse joins in $100,000 at one time to the child's account. The IRS assumes you will not give this beneficiary any more gifts over the next five years so it would be as if you had used your annual $10,000 gift exemption over five years.. So if you are a grandparent and want to get this new grandbaby's college fund off to a great start open it with a $50,000 contribution. Assuming an 8% return in 18 years she'll have $200,000 in her account. Now if she doesn't use it all for college she has until she is 30 to use it for graduate school. By the way the tax savings on the account would be close to $40,000.

For a great over view of 529 plans check out Joe Hurley's website **www.savingforcollege.com** and his book, The Best Way to Save for College. It has an easy to view comparison chart on all of the state programs and which ones that are available for nonresidents. Then contact the College Savings Plans Network at 877-277-6496 or visit their Web site at **www.collegesavings.org**. This site is run by the state treasurers association and you can click onto your state to learn even more about these plans.

Educational IRAs

Our legislators in Washington are really trying to make college affordable for everyone. They really are! They gave us Education IRAs in 1997, which can be established for children under 18 years of age, but there's a contribution limit of $500 a year. Well the tax act of 2001 changed all of that. As of 2002 you will be able to contribute $2000 annually to an Education IRA. The contribution is not tax-deductible, but the earnings will accumulate tax-free and will remain tax-free if used for the child's education expenses. Although this is called an IRA, it's a savings plan, not a retirement plan: the account earnings must be used for education expenses or they become taxable income. For taxpayers filing a joint return in 2001, there's an income ceiling that starts at $150,000 and phases out completely at $160,000. For single taxpayers, the ceiling starts at $95,000 and phases out at $110,000. Those numbers change only for taxpayers filing a joint return in 2002, the phase out begins at $190,000 and goes away with an income over $220,000.

Anyone can set up an Educational IRA for a child-not just his or her parents. So if you're above the income limit, you might be able to get the grandparents to set one up. Or set one up for your favorite niece.

The guys in Washington went one better with the Education IRA. Starting in 2002 the withdrawals from the Education IRA can be used not just for a college education but for K-12 expenses as well, including the purchase of computer technology or equipment or Internet access and related services. And if you have a special needs student, contributions are allowed above the age of 18.

If your little one is still in diapers and you are able to contribute $2,000 a year until she is 18 you could have a tax free windfall for her college education expenses. If we assume an 8% return, you you'll have $75,000 to use for her education. You will have invested $36,000 over those 18 years but it did earn $39,000 and if you are in the 25% tax bracket that is a tax savings of almost $10,000. Oh and by the way with the Education IRAs you get to choose how the money is invested.

Help from the Colleges Themselves

Financial help may come from the colleges themselves. Many students are eligible for some kind of aid. For most parents, much of the aid is in the form of loans or work-study programs. And if your family income is over $75,000 annually, don't expect to be eligible for such aid. Grants (which don't have to be repaid) are now harder and harder to get, and most often they're merit-based.

Financial aid is tricky, and you'll find advisors out there who will tell you that they can fix your applications so that you'll receive more aid. Beware! College financial aid officers read the same stuff you do and are aware of the methods being used. There are still scholarships available but they are harder to get. Check out **www.collegeboard.com** or **www.petersons.com** for information about available aid as well as other resources. You'll even find useful financial aid calculators online. Check out the Department of Education site at **www.ed.gov** as well as **www.finaid.org** for more information on financial aid.

Other Sources of Funding

When your little tyke started talking at an early age and she could count up to 20 with Big Bird, maybe you thought you had a genius on your hands and you could count on a college scholarship. Now, years later, here you are: your daughter is graduating from high school and the college of her choice tells you that your family's share for this year is $10,000. Where do you get it? You may have to borrow. Here are several sources you can check out:

- ✔ Stafford loans are subsidized by the federal government and are need-based. They allow you to borrow up to $35,125 for undergraduate work and $18,500 a year for graduate level work. The interest rate is variable and is based on the 91 day Treasury bill plus 1.7% and is capped at 8.25%.

- ✔ A Perkins loan, although subsidized by the federal government, allows you to borrow directly from the school at a 5% interest rate and no payments are due until 9 months after graduation. Unfortunately, not all students are eligible. Perkins loans are for students who have exceptional financial needs.

- ✔ Parent Loans for Undergraduate Students (PLUS) are available also from the federal government, and loan payments must begin within 60 days after the final loan disbursement. Interest is also variable and based on 52 week Treasury Bill plus 3.1% and capped at 9%.

- ✔ A last resort is to go to your local bank and see what it has to offer in the form of a private loan, also know as an alternative loan. Interest rates will be higher than the other loans mentioned, but there will no federal forms to fill out.

You do get some help with those loan payments. For the year 2001, there's a deduction available for the first 60 months of interest paid on qualified education expenses for a taxpayer and his or her spouse or dependents. The maximum deductions available is $2,500.

The deduction will begin to phase out between $40,000-$55,000 for single taxpayers, and for married filing jointly the phase out is between $60,000-$75,000. Not really much help for the middle-class taxpayer.

But starting in 2002, the rules change for the better. The deduction phases out for single taxpayers with an income between $50,000-$65,000 and for married filing jointly it is $100,000 to $130,000. And to sweeten the pie a bit more these income levels will be adjusted annually for inflation and the 60 month limitation will also go away in 2002. The deduction can be taken whether you file a long or short form 1040.

Don't forget about those credits we described earlier in the chapter. The Hope Education Credit and Lifetime Learning Credit can be used for all post-secondary students, but remember that the Hope Education Credit can be used only for the first two years of school. Figure 6-2 summarizes the phaseout range for different plans.

	Phaseout Range	
Provision	**Single Filers**	**Joint Filers**
Education IRA	$95,000 - $110,000	$190,000 - $220,000
Hope Education Credit	$40,000 - $50,000	$80,000 - $100,000
Lifetime Learning Credit	$40,000 - $50,000	$80,000 - $100,000
Student Loan Interest Deduction	$50,000 - $65,000	$100,000 - $130,000

FIGURE 6-2. PHASEOUT RANGES FOR DIFFERENT PLANS

So where else can you find the money you need? We repeat bank robbing is not a good idea, and it would be very embarrassing if you were caught and had to explain it to your kids. A home equity line of credit might be a good source. The interest is probably deductible, and if you have built up equity in your home, the bank will be happy to help you out. You may want to consider an open line of credit and then you can just write out the checks when needed.

As a last resort consider your retirement plans. Borrow from your 401(k) plan if borrowing is allowed. Is this ever a good idea? Probably not. Remember there are no scholarships given for retirement, but at least you will be paying yourself back. The term for 401(k) loans is five years and if you should lose your job during that time period the loan will be due. If you don't have the cash available to pay off the loan the government considers it a withdrawal and expects you to pay taxes and a 10% penalty if you are under age 59½. Tax law changes now allow you to tap into your IRAs for post-secondary educational expenses without incurring the early distribution 10% penalty. But income taxes will be due when you withdraw the money. And you can't ever put this money back into the IRA so you have lost out on the ability to have it compounding tax-deferred. With a Roth IRA you can pull out the after-tax contributions you have made and use them for college expenses without incurring a penalty or taxes.

Here's our last bit of advice on this subject. If money is really tight, your child can enroll in the local community college and live at home for two years (heaven forbid!) and then transfer to a four-year institution. If interested, your son or daughter might also consider an ROTC (Reserve Officers Training Corps) scholarship, which is not need-based. This includes training during the summer and a commitment to the armed forces after graduation. You can also check out co-op programs that allow students to work for one semester and attend school two semesters. It may then take your student five or six years to finish college, but these programs offer lots of different experiences to help the student make good career choices.

Paying for a college education can be a big bite out of your income and savings. If you have several kids, it may even be painful. The sooner you start saving, the better off you'll be and the more choices your family will have. There are very good state schools where you can get an education for under $10,000 a year. Don't wait until your child is a junior in high school to begin to think about college. Start while he or she is still in diapers. Planning early really pays off here.

The new tax law has added one more way to help parents. A deduction for tuition paid. What is the country coming to? If you are married filing jointly and your income is below $130,000 (filing single $65,000) you can deduct up to $3,000 for tuition and related expenses in 2002 thru 2004. That will increase to $4,000 in 2004. There is no phase out available. No one said that Congress had to be consistent here. You are not eligible to claim this deduction if you have used in the same year the Hope or Life Time Learning credits or have withdrawn funds from an Education IRA or monies from a 529 plan.

Teaching Your Kids About Money

If you've got kids or grandkids, read on. As parents we have a responsibility to teach our children about money.

But wait. You say you're just learning about money yourself. Well, kids learn by example. You probably picked up your parents' attitudes about money, the stock market, and savings simply be being around them. Your kids will do the same. So whether you know it or not, you are your kids' primary financial educator.

If you ask a child of four where money comes from, shc'll probably tell you "the ATM machine." And then, perhaps with some frustration, you say, "No, and it doesn't grow on trees either." Now your child is really confused. She's envisioning dollar bills and coins hanging from a tree and stuff coming out of a machine. Poor kid!

Money lessons can start as soon as the kid realizes that you exchange money for goods. So take any opportunity that comes up to teach your kids about money. If money fights occur in your family, the kids will pick up on the importance and the power of money. Sure, money is important, but you want to send the right money message. Explain that you go to work every day and, in exchange for the work you do, you get paid. You put your money in the bank, and then when you need it, you go to the bank and take some out. Depending on the age of the child, that may be the only explanation needed for a while. Don't overload kids with too much information.

Take the kids shopping with you. Teach them about buying items on sale and what 30% off really means. Teach them about value and using coupons. Have them clip the coupons, give them the job of searching for those items when you go to the store, and then share the savings with them.

Buy your children a small bank, preferably something made of transparent plastic or glass so they can see how much is in it and see it grow as they put more coins in. Then set a goal for when the bank is full, such as purchasing a new toy or video— something tangible so they see the rewards of saving and putting off immediate gratification. When they're old enough to read numbers set up a savings account and teach them about interest. Again, jointly decide on a goal for their savings—nothing as lofty as a college education that may be 10 years away since they won't stay interested that long. Make it something they want and something they can achieve in a reasonable amount of time.

> *Children have to be educated, but they also have to be left to educate themselves.*
> *—Ernest Dimnet*

Should children get an allowance? We think so. Children need to be able to have money of their own, money to spend, money to save, and money to make mistakes with. Mistakes? Actually, they need to make mistakes with money, because mistakes they make at age 10 with $15 they won't repeat at age 30 with $20,000.

Kids in the first grade are capable of handling an allowance. They understand exchanging money for goods. They're now bringing money to school to buy lunch or school supplies on a daily basis. Experts recommend a $1 allowance for every year of age, but if you expect your kids to pay for their entertainment, clothes, and lunches out of the allowance, you'll need to give them more than that. Check to see what the other parents are paying their kids. You don't want your kid to be getting the highest or the lowest allowance among her friends.

Pay the allowance on a regular basis. This is very important so they will learn about planning. If the child does the bulk of her spending on a Saturday at the mall give her the money on a Monday morning. She'll learn several lessons. She'll have to defer spending during the week so she'll have money for Saturday. She'll have to budget it all week if she is to buy her lunches as well. And here is where the real lesson lies—if she spends all of her money by Thursday—you can't bail her out. Help her pack a lunch for Friday but bite your tongue and don't say "I told you so!" She knows what happened. And don't give in on Saturday morning when she begins to whine and pesters you. No don't say "I told you so!" She knows what happened. And don't give in on Saturday morning when she begins to whine and pesters you. No matter how difficult it is and from experience we know, she will tell you, you are the stingiest and meanest parent alive. Don't buckle under fire. In the real world you may not be around to bail her out when she's an adult.

There's some controversy about whether or not allowances should be in exchange for doing chores around the house. If you decide to handle it this way, are you also going to withhold the allowance if your kids don't do their chores? Our philosophy is to give them spending money in the form of an allowance from the family budget and expect them to bring value to the family unit with household duties such as setting the table or keeping their rooms clean. And then if they want to earn extra money, find jobs they're capable of doing around the house that you normally would hire someone to do—such as washing windows, raking leaves, and cleaning the garage—and pay the kids to do these jobs.

Some families we've interviewed have set up a loan department. Kids can borrow from it, but they must sign a loan agreement and make weekly interest and principal payments so that other members of the family can use the loan fund when needed.

Your kids need to know how to handle credit and credit cards. Credit card debt among college students is soaring. More and more credit card companies are offering students pre-approved cards. Some students we talked with had as many as three cards maxed out and they felt they couldn't tell their parents. So they were paying just the minimum each month and digging themselves in deeper and deeper.

Talk about credit card debt with your kids whenever they see you use your credit card. Kids will understand if you explain that every time you use your card it's a short-term loan. And most important, explain you must pay it back—and that if you pay it back promptly, you don't have to pay interest. Take every opportunity you can to teach your kids about money. These are life lessons they will someday teach your grandchildren.

Chapter 7 | Retirement

How Much Will You Need to Stash Away?

Retirement is something we have come to expect, but it wasn't always that way. Retirement didn't exist at the turn of the 19th century. People worked until they couldn't work any longer and then they went home to spend time in their rocking chairs. Today retirement may mean travel, a different career, heading back to school, or volunteer work. Because of Social Security, yes, Social Security, we now think in terms of spending quality time in retirement. Social Security started it all in 1935 by offering older workers a steady income stream so that they could stop working at age 65. Experts now figure you could spend up to one third of your lifetime in retirement. So unless you want to live with your kids when you retire, you need to do some planning.

So here's that $64,000 question: How much will you need to stash away? And the answer is ... a lot more than $64,000! We know the answer you want is more defined but the quick and easy answer is you will need to save a lot.

Here's the good news; we're all living longer. Here's the bad news: we're all living longer. With life spans lasting 90 or even 100 years and medical technology being able to replace worn-out joints, transplant vital organs, and cure cancer, you need to plan financially for longer retirement years.

Here's a simple of way of figuring out how much you'll need. Work backwards. You need to know how much you're spending today to maintain your lifestyle and then carry the numbers forward, adding a bit for inflation, to see what you'll need in the future. If you are 40 and want to retire at 60, you have 20 years until retirement. Let's assume you find you could live quite comfortably on $50,000 a year. Let's see what a 3% inflation rate will do to that $50,000. Follow out 20 years on Figure 7-1 and see what you'll need in future dollars to maintain your lifestyle. It's $90,000! Now some of that future stream of income may come from your employer's pension plan and Social Security benefits, but you're on the hook for a good portion of it.

> One good thing about living in the past—it's cheaper.

Current Income	Years					
	5	10	15	20	25	30
$25,000	$29,000	$34,000	$39,000	$45,000	$52,000	$61,000
30,000	35,000	40,000	47,000	54,000	63,000	73,000
35,000	41,000	47,000	55,000	63,000	73,000	85,000
40,000	46,000	54,000	62,000	72,000	84,000	97,000
45,000	52,000	60,000	70,000	81,000	94,000	109,000
50,000	58,000	67,000	78,000	90,000	105,000	121,000
55,000	64,000	74,000	86,000	99,000	115,000	133,000
60,000	70,000	81,000	93,000	108,000	126,000	146,000
65,000	75,000	87,000	101,000	117,000	136,000	158,000
70,000	81,000	94,000	109,000	126,000	147,000	170,000
75,000	87,000	101,000	117,000	135,000	157,000	182,000

FIGURE 7-1. FUTURE INCOME NEEDS

There are several ways you'll be able to get a handle on how much more you need to save, but let's start with some basics. You first need to understand what your current living expenses are. So return to Chapter 2 and see where your money goes. How much do you need to maintain your current lifestyle? And is this the lifestyle you anticipate in retirement? Also, you may want to add a factor in here for health care needs. Yes, there's Medicare and Medigap insurance, but any retiree will tell you the co-pays do add up.

Financial planners estimate that individuals generally need to replace to 80% of their pre-retirement income to maintain their standard of living after retirement. We believe you may want to plan on 100%, especially in the early years of retirement. Social Security currently provides enough to replace 45% of pre-retirement income for a person earning $20,000, but less than 25% for a person earning more than $50,000. The balance must come from your savings or your employer's pension plan.

If you have an advisor, ask her or him to do some calculations for you. If you have a computer, there are some good programs that may interest you. Quicken, as part of its check-writing package, gives you the ability to do some forecasting on your own. If you've got a computer, make it work for you. Check out the Web sites of some of the major mutual fund families and see what they have to offer. The worksheet at the end of the chapter was developed by the the American Savings Education Council. You can access fill this form out online at **www.asec.org**.

This worksheet can help you estimate how much of your salary must be saved annually to accumulate enough assets to provide 70% of your salary after retirement. Keep in mind this is a simplified worksheet that only provides a rough estimate of your retirement savings needs.

Best Ways to Save for Retirement

Our advice right up front: start saving for retirement with your very first job and make use of the qualified plan that your employer offers allowing you to put away money pre-tax. Check with the benefits department and find out what your employer offers. If you're working in the public sector as a teacher or a state or city employee, you'll have either a 403(b) or a 457 plan available. If you're in the private sector, you may be eligible to participate in a 401(k) or SIMPLE IRA, depending on the size of your company. If you don't have a plan at work, you need to check out using IRAs. (We'll discuss all of those plans in Chapter 19.) And if you are one of those lucky souls with an employer who matches some of your contribution, saving becomes a slam-dunk.

The key here is the earlier you can begin to save and the longer you have until retirement, the less you will need to save. For example, Figure 7-2 shows you what can happen if we can get you to start early.

Age	One Time	Monthly Investment	Yearly Investment
20	$13,700	$100	$1,400
25	22,100	160	2,300
30	35,600	260	3,700
35	57,300	450	6,100
40	92,300	750	10,200
45	148,600	1,300	17,500
50	239,400	2,400	31,500
55	385,500	4,900	62,800
60	621,000	13,000	163,800

FIGURE 7-2. HOW TO SAVE A MILLION DOLLARS

All the people standing in line to buy lottery tickets will tell you why: they want to be millionaires. But there's another way and one that gives everyone a chance to be a winner. If you're 20 and can save just $3 a day, you could have over a million dollars in your retirement account when you retire. If you start at age 25, you need to save $6 a day. To achieve the same results starting at age 35, it's $17 a day to get your $1 million. (These results are based on the assumption that your portfolio will earn on average 10%.)

Let's compare ages 25 and 35 here. If you wait until age 35 to start, you will need to save almost three times as much as if you'd started at 25. A recent Harris Poll found that the baby boomer generation didn't start saving until age 34 on average. If only they'd had our book.

So you've just taken the pledge to start saving. Another key factor is being consistent in putting money away each month. That's why we like using qualified plans at work: the money comes right out your paycheck before you even see it. What you don't have you can't spend. So often we make these great plans and we vow we will save more, but it just doesn't happen. Why not? Because we are not consistent and saving has not become a habit.

And when you're investing in your retirement plan at work, you are using a concept called dollar cost averaging working for you. Check out Chapter 8 for more about dollar cost averaging and compounding. You're investing the same amount of money each month, but because of fluctuations in the stock market you're paying different prices for your investments. Dollar cost averaging is a great strategy for saving for retirement.

> *Retirement is the period in life when you stop quoting the proverb that time is money.*

Here's one more chart (Figure 7-3) to help make a believer out of you. We have two 25-year-old employees starting work at the same time. Jane immediately begins putting away $2,000 a year. Dick decides to wait until he's older to save, since he has what seems like an eternity to save for retirement; so he starts at 35. If, for some reason, Jane stops investing in the plan after 10 years and she never adds another nickel to it, she'll still have more money at retirement than Dick. But if she continues to save, look how her nest egg will grow. A chart is worth a thousand words! In the meantime we have John who diligently saves $2,000 every year, and you can see his results as well.

It's Never Too Late to Start Saving

OK, so you're discouraged. We knew our examples would do that to you. What we'd like is for everyone starting that first job to also start saving for retirement. But hey, you didn't have our book until now, so how were you supposed to know? Does that make you feel a bit better?

It truly is never too late to start saving for your retirement, even if you're planning to retire in five years or less. The reasoning behind that statement is that you're not going to use all of your retirement

Age	Jane's Contri-bution	Year-End Value	John's Contri-bution	Year-End Value	Dick's Contri-bution	Year-End Value
25	$2,000	$2,200	$2,000	$2,200		
26	2,000	4,620	2,000	4,620		
27	2,000	7,282	2,000	7,282		
28	2,000	10,210	2,000	10,210		
29	2,000	13,431	2,000	13,431		
30	2,000	16,974	2,000	16,974		
31	2,000	20,872	2,000	20,872		
32	2,000	25,159	2,000	25,159		
33	2,000	29,875	2,000	29,875		
34	2,000	35,062	2,000	35,062		
35		38,569	2,000	40,769	$2,000	$2,200
36		42,425	2,000	47,045	2,000	4,620
37		46,668	2,000	53,950	2,000	7,282
38		51,335	2,000	61,545	2,000	10,210
39		56,468	2,000	69,899	2,000	13,431
40		62,115	2,000	79,089	2,000	16,974
41		68,327	2,000	89,198	2,000	20,872
42		75,159	2,000	100,318	2,000	25,159
43		82,675	2,000	112,550	2,000	29,875
44		90,943	2,000	126,005	2,000	35,062
45		100,037	2,000	140,805	2,000	40,769
46		110,041	2,000	157,086	2,000	47,045
47		121,045	2,000	174,995	2,000	53,950
48		133,149	2,000	194,694	2,000	61,545
49		146,464	2,000	216,364	2,000	69,899
50		161,110	2,000	240,200	2,000	79,089
51		177,222	2,000	266,420	2,000	89,198
52		194,944	2,000	295,262	2,000	100,318
53		214,438	2,000	326,988	2,000	112,550
54		235,882	2,000	361,887	2,000	126,005
55		259,470	2,000	400,276	2,000	140,805
56		285,417	2,000	442,503	2,000	157,086
57		313,959	2,000	488,953	2,000	174,995
58		345,355	2,000	540,049	2,000	194,694
59		379,890	2,000	596,254	2,000	216,364
60		417,879	2,000	658,079	2,000	240,200
Total Investment	**$20,000**		**$72,000**		**$52,000**	

FIGURE 7-3. THE DIFFERENCE BETWEEN SAVING EARLY AND SAVING LATE (Chart assumes a 10% return)

nest egg the day you retire. You'll be drawing upon it over your retirement years and, if you've contributed the money to a qualified retirement plan such as a 401(k) or an IRA, those dollars are still compounding tax-deferred until you withdraw them.

Advice for 30-Somethings

We showed you what you can do if you start early, at age 25. But the reality is most people do not start saving early for retirement, for they are in an accumulation mode at age 25 as well as needing to pay back their school loans. So let's say you're now 30-something and you look at your net worth and say, "Oops, I forgot to start saving for retirement." You still have the luxury of 30 years or more to accumulate assets for retirement. Start by contributing as much as you can to your employer's plan. Be sure you are contributing enough to take advantage of your employer's match. Try to be doing the maximum allowed in your plan. If you are able to save $3,000 a year and we assume you will earn a 10% average return, your nest egg will be dazzling with over $500,000 in it at age 65. If you don't need it immediately upon retiring and want to wait until you must begin withdrawals at age 70½, your nest egg could grow to close to $875,000.

Advice for Those in Their 40s

So the above description doesn't fit you. You're a bit older, more like 45. And you've got only 20 years of accumulating ahead of you. So what should you do?

If you are already in a plan at work, be sure you are contributing the maximum to the plan. Don't fool around with starting out with a low contribution rate and increasing it over time. Bite the bullet and figure out a way to be putting away the maximum. Look at your cash flow and figure out where you can begin to cut corners, all of the corners count here.

You may be caught between saving for college for the kids and saving for retirement for yourself. Just a word of advice here: the last time we checked there were no scholarships out there for retirement. So you need to be saving for both goals at the same time and we know it isn't easy. If you want to have a nest egg of $500,000, you will need to save on average $8,000 a year to reach this goal. Again we've assumed an aggressive portfolio earning you a 10% return annually. Now some of you may be able to do this, so get with the program. But some of you are shaking your head and saying, "I can't do that." We know it's not easy, but give it a try. Begin to save; anything you save will make a difference in your retirement

For Those in Their 50s

OK, next! You're 55, you've not started to save, and you want to retire in 10 years. That probably won't work well unless you are expecting to inherit a bundle from your Uncle Fred or are willing to rev it up and start maxing out your retirement plan. Let's go with the latter choice.

If you're married with a joint income of $100,000 and contribute the maximum each and we assume a company match here of 3%, you'll be able to save 18% a year, a cool $18,000. Now $18,000 a year for 10 years will line your nest egg with $300,000. Again we have assumed a fairly aggressive portfolio with a 9% return (well, we thought you were getting a bit old so we added some bonds to your portfolio). Now if your life style allows it and you can squeeze another $4,000 a year in savings from your budget and contribute that to Roth IRAs, in 10 years you will have an additional $66,000 saved. So now the nest egg has grown to almost $366,000.

If that's not enough, then you have some other choices to make. Retire or continue working. Begin to tap into your savings or leave them to grow as long as you possibly can. So let's see what happens if we take the nest egg and leave it growing for another five years. At age 70 it could be worth over $563,000 and if you continue working and continue contributing you could amass over $700,000. But it means you must continue saving $22,000 a year for 15 years. That is not an easy feat under any conditions, but it does make for interesting reading.

There are other things you can do if you haven't saved enough. You can choose to work longer than age 65 and continue to contribute to your retirement plan. Delaying Social Security benefits if you continue to work will also increase your benefits when you do start to collect. You can find part-time work in retirement. You can lower your standard of living or you can hope Uncle Fred does have a fortune stashed away that he'll leave to you. If you choose to work there is some good news for you. According to the American Association of Retired Persons, there is a labor shortage projected due to the baby bust, so there will be jobs available for individuals who want to work. But the jobs available may not be as rewarding financially as the one you hold now.

Figure 7-4 shows you how much you'll need to save per year if you have a specific goal in mind. We've assumed a conservative rate of return of 9%.

Years Until Retirement	$250,000	$500,000	$750,000	$1,000,000
10	$15,000	$30,000	$45,000	$60,400
15	8,000	16,000	23,400	31,200
20	4,500	9,000	13,400	18,000
25	2,700	5,400	8,100	10,800
30	1,700	3,400	5,000	6,700
35	1,000	2,100	3,200	4,300

FIGURE 7-4. SAVINGS GOALS FOR RETIREMENT—HOW MUCH YOU NEED TO SAVE PER YEAR TO REACH YOUR FINANCIAL GOALS FOR RETIREMENT

Taking Distributions

OK, you've been dreaming about your retirement party and gold watch for the last couple of months so you know it's getting close. But now you need to do some planning on how to access your nest egg when it officially becomes yours. Our general rule is to deplete your taxable investments first and the retirement plan money last. That's because money grows faster when you're not paying current taxes on it.

When you take the distributions from your qualified tax-deferred retirement plans, you have to pay taxes on the full amount you take out at your current income tax rate, which today is 10% to 38.6%—this upper rate will decline to 35% by 2006. (The Roth IRA is the exception.)

If you sell stock or stock mutual funds in taxable accounts and have a lot of potential capital gains, the worst scenario is that you have to pay 8%-20% to Uncle Sam on the capital gains.

Here are some basic guidelines on managing and taking distributions from retirement plans and pensions. A good book that will help is J. K. Lasser's *How to Pay Less Tax on Your Retirement Savings,* third edition by Seymour Goldberg.

Pensions. If the option is available, take a lump sum distribution and roll it over into a separate IRA within 60 days. You can control how it is invested and take it only when you need it (subject to IRS minimum distribution requirements). Set up the IRA with a reputable brokerage or mutual fund company and request that your company do a direct transfer. Otherwise, your employer will have to withhold 20% for taxes and that amount becomes a taxable distribution unless you make up the amount. Put the money in a money market fund until you have a new investment plan for it.

401(k)/403(b) Plans. Upon retirement, roll the entire sum over into a new IRA at a mutual fund or brokerage firm. They will assist you and provide the paperwork for a direct trustee-to-trustee rollover from your employer. Otherwise, the same 20% withholding applies as with pensions.

457 Plans. If your retirement money is in a 457 plan you may want to wait until 2002 to retire for then you will have the ability to roll those dollars into an IRA. The rules are changing for 457 plans and as of this printing some of them need further definition by the IRS. If your plan does not allow rollovers, you may need to decide at the time you leave your employment or retire when you want to start receiving distributions. Not fair we know but those are the current rules. This start date is pretty much set in concrete so put some thought into the decision. You do not have to wait until age 59½ to start distributions from these plans, but if you do roll it into an IRA then you must follow the IRA rules and normally you don't have access to the money until you reach age 59½.

Employer Stock in Your 401(k) Plan. You may be better off taking the stock directly and rolling over the rest of the investments into an IRA, paying the taxes on the cost of the shares when they were originally put into your account, and holding them separately in a regular brokerage account. Then, when you sell the shares, you'll owe taxes only at the capital gains rate, not at your income tax rate. And there's no requirement that you ever sell them. The shares will be part of your estate (and estate taxes may be due) and then pass to your heirs with a new, higher cost basis.

Keogh Plan. When you retire, sell your business, or close it down, you can roll your Keogh into an IRA, although you don't have to do so. You can draw down your Keogh after age 59½ just as you would an IRA. In some states, a Keogh account has legal protection against creditors and legal judgments against you.

IRA. If you followed any of the above plans, now all your retirement plan money is in one or more IRAs. You are in control. If you can leave them untouched until the year after you turn 70½, your money will continue to grow tax-deferred. If you can live off your taxable savings and Social Security until then, do it.

Roth IRA. There is no required distribution for a Roth IRA because you will not owe federal income taxes on the money. You can also take the money whenever you want after five years or after age 59½ and owe no federal taxes or penalties. You may owe state taxes, however. Each state has its own rules for taxing retirement plan distributions (and Social Security payments), so check into the tax laws in the state where you reside when you take distributions.

Taking distributions from any retirement account at any time has tax consequences. If you don't fully understand the rules and options, consult a qualified tax professional. The variety of ways you can arrange to distribute the money is exceeded only by the variety of tax complications you have to negotiate. A spouse is usually the beneficiary in a retirement plan and a surviving spouse has a special privilege in that he or she can roll over the proceeds from an IRA, a Keogh, a 401(k), and a 403(b) into his or her own IRA. The IRS publication 590, Individual Retirement Arrangements, is worth reviewing. Call the IRS at 800-829-3676 or visit the Web site, **www.irs.ustreas.gov**.

How Long Will You Need It to Last?

How long you will need your money to last depends on so many things. When do you want to retire? The earlier you retire, the longer the retirement and the larger the nest egg you're going to need. If you're married, how old is your spouse? If you're in a May/December relationship, you know, where one spouse is a lot older than the other spouse, you need to do some fancy planning to be sure that if something happens the surviving spouse has enough income to live on in retirement.

Then you need to take into consideration your health, your genetic make-up, and your lifestyle. If you have longevity in your genes, you may need to plan on living to be 110. We know that sounds old, but check out *The Today Show* some morning when they celebrate viewers' birthdays. They're all over 100 years old. If you're over 50 now, you should plan on reaching 90, and if you are under 50, plan to reach the centennial mark of 100. If you have those longevity genes, then add some years. Our seniors are the fastest-growing segment of the population right now and that trend will continue.

Retirement ages have been dropping from age 65 to 62. Many retirees will tell you that they did not choose to retire. According to a Harris Poll, 76% of retirees would like to be working and an even greater number of retirees oppose mandatory retirement. So if we take an average retirement age of 65, most of us will need to plan for at least another 25 years of retirement living. If you have a partner, you will need to take into consideration his or her age also.

Let's take a look at a simple way of figuring out how much you can withdraw from your nest egg each year and not run out of money. There is retirement software available that will do this for you or get your financial planner to do it for you. How long your nest egg will last depends on two factors: the rate at which you withdraw funds and the rate your assets earn. The table on the next page (Figure 7-5) shows how long your money will last given a payout rate and an earnings rate.

If payout rate is 10% and the earnings rate is 7%, your money will last for 17 years. If the earnings rate is equal to or greater than the payout rate, your money can last indefinitely.

% Payout Rate	1	2	3	4	5	6	7	8	9	10	11	12	13	14	15
1															
2	69.4														
3	40.6	55.0													
4	28.8	34.7	46.3												
5	22.3	25.6	30.6	40.3											
6	18.2	20.3	23.2	27.6	35.9										
7	15.5	16.9	18.7	21.2	25.2	32.6									
8	13.4	14.4	15.7	17.4	19.7	23.2	29.8								
9	11.8	12.6	13.6	14.7	16.3	18.4	21.6	27.6							
10	10.6	11.2	11.9	12.8	13.9	15.3	17.2	20.2	25.7						
11	9.6	10.1	10.7	11.3	12.2	13.2	14.5	16.3	19.1	24.1					
12	8.7	9.2	9.7	10.2	10.8	11.6	12.6	13.8	15.5	18.0	22.7				
13	8.1	8.4	8.8	9.2	9.7	10.4	11.1	12.0	13.2	14.7	17.2	21.5			
14	7.4	7.8	8.1	8.5	8.9	9.4	10.0	10.7	11.5	12.6	14.1	16.3	20.4		
15	6.9	7.2	7.5	7.8	8.2	8.6	9.1	9.6	10.2	11.1	12.1	13.5	15.6	19.5	
16	6.5	6.7	7.0	7.2	7.6	7.9	8.2	8.7	9.2	9.9	10.7	11.7	13.3	15.0	18.7
17	6.1	6.3	6.5	6.8	7.0	7.3	7.7	8.0	8.4	8.9	9.6	10.2	11.2	12.5	14.4
18	5.7	5.9	6.2	6.3	6.6	6.8	7.1	7.4	7.7	8.2	8.7	9.2	9.9	10.8	12.1
19	5.4	5.6	5.7	6.0	6.2	6.4	6.7	6.9	7.2	7.6	7.9	8.4	8.9	9.7	10.5
20	5.2	5.3	5.5	5.7	5.8	6.0	6.2	6.4	6.7	7.0	7.3	7.7	8.2	8.7	9.3

% Earnings on Investment

If earnings rate is equal to or greater than payout rate, money can last indefinitely.

FIGURE 7-5. THE NUMBER OF YEARS YOUR MONEY WILL LAST DEPENDING ON THE EARNING RATE AND THE ANNUAL PERCENTAGE WITHDRAWN (Reprinted with permission of Johnson Charts, Inc.)

Let's explore another way to be sure you have the cash available to supplement your Social Security benefits and pension income in retirement. You will need to start this planning within five years of retirement. A conversion strategy would be to tuck away what you need to live on over five years into bonds and fixed income investments. So if you think you will need $20,000 a year from your retirement savings to live on starting in five years, then you should withdraw $20,000 a year for the next five years and purchase bonds or invest it in a money market mutual fund. That way, in five years, you'll have $100,000 plus in safe investments that will last you for the next five years. This is assuming you now have a portfolio of mostly stocks. If you already have a balanced portfolio of 60% stocks and 40% bonds and cash, you can shorten the time frame to suit your needs.

> *Money will not buy happiness, but it makes misery more comfortable.*

The rest of your portfolio you keep in stocks to keep pace with inflation. Don't forget to factor in taxes as you follow this plan. Each year after you begin your retirement, you should sell enough stock or stock mutual funds to cover 5 years so you will always have enough cash available no matter what is happening in the stock market. This can be shortened to a three- or four-year period.

Most people don't need income from their investments until they retire. Until then, any interest, dividend, and capital gain income should be reinvested to compound your returns. The mistake made too often at retirement is to change your asset allocation to generate income by investing much or all of the portfolio into income-oriented investments. Retirees don't need income; they need money from their investments to live on. Don't sacrifice the growth in your portfolio to get income or you'll run out of money, unless you're really loaded.

If you are married, you and your spouse should each fill out your own Ballpark Estimate worksheet taking your marital status into account when entering your Social Security benefit in number 2 below.

1. How much annual income will you want in retirement? (Figure at least 70% of your current annual gross income just to maintain your current standard of living. Really.) $_____

2. Subtract the income you expect to receive annually from:
   • Social Security--If you make under $25,000, enter $8,000; between $25,000 - $40,000, enter $12,000; over $40,000, enter $14,500 (For married couples, the lower earning spouse should enter either their own benefit based on their inco me or 50% of the higher earning spouse s benefit, whichever is higher.) $_____
   • Traditional Employer Pension--a plan that pays a set dollar amount for life, where the dollar amount depends on salary and years of service (in today's dollars) $_____
   • Part-time income $_____
   • Other $_____

   This is how much you need to make up for each retirement year: $_____

Now you want a ballpark estimate of how much money you'll need in the bank the day you retire. So the accountants went to work and devised a simple formula. For the record, they figure you'll realize a constant real rate of return of 3% after inflation, you'll live to age 87, and you'll begin to receive income from Social Security at age 65.

3. To determine the amount you'll need to save, multiply the amount you need to make up by the factor below. $_____

Age you expect to retire:		Your factor is:	
	55		21.0
	60		18.9
	65		16.4
	70		13.6

4. If you expect to retire before age 65, multiply your Social Security benefit from line 2 by the factor below. $_____

Age you expect to retire:		Your factor is:	
	55		8.8
	60		4.7

5. Multiply your savings to date (include money accumulated in a 401(K), IRA, or similar retirement plan). $_____

If you want to retire in		Your factor is:	
	10 yrs		1.3
	15 yrs		1.6
	20 yrs		1.8
	25 yrs		2.1
	30 yrs		2.4
	35 yrs		2.8
	40 yrs		3.3

Total additional savings needed at retirement: $_____

THE AMERICAN SAVINGS EDUCATION COUNCIL "BALLPARK ESTIMATE" RETIREMENT WORKSHEET— CONTINUED ON NEXT PAGE (Reprinted with permission of ASEC, www.asec.org)

Don't panic. Those same accountants devised another formula to show you how much to save each year in order to reach your goal amount. They factor in compounding. That's where your money not only makes interest, your interest starts making interest as well, creating a snowball effect.

6. To determine the ANNUAL amount you'll need to save, multiply the TOTAL
amount by the factor below. $_____

If you want to retire in		Your factor is:	
	10 yrs		.085
	15 yrs		.052
	20 yrs		.036
	25 yrs		.027
	30 yrs		.020
	35 yrs		.016
	40 yrs		.013

THE AMERICAN SAVINGS EDUCATION COUNCIL RETIREMENT WORKSHEET CONCLUDED

Part Three

What You Need to Know About Investing

P art Three will provide you with the basics of investing. It answers the question: What does it take to be an intelligent investor?

In essence, this means knowing the rules of the game, what to expect, and then where to put your money to get you where you want to go. If you don't get returns that are any better than inflation after taxes, that's clearly not a good investment strategy. You want and need to do better than that.

Emotions often play a big role when you're investing. Keeping them in check is key to avoiding bad short-term decisions. Many novice investors think that getting into and out of the market is how you make money. We'll show that's not the case: it's *time in the market* that matters, not *timing*. We'll talk about dollar cost averaging and compounding interest and show you that these strategies will ensure financial success.

It's hard to figure out what you want if you don't know what to expect in the way of investment returns. So we're going to give you a long and short perspective on just what investment returns to expect. Determining the time frame for when you need the money is probably the most critical decision when it comes to picking the right investments, so we narrow your choices down on the vast number of options available to you.

Asset allocation is a fancy term for how you've invested your money: which investments you've chosen to reach your goals. Over 90% of your investment performance is based on whether you decide on stocks, bonds, or money markets. As you get older and your wants and desires change then we will also tell you how to fine-tune this asset mix to adjust to your goals.

Chapter 8 | The Gospel of Investing

Seeking Returns: The Need to Beat Inflation

Most people think of successful investing as not losing money. Sure, that's important over time. But we feel that the primary financial goal for everyone is to maintain or improve his or her standard of living over the years. The only sure way to do that is to save and invest enough and to get a rate of return that beats inflation … after taxes. Anything less means losing purchasing power: your standard of living will slowly decline every year.

Will Rogers said, "It's not the return *on* my money I worry about, it's the return *of* my money." That makes sense: we all want to get back the dollars that we invested. But if we get back only our investment principal, we've actually lost some of that principal—not to a risky investment, as Will Rogers might have feared, but to inflation.

The biggest risk in investing is that the real value of your money, its purchasing power, might decline over time. Then you might not fully achieve all your goals—a home, education, and retirement. So, how can we beat inflation?

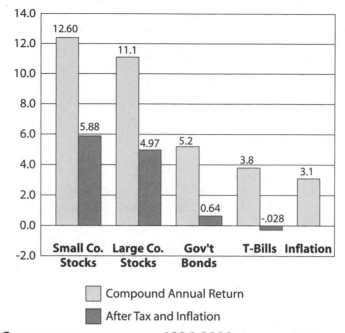

FIGURE 8-1. COMPOUND ANNUAL RETURNS 1926-2000 (Assumes 25% tax rate and actual inflation. Return and inflation data from *Ibbotson Associates Yearbook.*)

Let's take a look at what has worked in the battle against inflation. Of course, there's no guarantee that history will repeat itself, but we certainly can learn from the past. As Figure 8-1 shows, stocks were the best-performing asset class over the last 75 years (1926-2000). And look at what happened to returns after taxes (we used a 25% tax rate as a blended historical average) and the 3.1% average annual rate of inflation. Ouch! Inflation doesn't reduce your return like taxes do. Inflation simply reduces your buying power.

> *Inflation is when the buck doesn't stop anywhere.*

You can see that taxes and inflation cut long-term stock returns by more than half and reduced returns on U.S. Government Bonds by almost 90%. In the "safest" investment, U.S. Treasury Bills with a maturity of one year or less, investors actually appear to have lost money.

Your return on investment after taxes and inflation must be high enough to increase the buying power of your investment over time. This means you need to aim for an average annual return of 3% after taxes and inflation. This includes your tax-deferred retirement accounts because, except for the Roth IRA, you'll be paying taxes when you withdraw from those accounts. To get a long-term return better than inflation after taxes, to maintain or improve your future standard of living, stocks are the only thing that give you a shot.

Eighth Wonder of the World: Compounding

There are seven wonders of the modern world, which most of us can't remember. We'll add an eighth wonder—compound interest.

Compounding is like planting a small apple tree. As a sapling, it doesn't produce very much fruit. But over time it produces more apples every year. Yet there still aren't enough to make all the cider and pies you want. Then this tree reaches maturity and it yields not only enough apples for you, but also enough for your whole family and your neighbors, as long as you spray the tree and care for it. A tree that grows 10% more apples every year makes a lot of pies, cider, and strudel after 30 years.

The key to compounding is *time*. Figure 8-2 shows compounding over 5, 10, 15, 20, and 30 years. The differences aren't great for what seems like a long time: things don't really start to take off for at least 10 years.

So what does this mean to you in real dollars today? When you reinvest your earnings—interest, dividends, and capital gains—they generate more earnings. This compounding allows your money to

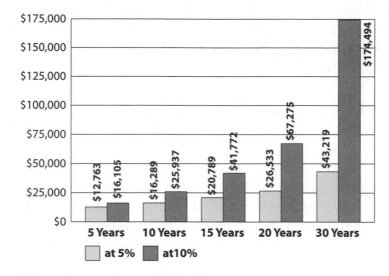

FIGURE 8-2. COMPOUND GROWTH OF $10,000

work harder and harder for you. That's why automatic reinvestment of earnings of any kind is so important. You don't have to think about it and you're not tempted to spend it. Only through compounding will you be able to accumulate serious wealth over time.

Obviously, the stock market and your investments won't go up 10% each and every year. The long-term history of market returns suggests that a 10% to 12% average annual return is a reasonable expectation over a period of decades. Some years returns may exceed 30%. Other years they may be much lower. But, historically, the stock market has gone up two out of three years on average over a long period. Putting some money in every month or every year and leaving it alone to compound is the best way to reach your long-term goals. The earlier you start, the longer your earnings compound and the better off financially you will be in the future

Time in the Market, Not Timing the Market

To meet your long-term goals, it's essential to have a long-term view of investing. If you can match your investment outlook with your goals, you will be able to see the markets' gyrations differently. Over a 10- or

20-year period, short-term volatility is smoothed out. Some bad years are more than balanced by good years. The amount of time you are invested in the market is your biggest ally.

Here's what three legendary investors have to say on the subject:

Warren Buffet: "We don't have, never have had, and never will have an opinion about where the stock market, interest rates, or business activity will be a year from now."

Peter Lynch: "I have no feeling for the direction of the market over the near term, or the next three to twelve months—and that has always been my position."

Sir John Templeton: "Ignore fluctuations. Don't try to outguess the stock market. Buy a quality portfolio and invest for the long term."

Time in the market eliminates most of the risk. With a long-term investment horizon, you can afford to ride out the inevitable down markets, even the scary ones. You don't need the money tomorrow; you need it years into the future. You can lose money only if you sell when markets are down. After every correction and bear market, stocks have bounced back and gone up to new highs. Patient, long-term investors come out the winners. Those who panic and forget the long-term picture do serious damage to their portfolios.

> *The patient man realizes a profit on his investment whereas the only thing an impatient man realizes is his mistake.*

Market timers have to be right twice—when to sell and when to buy. The biggest danger of market timing is that you're out of the market when the big moves are made. If you're out of the stock market during the best month each decade, you reduce your return by half. No one ever consistently sees the big moves, up or down, ahead of time. A *Smart Money* magazine article in October 1996 reported a study of perfect market timing by a hypothetical investor from 1989 through 1994. The combination of taxes and loads or commissions did more damage to a portfolio than the market corrections! So, even if you guess right all of the time, you can still lose.

To see how time in the market reduces volatility, we reviewed all of the 20-year rolling periods from 1958 through 1999. For the 23 periods:

✔ Stocks never lost money in any 20-year period.

✔ The worst period for stocks was 1962-1981, when they gained only an average of 0.89% per year.

✔ Bonds lost money in two of the 20-year periods.

✔ The worst period for bonds was also 1962-1981, when they lost an average of 0.66% per year.

✔ Over the 42 years, 1958-1999, stocks beat bonds better than 3 to 1 after inflation.

Of course, there's no guarantee that the next 40 years will turn out the same way, because no one has a clue about the future. But you can see how time in the stock market can reduce risk and allow your money to grow substantially.

Dollar Cost Averaging

Dollar cost averaging is a simple investment strategy that many people use without knowing it. You invest a fixed dollar amount at regular intervals regardless of market prices. Employees in 401(k), 403(b), and 457 plans follow this strategy automatically on a weekly or monthly basis. What happens if you invest the same amount at regular intervals? When the market is going down, you buy more shares at a lower price. When the market is going up, you buy fewer shares at a higher price. You don't worry about the market; you just keep buying regularly, automatically averaging your cost as you go. Maybe you're wondering why you would want to buy shares when the market is down. Think of it as the share prices going on sale. You get more for your money. When good companies get battered in the market, that's the time to buy them.

If you happen to get a large lump sum to invest, such as a bonus or an inheritance, you could invest it all at once. The odds are about 2 to 1 that this will give you the best return, but at a higher risk, according to an article by Richard E. Williams and Peter W. Bacon in the April 1993 issue of *Journal of Financial Planning*. How would you feel if the market dropped 10% or 20% a month later? If that wouldn't bother you, go ahead and invest your wad. But if such a drop would upset you, put it into a money market fund and then draw out an equal amount every month for the next year or two to invest in the market.

Dollar cost averaging just may allow you to sleep better at night. But make sure to follow the plan every month, no matter what the market is doing. You can easily set up an automatic investment plan with a mutual fund company.

Dollar cost averaging as a strategy accomplishes several things:

- ✔ It is a disciplined plan to save and invest regularly.
- ✔ It gives you the opportunity to buy more shares at a lower price when the market is down.
- ✔ It puts your average cost per share below the average transaction price per share.

Emotions Are Your Enemy in Investing

As advisors, we've learned that managing money is important, but managing emotions is even more important—much more. Why? Because emotions running amuck will more than likely cause damage to a portfolio.

How do you make investment decisions? With your *head* or with your *stomach*? As human beings, we create investment risks through our fear, greed, and ignorance. We are our own worst enemies! Much of the short-term volatility in the markets is a result of the collective emotional turmoil of traders and investors. Too often, emotions *push* us to do something we *shouldn't* do or *prevent* us from doing something we *should* do. When investing, you need the ability to balance an emotional reaction with a rational point of view.

A few years ago, Morningstar reported a study of investors in growth funds that averaged over 12% return for five years ending May 1994. Yet the actual investors lost 2% per year. How could that happen? Fear and greed. Too many people bought the mutual funds when they were high after the fund had a good year and then, when it cooled off and went down temporarily, they sold—and then bought into the next hot fund.

The roller coaster ride (Figure 8-3) represents the emotional ride that can result from a short-term investment perspective.

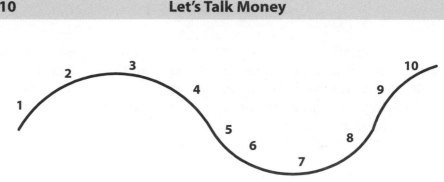

FIGURE 8-3. INVESTING: IT CAN BE AN EMOTIONAL ROLLER COASTER RIDE (Reproduced with permission of Dover Partners)

1. You watch a stock moving up. (Anticipation)
2. You make the buy. (Greed)
3. You check the newspaper daily as the stock goes sideways. (Impatience)
4. Then what happens? Right! The stock goes down. (Concern)
5. It continues to go down. (Fear)
6. It goes below the price at which you started watching it. (Panic)
7. You sell. (Relief)
8. You check the newspaper daily as the stock soars in price. (Anger)
9. It goes above the price you paid for it. (Anticipation)
10. You make the buy again. (Greed)

What kind of investor are you? When trouble pops up, does your mind immediately kick into gear and tell the rest of your body, "Just cool it! I'm in charge here"? Or is it the Maalox moment as your stomach says, "Enough of this stuff, I'm outta here!" Do your emotions drive your intellect? Or does your intellect drive your emotions? For most of us, it's a little of both. Not knowing your "decision patterns" will probably get you into trouble when it comes to the financial markets. You really need to lead with your head. Patience and discipline are key components in attempting to meet your long-term goals and objectives.

Investment decisions are no different from all the other decisions we make in life. Too often though, we don't think—we just react. With all our time constraints, we're on autopilot. We're running on instincts with our spouse, our kids, our work, and our friends. Why would our investment decisions be any different?

We learn to develop good financial habits by consciously thinking about them. Then, every once in a while, we need to run a system check to see if things are still in order. Often, our good habits are driven by our minds, but bad ones develop when we let our emotions take over. We would need an entire book to tackle this emotional vs. intellectual decision process. There's also a basic theory about left-brain and right-brain thinking. The left brain is for the analytical, logical, concrete, and linear thinking processes. The right brain uses a more creative, intuitive, and holistic way of thinking. Sometimes we use both sides and sometimes we don't!

Always keep in mind that the markets are just made up of other people like you, so it would be foolish to think that markets wouldn't have all the emotions of humans. In fact, we tend to talk about the markets as if they were beings with emotions. The markets are driven by rumors, greed, fear, and worry. Sure, you want to yell and sell in panic when the market plunges, to get out before it goes down even further. But the fluctuations in the market are the inevitable consequence of higher returns over time. This volatility provides you with opportunities and rewards. The age-old advice to buy low and sell high works better in volatile markets—you just have to have the guts to buy when prices are falling. And you will never know at that exact moment whether it's as low as it's going to go.

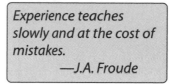

Experience teaches slowly and at the cost of mistakes.
—J.A. Froude

The No. 1 one reason for poor investment performance is the inability to maintain the discipline to follow a plan. Is this beginning to sound familiar here? Financial planning allows you to create a plan and gives you the motivation to discipline your habits and emotions because you want to achieve your objectives. Your actions—how you handle your money, spend it, save it, and invest it—will make or break your financial future. You can't control the markets, but you can control how you act and react to them.

Chapter 9

Great Expectations

How Much Can You Make?

Y ou can make money investing in stocks and stock mutual funds, but you shouldn't expect to regularly make 20% to 30% per year! Many financial planners, mutual fund companies, and the press have found that the investing public has come to expect these large returns every year, based on the last 15 years in the stock market. We're here to tell you that this is not realistic. It simply can't happen!

Figure 8-1 in the last chapter showed the long-term compound annual returns from 1926 to 2000 for major classes of investment. Figure 9-1 looks at total returns (reinvesting interest, dividends, and capital gains) for three classes of investments, plus inflation over periods of time in the last 75 years.

The figure shows that when we go back to the 75-year returns, the returns get lower. That's another way of saying that it doesn't get as good as the last fifteen years very often. But it doesn't mean that we must return to the 75-year average of stocks of just over 11%. We

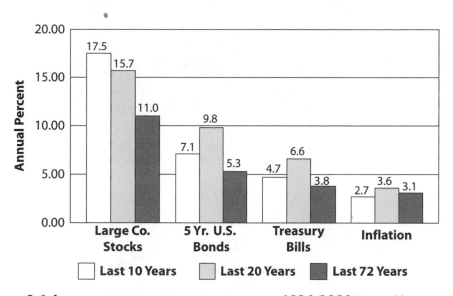

FIGURE 9-1. LONG-TERM COMPOUND ANNUAL RETURNS, 1926-2000 (Data: *Ibbotson Associates Yearbook*. Chart: Flewelling Associates)

might, but there is no rule that says we must average 11.4% over every long-term time frame.

There certainly will be market downturns-maybe some nasty ones. And it may take six months to two years to recover from the bottom. There will also be more great bull markets in the future. You should know that what distinguishes prudent long-term investors is that they don't worry too much about the market in any particular year. In 10, 20, or 30 years, when you need the money, the long-term average return is the tool that you can rely on to help you reach your goals.

There certainly will be market downturns—maybe some nasty ones. And it will likely take six months to two years to recover from the bottom of a nasty downturn. There will also be more great bull markets in the future. You should know that what distinguishes prudent long-term investors is that they don't worry too much about the market in any particular year. In 10, 20, or 30 years, when you need the money, the long-term average return is the tool that you can rely on to help you reach your goals.

And don't forget that the good times have tended to outpace the bad times by about 2 to 1. About once every three years, you'd have been better off leaving your money in the bank rather than taking the

risk of having it invested in the stock market. It's just unfortunate that no one has been able to actually figure out which year it's going to be. The only thing we can say is that the ride up in the two good years is almost always worth the Maalox of the ride down in the third.

So in this section we've looked at the really long 75 year performances and compared them to the last 10 and 20 years, but the questions still is what should rate of return should we anticipate? Here's where we split the difference and suggest you use 40-year numbers as a realistic guide going forward. The returns from 1961-2000 look like this according to Ibbotson data:

Large company stocks, total return	11.9%
Small company stocks	14.5%
Long-term corporate bonds	7.3%
20-year U.S. Treasury Bonds	7.0%
5-year U.S. Treasury Notes	7.3%
Treasury Bills (30-day)	6.1%

A prudent investor would use the last 40 years' returns to guide expectations for the long-term future. But remember that the last 40 years doesn't include the four years from 1929 through 1932 when large company stock prices dropped almost 72%. We can also hope that we never see periods of inflation like the four years of 1978 through 1981, with just under 11% inflation per year on average. But of course lightning could strike twice. Just remember that severe economic waves, both good and bad, can happen.

The bottom line is that big company stocks should give you 10-12% returns, smaller company stocks about 12-14%, and bonds about 6-8%. Anything more is a bonus, and anything less should eventually catch up. Remember that these are only guidelines to use for your financial planning over the next 20 to 40 years. We can hope the results exceed these, but we won't be surprised if they don't.

Don't forget the magic of compounding. At 10% per year compounded, your money doubles in 7.2 years. But that's before Uncle Sam gets his share and inflation nibbles at it.

To find out how long it will take an investment to double at a given rate of compounding, divide the rate into 72. For example, to double at 6% would take 12 years (72 ÷ 6 = 12). Conversely, to find out what rate it takes to double an investment over a fixed number of years, divide the years into 72. For example, to double in 8 years would take 9% (72 ÷ 8 = 9). This is referred to as the *rule of 72*.

What Past Performance Means

Performance analysis is only the very beginning for figuring out where to invest your money. Investing based on past performance is like driving down the road by looking in the rearview mirror. It tells you only where you've been, not where you're going. One of the first things you see in any mutual fund prospectus is the great American disclaimer, "Past performance is no indication of future results." Believe it. So why bother looking at past performance?

> *Remember: Stocks don't perform; companies and those who manage them do.*

We can use past performance as an indicator when we compare it properly and figure out where it came from. The people who manage the funds are a key element in analyzing performance. Knowing who runs the company or manages the money is a must. The corporate world is run by people, and companies or funds take on the characteristics of the people who run them. So learn about the people in charge. If these key people are no longer around, then all bets should be off regarding future performance. The point here is that, when you're invested in a company or are considering investing, you need to find out how the management of a company thinks and operates.

You want to know how the manager earned the performance record. How much volatility did the fund experience? Did the volatility swing twice as much for one manager as for the other? Was there one big year because the fund got hot, while the rest of the years were mediocre at best? Did the manager focus the entire portfolio on just a few stocks? Was there a change in the style and discipline as the manager tried to get better performance? Did the size of the assets under management or the earnings change drastically? All these questions need to be answered before you go to the performance numbers to make your decision. We'll talk more about this in the investing chapters in Part Four.

> *One way to get burned is to purchase hot stocks.*

Looking at just stock indices (big, small, and international) over five-year rolling periods from 1979 to 2000, we find 6 instances out 13 periods where the best-performing category became the worst over the next five years. Five times, the worst then became the best. Only once did the winner over five years stay on top.

Buying last year's hot mutual fund or stock is a good way to sink a portfolio. Often, what has recently gone *up* a lot is *more likely* to go *down* the most in the next year. If you didn't own it when it had a big runup, assume that you missed the party. Why? Because it's very difficult to consistently pick stocks that will go up more than an average amount. Further, the companies whose stocks have most increased in value often find it difficult to sustain the growth and profitability that drive stock prices.

Bond markets are simply playing "follow the leader," following inflation expectations and interest rates—in reverse. When interest rates rise, bond prices decline and vice versa. We don't remember when predictions agreed on the direction of interest rates, let alone on an actual number. Predicting interest rates is riskier than predicting the stock market. The only ways a bond fund manager can significantly outperform his or her peers is through lowering expenses, taking greater risks in lower-rated debt or foreign debt, or using some kind of derivatives (complex investments whose value is based on the value of an underlying security). These investment choices also mean the fund can underperform if one of these gambles blows up—as it can, even for the most savvy managers.

Now, let's look at how to use specific past performance numbers properly when evaluating mutual funds and benchmarking your investments in future chapters. Just remember: performance is relative, and it's only the starting point of good research and figuring out how to invest for the future.

Long-Term Investing

Earlier we mentioned that what's important *is time in* the market, not *timing* the market. We define long-term investing as anything over five years. *Short-term* is three years or less. Between three and five years is the "twilight zone."

The reason for distinguishing between long-term investing and short-term investing is to properly match them to your goals and financial objectives. When your time horizon for a particular objective is less than five years, you want to invest appropriately to make sure the money is available when the time comes. We'll look at short-term and "twilight zone" investments in the next section.

> I buy [stocks] on the assumption that they could close the market the next day and not reopen it for five years.
> —Warren Buffett

The 55 rolling five-year periods beginning in 1941 for the S&P 500 Index show only two periods when you would have lost money before inflation if you'd reinvested the dividends. Time in the market allows your portfolio to ride out the rough years and recover.

Good investment decisions are based on your financial plan. You need to know three things to start your plan:

✔ What do you want?

✔ When do you need it?

✔ What does it take to get there?

Without a plan, you won't know where you are going or when you'll get there. Investing to meet a goal without a time horizon is risky because your investments may not be appropriate to meet your need in the future. Neither you nor anyone else can determine whether any particular investment is a good one for you without knowing these basics. Once you've figured these out in some detail, you can then answer the next two questions:

✔ How much do you need to save now?

✔ Where do you invest it?

Most people are investing for a lifetime of goals. Long-term investing for goals five to 40 years or more in the future requires investing in stocks and stock mutual funds to allow you the best chance to meet those goals and beat the twin evils—inflation and taxes. Most of the risks we see in the short term in the stock market disappear in the long run. You can afford to ride out any severe market drops because you don't need that money for many years.

As a long-term investor, you can afford to take more risks with your money. That's because the biggest risk you face is that you won't beat inflation and taxes, that you won't have enough money when you need it. Most of the other risks, such as the risk of losing money in stocks, decline over time to near zero after 20 years. The results of investing too conservatively because market drops are scary may be that you won't have the money you need in the future.

Of course, everybody is a long-term investor until the market tanks. Fear then takes over and a voice screams, "It'll go down and stay there forever!" Panic quickly sets in and yells, "Sell!" In part, that's what makes market downturns worse—everyone panics. (Years ago, big market drops were actually called "panics.") Investors with long-term horizons, some understanding of the market, and self-discipline don't sell out of fear. The long-term investor feels the pain when the market drops, but understands that selling only makes the pain permanent.

As you get closer to your long-term goals, you'll need to change your portfolio to reflect this. With less than five years left, you'll need to begin to use short-term investments. However, not all of your goals will require the whole pile to be available at once. College education takes big bites over four or more years. Retirement can go on for decades, and you're likely to need more money in the later years than in the early ones.

Short-Term Investing

When people call the market a gamble or a crapshoot, they're actually right—in the short term. In the long run, the stock and bond markets are your only protection against inflation and taxes. But in the short term they're a mystery. A short-time horizon is just a period in which you want to protect your principal and maybe pick up some interest along the way. It's a holding pattern for your money.

Why not invest in the stock market to meet objectives in less than five years? After all, a year or two of 20%-30% gains will grow your money faster. Good question. Our answer: Sure, go ahead and take that chance if you want. You just have to answer one question: How much longer will

> *The short term is always unpredictable. But in the long term, everything always averages out.*

you have to save if the stock market goes *down* 20%-30%? It may take you several years to make back the money you lost, thus extending your time horizon.

The stock market periodically goes down 10% or more. Since 1958, once every six years on average it has gone down at least 20%, even as far as 48%. That's called a *bear market*. The last seven bear markets took a year, on average, to finally hit bottom and almost two years more to recover to the previous high. During those periods, if you happened to need the money you'd invested in the market, it wouldn't be all there. Bad luck? No, bad planning. Because no one knows when the next big decline will occur or how long it will take to recover, short-term money isn't safe in the stock market.

The bond market can be scary, too. During the last 40 years, bond market declines of 15% or more lasted over two years on average. The declines also occur on average once every four years. Long-term bonds, which pay the highest interest rates, fall the most. (As we mentioned earlier, when interest rates go up, bond prices drop.) If you have to sell a bond or a bond fund after interest rates have gone up, you'll suffer losses just like in the stock market (check out Chapter 14).

The biggest mistake you can make here is to take a higher risk in the stock market for a short-term goal. It's double jeopardy if the market goes down. Not only will you fail to achieve your goal on time, but it'll actually take you longer. How would you feel if you lost the down pay-ment on the house that your growing family needs because you decided to chance it by investing the money in the stock market that year?

Sure, life is a gamble. But when we can reduce our risks, it usually pays to do so. There's a lot we can't control in life, so we want to put the odds in our favor whenever we can. Short-term investing strategy says it's better to be safe than sorry. When it's your hard-earned money and your goals on the line, don't risk them.

We said that three to five years is the "twilight zone" because we don't have a clue what might happen over that short a time frame. If you want to push it just a little in this range, you can put up to half the money into a short-term bond fund or a good, balanced mutual fund. A balanced fund holds about 40% or so in bonds and cash, with the rest in large company stocks that pay dividends. You may make a couple percentage points more. Then again, you may make a couple less!

In theory, the bonds will cushion the damage done to the fund if the stock market goes down for any length of time. However, both the stock market and the bond market can lose money at the same time. Four of the last seven bond market declines of over 15% occurred when stocks were in a bear market averaging 36% losses! So this is a riskier strategy. If you try it and the fund is up for the first couple of years, bail out and put that money in safe, short-term investments. On the other hand, if it's down after a year or two, leave it in. The odds are it will recover by the time you need it. If not, that's the greater risk you take with this strategy.

Invest money needed for goals within the next five years very con-servatively and sleep well at night. There's no way to time market moves and make money. Invest your long-term money in the stock market and ignore the short-term fluctuations as much as possible. Over the long term, markets will behave according to underlying eco-nomic conditions. Investors have to be optimistic that over many years the U.S. economy and the world economy will continue to improve. Although there have always been difficult periods, such as depressions and world wars, the economy and the markets have always recovered.

Chapter 10 | Asset Allocation

What Is It and How to Use It

Asset allocation has been the buzzword for the 1990s. Yet the concept is as old as investments themselves. It's best represented by the old adage: "Don't put all your eggs in one basket." The alternative to this is: "Put all your eggs in one basket and watch it like a hawk." Believe it or not, both of these styles can make sense in different situations.

Some of the richest men in the world have followed the one-basket strategy and it works for them. The classic example is the richest man in the world, Bill Gates, and his host of millionaire partners and workers who put all their efforts into a company and then focused on nothing else to make the company and themselves successful and rich. In fact, most of America's richest people have made their money by running or building a company and having the bulk of their net worth in the stock of that company. These people were able to control the direction of the company as active investors and managers. They truly hold their destiny in their hands and all of their eggs in one basket.

Most of us don't own a company. We put food on the table by working in someone else's company. Neither are we able to be full-time investors. So the answer for us is to put some of our eggs in different baskets and try not to drop them.

Here's where you start learning to develop an investing program that works for you. Asset allocation is a fancy investment term that simply means you determine what percent or range of percent of your portfolio is invested in each general class of assets, stocks, bonds, cash, and real estate (including your home). Your asset allocation is a key part of your long-term strategy.

All investments provide varying degrees of stability, income, or growth. You can't get all three of these in a single class of investment. Each class provides more of one than of the other two, so you have to examine the tradeoffs among them. You design your portfolio to give you the approximate amount of stability, income, and growth you need to get to where you want to go over the long run.

Allocation balances your portfolio so not all of your money is invested in one asset class. This means that when stocks hit a rough period, your whole portfolio doesn't suffer. The same is true with bonds or other investments. At any given time, at least some of your money is in the right place. Because no one knows ahead of time where the right and wrong places will be, asset allocation reduces the short-term volatility of your portfolio.

> *Never invest your money in anything that eats or needs repairing.*
> *—Billy Rose*

What you're really interested in here is the performance of your portfolio as a complete unit, because that's what's going to get the job done for you over time. The individual components are significant only as they affect your portfolio. Don't focus on individual investment performance in the short term and lose sight of the long-term big picture.

Asset allocation is your long-term strategy as an investor with various goals. The time horizon is from one year to however long you expect to live. Investing is not a race like a 100-yard dash. Think of it more like a marathon: your goal is to finish. Since you get only one chance to run this marathon, it makes sense to plan how to pace yourself so you can cross the finish line rather than drop out along the way. That's what asset allocation is—pacing your investments so they're always working for you.

At various points in your life cycle, your allocation may need to change. The portion allocated to stocks can range from 50% to 90% depending on the age of the investor, with younger investors having a larger proportion of stocks in their portfolio. The mix of styles within the classes may also change. We'll look closer at these styles and strategies throughout this section and the next. The cash portion is based on your emergency fund and your short-term needs.

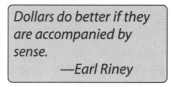

Dollars do better if they are accompanied by sense.
—Earl Riney

This allocation is just the beginning of how you structure your portfolio. Within the asset classes, you have a variety of styles of investing to use to diversify your holdings. A basic allocation might be as shown in Figure 10-1.

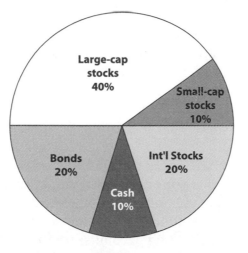

FIGURE 10-1. AN EXAMPLE OF THE ALLOCATION OF ASSETS IN ONE PORTFOLIO

Within this allocation you might have aggressive growth funds or more conservative value funds. Your foreign stock funds could be in emerging markets or developed countries. The bonds could be high-yield corporate bonds or intermediate-term U.S. treasuries. The combination of styles within the asset classes determines whether the portfolio is more conservative or more aggressive. Rather than change the allocation, you can change the style mix within each class to adjust your portfolio to meet your long-term needs and comfort level at various stages of your life cycle.

Just remember that "one size fits all" portfolios don't work. You need to have your portfolio tailored to your specific needs, not a pie chart from a mutual fund brochure. An investor with a $10,000 portfolio should not have the same asset mix as someone with a $100,000 portfolio.

How Many Baskets Do You Need?

So with which of these major categories—cash, bonds, and stocks—should you fill your baskets? The Brinson Associates study showed that, on average, 92% of investment returns can be explained by the class of assets in which the money was invested—stocks, bonds, or cash. Only 5% of the average return was due to the specific investment—which particular stocks or bonds were bought. Less than 2% of the returns came from market timing—but we've already emphasized that trying to time the markets is not for mere mortals.

When designing your asset allocation to meet your needs and goals, this simply means that you create a balance among stocks, bonds, and interest-bearing cash investments in the proportion necessary to generate the long-term returns you need. The research says that it's much less important in the long run which stocks, bonds, or funds you choose because that makes only a small difference in your total return.

Everybody has to have some cash in one basket. You use the cash for short-term needs, like your emergency fund, living expenses, or any other commitments that call for cash. Some examples of cash holdings are money market mutual funds, tax-exempt money market funds, CDs, savings accounts, checking accounts, treasury bills, your piggy bank, and, of course, the proverbial mattress. These are all the places where you can get to your cash in a hurry and not worry about losing your principal.

Bonds are the second asset class you'll need to learn to deal with. These are a little bit trickier than cash. You need to know that all bonds are not created equal. Bonds are used because you need money at the end of a specific period of time and you want it to be there. Many people use bonds because they want less volatility than with the stock market, although in some years bonds have actually been more volatile than stocks. When you buy bonds, you're making three basic assumptions:

✔ You won't need the money until the bonds mature.

✔ You're going to get all your cash back at maturity.

✔ The interest rate you receive will beat inflation.

We'll discuss the details of bonds in Chapter 14.

Stocks are the asset class that brings growth to your portfolio over the long term. Stocks and stock mutual funds are the only class of assets that give you a chance at beating both taxes and inflation over time. There are many strategies and techniques to investing in stocks. Some work better long term than others, and some require less attention and work than others. We'll take a closer look at some of these you can use in Chapters 12, 13, and 15.

Rebalancing Your Portfolio

Rebalancing your portfolio is a lot like rebalancing and rotating the tires on your car. The best strategy is preventive maintenance. It's the same for your investments: they need to be rebalanced periodically. Most of us are not disciplined to do this, so we just let it go, trusting that things will be OK—till we have a problem, and then we hope the spare tire has air in it.

Your portfolio becomes unbalanced over time because the various asset classes perform differently. When you review your portfolio annually and find that the allocations have strayed from the range you set for them, it's a good idea to return each asset class to within its specified range. Remember: your asset allocation is created to serve your financial objectives, so it's your investment guide.

If you've figured that your long-term needs call for 10% cash, 30% bonds, and 60% stocks, then just change your mix every time one of those categories gets 5% to 10% higher. For example, let's assume the stock market went up and the value of your stock portfolio is now 70% of your net worth. Your cash is still 10% of your portfolio, but your bonds are now only 20%. One effective strategy is to sell 10% of the stocks and shift them into bonds.

This strategy we call contrarian optimism. You take some of your gains and reinvest them in the class that hasn't performed as well.

> Take calculated risks.
> That is quite different
> from being rash.
> —George S. Patton

Sooner or later, it will rebound, while the better-performing class may slow down. It's the secret of the market strategist who believes that you have to buy low and sell high. It forces you to sell at least some of your winners when they've done well and put new money into the asset classes that have been under-performing.

In this case, the stocks had trampled the bond portfolio, so your natural inclination is to buy even more stocks. But having sound investment guidelines allows you to take the emotions out of managing your portfolio, and this will improve your long-term results. By selling the winners and buying the losers, you allow the portfolio to benefit from the wisdom that the losing investments over most three- to five-year time frames often tend to be the winning investments over the next three to five years.

We went back to 1979 when there was good data on small companies and looked at four places you could have put your money: stocks—big companies, small companies, and international—and five-year U.S. Treasuries. The results were striking. In 8 out of 13 periods either the worst performing group became the best or the best became the worst or, sometimes, even both happened. Only once did the winner over the last five years beat the pack over the next five. Yet in the interest of full disclosure, it was big company stocks in the five-year periods ending 1997 through 2000 doing a repeat on the top. So we'll let you decide if this is a new trend developing.

When rebalancing in taxable accounts, you'd rather not do anything that generates a tax bill if you can help it. If you can't adequately rebalance using non-taxable retirement accounts, then direct your stream of new investment money into the asset class or classes that are below their range. In the example above, you would put all your new money into bonds or bond funds. Over time, your portfolio will return to its proper allocation. If, however, it's too imbalanced due to a great stock market run, you may want to take some profits and pay Uncle Sam his due.

Reallocation: When Your Goals Change

Your current asset allocation plan needs to change when major alterations occur in cash flow, time horizons, or goals. As you pass significant life events and achieve some of your goals, your position in your life cycle shifts. This, too, calls for a review of your allocation to make sure you can reach your remaining objectives or any new goals you may set.

Sometimes, lifestyle changes are not always intentional. Some big changes can catch us by surprise. Events such as a job loss, a disability, a divorce, health problems, and a family member in need may force your hand. Positive events, such as an unexpected promotion and raise, a lucrative job change, an unplanned inheritance, or other good news, may also call for an allocation change.

Two questions arise here: (1) How much change is required? (2) How do you make the change? The amount of change required depends on how much the lifestyle change alters your basic plan and how long you expect the effects of the change to last. If the change is big, your original allocation may no longer fit the new plan. Review the basics. What do you want, when do you need it, and what will it take to get you there? This will tell you what changes are needed.

If the change in your life is a temporary one, then maybe only minor alterations are needed, if any. Losing a job, health issues, or aiding a sick friend or relative may all be changes that you can reasonably assume will be over in six months or a year. If you need to increase the cash in your emergency fund to tide you over, take some funds from your long-term investments. Keep the remainder of your long-term money in your long-term portfolio. If the effects of the change run longer than anticipated, you may need to shift more money over to your emergency fund. On the other hand, if the situation is resolved sooner than expected, you can return everything not needed in your regular emergency fund balance back into your long-term investments.

It's different when changes are permanent. If the change leads to a reduction in your income, you need to change your lifestyle first rather than your portfolio. In other words, don't cash in the assets in your portfolio to maintain a lifestyle you can no longer afford. And if you

> *A dollar will not go as far as it used to, but it will go faster.*

can no longer add money to your savings, you'll have to scale back your goals and push back time horizons until the picture gets into balance again. If the changes in your life are positive to your cash flow, then you may add new goals or upscale the ones you have. A bigger house, a fancier car, or earlier retirement may be possible. Either way, whether the changes are positive or negative, it's imperative to review and re-evaluate your financial plan when long-term changes affect your life.

When you're within three to five years of needing money for a long-term financial goal, the time horizon has become short-term, as we discussed earlier. You want to be sure of having the money available when you need it. A strategy that works here is to start selling off some of your stock winners and to begin using bonds and fixed income investments as a holding place, so when the kid starts college or you reach retirement age the money will be available.

The rest of your portfolio you keep in stocks to keep pace with inflation. Don't forget to factor in income taxes as you follow this plan. When you sell long-term investments, you will hopefully have a capital gain, for which the taxes can be paid either out of the proceeds or with other funds you have available.

How to Pick the Right Investments for Your Goals

This part is all about the big picture of investing and understanding where to put your money and how the game is played. Here we get into the specific investment choices you will have to make in setting up your investment portfolio. We'll cover the gamut of investments, starting with the best-yielding guaranteed returns and going all the way to high-flying growth and international stocks. Putting them in perspective is also part of the plan, as you must understand that those higher returns usually mean higher risks.

We'll start with using banks and money market funds. Then we'll move into stocks and bonds.

Bonds can be an important part of a portfolio for helping to provide income in retirement. We'll cover when to buy, but even more important, we'll cover when to sell an investment.

For most of you, stock investments will be the workhorses of your portfolio and will ultimately give you the best returns. The problem is figuring out which one particular investment makes sense for you out of the thousands of stock and stock mutual fund options. So we'll sort out how to make good choices when buying stock mutual funds as well as individual stock issues.

For the average investor, individual stocks are a higher-maintenance approach, but we'll show you how the stock market works. Focusing on style is also a key element to investing, so we sort through the process of having the right mix of specific investment styles and disciplines.

Chapter 11 | Banks and Money Market Funds

Bank Checking Accounts and Services

As children the first thing we learn about money is how to spend it, by watching the adults around us. The second thing we learn about money is that it's important to save it, because the adults in our life told us so. And usually some well-meaning adult gave us a piggy bank and told us to save our pennies for a rainy day or even helped us open a passbook savings account at the local friendly bank.

> I don't know how much money I have in the bank. I haven't shaken it lately.
> —Milton Berle

Now for most of us that local friendly bank doesn't exist anymore. We may have more interaction with an ATM than with a live teller—and yes, they still call them "tellers."

The role of banks is changing. The way that banks made money years ago was to lend money at the highest rates and pay the lowest interest rates on deposits. The difference between the rates is called the *spread*. The bigger the spread, the higher the potential profits. Now, banks want to be players in all the areas of financial services.

But not all things have changed. The one thing most people still use banks for is checking and daily money needs. Banks do a good job in meeting those needs.

Choosing Your Bank

With so many banks competing for our money, the fees are becoming more competitive, but you still need to shop around for a bank that shows it wants your business. There are things that you need to look for, because all banks are certainly not created equal.

Size is usually the best way to categorize your options. You have big commercial banks (that continue to get bigger), local or regional banks, and credit unions. All three are fine places to do business, but if you're more interested in the personal touch and people who know you, then you might want to start with local smaller banks. The big banks give you the latest technology and a broad array of services, but they're not overly friendly. It costs money to be friendly.

Most people just open a bank account at the nearest location. Comparison shopping is usually not a top priority for most people. But a bunch of small fees every month can really add up. A little legwork can save hundreds of dollars in fees. That's not bad for a couple hours of work.

One of the things you might want to look for is a bank that pays interest on your checking account. Unfortunately, all checking accounts don't pay interest, and even if they do, it's about the lowest rate you'll find. Still, it's worth considering. The down side on interest-bearing checking accounts, however, is that you may be required to keep a minimum balance.

Keep as little in your checking account as possible—just enough to pay your upcoming expenses. If you can get a free checking account with a $2,500 CD, it's usually worth it. If you add the $150 or so in fees you save to the competitive interest rate on the CD, you're earning a healthy return. A six-month CD that you roll over at maturity every time can be part of your emergency fund. Don't use a one-year or longer-term CD. The cost of redeeming it early if you need the money is too high. There are better places to put your emergency fund.

If you can get a no-fee checking account when you keep a minimum balance and if you can discipline yourself not to spend that minimum, then you don't need the CD. Set your checkbook balance to zero when the balance is at the minimum and don't write checks that dip into the minimum. You might also get free checking if you keep a balance in a savings account or if the combined balance of checking and savings accounts meets a minimum. As long as the amount required isn't more than $1,000 or so, then it may be worth it. Savings accounts don't pay nearly as much as a CD.

If you're not earning interest on your checking account, just keep what you need to cover the bills coming due and write a check for the balance to a money market mutual fund. Bank savings accounts and "money market accounts" pay about half the interest rate of a money market mutual fund—about 2% per year versus 5% at the moment. We'll look at these types of accounts in the next section.

The Federal Deposit Insurance Corporation (FDIC) insures deposits up to $100,000 in commercial banks, savings banks, savings and loans, and mutual savings banks. These banks must be approved by the FDIC and meet certain standards of safety and use sound banking practices. Banks covered by the FDIC will display a sign as evidence of this coverage. If you don't see it, ask.

All types of deposit accounts made at FDIC-insured banks are covered. This means checking or NOW accounts, savings accounts, certificates of deposit, and money market deposit accounts. Other products sold by a bank, such as mutual funds and annuities, are not covered. FDIC insurance covers you as a depositor based on the name on the account. All accounts in the same name at one bank are insured up to $100,000. You can open other accounts at another bank and the insurance will cover $100,000 there. In addition, any joint accounts are separately insured up to the same amount.

Retirement accounts and custodial accounts held by a bank in trust or as custodian under the Uniform Transfers to Minors Act or Uniform Gifts to Minors Act are insured separately from your regular deposits. But the FDIC insurance coverage is only for deposit accounts here, too. If you have a brokerage account in your retirement plan through a bank, that balance is not covered by the FDIC.

Credit unions are different from banks in that they are legally nonprofit. They were originally set up to serve the needs of people who often were unable to get regular bank services. Today, they are no-frills operations that usually pay higher interest rates on accounts and charge lower rates on loans to members. You can join through a close relative if you don't belong to an association or employee group that's covered.

> *The drive-in bank was established so that the real owner of a car can see it once in a while.*

However, make sure it's a federally chartered and regulated credit union rather than a state-chartered credit union. Federally chartered credit unions are covered by National Credit Union Administration (NCUA) insurance, also in the amount of $100,000. Some states' regulations and insurance coverage are weak. If a credit union is shaky and the state isn't paying close attention, it could become insolvent. If it can't return your money, then the state insurance fund is called in. The problem is that some state insurance funds may not be able to meet that demand created by insolvency. Your money could be tied up for years; in fact, it may take a special act of the legislature to use tax money to compensate your loss! The safety of your money is important to you, so be careful if you choose a credit union.

Bank Savings Accounts and CDs

Currently there is roughly $1.9 trillion in savings accounts in the country and the bulk of this money is earning less than 2%. These accounts are good for some purposes, but they may not make sense for others. Savings accounts don't pay enough interest to grow after taxes and inflation. Your money may even lose purchasing power over time.

CDs can serve as a good short-term investment and maintain purchasing power if inflation doesn't rise much. Let's look at the numbers (Figure 11-1). If you compare these two options over a number of years, you'll see that returns from CDs far outpace returns from savings accounts.

CDs can be used very effectively as an alternative for people who want to ladder a portfolio of bonds, either to reduce volatility or to generate retirement cash to live off. They're extremely safe and usually

Year	6 month CD Rates	Passbook Savings Rates
1991	4.95	4.90
1992	3.27	3.13
1993	2.88	2.38
1994	5.40	2.16
1995	5.21	2.35
1996	5.21	2.24
1997	5.71	2.13
1998	5.34	2.12
1999	5.43	1.67
2000	6.64	1.64
Average	**5.01**	**2.47**

FIGURE 11-1. THE DIFFERENCE BETWEEN CD RATES AND PASSBOOK SAVINGS RATES (Data: Passbook Savings Average Annual Rates courtesy of *Bankrate Inc.*, 6-month CD data courtesy of The American Funds Group®)

come in a variety of maturities. They're also very competitive, which means you can find a good deal if you shop around. Any bank can give you a competitive rate of return in just about any maturity you want. Interest rates are also competitive with U.S. Treasury notes (government debt of less than ten-year maturity, which we'll discuss in Chapter 14).

The safety factor is great, because CDs in banks are covered by FDIC insurance up to $100,000 per account in each institution. Only Treasury bonds from the U.S Government are safer. Although you hope never to use the $100,000 insurance, banks sometimes do go under.

In the late '80s there were a lot of banks that didn't survive. In hindsight, we recognize as one of the telltale signs the very high CD rates they were offering to attract new customers. If one bank is paying much more than the others, you better find out why before you purchase that CD. It could just be a "teaser rate," good only for a short period of time, after which it will go down (much like the teaser interest rates offered by credit cards, that then go up substantially). A high rate could also mean that what you're buying from the bank is an actual bond, not a CD. What's the difference, if you're earning a good return? Well, the FDIC does not insure the bank's bonds, and this also happened in some fraud cases in the late '80s.

No Free Lunches—or Toasters

Most of us have seen the free toaster marketing campaigns. The bank offers a free toaster when you buy a CD. Sometimes that can be a very expensive toaster. Let's suppose you had $10,000 in a CD and locked it up for three years. If you didn't shop around and missed a return that was only ¼% better, that toaster cost you $75. If you got a return that was 1% lower, then the toaster price tag would be $300.

If you want a free toaster, that's fine. Just be sure you're getting a competitive rate. You should also know that most CDs have an associated cost if you redeem them early. You may lose some interest and maybe even pay a penalty. That's why you don't want to put money for your emergency fund in a long-term CD.

Bank Mergers

Today, banks are merging at a frantic rate. That may mean that some of the rates that were offered by your old bank may not be honored by the new one. So be a little careful of locking in your rates for a long time. If your bank becomes involved in a merger, you should watch for changes in the account minimums, interest rates, and charges.

Other Bank Services

Trying to distinguish among banks, brokerage houses, mutual fund houses, and insurance companies is getting more difficult. It's best to know what each institution can do well and what it's just getting into. It might be convenient to get all your financial needs met by one institution, but that convenience could come at a high price.

Many banks are currently offering one-stop financial shopping. Historically, it's been their job to lend you money to help you reach your life goals and handle your CDs, savings, and checking accounts. They also have experience in handling trusts that need to be managed by a professional trustee. Now, banks are trying to become full-service money managers, financial planners, brokers, and insurance agents as well.

Needless to say, that's hard for any organization to learn to do well in a short period of time. With all of these services, it comes down to the value-added question: Is this institution helping you make good investment decisions at a reasonable cost? The answer is ... maybe. That's because it's the person providing those services who either makes or breaks the relationship.

What kind of relationship do you want with these services? If you want a sounding board or a financial partner, then interview the person you'll be dealing with. Hold him or her up to the same scrutiny you would for any of the advisors that you might work with, such as financial planners, stockbrokers, insurance agents, and money managers. Don't just go with the person for convenience, like your checking account. Ask all the questions we go over in Chapter 27. If the person stacks up, hire him or her. If not, go elsewhere.

All these bank services have a fee attached somewhere—loads, commissions, management fees, origination fees, and so on. The banks don't always tell you about them up front, so ask. Then you can compare the cost of their services with the costs of doing business with other institutions. There's nothing wrong with paying for service, advice, and management. What you want to avoid is making important financial decisions based on the expertise of a person who was a teller three weeks earlier and then had just a week's training as a "personal banker." You want someone with knowledge and experience who will take the time to look at your situation with you, answer your questions clearly, and be there the next time you come in.

A few big banks have their own mutual funds. They're not insured or guaranteed through the bank. They may also have higher expense fees, so you need to compare their long-term performance with the performance of similar styles of funds. Some bank-sponsored funds have very good track records, but it's up to you to do your homework before investing in such funds. Check out Chapter 16 for more information on picking a mutual fund.

What Are Money Market Funds?

Money market mutual funds really are the greatest thing since sliced bread—well, almost! New federal laws in the early 1970s gave consumers an alternative to the low-interest bank accounts. Hundreds of millions of dollars flowed into the new funds. Eventually, banks were allowed to pay market-rate interest on deposits, too, but as we noted earlier, they usually don't.

A money market mutual fund is as close as you can get to a no-brainer in the investment world. They are simply mutual funds that invest in and manage a variety of very short-term (less than one-year maturity) bonds and other interest-paying securities. The manager of a fund is hired to maximize the return on the money invested in the fund while minimizing the risk of any borrower defaulting on the debt. Interest is calculated on the balance daily, so you can buy and sell without worrying about timing, although the interest is actually credited to your account monthly.

The funds cost $1.00 per share all the time, whether you're buying or selling. No consumer money market fund has ever "broken the buck," that is, given the investor less than $1.00 per share. It has happened that the value of a fund has sunk below $1.00, due to a risky investment that went bad. The fund distributor made up the difference and no one lost any money. That doesn't mean that it can't or won't happen, but the fund companies go to great lengths to prevent it. Also, new government regulations restrict investments now to relatively safe types.

There are three basic styles of these funds: *regular, government,* and *tax-free*.

✔ *Regular* money market funds invest in short-term corporate debt called commercial paper and notes as well as short-term jumbo bank certificates of deposit and some government debt.

✔ *Government* funds primarily invest in short-term debt of federal agencies, such as the Federal National Mortgage Association and the Federal Home Loan Bank. A subset of government funds is labeled Treasury funds. They invest only in short-term debt issued by the U.S. Treasury. You'd use these for lock-tight absolute safety and for income that's exempt from state taxes, but the interest rates they pay are a little lower than the rates for the other funds.

✔ *Tax-free* money market funds buy short-term debt issued by state and local governments and U.S. Territories such as Guam and Puerto Rico. Most of the interest is exempt from federal tax and the rates are about 40% lower than for regular funds. You can also find state tax-free funds that invest only in the municipal debt of a single state and other governmental units in the state. If you live in that state, your interest is generally both federal and state tax-exempt. This kind of fund works best if you're in a high-tax state and in a 31% or higher federal tax bracket.

Today, U.S.-based money market funds hold about $2.0 trillion. They are closely regulated by the Federal Reserve Bank and the Securities and Exchange Commission. Although the funds are not government insured, they are held as trusts, subject to strict legal requirements designed to protect the money. Investors are insured against fraud and theft by the Securities Investor Protection Corporation (SIPC) through the fund companies that sponsor the funds.

The debt held by money market funds is short-term, which means it's due to mature in less than a year, and the fund will get its money back. Because these funds invest only in short-term debt, the value of their holdings doesn't change very much. As interest rates go up and down, fund managers quickly adjust the rate the fund earns and can pay the market rate by buying and selling securities. This is great when rates go up, but not so great when rates are going down. You don't lose any money; you just get paid a lower interest rate within a month or so. The Federal Reserve Bank pretty much controls the market interest rate within a narrow range at this level of debt.

It's important to recognize the difference between a money market mutual fund and a money market deposit account at a bank. A bank's function is to borrow money from depositors at the lowest rate that attracts the amount of money it needs or wants to lend. When a bank can get cheaper money elsewhere, it pays lower rates of interest than money market funds. The only advantage to the bank money market accounts is the FDIC insurance, but that's not worth 2% or more per year.

Year	Bank Money Market Rates	Money Market Mutual Funds
1991	5.11	5.83
1992	3.22	3.45
1993	2.49	2.72
1994	2.41	3.73
1995	2.82	5.53
1996	2.66	4.94
1997	2.61	4.71
1998	2.47	5.10
1999	2.07	4.74
2000	2.07	5.94
Average	**2.79**	**4.77**

FIGURE 11-2. A COMPARISON OF BANK MONEY MARKET RATES AND MONEY MARKET MUTUAL FUNDS RATES (Data: Bank Money Market rates courtesy of *Bankrate Inc.*, Lipper Money Market Funds Index)

Money market funds pay market rates of interest subject to two factors: how much the fund company charges to manage the fund and the average length of maturity of the debt the fund holds. The average fee is 40 to 60 *basis points*. A basis point is 1/100th of a percent (0.01%). If the fund earns 5.5% and the fee runs 0.40% (forty basis points), you would earn 5.1% per year. Fees can be as low as 0.20% and a few actually charge over 1.0%! So look for the money market funds that take less than 0.60% in fees. You'll find this information in the first couple pages of the fund's prospectus.

Occasionally, some funds will absorb the fees or part of them, so their advertised yield is higher. And they'll pay more until they impose a fee or raise it. Once they have enough money, they'll start charging fees again and perhaps you won't even notice. Unless you have a huge amount of money in money market funds, it isn't worth your time to continually hunt for funds that temporarily charge no fee or very low fees and keep switching as fees change.

Using Money Market Funds

Money market funds have a variety of uses because they're so flexible. They're a great place to start as an investor. You can earn market interest rates while you decide where to invest the money for a longer term. For dollar cost averaging lump sums, you can feed the money monthly into the stock market from a money market fund. Many fund companies will help you set up an automatic program to do this. Savvy investors use money market funds to stash their cash temporarily while they wait to buy other investments.

A money market fund works well as a core account at your brokerage or mutual fund company to help you keep track of the flow of your money. When you sell a stock or a bond, you can have the proceeds automatically go into this fund while you decide what to do next. You can have stock dividends and interest payments automatically flow here, too. However, you should automatically reinvest your stock and bond mutual fund dividends to take advantage of compounding.

You can also use a money market fund to organize practically your whole financial life. It can be your checking account and your debit and credit card account with automatic payments made for you each month as well as your core investment account. Finally, it's a good place to hold cash for short-term needs and for a significant part of your emergency fund.

There's a complete listing of money market funds, both taxable and tax-free, in *Barron's*, a Dow Jones weekend newspaper. Your Sunday newspaper may list many of them in the business section, as well. You'll find the current 7-day and 30-day compound rates listed as well as the average maturity as of the previous week. Most mutual fund companies and brokerage houses have money market funds that will meet your needs.

The money market fund listings are also a great short-term indicator of where professional money managers think interest rates are heading. The consensus is not always correct, but it's a good reading of market sentiment. Look at the average maturity of all the funds (usually at the beginning or end of the listing). If the days-to-maturity is rising toward 60 or even above for several weeks, managers are locking in longer-term higher yields because they think rates are declining soon. If the number is below 60 days and falling, they expect rates to increase. The managers want to roll over into higher-yielding debt sooner if that happens.

Just as with CDs and bonds, short-term debt interest rates are based on the amount of time to maturity. Overnight debt (yes, banks borrow money overnight) is the lowest, while 52-week maturity debt is the highest, unless rates are climbing. If that happens, the shorter new debt may pay as much as or more than the older, longer-term notes. A few basis points may not mean much to you, but these managers are investing hundreds of millions, even billions, of dollars. So the basis points at those levels add up fast into real money.

When interest rates are going up, a money market fund is a good place to have some money, because you will soon earn the higher rates. On the other hand, when rates are going down, money in longer-term debt such as CDs and bonds is better, because you earn interest at the higher rate until maturity. And we won't predict which way the rates will be heading.

Chapter 12 | Stocks: Owning a Piece of the Company

What Is a Stock?

When you own stock in a company, you're a part owner of the business, even if it's just one share. Most of the richest men in the world have made their fortunes by owning a company and benefiting by the rise of that company's value. Let's face it, wouldn't most of us want to have the buying power of Bill Gates (Microsoft founder), Ted Turner (CNN founder), and Warren Buffet (who actually made his billions by picking stocks), currently among the richest men in the world? We can't all own our own company, at least not huge ones. But you can own small pieces of great, large companies and benefit from their rise in value.

A share of stock is a legal document that represents direct ownership of a small piece of a company. Traditionally, shares were represented by fancy engraved certificates usually kept in a safety deposit

box or other secure place. Today, shares are usually held in your account at a brokerage firm and registered in the firm's "street name." The information on ownership is kept electronically by the brokerage firm, the custodian (a bank or trust company not affiliated with the brokerage firm), and the company's transfer agent. This is more convenient for everyone, since you would need to present the paper certificate at the broker's office within three days of selling shares. With over a billion shares traded every day, Wall Street would drown in paperwork.

Being an owner gives you a few limited rights, such as:

✔ Voting on candidates for the board of directors

✔ Voting on some matters that affect your ownership, such as mergers

✔ Attending the annual meeting of the company's stockholders

✔ Receiving any dividend that the board may declare

✔ Receiving the annual report and proxy materials for the annual meeting

Rather than attend the annual meetings in person, most stockholders vote by proxy on the ballot sent with the information on the meeting. If you really have the desire to delve into the workings of the company, then pore over the proxy material and annual reports.

Although the annual report is intended to put a positive spin on the company and its activities, there is plenty of useful information there. Always read the footnotes, since they usually contain some interesting stuff. Additional information is also available upon request. Call or write the company's investor relations office and request the company's most recent 10Q quarterly reports and the annual 10K report to the Securities and Exchange Commission (SEC).

As a part owner of the company, you're taking more risk than if you were to loan the company money in the form of buying some of its bonds. Unless the company goes bankrupt, lenders get paid interest on their bonds and receive their principal back. Stock owners get absolutely no guarantees. Your stock price will go up and down with the whims of the market and you will get back whatever the market is willing to pay when you sell. If the company goes bankrupt, the lenders have priority over the owners. If there's anything left after the IRS, employees, lawyers, and lenders get paid—and there often isn't anything—then the stockholders divvy it up. Fortunately for all of us, most companies never get close to bankruptcy.

> The safest and fastest way to double your money is to fold it over.

When a company is successful, the market will recognize that fact sooner or later. More people will want to own the stock and this demand will increase the price. That's where your compound annual returns come from. Sometimes, the return for companies can be higher than the 10% to 12% long-term market average, even a lot higher. That's the reward you get for taking more risk than the lender.

Most companies start out as private companies, except for a few that are spun out of companies that are already publicly traded. The owners and original investors supply the capital and the management. Most companies stay private, though the ownership may change from time to time in private transactions. Some companies decide to "go public," to sell some shares in the stock market to anyone willing to pay the price that is set initially. The new "public owners" are then free to sell their shares as they wish in the open market. The price of the shares changes, often from minute to minute, based on the collective desires of buyers and sellers to hold the stock or not.

Over the long run, the price of a share will reflect the relative success of the company in meeting the demands and challenges of the market-place for its goods or services and on the stock market's view of the future success of the company. Not surprisingly, everyone has an opinion of that future. It's these differences in opinions that make a market.

If you want to participate in the long-term success of the stock market, you can do so by owning shares in stocks of companies or shares in a mutual fund that buys individual stocks. Today, more than one out of three households participates in the stock market, either directly or through mutual funds.

Markets for shares in companies have existed at least since the 1600s, when shares of The East India Company traded in coffeehouses in England. Here in the U.S. in 1792, men met under a buttonwood tree at the corner of Wall Street and Broad Street in Manhattan to trade shares. The market that started there is now the largest in the world, trading over $50 billion worth of shares every day of the work week.

Owning Individual Stocks

Until the last twenty years or so, most people participated in the stock market by owning shares *directly*. The recent rise in the popularity of mutual funds shows that many people are now participating *indirectly*. Even though mutual funds as we know them have been around since the 1920s, they were not as accessible to the average person as stocks were. Households still own more stocks directly, but mutual funds are quickly catching up. Each approach to investing has advantages and disadvantages.

Can a small investor have any chance of buying stocks and doing as well as or even better than the market? Yes. However, most don't. Most professional fund managers don't beat the market averages consistently either. If you want to invest directly in stocks, you can learn to achieve exceptional returns over time. Contrary to what you may hear or read, there are no tricks, no easy methods, and no sure, quick ways to get wealthy in stocks. It takes time and hard work over many years. People who have the time, who are willing and able to do the work and enjoy it, and who can discipline themselves to follow a plan may succeed. The rest need assistance of some kind.

Time is a critical element for stock investing. Don't even think of putting your money into the stock market unless you won't need that money for at least five years. Over shorter periods of time, you're not *investing,* you're *speculating,* and the odds aren't in your favor with the volatility of the stock market.

The key to investing successfully in stocks is to learn to buy shares in good companies at reasonable prices and then hold them. Each stock, while subject to the tidal pull of the market's direction, trades in its own market in ways unique to that stock. Picking good companies is essential. Just buying a bunch of stocks at random without a disciplined approach and a plan will not yield very good returns.

The plan and style of investing you choose and the discipline with which you stick to that plan are critical. It doesn't really matter what your plan is as long as you follow it consistently. Successful investors have chosen many paths to become wealthy. The path you choose should be the one you're most comfortable following.

Assembling your own portfolio of stocks is like creating your own mutual fund, a well-diversified selection of stocks that you follow closely and manage. The ideal diversification is ten companies, each in a different business or industry. This

> *Success is sweet, but its secret is sweat.*

reduces the volatility of your portfolio and reduces your risk of one company's fortunes or one industry being adversely affected by the economy. By minimizing any overlaps among your companies, you reduce what is called *market correlation*, the amount that one stock moves in relation to another.

In practice, twelve to fifteen stocks in different industries will provide a portfolio that approaches this level of protection. Your portfolio value will still move up and down, but this diversification will protect you if one of your stocks gets hit. If you only own four stocks in roughly equal dollar amounts and one of them goes down 50%, the value of your portfolio will drop 12.5%. If you own fifteen stocks, the effect on your portfolio of that one stock dropping by 50% is only 3.3%.

To own 100 shares each in this many companies might take at least $50,000. If you can't afford this level of investment, stay with mutual funds to get the protection their diversification provides. With more money, you can increase the number of stocks as high as thirty with some industry overlap. But you'll need a lot of time to research and follow that many companies and industries. You're probably better off limiting your investment to the twenty best companies and then adding your new money to those positions.

To build your own portfolio, you need to take the time to do thorough research, called fundamental analysis, of dozens of companies in many different businesses, in order to identify the best potential investments for a diversified portfolio. Then, you have to follow those stocks closely to make sure they perform in line with your expectations. You also need to tightly control your emotional reactions as your stocks make large gains or losses. You need the patience to allow your companies to perform over time as you've anticipated.

Investors who don't do sufficient research and analysis of the major factors that affect their companies are continually whipsawed by rumors, misstatements in the press, and other short-term factors that drive prices up and down. Confused and unwary investors are often panicked into making unwise decisions if they haven't done their homework and are not fully committed to their long-term positions and plan.

If you are unsure about buying and selling based on your own research and judgment, you should find and pay for outside, competent advice or you will get hurt. You will constantly be swayed by the actions of the market and the opinions of others one way or another. Your level of stress will rise and the value of your portfolio will inevitably suffer. Chapter 27 will help you find the right kind of assistance you need.

> *Bulls and bears aren't as responsible for as many stock losses as bum steers.*
> *—Olin Miller*

There are some tax benefits to owning individual stocks rather than mutual funds. You're in control of when you sell and take the capital gain or loss. If the stock pays a small dividend, you owe tax on that at your ordinary income tax rate, up to 39.6%. But you won't get that "January jolt" that comes when a mutual fund sends out a 1099 reporting annual distributions that forces you to scramble for money to pay the additional taxes. Of course, if your stocks or funds are in a tax-sheltered retirement plan, you don't need to worry about taxes until you take them out.

Mutual funds may trade a lot and will hit you with short-term capital gains. These are taxed as ordinary income. You can escape short-term gains altogether if you buy individual stocks and hold them at least a year. Then all your gains are taxed at lower, long-term capital gain rates of 10% or 20%. And if you find you've made a mistake (and you will), you can cut your losses early and take advantage of the tax break for short-term capital losses. They're deductible at your top rate of tax, unless you hold the stock in a retirement plan. In that case, you can't share your loss with Uncle Sam.

A final benefit of owning stocks: you save the management fees that mutual funds charge, which could range from 0.5% to 1.5% annually on the value of your portfolio.

Managing your own portfolio of stocks has its rewards, financial and otherwise. But there is a higher maintenance level required than

> *In Wall Street the only thing that's hard to explain is—next week.*
> *—Louis Rukeyser*

with mutual funds. This includes keeping up with your companies, doing the ongoing research to buy and sell, and living with your decisions. A book you might wish to add to your resource library is *The Basics of Stocks* by Gerald Krefetz.

Stock Market Mechanics

It's amazing how Wall Street is able to match all the buyers and sellers of hundreds of millions of shares of stock. Billions of dollars of capital changes hands virtually without a hitch. It is definitely the most efficient market in the world, even though to an outsider it may look like chaos.

Buying and Selling Stocks

To buy or sell stock, you first need to set up a brokerage account. You call a broker, give him or her some basic information (including your name, Social Security number, and address), and fill out some paperwork. Brokers need to follow the NYSE Rule 405 and NASD Conduct Rule 3110, which are the "know your customer" rules. That's why brokers ask about your investment experience, income, net worth, and objectives. The reason is to make sure investors aren't clueless and about to shoot themselves in the foot. If you don't wish to disclose this information, that's your prerogative and is so noted by the brokers.

Once you have a brokerage account, you're free to place orders to buy and sell. Then what happens? Let's take a quick look at how your order works its way through the system.

You tell your broker to buy 100 shares of General Electric (GE) "at the market price." The broker writes up the order and sends it to the firm's floor broker in the New York Stock Exchange. The floor broker goes to the "specialist" who is responsible for trading all the stocks of this company and they complete the transaction. It's then reported back to the broker, who calls you and verbally confirms the trade.

You can also place your order at a "limit" price, a specified price at which you want to buy or sell, either for that day only or "good 'til canceled." Your desired buy ("bid") price may be at or below the current market price and your sell ("ask") price at or above the market price. You have created a "bid" or "ask" price in the market. Your order awaits execution until the stock in question hits your limit price. Your risk with placing an order at a limit price is that the stock might move away from your price and your order will never be executed.

In a few days, you'll receive a confirmation statement of the exact cost of the transaction, including any fees and commissions. The day the trade gets done is the *trade* date. The money (if you're buying) or the shares (if you're selling) are not due until the *settlement* day, which is always three business days after the trade date. This three-day lag is to allow for money and shares to physically change hands, if necessary. You must have the money or the shares at the broker's office by the settlement day, which may be before you get the confirmation in the mail.

If the broker is holding the shares for you, they are called "street name" holdings. The shares are held in the name of the securities firm for your benefit and insured against theft by the Securities Investors Protection Corporation (SIPC). The broker will send you statements, either monthly or quarterly, as proof of your holdings and detailing any transactions.

Arenas and Players

There are two major stock exchanges in the U.S., the New York Stock Exchange (NYSE) and the NASDAQ (which recently merged with the American Stock Exchange), which is run by the National Association of Securities Dealers. There are also a number of smaller, regional exchanges.

The NYSE is the largest stock exchange. Each stock listed on the NYSE has a station and a "specialist" responsible for all buys and sells. It's that person's job to maintain an orderly market—although if you've ever seen a trading floor, you might consider "orderly market" to be an oxymoron. Being on the NYSE used to be a big deal, like making it to the major leagues. Today it's a still a sign of quality, but many of the modern technology giants, such as Microsoft, Intel, and Cisco—companies that are much bigger than most of the NYSE stocks—are on the NASDAQ and would rather remain there.

The NASDAQ is a quote system—the "AQ" stands for "Automated Quotation"—for market makers, and it tracks the trades and prices. OTC ("over-the-counter," from its historical basis, when stocks were bought and sold over the local broker's counter) is a networked computer system that posts all "bid" and "ask" prices and tracks trades among all brokerage firms. OTC is, by definition, how any stock not listed on an exchanges such as the NYSE or AMEX is traded.

In popular street usage, NASDAQ and OTC are used interchangeably. The NASDAQ is the evolutionary descendent of trading "over-the-counter," but we use electronic systems now. The NASDAQ is the means by which OTC stocks trade.

The Small Order Execution System (SOES) is integrated into the NASDAQ system. It allows automatic execution of market orders of 100 shares or less at the quoted bid and ask prices from market makers. This automates the process for small investors and creates the phenomenon of "day-trading" for individuals, but they are still buying OTC.

Finally, we have the regional exchanges in Chicago, Philadelphia, Boston, and Los Angeles (Pacific). These exchanges just take the spillover of NYSE trades or specialize in OTC stocks that are usually located in their geographic part of the country.

So much for the arenas of the stock world. Now, who are the players and how do they play this stocks game?

Brokerage firms actually maintain an inventory of stock, just like a store would have a rack of suits or dresses. Firms that inventory certain stocks are called "market makers," but the firms are not required to keep an inventory of the shares so, when things get hairy in the stock market, these shares get tougher to trade. In the NYSE, it is one person's job to maintain an orderly market in turbulent times. In the NASDAQ, the market makers could bow out and say "it's not my job," causing even more volatility in the markets.

Earlier we referred to bid prices and ask prices. A bid price is what a buyer is willing to pay and an ask price is what a seller wants for the stock. The volume of shares traded usually determines the difference ("spread") between bid prices and ask prices. The price at which a stock is bought or sold—when bid price and ask price meet—is called (logical-ly) the "sale" price or last trade price in the markets. If only a few shares of a stock are traded, then the difference between the bid and ask is wide, which Wall Street calls a "big spread." If the stock is traded active-ly, then the spread is narrow, perhaps only a penny. Specialists and mar-ket makers generate their income from the spread and from any appreci-ation of their inventory when it's sold.

In 2001, all stocks began trading in the familiar decimals—plain dol-lars and cents—rather than fractions. Some stocks may only have a spread of a penny while small issues that don't trade in much volume will still see wide spreads.

Stock Splits

We mentioned earlier that stock prices rise and fall according to supply and demand. There's an exception to that basic rule of the stock mar-ket: the split.

When a company declares a 2-for-1 stock split, you do not double the money you have in that stock. You simply have double the number of shares. For examples, if you own 100 shares of XYZ at $50 a share and XYZ declares a split, you're going to own 200 shares of a $25 stock. It's still worth $5,000: your position isn't worth a penny more than before the split. But then if the stock goes up 1 point tomorrow, you make $200, instead of the $100 that a 1-point rise would have been worth yesterday.

Why split a stock? The board of directors makes that decision if the directors want to make the price of the company stock more afford-able. The theory is that a lower price per share makes the stock more attractive to small investors. In practice, news of a stock split excites the market and the price often rises. Since the occasion to split the stock arose because the price had been going up for a while, the announcement indicates to some that the directors have confidence in the future of the company and the price will keep going up to reflect future value.

Dividends and Gains

You make money from stocks in two ways: dividends and gains. The difference is fundamental to stock investment strategies.

Dividends

First, many companies, especially the larger, mature ones, pay out a part of their earnings each quarter as dividends. The board of directors fixes the amount and votes to pay it. You get a check for the amount per share times the number of shares you own as of the *date of record* (meaning who is recorded as owner of the stock as of that date). Periodically, most companies that pay dividends will raise the amount if their earnings justify doing so. On the other hand, companies doing poorly may cut the dividend or eliminate it altogether for a time, if they need the cash.

Some investors prefer a good dividend for the income it provides. Dividends may also cushion the fall when the market drops and the stockholder gets paid to wait until the price recovers.

The annual dividend as a percent of the price of a stock is called the *dividend yield*. Today, dividend yields are the lowest in history. Many growth companies pay no dividend, so they can reinvest all of their money to keep the growth going at a higher rate.

Until 1958, dividend yields exceeded the yield or interest paid on bonds by an average of 1.3% a year. Since then, this relationship has reversed: bond yields have exceeded stock yields by an average of 3.5%. Most people buy stocks now for their potential growth in price, not for the dividend.

It's worth noting that the 11.0% average annual compound return of large company stocks since 1925 has included automatic reinvestment of dividends back in the market. Without this, the return over the last 75 years drops to about 6.4%! That's a big difference!

Most stocks that pay dividends today pay them at a rate of only 1% to 2%, so the difference in reinvesting may not be quite so much in the future, but it is still significant. If the market drops a lot, the yield will rise again, and the compound return from reinvesting will rise as well. Dividend reinvestment is just a modified form of dollar cost averaging.

Stockholders of individual stocks should periodically buy more shares in order to reinvest their dividend dollars. Some companies make this easier by paying dividends in stock.

Over 1,000 companies offer dividend reinvestment programs (DRIPs) that allow stockholders to buy more shares with their dividends at a price a little below market at little or no extra charge. Some companies will also allow stockholders to buy additional shares at the same time and on the same terms without paying a commission. You can even sell your shares through some of these programs.

This sounds like a pretty good deal, but there are a few problems you need to know about first. You have to fill out forms each time you want more shares. You also need to keep careful records of how many you bought, at what price, and when. The actual price at which you buy and sell is out of your control. The company batches the orders and periodically executes them all based on that day's market price.

Bigger problems may arise at tax time if you hold the shares in a taxable account. You still owe taxes on the dollar amount of the dividend plus the discount, if any, from the purchase day's market price. When you buy additional shares through the DRIP, you are required to report the total value of any discount as taxable dividend income for that year. In both cases, your tax basis in the shares becomes the actual market price on the transaction date, not the discounted price. That way you don't get taxed twice on the same discount, but the record-keeping you have to do can get pretty complicated if you do this often.

Finally, you have to track each separate purchase until you sell, in order to calculate the correct capital gain or loss. It's wise to think this through and talk with your tax advisor, to make sure it's really worth your trouble before you go ahead. If you hold the stocks in a self-directed IRA, then all of this is much simpler and may be worth doing.

Gains

The second way you make money owning stocks is through gains (or increases) in the value of the stocks. When you eventually sell a stock that has gone up in price over the years, the difference between what you paid, including commission, and what you receive, less the selling commission, is a capital gain. Currently, long-term capital gains are defined by the IRS as gains on securities held over one year. These gains in taxable accounts are taxed at a lower rate than ordinary income. Gains on sales of securities held for a year or less are short-term gains and are taxed at ordinary income rates.

You may also have stocks you sell at a loss—unless you're batting a thousand. It happens to the best of investors, so learn to accept loss as part of the process. In taxable accounts, these losses are netted against any gains for the year on Schedule D of Form 1040 to calculate net taxable gain or loss. You can take a net loss of $1,500 ($3,000 if married, filing jointly) against other income each year and carry over any additional loss to the following year. This takes some of the pain out of losses.

Chapter 13

Finding Stocks to Own

Value vs. Growth

You remember the parable of the tortoise and the hare. Well, here the hare is like the growth style of investing, quick out of the box with a penchant for speed. When it's on, it's a sight to behold. The tortoise, well, he's like the value style of investing, a bit beaten down but not about to give up; he just plugs along and will eventually come into his own.

These fundamentally different investment styles alternate in market performance in multi-year cycles. Over long periods of time, they run almost neck and neck in total return. Value stocks are less volatile and require more patience from an investor. Growth stocks need more attention.

If you look at a 15-year history of growth versus value (Figure 13-1), you can see that at times one style is usually dominant over the other for the year. And over that same 15-year period, the total returns were 21.5% for a growth portfolio and 17.6% for a value portfolio.

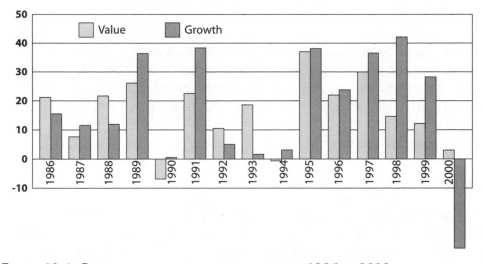

FIGURE 13-1. GROWTH VS. VALUE STOCKS, TOTAL RETURN 1986 TO 2000
(Source: Barra S&P Growth vs. Value Index)

Value Stocks

Many companies occasionally fall on hard times. Wall Street hates a loser, so when companies don't deliver on earnings, investors may express their disappointment by selling, sometimes in large numbers, so the stock price falls. This drop in price allows savvy value hunters to grab some bargains: they check out the true condition of these out-of-favor companies and buy the promising ones. Some companies rally and return, while others just fall by the wayside. The job of a value investor is to find those that will get back on their feet. Biases on Wall Street last just a short while, so if you can look a few quarters into the future and be patient, value investing can pay off well.

You can find examples of these companies in very cyclical and volatile industries that have their stocks beaten down because of an economic trend. Yet most will rally back in the next business cycle. Other companies may be late with a new product or mess up in introducing a product, so their earnings might suffer for a quarter or so. Whatever the reason, a value stock is unloved and undervalued by the market. The value investor seeks to determine the reason and find out how the management will correct the situation. If the analysis is correct and the company gets back on track, the market will eventually "discover" the stock and propel it higher.

Meanwhile, as you wait for the turnaround and renewed interest, the stock is not likely to decline much further during market corrections. Eventually, at some point in its recovery, a value stock can actually flip-flop to become a growth stock. The true value investor will then sell it while the growth investor is buying it in the belief that the fundamentals will drive the price even higher. It's not true that in every transaction there has to be a winner and a loser. The market depends on investors with different disciplines and plans to keep it alive.

Growth Stocks

Growth stocks are Wall Street's darlings. They're companies that are consistently increasing their earnings, providing good products and/or services, and are riding on strong momentum. They're exciting when they're moving and they grab all the attention. But when the momentum stops, every stockholder tries to be the first to sell—or at least to get out while there are still people willing to buy!

Some companies seem just like the Energizer bunny. They just keep going and going with nary a stumble. Usually, they are very recognizable brand name companies that are leaders in their industry. Companies like GE, Coke, Gillette, and Microsoft can go for years without a correction. But when the market as a whole takes a tumble, they go down, too. Often, these occasions are opportunities for savvy investors to buy some stock or more of the stock, if you believe there's nothing fundamentally wrong with the company. Corrections are part of the market. But research is still the key here. The company may still be overpriced relative to its growth. (See the section on Valuing Stocks in this chapter.) You can't buy just because the price goes down.

Different Goals, Different Strategies

Which style of investing is best, value or growth? Good news! Neither style is better than the other. Over long periods of time, as we mentioned earlier, they perform about the same. It's just that Wall Street is fickle and trendy, so you'll always find these two strategies in flux. When value is hot, growth is not. When growth calls, value falls. But you can never time which one is going to be in favor. You may just decide you're more comfortable with one style or the other and stick to it.

We suggest that you combine growth and value strategies to diversify your portfolio. This provides the best long-term performance and more consistent returns year after year. Split your portfolio 50-50 and manage each style separately. Buy good companies within each style when they are out of favor and be patient. This isn't the same as switching between styles, trying to time the market. It's part of a consistent plan and an investing discipline.

Researching Companies

Ten years ago it was tougher to get information on companies. Today, there's plenty of information. But what do you use? Here are some of the questions you need to ask about a company, both before you buy and while you own the stocks. We're just scratching the surface on this subject. You will need to explore this much further as you plan your strategy.

✔ What's the outlook for the industry?

✔ Who is the competition?

✔ Does the company have a product cycle? If so, where is it now?

✔ What do the numbers look like?

✔ Who are the people who run the company? What are their backgrounds and experience?

The outlook for an industry is not an easy thing to figure out, so you have to either depend on professionals (Wall Street analysts) or know the business from your own experience or through a friend. If you can't figure out the industry, then just invest in basic areas you know people will continue to use—things like retail stores (we'll always be buying new things), drug compa-

nies (especially as all the baby boomers age), food stocks, or banks. Just bear in mind that there is never going to be an easy way to forecast industry results. Many Wall Street analysts have a tough enough time figuring this out, so you'll need to use a little instinct to go with your research.

A key to understanding a company is the *competition*. The single best question to ask any company official or analyst is "Who are the three most formidable competitors?" Then,

> *The man who saves money nowadays isn't a miser, he's a wizard.*

before you buy, see if you're buying the best company. In many cases, you can check out a company and its competitors by just walking into a mall, since two-thirds of our economy is stuff bought by consumers. Ask questions of the salespeople about which product is better or sells better. Go to several stores and compare the answers. It's very much like doing comparison shopping to find the best product at a good price. Most important, do you or would you buy what the company makes?

Many companies and industries are up and down with the economy. They're called *cyclical* companies. Others have their own internal cycles based on product development and the introduction of new products and models. This can greatly affect earnings and, therefore, stock prices. Try to find out if this is true for the company you're interested in and where the company is in its product cycle. You'd rather buy early than after a great new product has Wall Street all excited and already driven up the stock price.

The numbers are not for everybody to scrutinize; that's why you have brokers, analysts, financial planners, magazines, newspapers, and newsletters to help you. Just know that the only long-term number you need to know is earnings. Will the company make money and how much? That's what Wall Street really cares about. What's the recent revenue and earnings trend? Is it expected to continue? Why? What should you look for to find out if the trend is in danger of changing direction? The rest is just interesting tidbits.

One of the most important factors is who runs the company. It all starts in those corner offices and works its way through the company. Every company has its own personality and you can bet it's the top people who have developed this personality based on their own. If they're doing the job that they collect the big bucks for, then they must have a well thought-out plan. They've got to do what they say they're going to do and gain market share and profits. The best way to get to know the top brass is to go to the annual shareholder meeting. Every company has one and it's a great way to get an up-close reading on the people running the show.

There's no single best source of information, because it's all based on how much time you want to spend researching companies. If you want to do daily and weekly work, then read *The Wall Street Journal*, *Investor's Business Daily*, and *Barron's*. If you're pinched for time, there are also single-page or shortened reviews. Morningstar, Value Line, or Standard & Poor's reports are available at many libraries and from full-service brokerage firms. Then there are the rest of the magazines, newsletters, and market reports that come spewing out by the hundreds. So scan the horizon and see if there's one that you like.

The final frontier is being built as we speak—the Internet. Finance and investing are certainly the hottest sites for 'Net browsers. The problem is knowing who's touting what and what is their track record. There's a lot of garbage and misleading info online, so caveat emptor if you don't recognize the source. Places we would recommend to begin your search: **www.morningstar.net**, **www.investor.msn.com**, **www.quicken.com**, **www.edgar-online.com**, and **www. bigcharts.com**.

The single best source may be your friends and neighbors. They work in the various industries and would be glad to share their experiences with no ax to grind. You're not looking for hot stock tips or inside information; you want their knowledgeable perspective on their industry and the companies in it as part of your research.

To formalize that help, you could consider setting up an investment club. It's a good way to pick the experience of others at no cost and share the research work on companies. You can learn how to set up one of these clubs by contacting this organization:

National Association of Investors Corporation (NAIC)
P.O. Box 220
Royal Oak, MI 48068
Phone: 877-275-6242 or 248-583-6242
Fax: 248-583-4880
Web: **www.better-investing.org**

Here's another organization you should consider joining:

American Association of Individual Investors (AAII)
625 N. Michigan Avenue
Chicago, IL 60611
Phone: 800-428-2244 or 312-280-0170
Fax: 312-280-9883
Web: **www.aaii.com**

Valuing Stocks

What's a stock worth? Whatever anyone is willing to pay for it.

Once we accept that this is how the markets work, then we can crunch the numbers and try and get some sort of evaluation of the information. As Mark Twain told us, there are lies, damn lies, and statistics. So valuing stocks by the numbers is important, but by no means everything—and those numbers could be misleading.

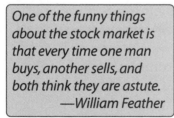

One of the funny things about the stock market is that every time one man buys, another sells, and both think they are astute.
—William Feather

These numbers, when calculated, are just historical numbers, not indicative of any future results. Understand that every number you review is relative to the current state of the market as well as other companies in the industry. Every industry has different needs and dynamics, based on how much money it takes to run and grow the companies in it. Thus, the numbers can be interpreted in different ways and from widely differing perspectives. It's the mood and the temperament of a market that dictate the prices of stock in the short term. In the long run, the economic realities win out.

Hundreds of books and articles have been written on valuing stocks. Their main theme is to buy low, sell high. That sounds simple enough, but most people find it hard to do. The trick is figuring out what is *low* and what is *high*.

But buying low is more than just buying cheap stocks. A smart investor wants to buy fundamentally good companies whose stock prices are low in relation to where they expect them to be in the future. That means research. Why is the price low? What will convince the market to raise the price? How likely is that to happen? And in what time frame?

Stocks may frequently be undervalued or overvalued relative to the market or to the long-term view of their prospects because many people invest with more emotion than logic. Too often, they also have a short-term horizon: they hope to make a quick killing. Rational investors who have done their homework can take advantage of this to buy "good stuff cheap" and hold on for the long term. To do this successfully requires experience and patience. New investors need to learn this just as much as they need to learn how to do valuations.

Part of the discipline is finding good companies and continually monitoring their prices and activities over time until they may become undervalued and worth buying. Buying a good company when the stock price is too high just won't work. While it's more an art than a science, fundamental analysis is the tool to uncover potentially good investments and to evaluate them regularly after they become part of your portfolio. So here's what to look for.

Earnings

This figure shows whether a company is growing and profitable. There are bound to be quarterly disappointments, but make sure the trend is up. If not, then quickly move on. The higher the growth rate the better, but extremely high growth rates are not sustainable. Figure out what the long-term growth rate is of your respective benchmark and compare your prospective company against that number. More about benchmarks in Chapter 21.

In looking through financial statements, you'll notice that there are *net* earnings (after any special write-offs for restructuring or mergers) and there are *operating* earnings. The latter is the income from operations after normal expenses but before any charges and write-offs. Many companies will take some of these charges in calculating operating earnings. You may have to extract these numbers yourself and calculate net operating earnings to get an accurate figure. The operating numbers are often more useful to track the long-term trends.

P/E Ratio

This figure is the *price* per share of the stock divided by the *earnings* per share. It's what the market is paying for every dollar of earnings the company makes. So if a company is trading at $20 a share and earned $1 a share for the last twelve months, it's trading at 20 times earnings or a P/E ratio of 20.

You want to see if the P/E ratio is in line with the earnings growth of a company. If the earnings are growing at 20% a year, for example, then a P/E ratio of 20 is in line. If this company is growing its earnings at only 10% a year, then you're overpaying for the earnings. In the best case, a company is growing at 20% a year and trading at 10 times earnings. This stock is a bargain, because its P/E is one-half the growth rate. So remember that P/E ratios are not good or bad by themselves; they're just a barometer of the earnings of the company relative to the market price on any given day.

Markets trade more on anticipated future performance than on past performance. A forward P/E is based on projected earnings over the next twelve months. Herein lies a danger. Predicting earnings a year or more in advance is difficult to do accurately—even for the officers of the company. No one can predict the sales, expenses, and earnings consistently. The analysts whose job it is to do this even can be far off. They adjust their forecasts as each quarter draws near and again after each quarter if they see a reason to do so. So a P/E based on future projections should be taken with several grains of salt.

Book Value

This figure is what the company would be worth if you added up all the assets and subtracted all the liabilities. If you were a liquidator and were told to take this company apart and sell it off, then this would be what you might get for the parts. So the lower the price of the stock compared with the book value, the better.

In recent years, it's rare to find a healthy company selling near book value (market cap to book value). Market cap (capitalization) is the market price of a company, calculated by multiplying the number of shares outstanding by the price per share. Some multiple of book value is the norm. This ratio is more important for a company that invests a lot of capital in plant and equipment. Service companies and most technology companies invest their money in their employees. These assets don't show up in book value.

Debt/Equity Ratio

What does the company owe to lenders and how much have the owners invested? Just as you can leverage your down payment to buy a house by getting a mortgage, a company can borrow and invest the money in its growth. The higher the debt/equity ratio, the more leveraged the company. Companies must have sufficient cash flow to cover the interest expense, repay the debt, and have enough left over to invest in growth. Too much debt would make it harder for a company with a lot of interest expenses to weather the bad times. (Does that sound familiar?) A rule of thumb in many industries is that long-term debt shouldn't exceed the amount of shareholders' equity.

There are dozens of other financial ratios investors use to analyze companies. They can all add to the evaluation process. But you need to keep in mind that they are also all historical numbers. You can't just project them into the future. Companies, markets, and economies are always changing and no one can predict what will happen in the future.

Keep all the numbers in perspective and just remember the bottom line—the beauty of a stock is in the eye of the shareholder. Two good books to help you research companies are *Security Analysis on Wall Street* by Jeffrey Hooke and *The Craft of Investing* by John Train.

Buying and Selling Stocks

There's no secret formula for buying and selling stocks. All the guidelines and strategies can be found in hundreds of books and articles. Some seem to work better than others ... some of the time. Through reading and experience you'll find one that works best for you over time because it will fit your style and investing personality. To cite a common phrase, you can beat *some* of the markets *all* of the time, and *all* of the markets *some* of the time, but you can't beat *all* of the markets *all* of the time.

You'll always make mistakes no matter how much work you do. The future is unpredictable. The professionals are often quoted as saying that they aim to be right 60% of the time. You can make money if only four out of every ten of your stock picks go down and you cut those losses early enough. The pros also say that in every successful portfolio there's one big winner, a bunch of average winners, and a bunch of losers.

Like a baseball player, try to hit enough singles, be grateful for the occasional home run, and try not to strike out too often. Self-discipline and experience keep a lot of players in the game. If you can get a hit 60% of the time in stocks, you'll make money over the years.

Here's a list of good suggestions to get you started.

✔ Study the fundamentals of a company—its earnings, growth, operations, products, markets, competition, and management.

✔ Find and read analyst reports on your companies and follow the companies through newspapers and trade publications.

✔ If you don't understand the company and how it will make money, don't buy it.

✔ Be contrarian: don't follow the "prevailing wisdom." If everyone agrees with you, the odds are you may be on the losing side. Do the opposite if your research objectively supports doing so.

✔ Look at companies that are out of favor due to market reaction or market conditions.

✔ Buy good companies and plan to hold them.

✔ Know where a company fits into your portfolio and why you are buying it.

Getting Out

Buying good stocks is generally easier than knowing when to sell them. If you listen to Wall Street, you'd be lucky if there is one sell for every 20 buy recommendations. So we feel it's absolutely a tougher decision to sell than to buy. There's no "right" method, but here are some guidelines to use for different situations.

If you don't know why you bought a stock and why you own it, you won't know why and when to sell it. The selling decision is made easier by an intelligent buying decision. Just because a stock goes down, that's not in itself a reason to sell. Figure out why it went down and then determine whether or not you still want to own the company.

Give your ideas at least two to three years to show results. If after this period the company hasn't made the progress you expected, then accept your mistake and sell it. Don't let your ego get in the way. Don't wait and hope you'll get back to break even; it may never happen and your money will waste away.

When a stock reaches the price/value target you set when you bought it, look closely to see if there are new fundamental reasons to raise your target. Any decision to change your target must be rational, not emotional. List the good news on one side of a sheet of paper and weigh it against the bad. Would you still buy that stock today? When a company's stock price gets considerably ahead of its growth rate due to market exuberance, count your blessings and take some or all of your money off the table. You can always buy the stock back later if the value gets more reasonable.

When a company and its industry are mature and no longer capable of growing faster than the economy, it may be time to look for greener pastures. Are there other companies that you think will perform better than the companies you currently own?

When a company begins to show signs of fundamental problems, it's time to sell. But it's essential to know the difference between fundamental problems and short-term problems that management or time will correct.

Most financial planers would recommend that you sell part of your holdings in a company when the stock makes up more than 10% of your total net assets. But if we had given Bill Gates that advice, do you think we'd still be his advisors? Just be aware that it is probably not prudent to hold more than 25% of any company in your portfolio. But it's not a hard-and-fast rule! Finally, when a company no longer fits in your portfolio, due to a change in your time horizons, goals, or allocation plan, it's time to sell and put your money elsewhere.

Chapter 14 | Bonds— Lending Your Money

What Is a Bond?

A bond is a debt instrument issued to raise capital by borrowing. Basically, a bond is an IOU, a contract to pay back money borrowed at some point in time. There's usually a guarantee to pay interest while you wait to get your principal back at maturity when the bond is due. Problems arise when the borrower can't pay you back, interest rates go wild, or you need the money before the bond matures.

Bonds are issued by the U.S. Government, foreign governments, corporations, and the states and municipalities. Within these four general categories, there are a whole bunch of sub-categories, each with different characteristics. Each sub-category serves different purposes for investors, offers a wide range of time frames (maturities), and trades in a different market.

Investing in bonds or bond funds as a strategy can serve three goals.

The most important goal is *stability*. By diversifying a portion of your portfolio into bonds, you reduce the overall volatility of your portfolio because bond prices don't always move in the same direction as stock prices. Bond total returns do not fluctuate as much as stock returns if you invest across the maturity spectrum of one to twenty years. This is especially true if you concentrate on intermediate term bonds (one- to ten-year maturity).

The second goal is to *preserve buying power*. From this perspective, the five-year U.S. Treasury notes, which are the best-performing category of bonds over time, barely managed to succeed over the 40 years from 1958 to 1997. $10,000 in 1958 dollars would have the buying power of $11,273 at the end of 1997. People who invested in bonds in 1958 and held them for 40 years had their money successfully warehoused and its value returned, plus a bit more.

The third goal is *income*. Getting the check in the mail certainly helps you pay the bills.

Bond Interest Rates

Interest rates are really just the cost of renting money at any given time. They are adjusted by the market for inflation and inflation fears, for perceived risks of default, and for the term of the rental period. A longer term usually calls for higher rates to compensate for the unknowns between the date of issue and the date of maturity. The idea is to try to retain the value, the buying power of the money invested over time, through balancing the perceived risks with enough reward to persuade investors to lend their money.

In general, market interest rates rise on the expectation of an increase in the rate of inflation and drop when the rate is expected to fall. Lenders want to be assured that they receive a real return on their money that exceeds inflation by at least 2%, because they know that, due to inflation, the dollars they get back will be worth less than the ones they loaned out.

The additional rate of interest that lenders demand over the expected rate of inflation depends on the perceived risk of not getting back the money. Since we all expect the U.S. Government to repay its debt, investors are happy with a 2% to 3% real return over inflation or anticipated inflation. As the risk of losing the principal rises, so does the margin. Treasury rates may be dropping as the rate of inflation is expected to decline when the economy is in recession, but corporate rates, especially for junk bonds, may be rising. A recession increases the risk of lending money, since some companies may not survive a recession. The higher rate compensates investors for the risk of a company defaulting on the loans.

Historically, bonds have a strong positive real return, after inflation is considered, only when interest rates are falling. Stable rates, whether high or low, have not always been positive for bonds.

Bond Mechanics

The bond market has its own language. Here's a list of key terms you need to understand so you can talk the talk:

- ✔ **Basis point:** one-hundredth (1/100) of one percent of yield; 0.01% is one basis point
- ✔ **Coupon rate:** the stated annual rate of interest paid to the holder of a bond
- ✔ **Yield:** the total return on a bond based on its purchase price and the coupon rate
- ✔ **Yield spread:** the difference in the current yield between two fixed income securities
- ✔ **Average maturity:** the average length of time to maturity for all bonds in a portfolio
- ✔ **Maturity risk:** the risk that the price of a bond will go up or down based on a change in market interest rates
- ✔ **Credit risk:** the risk that the issuer of the bond may be unable to pay the interest on a timely basis or become unable to repay the principal at maturity
- ✔ **Call:** the option of an issuer to redeem the bond before maturity
- ✔ **Par:** a bond priced at 100 is trading at par. Bonds trade in units of $1,000 so a bond at par with a price of 100 trades at $1,000
- ✔ **Premium:** a bond trading at a price higher than 100 is priced at a premium

✔ **Discount:** a bond trading under 100 is selling at a discount

Bonds can be more complex than stocks because they come in more varieties, they're tougher to research, and there's also a bunch of jargon that makes learning Japanese look easy. All you really need to understand to get a handle on bonds are seven things:

✔ Issuer
✔ Quantity
✔ Coupon
✔ Maturity
✔ Price
✔ Yield
✔ Rating

It's the interactions of these factors that define the bond market and create the confusion.

The Issuer is who issued the bond and is borrowing the money with the bond and is going to pay you back. It could be the U.S. Government or its agencies, a private corporation, or states and municipalities. The jargon often used here is "Govies" for government bonds, "Corporates" for corporate bonds, and "Munis" for bonds issued by states and municipalities.

The Quantity is almost always in units of a thousand dollars. So ten bonds means $10,000 worth at face amount. Just keep in mind that on rare occasions some issuers do have "baby bonds," which are issued for less than $1,000. Bonds are usually bought and sold in minimum blocks of five or ten ($5,000 or $10,000). Just be aware that with small lots of bonds (under $100,000) your commission can be 1% to 3% depending on the maturity. So if you don't have that much, then head to bond mutual funds to invest. (We'll get to those in Chapter 15.)

The Coupon is the stated percent of interest paid each year on the face amount of the bonds. If you had ten bonds ($10,000) at a 6% coupon, that would be $600 a year in interest. The term "coupon" is historical. In years past, bonds were issued with tear-off coupons that bond owners had to send in every six months to get the interest payment. Just keep in mind that most bonds pay their interest every six months, with the final payment at maturity.

Maturity is when the face amount of the bond, known as the principal, is paid in full. So if you own ten bonds with a 6/1/03 maturity, it means that on June 1, 2003 you get $10,000 plus the final interest payment. Some bonds, excluding most Treasuries, are subject to early redemption at the option of the issuer if interest rates drop. You usually get paid a small premium if this happens, but be sure to check this before you buy a longer-term bond.

The Price is where the fun comes in. This is what you would get if you had to sell the bond before it matures or what you would pay to buy a bond in the market after it was issued. There's a difference, or spread, between the bid price and the ask price, just as with stocks. Beware that the price swings can be violent, depending on what's going on in the world of interest rates. Any value before the maturity date (or the call date, if the issuer decides to redeem the bonds early) is going to be determined by the outside influences of inflation and interest rates also referred to as the cost of money.

The actual price number you see quoted in the newspaper represents a percentage of the face value. A price of 99 is 99% of the face value, which for a bond with a face amount of $10,000 would mean $9,900. Government bond prices are quoted in increments of 1/32. A quote of 99.13 is 99-13/32 or $9940.63 on a $10,000 face value bond. Corporate bonds are quoted as fractions like stocks.

The Yield is a little slippery to define, because you have to ask the right question here. Is it the yield to maturity, yield to call, or current yield? The *yield to maturity* is the total rate of return you get when you figure out the price you pay for a bond and hold it until the bond pays its principal back. Then there's the *yield to call*. It is important to know that bonds can be called before they reach maturity. (The possible call dates are specified in the *indenture*, the written agreement between bond issuer and bondholders.) If a bond is called, this will affect your total yield if you bought the bond for more or less than the face amount. The *current yield* is a tricky number, because this too does not take into consideration the price that you paid for the bond when figuring out how much money you made. So the bottom line here is to always ask what the yield to maturity and the yield to call are.

The Rating is an assessment of the quality of the bond issuer, as determined by an outside rating service. The two major rating agencies for bonds are Standard and Poor's and Moody's. Because most of us don't have the time or skills to go over the books of each company or state or government agency, we have to rely on some expert to keep an eye on the issuers to make sure there's no danger on the horizon. It's the job of these rating agencies to keep the market posted on what's going on. Each has its own slightly different rating marks, from AAA or Aaa (the best) to D (in default). Anything less than BBB or Baa is considered non-investment grade, sometimes called "junk bonds." Check out **www.moodys.com**, **www.bondsonline.com**, and **www.rate.net** for some evaluation of bonds.

Regardless of what's going on in the world of interest rates, if you just buy a bond and hold it till maturity, you will get your face amount back and the rate of return you signed up for.

As we keep pointing out, bonds can be very complicated investments. A good book for the bond investor is *The Basics of Bonds* by Gerald Krefetz.

U.S. Government Bonds

Government bonds are issued by national governments and their agencies. U.S. Government bonds are considered among the safest in the world in terms of credit risk. For this reason, Treasuries are the benchmark against which all other bonds are measured. U.S. Treasuries are direct obligations of the United States Government.

✔ Treasury *Bills* are issued with maturities of 13, 26, and 52 weeks.

✔ Treasury *Notes* are issued in 2-, 3-, 5-, and 10-year maturities.

✔ Treasury *Bonds* are issued only in 30-year maturities.

All are actively traded, so you can buy whatever maturity you need in the market. U.S. Treasuries are not taxed by state and local governments, but you will owe federal tax on the interest you earn.

In 1997, the U.S. Government introduced inflation-indexed Treasury bonds in 10-year and 30-year maturities. The coupon rate is lower than for regular Treasury bonds because the driving force behind interest rates is inflation. The principal of the indexed bonds is adjusted each year for the damage done to the value of the principal by inflation. If inflation is 3% the first year, for example, a $10,000 bond becomes a $10,300 bond, and the interest rate applies to the new amount for the next year. This can be a good deal, because both your principal and the interest you make are protected from inflation by the adjustment. The only bad news is that you also owe federal income tax each year on the annual adjustment to principal as well as on the interest.

A variation on Treasury bonds is the zero-coupon bonds called STRIPS. The government doesn't sell STRIPS; brokerage houses buy government bonds, separate the interest payments from the bond, and sell both parts separately. (As you might have guessed, the term is an acronym—for Separated Trading of Registered Interest and Principal of Securities.)

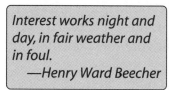

Interest works night and day, in fair weather and in foul.
—*Henry Ward Beecher*

The zero-coupon bond sells at a steep discount to the face value and pays the face value at maturity. The difference between the discount market price and the face value represents the total interest, which accrues annually. But even though you collect this interest only at maturity (or when you sell the bond in the market before maturity), you owe federal tax on the "imputed" interest earned and automatically reinvested each year. That's the bad news. The good news is that the IRS has a schedule to calculate the interest.

You can buy Treasuries directly from the U.S. Treasury in $1,000 amounts when it holds its auctions. You submit a "non-competitive bid" and get the bonds at the average interest rate at the auction. Contact the U.S. Treasury for a "Treasury Direct" information package and application:

The Bureau of the Public Debt
Division of Customer Services
Washington, DC 20239
Phone: 202-874-4000

The U.S. Treasury also maintains a Web site: **www.publicdebt. treas.gov**. You can even buy the bonds through the Internet. In all cases, the Treasury will also hold the bonds in an electronic account for you, forward interest to your bank or money market fund, and automatically reinvest the money at maturity if you instruct the agency to do so ahead of time. Finally, if you unexpectedly need to sell a bond before maturity, the agency will arrange it with a broker for a small fee and forward the money to your account. Remember that when you sell any bond before maturity, you get only what the market thinks it's worth that day plus your accrued interest to date.

Government Sponsored Enterprise (GSE) bonds are issued by independent organizations sponsored by the U.S. Government. These are the Federal Farm Credit Banks, the Federal Home Loan Bank System, and the Student Loan Marketing Association (Sallie Mae). GSE bonds carry an implied guarantee by the U.S. Government, and their interest is tax-exempt in most states.

Agency bonds are issued by entities that are legally separate from the U.S. Government. They include the Federal Home Loan Mortgage Corporation (Freddie Mac), the Federal National Mortgage Association (Fannie Mae), and the Tennessee Valley Authority. Agency bonds come without any government guarantee, and the interest on them is taxable in most states. Freddie Mac and Fannie Mae bonds are publicly traded.

U.S. Government agencies issue debt securities at slightly higher coupon rates than Treasuries of the same maturity. The government does not explicitly guarantee agency debt, but it is believed that the government would bail out any agency that ran into financial trouble. Most small investors don't buy Agency or GSE bonds directly, but they are major components of government bond mutual funds.

Several agencies and GSEs issue pass-through securities. These are backed by bundles of consumer mortgages. (A pass-through is a security representing pooled debt obligations that passes income from debtors to shareholders.) The Government National Mortgage Association packages and sells mortgages issued by the Veterans Association and the Federal Housing Authority. These are often referred to as "Ginnie Mae" bonds (Government National Mortgage Association). The Federal Home Loan Mortgage Corporation ("Freddie

Mac") and the Federal National Mortgage Association ("Fannie Mae") issue pass-throughs backed by private mortgages bought from banks and mortgage companies. These are not direct obligations of the U.S. Government and are taxable at the federal, state, and local levels.

Each payment received by the consumer represents interest plus a return of principal, so there's no big payoff at maturity. When interest rates fall, many people refinance their mortgage and pay off the old one. This money is returned to investors earlier than expected. In recent years, 30-year pass-throughs have returned all the principal in about 10 years or so. For this reason, pass-through securities are good candidates for mutual funds rather than for direct ownership. Ginnie Mae funds are available from many fund families.

U.S. Savings Bonds

The U.S. Government also sells U.S. Savings Bonds. Don't confuse these with the other government bonds; they have their own rules and the government controls the market.

Savings bonds are issued in three different types: Series EE, Series I, and Series HH.

Both Series EE and Series I Bonds are issued in denominations of $50, $75, $100, $200, $500, $1,000, $5,000, and $10,000 at a price of one-half the face value. You can buy up to $15,000 each year per per-

son. Most financial institutions such as banks sell savings bonds. They'll take your payment and order form and send it to the Federal Reserve Bank. You'll receive your bond by mail within 15 business days.

Series EE and Series I bonds accrue interest for 30 years. They reach face value in 17 years or less, depending on the interest rates, but they continue to earn interest until maturity. The interest is exempt from state and local taxes and the federal tax is deferred until you redeem them or until they mature.

Series EE bonds pay 90% of the average yield of five-year Treasury notes for the preceding six months. Interest rates are adjusted accordingly on May 1 and November 1. Series I bonds pay a fixed rate plus an adjustment every six months, based on the Consumer Price Index change for the previous six months, so the rate is indexed for inflation. This feature makes them attractive during periods of increasing inflation.

If you think education is expensive, try ignorance.

You can redeem either of these bonds after six months, but there's a three-month interest penalty if you redeem them within five. Interest is added to the bond's value every six months after you purchase it. It is wise to find out when the interest is added to the bond before you redeem it, so you don't lose out on the last few months' interest.

The interest earned on Series I bonds and Series EE bonds issued after January 1, 1990 may qualify for exclusion from taxes if it's used to pay post-secondary education expenses. Only bonds issued in the name of a person who was 24 or older when the bond was purchased can be used for this exclusion. In essence, Uncle Sam is saying these bonds must be in the parents' name to qualify for the exclusion. So all of those bonds the kids received from grandma in their names can't be used tax-free.

Also there are income limits. For 2001, the exclusion is phased out between $55,750 and $70,750 if you are single and between $83,650 and $113,650 for joint filers. The income limits are indexed to inflation and have been rising annually. Get IRS Publication 550 (Investment Income and Expenses) and Forms 8815 and 8819 (Exclusion of Interest from Series EE U.S. Savings Bonds and Dollar Election Under Section 985) for detailed information about rules and eligibility by calling the IRS at 800-829-3676. The exclusion amount must be adjusted by the expenses taken into account when using the Hope Scholarship and the Life Time Learning Credit. So our advice would be to look for other places to invest the college savings.

Series HH bonds are issued for 10 years at a low fixed rate. They may be renewed for another 10 years at a new rate then in effect. They are issued at face value and pay federally taxable interest semi-annually, directly to your bank account. The only way to get Series HH bonds is to exchange Series EE bonds for HH bonds in multiples of $500 anytime between six months and 31 years after issuance. You get to roll over the accrued interest and defer federal taxation until the HH bond matures or you redeem it. The advantage here is to convert non-interest paying bonds to income without having a big tax hit.

For more information about savings bonds, contact:

Bureau of the Public Debt
Savings Bond Operations Office
200 Third Street
Parkersburg, WV 26106-1328
Phone: 304-480-6112
Web: **www.savingsbonds.gov**

If you don't mind paying a few dollars for someone to get the information for you, then contact:

The Savings Bond Informer, Inc.
P.O. Box 9249
Detroit, MI 48209
Phone: 800-927-1901
Fax: 313-843-1912
E-mail: bondinform@aol.com
Web: **www.bondinformer.com**

Foreign, Corporate, and Municipal Bonds

Foreign Government Bonds

Government bonds issued by foreign governments are also available in the market. They are usually denominated in the currency of the issuing country. Investors in foreign bonds take on two additional risks.

First is *country* risk. How likely is the government going to be around in the future to fulfill its obligations? Will it be financially sound enough to pay what it owes? This is especially true for emerging market countries.

The second risk is *currency* risk. Even if you pick the right country and get a good rate of interest, you could still lose money if the U.S. dollar appreciates a lot in value. The foreign currency of your bond may buy fewer dollars at maturity than you invested. On the other hand, if the dollar drops in value relative to that currency, you could get back more than you invested. If you decide to invest in foreign bonds, find an established mutual fund with an experienced manager.

Corporate Bonds

Companies that need to raise money to invest in their operations or to buy other companies issue corporate bonds. The contract for interest and repayment is between you and the company. There is no outside guarantee.

Here's where bond ratings come into play to determine credit risk. Top ratings go to financially healthy companies. Independent bond rating agencies such as Standard and Poor's and Moody's rate a company when it issues bonds and then follow the company's finances closely. They will issue upgrades or downgrades of existing debt based on changes in the company.

As we mentioned earlier in this chapter, the highest rating is AAA or Aaa. Anything less than BBB or Baa is not considered investment grade. Below this are high-yield bonds, also known as junk bonds. A rating of D means the company is in default, behind on interest payments, perhaps unable to repay the loan, and in or on the brink of bankruptcy.

> Gentlemen prefer bonds.
> —Andrew Mellon

The yield on corporate bonds rises as the rating decreases. That means a downgrade in the rating causes the price to drop and the yield to rise. When the rating rises, the price of the bond goes up and the yield goes down. Just remember that the actual dollars paid in interest does not change; it's just the price movement that changes the yield.

Corporate bonds are primarily purchased by companies that get a tax break on the income and by institutions, including mutual funds. It's a complicated venue for small investors.

A strange hybrid of the corporate bond market is known as a *convertible* bond. Up front, you get a straight bond that pays interest. You also get an option to convert the bond into common stock of the company at some future point and at some fixed conversion rate. The "strike price" at which it can be profitably converted is usually higher than the current stock price. A buyer gets the benefit of a bond with the possibility of a capital gain if the stock price rises enough in the future. The market price of this bond is determined by the rating, the interest rate, the conversion ratio, the time to conversion, and the stock price.

Municipal Bonds

Municipal bonds are issued by states, counties, cities, towns, and authorized agencies of these governments to fund projects such as water and sewage treatment plants, transportation systems, schools, hospitals, airports, and industrial development to serve a public purpose. Income from these bonds is generally exempt from federal income tax and exempt from state and local taxes for residents of the state in which they were issued.

Interest rates are lower on most municipals, because they are usually federally tax-exempt. Municipal bonds make sense only if you are in a 31% or higher federal tax bracket. If you also live in a high-tax state, then municipal bonds issued in your state or a single state bond mutual fund will generally give you a higher return than the after-tax yield on a regular bond or bond fund. Taxpayers in federal brackets of 36% and 39.6% will generally come out ahead with municipals regardless of state tax.

Municipal bonds are also rated by agencies based on the financial health and ability of the issuing government to meet future obligations. General obligation municipals are usually rated higher than issues for specific purposes, because they are backed by the ability of the issuer to raise taxes to meet the obligation. Special purpose munis, such as an airport, depend on the revenue from the purpose for which the bond was issued. If this facility gets into financial difficulty, it may not be able to make payments on interest or principal.

Municipal bond issuers can also buy insurance to guarantee timely payment of interest and principal. Insured munis are rated AAA for that reason. The risk is now transferred to the insurance company. This adds another complication, because the insurance company must now be rated, too.

There is an additional risk with single state municipal bonds and funds—the concentration of credit risk. If the state falls on hard economic times, its credit rating may drop and some of the municipal issuers may default. Either event will reduce the market price of the state's bonds, and default brings up the question of paying back the principal.

Bond Ladders

We've made bonds sound pretty complicated so far. But that's not our fault—bonds are complicated. And we've just scratched the surface.

But there are simple strategies you can use that reduce the interest rate risk, diversify your fixed income portfolio, minimize volatility, and preserve your capital. A bond ladder is one of the best ways to invest in bonds, whether you're retired or not.

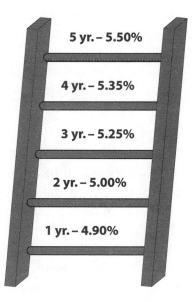

5 yr. – 5.50%

4 yr. – 5.35%

3 yr. – 5.25%

2 yr. – 5.00%

1 yr. – 4.90%

FIGURE 14-1. A FIVE-YEAR BOND LADDER—AVERAGE YIELD: 5.20%

A bond ladder is a series of bonds that mature at regular, fixed intervals over a period of years. We'll use Treasuries in this discussion: they're the best choice for your bond ladder because they're the safest bonds. They're also easy to buy, with a low transaction cost, and you can sell them quickly if you really need to. Here's one ladder you can build:

With this ladder, your average maturity is only 2½ years and your average rate is 5.2%. Every year, one bond matures and you automatically reinvest the money in another Treasury with a five-year maturity to maintain the ladder. This process allows you to buy a higher-yielding note if rates go up within the next year. If they go down, you still have four others paying higher rates. Just keep them rolling without worrying about where rates are or where they're going. This low-maintenance strategy keeps your portfolio reasonably current with the market.

If you want a taller ladder, you can build one using two-year intervals, such as 2-, 4-, 6-, 8-, or 10-year maturities, and roll into a new 10-year Treasury every two years. It doesn't usually pay to extend the ladder beyond 10 years, unless rates on longer bonds are quite a bit higher.

You want to reinvest the interest payments in order to compound the return of your bond portfolio—unless, of course, you're retired and need the cash. With five bonds, you get a total of 10 payments every year. If you funnel this money into a money market fund, you earn a short-term rate of interest while it accumulates. Then, when the next bond matures, add this money to your new rollover bond investment. Treasuries are now sold in $1,000 face value amount, so reinvest in as many additional bonds as the interest payments will purchase.

Bond Mutual Funds

Bond mutual funds are really very different animals than bonds.

First, you don't have a contract with the borrower; you buy shares in a fund that can hold all kinds of debt securities. The name of the fund usually indicates what kind of debt the fund concentrates on and sometimes what the maturity range is, such as intermediate or long term. But to be sure, you really need to read the prospectus to find out these key facts.

Second, bond funds never mature, except for a few that only hold long-term zero-coupon bonds maturing in the same year. This means there is no fixed point in the future when you are sure to get back your principal, as there would be if you owned a bond. The price per share of the fund, its net asset value, changes daily, depending on the market. You also can't count on getting a known interest payment. The funds pay dividends monthly, but the amount may change as the bonds in the fund change. The rate isn't fixed.

Third, there's more than one yield to a bond fund, too. The most important yield is called the *SEC yield* (named after the Securities and Exchange Commission regulation requiring the method to calculate the yield). The SEC yield is the average, weighted yield to maturity of all the securities in the fund at a fixed point in time, less the fund expenses and sales load, if any.

The second yield is based on the income the fund has paid out to shareholders as dividends over the past 12 months, known as the *distributed yield*. This number can be quite a bit higher if the fund owns premium bonds that pay higher rates. But the fund likely paid a high price for these bonds, more than face value, because of the high rate, unless it bought them many years ago when rates were sky-high. Their yield to maturity is much less than the coupon rate because at maturity the fund gets back only face value. In effect, a fund dividend is giving you back some of your own money, which gets subtracted from the fund share price and you pay taxes on it.

Bond funds also pay capital gain dividends if they have more gains than losses from their bond trading. Fund managers may also try to improve the quality of the bonds they hold or change the duration of the portfolio if they think rates are going to change. Long-term capital gains dividends result and these are part of the total return of the fund. Unless you hold the fund in a tax-sheltered retirement plan, you will owe taxes on these gains (and this includes tax-free municipal bond funds).

Bond funds charge a fee for managing the portfolio and they also run up various expenses. These costs are paid out of the interest the bonds generate and are subtracted from income. Then the shareholders get paid. For any given maturity and style, there isn't a lot a fund manager can do to beat the benchmark by very much, so you want funds with low fees and expenses. Bond fees range from about 0.2% to 1.0% or more of the assets under management. On a fund that generates 6.0% from interest, a 1% fee cuts your take to 5.0%. It's tough for the manager to make this up with smart trading.

If you have at least $100,000 to invest in your fixed income allocation, you'll save on fees by creating your own "fund," using the bond ladder in the last section. For amounts under $100,000, funds may be less expensive if you get ones with low fees and you also get good diversification with a smaller amount of money. Those are two of the reasons people use bond funds rather than buy bonds directly.

There are other good reasons to use bond funds. Short-term funds can be used for money you need in three to five years. You'll get a higher return than money market funds with only a small risk of principal loss if interest rates go up. Funds are less work than maintaining your own bond portfolio and you can redeem shares at the end of each business day at the fund's net asset value with a phone call before the market closes. That's easier than selling a bond and paying a commission plus the bid/ask spread. Tax-free municipal bond funds are usually more efficient than buying and selling muni bonds, because the market isn't as liquid so the spreads are higher.

Finally, for non-U.S. Government debt, the fund manager and analysts do their own credit analysis of the issuers of the debt and they're on top of the situation when something changes. Credit risk isn't something individual investors can evaluate easily. That's why we recommend mutual funds for non-U.S. government debt.

There are 29 categories of non-money market "fixed income" funds listed by Lipper Analytical Services, not counting single state municipal bond funds. That means there's a fund for just about any purpose. You can use bond funds to simulate a bond ladder by selecting a short-term bond fund, a short-intermediate fund, and an intermediate-term fund. If you wish to extend your ladder, you can add a long-term fund. Investors can construct a more diversified and flexible portfolio using bond mutual funds than through buying individual bonds. That comes at a price, though, so watch your fund fees and charges.

Chapter 15 | Mutual Funds

What Is a Mutual Fund?

Mutual funds are the investment community's form of mass transit. It's a way for people to climb aboard and leave the driving to someone else. The good news is that they give you a comfortable ride with very little effort on your part. The bad news is that you have absolutely no say in terms of where the bus is going or how the bus is being driven. Your only choices are to take the ride or to get off at the next stop, so you have to know how to make those choices.

A mutual fund is an investment company registered with the Securities and Exchange Commission that holds a portfolio of securities. Mutual funds allow investors to pool their money and let a professional money manager make the investment decisions. The manager invests the money in stocks, bonds, or money market instruments according to the objectives of the fund. Those objectives vary a lot among mutual funds, so you have choices.

With mutual funds, you get instant diversification, lower costs through economy of scale, protection from fraud, and daily market values. The toughest part about buying a fund is to figure out which one meets your needs.

Mutual funds have gained remarkable popularity over the last two decades. In 1978, there were only 505 funds, with $55.9 billion under management. By early 2001 there were almost 13,000 funds (including 1,590 money market mutual finds), with $5.9 trillion under management. There are plenty of reasons for their popularity. It seems that we're all busier these days, so we want to have a low-maintenance approach to our investments. Also, more people are investing in retirement plans, such as IRAs and 401(k)s, and we're all more aware that the only chance to reach our long-term goals is by saving and investing.

And where are all those mutual funds investing our money? Figure 15-1 shows how the money is roughly spread out among stocks, bonds, stock-bond balances, and money markets.

The major attraction of mutual funds is *professional management*, because we're living in a very specialized and more sophisticated world. So it's just natural that we would want to rely on the experts to keep a close eye on our money for us.

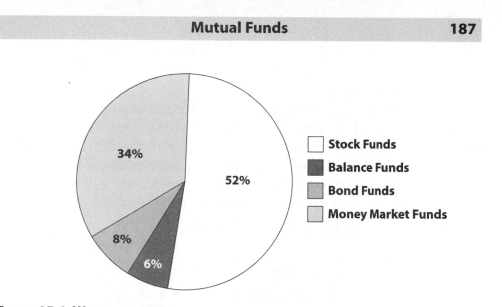

34%

52%

8%

6%

- ☐ Stock Funds
- ■ Balance Funds
- ▨ Bond Funds
- ☐ Money Market Funds

FIGURE 15-1. WHERE THE MONEY IS IN MUTUAL FUNDS

Another attraction is *safety*. The actual securities owned by the fund are held by a custodian, usually a large bank's trust department. Your investment in a fund is insured against fraud and theft up to $500,000 by the Securities Investor Protection Corporation (SIPC), a nonprofit corporation formed by Congress under the Securities Investor Protection Act of 1970 to protect customer accounts. Usually, the brokerage firm or mutual fund company also carries insurance, to cover amounts over the SIPC limit.

The Investment Company Act of 1940 includes numerous safeguards for mutual fund investors. Even if the fund sponsor, distributor, or underwriter gets in financial trouble, the securities in the fund are separate and safe. The only thing you're not protected against is the volatility of the stock market and its effect on the value of the mutual fund securities.

The market value of a mutual fund varies daily, based on the market prices of the individual investments the fund holds. However, because of the diversification of a mutual fund, that value is unlikely to fluctuate as much as an individual stock.

Much of the basic information about a mutual fund can be found in its *prospectus*. This is the official offering document you should read before investing any money in a fund. It tells you everything the SEC thinks you should know about the fund. You can learn about the fees and expenses, the investment principles and objectives, and the past performance numbers.

That's usually enough for many investors. But if you want to know more about a fund, you can also call the fund distributor and request the "Statement of Additional Information," a document that contains more detailed information about what the fund is allowed to invest in as well as who's on the board of directors.

The advantages of investing in mutual funds include:

✔ Professional management and research
✔ Diversification
✔ Variety of types and styles
✔ Ability to invest in markets all over the world
✔ Ease of buying and selling

For most investors, *diversification* is the single most valuable benefit of mutual funds. If you manage your own portfolio of stocks and bonds, you have to work at establishing and maintaining diversification. But diversification is almost automatic with mutual funds, because a diversified mutual fund cannot put more than 5% of its money in any one company. Therefore, by definition it has to own at least 20 different stocks or bonds.

But that's just the minimum. Stock mutual funds generally have a hundred and often many hundreds of different stocks in their portfolios at any time.

> *Buy when everyone else is selling and hold until everyone else is buying. This is not merely a catchy slogan. It is a very essence of successful investment.*
> —*J. Paul Getty*

Note that we said that diversification was *almost* automatic. Just beware that there are also non-diversified funds, which can put very large chunks of the portfolio in a few stocks or concentrate on one style or sector of the market. That can mean the possibility for rapid gains, but you also lose the safety of diversification.

Mutual funds have visibility, so people can keep an eye on their money. Their prices are listed in the paper every day, just like individual stocks, and most newspapers even give you a performance number so you can compare the funds. The number you see in the paper is called the *net asset value* or NAV. It's the total value of all the individual stocks in the portfolio divided by the number of shares of the fund. So if the value of the fund is $1,000,000 and there are 100,000 shares outstanding, then the NAV is $10 a share.

The bible for mutual fund investors is Morningstar's reports. This rating company based in Chicago was a pioneer in making mutual fund information available to both financial planners and consumers. Morningstar periodically issues reports on mutual funds and provides a comprehensive one-page report on some 1,700 mutual funds, with all of the pertinent information you need to know to evaluate funds. Many libraries subscribe to Morningstar's services, so check with your reference librarian. You can also contact the company by phone (800-735-0700) and through its Web site: **www.morningstar.com**.

Most mutual funds today are *open-end* mutual funds. That means that the fund will issue or redeem its shares for the shareholders at the NAV. Investors are free to come and go as they like.

Sometimes a fund will close its doors to new investors, either temporarily or permanently. It is then considered a *closed* fund. It will no longer sell shares to investors who do not already own shares. It will usually, however, allow current investors to continue to buy shares.

Then there's a third type of mutual fund—*closed-end*. A closed-end fund is a horse of a different color. It has a fixed number of shares outstanding. The shares are traded through brokers, just like stocks, at market prices. The fund will not redeem shares at the NAV. Since a closed-end fund is traded like other securities, the market price of the fund is different from the NAV. Closed-end funds are complicated, since their prices may fall below the actual market value of the stocks they hold.

Load vs. No-Load

A load is a commission you pay to buy a mutual fund. So, which is better, load funds or no-load funds? The answer: both. It depends on how much help you need.

If you know what you're doing and you don't want a financial advisor, then you'll save yourself the load by selecting no-load funds. When you buy a *no-load* fund, it is assumed you understand what you are purchasing and can do it yourself. Many people take this path.

If you feel you need some help establishing goals and objectives and need face-to-face help to learn about your options, then choose a load fund or fee-based no-load fund (the advisor doesn't charge a commission but takes an annual fee, usually around 1 to 2%). Don't feel guilty about asking for help, because according to 1998 data compiled by the Boston-based Financial Research Corporation, load funds and no load fee-based funds account for about 66% to 82% of all mutual funds sold. The variance is because it's hard to determine if 401(k)s are considered advisor-assisted or not.

Neither approach is right or wrong. You just have to know the difference and realize the fees or commissions are more expensive than a pure no load fund with no advisor.

Never think that a no-load fund is a no-*cost* fund. Even if you don't pay a commission, there are still management fees and operating expenses built into the fund expenses. And there may be some additional expenses as well. Instead of paying brokers or planners to market their funds, as load funds do, no-load funds use some of the management fees to sell directly to the public through newspaper, radio, magazine, and TV ads.

Because of that media exposure, novice investors are generally more likely to recognize no-load mutual funds. Just keep in mind that just because you recognize the name of a fund doesn't mean it's a better investment. In the same light, just because your load fund advisor recommends a fund doesn't mean it's a good one for you, either. So keep your antennae up when it comes to ads and recommendations. It's you—and not the marketers and brokers and planners—who are responsible for your money and how it's invested.

No-load funds customer service representatives are usually patient and trained to be able to answer most questions you may have about their funds. They tend to be low-key and don't put any pressure on you because they're not paid by commission. Their information is confined to the particular funds offered by the company; they are not trained and licensed to give you specific recommendations based on your financial situation. They also don't offer any follow-through or continuity on a person-to-person basis.

The load advisors are almost always more expensive, in terms of the fees and commissions. Load funds may add a percentage markup to the NAV when you buy the shares (a *front-end* load) or deduct a percentage when you sell the shares (a *back-end* load). For some classes of shares, the load is added to the fees and expenses and is paid before the shareholder gains are calculated. All these types of loads are clearly stated in the prospectus. You may have several choices as to how you pay the load, depending on which class of shares you select.

When you choose a load fund, you have to figure out if you're getting what you paid for. If an advisor sells you a mutual fund and charges you a 5% load, then the fund goes down and you never hear from the advisor again, well, it seems obvious that you didn't get what you paid for. Yet if the fund goes up or down and your advisor contacts you in the good times and the bad times, tells you what's going on, and continues to help you define your goals and objectives, then it's definitely worth it. You are going to have to pay for attention and hand holding.

The bottom line here is not *load* or *no-load*, but *help*. If you have an interest in researching mutual funds, then maybe you ought to go it alone and invest in no-load mutual funds. On the other hand, if you don't mind delegating these things because you don't have the time or the desire, then go find a good advisor and pay a load. There is no right answer. It's just a matter of what you like to do and how much you're willing to spend of your time or your money.

Index Funds

An index fund is simply a mutual fund set up to match the performance of a broad market index. That's simple enough.

But what's a *market index*? It's a list of stocks that represent, in one way or another, aspects of the stock market in general. You've probably heard stock market reports mention the Dow Jones Industrial Averages, an index of 30 stocks updated by the editors of *The Wall Street Journal*. When it's announced, "The Dow closed up today" or "The Dow declined," it means that stocks in general rose or fell. At the other end of the market index spectrum, providing the broadest coverage, would be the Russell 2000 and the Wilshire 5000.

A good example of a broad market index is the Standard & Poor's 500 Index. It's certainly the most popular index to imitate. The S&P 500 is an index of the 500 largest companies in the U.S. In the 1990s, S&P 500 Index funds became increasingly popular as large-cap stocks had their day in the market sunshine. The top 35 stocks, jumbo-caps really, make up the bulk of the index value, because the index is market cap-weighted. In other words, instead of these 35 shares representing 35/500ths of the 500 shares indexed, they represent more than half the value. As billions of dollars poured into the S&P 500 Index funds, these jumbo-cap stocks went up and up, attracting even more money.

Retail mutual fund money is still a minority of all indexed institutional investment, despite its rapid growth in recent years. More and more money going into indexed funds, primarily into funds indexed to the S&P 500, drives up the prices of the top 35 jumbo-cap stocks. In turn, the higher the prices, the better the funds perform and the more money they attract. This investing circle has become a self-fulfilling prophecy where, at least for a time, future returns *are* related to past performance.

How long will this go on? These jumbo-cap stocks become more and more overvalued relative to the rest of the market and to their underlying fundamentals, including sales and earnings growth. Historically, these bubbles end badly. This jumbo-cap bubble may eventually explode, as it did in 1973-74 when the "nifty-fifty" large-cap stocks fell as much as 90%.

Meanwhile, many actively managed mutual funds don't buy these "jumbo-cap" stocks because their managers believe they are too overvalued. They can't rationally justify investing in them. So, since 1994, most mutual funds have experienced lower returns than the S&P 500 Index funds. However, large-cap stocks have rarely outperformed the market for three years.

So, that's the S&P 500 Index in brief. As we mentioned, there are other market indices, all representing the stock market in various ways.

An index fund is a mutual fund set up to produce the same return for its investors as they would get if they each owned all the stocks in a particular index. There are several hundred index funds that seek to match the returns in 25 categories, such as small-cap, mid-cap, value or growth, and various foreign stock indexes. There are also funds that index the market as a whole, to match the Wilshire 5000 or other total market index. They cover all sizes of companies except the micro-caps. This is a less risky way to use index funds than through an S&P Index fund, for example. Diversification lowers both your long-term risk and the shorter-term volatility.

Index funds are not actively managed. After all, the stocks in an index don't change very often. This keeps the fees and expenses very low, compared with other funds. Index funds are also tax-efficient, because they have low turnover and they produce very little dividend income. This allows you to defer much of the capital gains over many years and to compound the gains.

So, for these reasons, index funds may have a place in long-term portfolios. You won't ever beat the benchmark index with these funds, but you won't do much worse than the index either. We expect there will be years when many good, actively managed mutual funds will beat the index funds regularly, as they did prior to 1995.

Fees and Expenses

As we noted at the start of this chapter, one of the major advantages of mutual funds is that a professional money manager makes the investment decisions. As much as those managers like what they're doing, they don't do it for love alone. Every mutual fund has fees; they couldn't stay in business otherwise.

Managers of funds with high fees will say that they're worth every penny. Managers of funds with low fees may point out how efficient they are. Fees are an important considera-

> *The cost you're willing to pay for something is a measure of the value you put on it.*

tion for the mutual fund investor, but *performance* is still the key factor. In many cases the style of the manager and the size of the portfolio determine the fees. International funds have a bit more in record-keeping and administrative expenses, so they tend to have higher costs. Small-cap funds often have higher fees because the funds are smaller and because it's more difficult to research so many small companies.

The fees and expenses of a fund may also include commissions to advisors, planners, and brokers. As we mentioned in discussing load funds and no-load funds, commissions should generally be paid on those funds that give you the help of a personal advisor. The key here is to know where to find those commissions and fees. They are in the first two pages of the prospectus. You can request the prospectus for any fund by calling the mutual fund, your broker, or your financial planner. We strongly suggest that you read the prospectus to find out the fees, the investment style, and how to buy and sell the shares of the fund. Morningstar also provides this information in its reports.

The key to understanding commissions is to know your ABCs. Just about all commissioned funds have classes of shares called A shares, B shares, or C/D shares. There are also some institutional classes as well.

For *A* shares, you pay a commission up front that ranges from 1% to 8.5%, with the average being around 4%. This means that you buy the fund shares at a price higher than the NAV.

The B shares have no charge up front, but usually impose back-end charges if you leave within five to seven years. An example might be a redemption or contingent deferred sales charge of 5% the first year, reduced by 1% each year thereafter.

The *C* or *D* shares have an asset-based charge. That means that, although there's usually no charge up front and no redemption fee if you hold them for a year to two, the commission or load shows up in what is called a *12b-1* fee. Funds are allowed to charge you this fee each year for advertising and distribution costs and to compensate your advisor for the service and advice you receive. For C/D shares, this can run to 1% annually, on top of a fund's regular expenses. The 12b-1 fee is much smaller for A and B shares, on the order of 0.25% to 0.50% per year. In these cases, the fee is charged to compensate your advisor for continuous account assistance and service.

To summarize: the A shares have the highest up-front charge but the lowest fees, while the B and C/D shares charge more in annual fees but you don't have to pay a big up-front commission. So there's no best or worst type of mutual fund, in terms of the fees and expenses. Just know ahead of time how much you're going to pay, when, and for how long.

If you don't understand the charges, then have the salesperson or advisor explain them to you until you get it. You shouldn't pay any commissions unless you need someone to help you. But when you want help and you're paying for it, make sure you get it. If you plan on staying in the fund for more than five years, the A shares are going to be the least expensive way to invest, at least in most cases. But don't refuse to invest in a fund with a load or commission if it's a fund that meets your financial objectives. After all, you're investing to achieve your objectives, not to minimize investment charges.

Let's take a look here at just what you pay when it comes to total expenses. The *expense ratio* is all the charges as a percentage of the value of your account. So an expense ratio of 1.25% would mean that you pay $125 in fees for every $10,000 of your investment value each year. (These expenses are actually deducted on a daily basis, rather than once a year.) According to Morningstar, here's a sampling of what you would pay in annual fees in these categories:

Category	Average Expense
all-stock funds	1.53%
growth funds	1.44%
international funds	1.85%
bond funds	1.08%
index funds	0.58%
small-company funds	1.50%

When your funds are making 15% to 25% a year, you're probably not concerned with the fees and expenses—but you should be. There will be years when you make only 5% or even lose money. These expenses will make a big difference to you then.

If you just want the cheapest funds, then stick to the index funds, because there's no cost to hire highly paid portfolio managers to make investment decisions. Otherwise, decide on the type of fund you want, fitting fund performance with your objectives. Then aim for expense ratios in the lower half of the expense range for that type of fund. Higher expenses don't equate to better performance. In this case at least, you don't necessarily get what you pay for.

Taxes on Dividends and Profits

For everything we do in the world of investing, mutual funds included, there's some form of ultimate tax ramification. If the money is in a retirement account, we don't have to worry about the taxes until we take the money out or we die. (Of course, in the latter case we won't be around to worry!) On the other hand, if the money is not in a tax-deferred account, then those 1099 tax forms come rolling in every year so Uncle Sam can get his share.

A mutual fund is a portfolio of individual stocks or fixed-income securities such as bonds. If you owned these directly and received dividends from each of those stocks or interest from each of those bonds, you would have to pay taxes on this income each year.

The same holds true with a mutual fund. After the end of the year, you receive a single statement from the mutual fund company or your brokerage firm, a 1099-DIV, that tells you the amount of the dividends paid by the fund to you. You pay the taxes on that income, based on your income tax bracket. Even if you reinvest the mutual fund's dividends, as most investors do, you still have to pay the taxes on them.

Most years, mutual funds will also distribute a capital gains dividend at least once if not twice during the year. This happens because the fund has realized a net gain on the securities it sold, even if the NAV of the fund has decreased. The fund or the broker will either break these gains out on the 1099-DIV form you receive as *long-term* capital gains (for securities the fund held over a year) or lump them in with the ordinary dividends as *short-term* capital gains (for securities held less than a year). This difference between long-term and short-term has nothing to do with how long you've owned shares in the fund. By law the mutual fund company must make these distributions to you at least annually.

If you're thinking about buying a fund late in the year, be aware that you could be buying a tax burden. If you buy the fund on December 1 and the fund declares a taxable gain on December 2, you would have to pay the whole year of tax liability, even though you owned the fund for only one day. That may not strike you as fair, but it's the law. So, if you're buying funds near the end of the year, be sure to ask about the potential tax liability or the date when the fund will declare the dividend. You may want to wait a week or two before you buy. Don't get too upset if you get snagged here, because you still get to increase your cost basis of the fund by the amount of the distribution, which will reduce your taxes if you sell.

Bond mutual funds usually pay a monthly income dividend representing the interest earned by the fund less fees and expenses. After the end of the year, the fund will advise you how much, if any, of the income is tax-exempt at the federal and state levels. Once a year, a bond fund may also pay a capital gain dividend, if the net trading has resulted in a profit. This dividend, unlike the income dividends in a bond fund, is deducted from the fund's NAV.

Dividends

There's a common misperception about mutual funds. It may appear that after a fund pays a dividend you lose money, because you see that the day after the dividend the fund is down. You don't lose anything; it's just that a dividend of $3.00 reduces the price of the fund by $3.00 that day. So if you're reinvesting the dividends, you now have more shares—for the exact same total value. If you're not reinvesting the dividends, then you'll be getting a dividend check in the mail for $3.00 per share.

Dividend payments have a second tax consequence. The biggest problem for most mutual fund investors is keeping tabs of all the dividends the funds have paid over the years. You want to keep track of these because every dividend adds to your tax cost basis. For tax purposes you want to have a high cost, because the capital gain is the difference between your selling price and the total adjusted cost basis.

Here's an example. You buy shares in a fund for $10,000. You hold the shares for 10 years, reinvesting $5,000 in dividends over that time. Then, you sell the fund for $20,000. What's the taxable capital gain on that transaction? It's only $5,000, not $10,000, because it's $20,000 minus your adjusted cost basis. Since you've already paid taxes on the $5,000 of dividends as they were distributed over the years, you add them to your tax cost basis. So be sure to keep good records of your dividends.

If you didn't automatically reinvest your dividends, then your gain is simply the difference between what you paid for the shares (including any load) and what you sell them for. In the above example, if you took the $5,000 in dividends as they were distributed, paid the taxes on them every year, and then sold the shares for $15,000, your taxable gain would still be $5,000.

For help in figuring out your gains, request Publication 564, "Mutual Fund Distributions," from the IRS at 800-829-3676.

You may want to be sure the funds that you own in taxable accounts are "tax-efficient" so that you don't get hit with surprises from your mutual fund company every January. To get a feel for what a fund has done in terms of its after-tax rate of return, check out the Morningstar analysis sheet for the fund. Just go to the section on taxes called "Tax Analysis" to find the after-tax rate. You want a fund that has an after-tax return of 85% or more of its pre-tax total return.

It's important to remember that, if you exchange from one fund to another in the same fund family, it's a taxable event. You may not consider that exchange to be a sale, but that's what it is for the IRS.

We'll take a closer look at taxes on investments in Chapter 24. For now, the key to remember is that you can defer taxes on the buildup of gains in your fund as represented by the increase in the NAV until you sell the shares. You can control when you pay taxes on the buildup by investing in the fund for the long term.

Chapter 16 | Building Your Fund Portfolio

Invest with Style

At one point in time, figuring out fund categories was easy. You were buying a *stock* mutual fund, a *bond* mutual fund, or a combination of the two in a *balanced* fund. But that was back in the olden days when there were a lot fewer mutual funds.

Today, with over 11,500 mutual funds available, it's gotten complicated. But there are services out here to help small investors. One of your best sources for research is Morningstar Mutual Funds, a mutual fund and stock rating service located in Chicago. You can find Morningstar at most libraries, call 312-696-6000, or visit the Web site at **www.morningstar.com**.

Morningstar uses the *style box* to help investors better understand a fund's true investment strategy. Without this tool, categorizing funds can be perplexing. The style box provides an easy way for the investor to see what a fund's dominant investment style is.

The equity style box (Figure 16-1) is a nine-box matrix that summarizes a portfolio's characteristics and allows the investor to more accurately determine a particular fund's investment objectives. Along the vertical axis you have the market-cap size of the companies in the fund. Morningstar ties market cap to the relative movements of the market. The top 5% of the 5,000 largest domestic stocks in Morningstar's equity database are classified as large-cap, the next 15% of the 5,000 are mid-cap, and the remaining 80% are small-cap.

> *Style in a mutual fund has little to do with fashion.*

Morningstar then determines a fund's market cap by ranking the stocks in a fund's portfolio, from the largest market-capitalized stock to the smallest, and then calculating the average weighted market capitalization of the stocks in the middle quintile of the portfolio. After determining a fund's market cap, Morningstar places the fund in the large-cap, mid-cap, or small-cap group.

Along the horizontal axis, there are three types of investment styles—value-oriented on the left, growth-oriented on the right, and a blend of the two in the middle.

Equity Style

	Value	Blend	Growth
Large-cap	Large-cap Value	Large-cap Blend	Large-cap Growth
Mid-cap	Mid-cap Value	Mid-cap Blend	Mid-cap Growth
Small-cap	Small-cap Value	Small-cap Blend	Small-cap Growth

☐ Low risk ☐ Moderate Risk ☐ High Risk

FIGURE 16-1. EQUITY STYLE BOX: THE NATURE AND RISK OF A FUND

The example on the right is what you'll actually find on a Morningstar fund fact sheet. One of the boxes will be shaded to indicate the current style of investing. In our sample we have a large-cap growth fund.

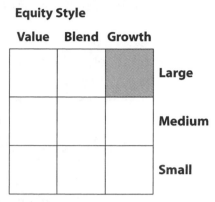

Equity Style

Value	Blend	Growth	
			Large
			Medium
			Small

Starting with the large company value funds, you would put your money here because you can buy some of the biggest and best-run companies in the world when most investors don't want to own them. These basically good companies have generated some temporary bad news or are in business sectors that are out of favor currently.

Large company growth stocks are companies that are growing faster than the S&P 500. They are usually brand name companies such as Microsoft or Dell, names we usually recognize as products or services we use.

Small and medium-sized value companies most investors may not recognize because they operate in niche markets. There are so many small and medium-sized companies that they're often overlooked by Wall Street, which tends to focus more on the bigger companies.

Small and medium-sized growth companies are usually cutting-edge companies that are growing their earnings by as much as 25% a year or more. They're usually in a sexy business like technology.

There are good reasons to invest in all of these areas. At any point in time one or more of these styles will be hot or ice-cold. The secret is to decide the mix you feel comfortable with and stick to your boxes. Don't try and flip-flop between styles in anticipation of making the next style call, because that's just trying to time the market. And never, never have all your funds in just one style box. In fact, if you find that all your funds are doing well at the same time, your portfolio probably isn't diversified enough. So spread your money around to three or more styles. At any time one of them will be doing better than the others. We just never know in advance which one or when.

International companies have their own nine categories with pretty much the same definitions as above. The only difference is that Morningstar classifies funds as large-, mid-, and small-cap based on fixed market cap boundaries. If the median market cap of an international fund is above $5 billion, then it's noted as a large-cap fund. Between $1 billion and $5 billion, the fund is classified as mid-size. A fund below $1 billion is classified as small-cap. Good solid information is often not available for smaller foreign companies, so the style box may be less informative for this type of fund.

Bonds Have Style Too

Most people don't buy individual bonds; they invest in bond funds. There's $808 billion invested in bond funds, which is about 12% of all the mutual fund money outstanding. In other words, you have a lot of company when you invest in bond mutual funds.

The style box for fixed income funds offers a different interpretation of the way a fund company chooses to position a fund. You may be confused by such indications as a fund's name or the marketing material. Style data often proves to be a more accurate assessment of a fund's investment approach, because it's based upon the fund's actual holdings. So it's actually pretty easy to get a handle on the style of bond fund managers. All you have to look at is the quality of the bonds and the average length of maturity (the duration).

If we look at a bond fund's style box (Figure 16-2), we see that

Fixed Income Style

	Short	Inter.	Long
High	Short-Term High Quality	Inter-mediate High Quality	Long-Term High Quality
Medium	Short-Term Medium Quality	Inter-mediate Medium Quality	Long-Term Medium Quality
Low	Short-Term Low Quality	Inter-mediate Low Quality	Long-Term Low Quality

☐ Low risk   ☐ Moderate Risk   ■ High Risk

FIGURE 16-2. FIXED INCOME STYLE BOX: THE RISK IN BOND FUNDS

Morningstar lists the quality of the bonds along the vertical axis—high-, medium-, and low-quality—and the general maturity of the bonds in the portfolio along the horizontal axis—short-, intermediate-, and long-term. Generally, bond funds with durations of less than 4 years are considered short-term, intermediate bonds are 4 to 10 years, and long-term bonds have maturities of over 10 years.

The example on the right is what you will actually find on a Morningstar fund fact sheet; only one of the boxes will be shaded to indicate the current style of investing. In our sample we have a short-term bond fund containing high-quality bonds.

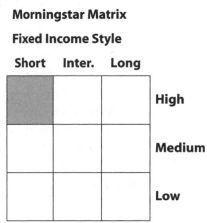

Once you figure out which styles fit your financial objectives, you can narrow down your search to the funds in those style boxes. Don't make the mistake of reaching for higher yields and total return performance numbers with money you know you will need in three years or less. Stick to short-term funds for your short-term money and use the intermediate funds for money you won't need for at least five years. Long-term bond funds can also play a role for long-term money, but the volatility can be as great as in the stock market.

The returns on all of these funds will usually be dictated by the change in interest rates in the real world. If rates go up, then short-term bond funds are hurt the least and long-term bond funds get whacked the hardest. On the other hand, if rates go down, then long-term and intermediate bonds cash in more than the short-term funds.

In periods of economic uncertainty and in recessions, credit quality will play a key role in how these funds perform. The quality of bonds other than U.S. Treasuries is determined by the rating services.

The quality standard of the portfolio is decided by the individual mutual fund's manager. The quality range is within the stated objectives of the fund, so read the prospectus before you invest to understand the quality standard of the portfolio. If you own a government bond fund, make sure that it's a U.S. government bond fund and not a specialty fund that invests in foreign government debt.

The bottom line with bond funds is that quality and maturity rule bond performance. So be sure to know what you own.

How to Pick a Mutual Fund

Investing is not a competitive sport for individual investors. The most important factor is to select funds that are appropriate for your personal financial plan and objectives. Your plan can tell you how much you need to invest in stock mutual funds and how much in bond funds. It also guides you toward certain styles, in combination with your expected future cash flow and your comfort level with the various styles.

With so many funds to choose from, you need a disciplined procedure to whittle down the number. Ideally, you want to invest in three to six funds, depending on how much money you currently have to invest, that represent three or more styles, based on the style boxes in previous sections. You want to stay in these funds, adding to your investment for many years, as long as the funds perform well compared with their benchmarks. (We'll discuss benchmarks toward the end of this chapter.) Therefore, it's worth taking some time to select these funds.

Seven Guidelines for Selecting Mutual Funds

It's easy to have a disciplined approach to selecting mutual funds. To begin your search, look for:

- ✔ A manager with a good three- and five-year performance record
- ✔ A below-average expense ratio
- ✔ A below-average annual turnover ratio
- ✔ A below-average price/earnings (P/E) ratio
- ✔ A beta rating that represents your risk tolerance
- ✔ An above-average Sharpe Ratio
- ✔ Minimum investment level

Those are your criteria. Now, let's discuss each of them briefly.

You should compare the *performance* of the fund and the manager relative to the style benchmark, not necessarily to the S&P 500 index.

You're interested in the comparative performance over three- and five-year periods, since very few funds have a 10-year performance, especially with the same manager these days.

Check the fund's performance each year for the last five years in the Morningstar page; don't check only the overall performance number. You want to see that the fund's annual return was consistently in the top 50% or even top 25% of all funds of that same style. One great year and several poor years is not consistency; it may be just luck. That's why one-year ratings are not very meaningful.

We looked at *fees and expenses* and saw the difference they make in your returns. Fees and expenses are not necessarily bad, but you should be getting something of value for those costs.

Turnover also increases expenses, as the manager buys and sells securities. The idea is that the manager sells something at a high price and buys something else at a better value. As long as this works most of the time, you come out ahead. Turnover is a measure of *activity*; what you want, of course, is *results*. If higher activity does not bring better results, if the returns are not commensurate with the turnover, you're paying for activity. That's why you need to pay attention after you buy the fund. You'll find that growth funds, especially small-cap growth

> *Investing is a lot like learning to swim. Take it slow at first and know what you're doing. Don't jump into the deep end of the pool.*

funds, have the highest turnover. Compare each fund's annual turnover ratio with the turnover for other funds in the same style.

The *price/earnings ratio* is also important here. A fund's P/E ratio is the average of the P/E ratios of all the stocks in the fund. If the ratio is higher than the ratios of other funds of the same style, the future performance may be affected. This is a tougher call, because funds don't usually release their list of holdings until months later. The manager may have sold the high P/E stocks by the time this information is available. But it helps to use this criterion to get some idea of how the manager operates within the chosen style.

Volatility can be measured by a statistical tool called *beta*, which represents how much a fund or a stock moved up and down compared with the market over short periods in the past, usually a year. The market's volatility is represented by a beta of 1.0. Funds with a higher beta went up and down more than the market while funds below 1.0 went up and down less than the market. However, studies show that volatility in the past doesn't have any relation to volatility in the future. If you don't like the ups and downs in the market, you may want to select funds where the beta was below 1.0, though there's no promise of a smoother ride. Keep in mind, however, that there does seem to be a positive relationship between higher volatility and higher long-term performance.

The *Sharpe Ratio* combines beta with the return of the fund over the same period. It measures whether the amount of volatility the fund experienced was justified by the return of the fund compared with the return of Treasury bills, which aren't very volatile because they mature in less than a year. A Sharpe Ratio greater than 1.0 means the manager got a bigger bang for the bucks in the fund than the volatility would indicate. According to Professor William Sharpe, the 1990 Nobel Prize winner for Economic Science who created the ratio, this measure has a weak predictive value. So use this measure cautiously.

Another factor relates to the size of your initial investment in the funds and your ongoing additional investments. Funds have widely varying minimums for both entry and subsequent investments. Most also have lower minimums for qualified retirement plans such as IRAs. You need to find out whether the funds you're interested in take contributions in the amounts you plan on making.

The Convenience Factor

Once you've narrowed down the universe of funds using the seven guidelines above, you probably still have more funds than you need. Take your search one step further and look at the ease of purchasing the funds. Can you use one of the supermarkets, which are self-directed brokerage accounts with Fidelity or Schwab? Or does one fund family fit your needs in the beginning? You should also consider the ease of selling or transferring. Make sure that whatever fund family you chose has a money market fund. Selling your fund or transferring the fund will be so much easier if you have a money market fund to use as a holding place.

How do you find out more about the funds that you're considering? All of the mutual fund companies now have Web sites that you can visit to get more information. There's also a magazine dedicated entirely to mutual funds, *Mutual Funds Magazine*. Other good sources of information would be *Money Magazine* and *Kiplinger's Personal Finance*. These magazines are also a great source to keep you updated on the tax law changes that will affect your investing.

Building a Portfolio of Funds

The right way to build a portfolio of mutual funds is from the ground up, based on your financial plan. Let's start with some simple math.

There are three distinct areas of mutual fund investing: bonds, domestic stocks, and international stocks. There are nine fund styles from which you can choose, as we explained earlier in this chapter. That means a total of 27 potential styles boxes (three areas times nine styles each).

You don't want to be in all of the boxes and own 27 funds. How many funds you own is partly a function of how much money you have to invest. You have to observe the various fund minimums, and you want enough money in each fund to make an impact on your portfolio's overall performance.

What we recommend is a six-pack of mutual funds, such as in Figure 16-3. The six funds that you select, of course, should reflect the objectives of your financial plan.

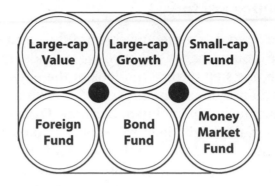

FIGURE 16-3. MUTUAL FUND SIX-PACK

As your money available for investing increases, limit your fund choices to a maximum of a dozen. If you own more than that, you're not *diversifying*, you're *deworsifying*. As you add more funds, you just end up getting closer and closer to an indexed portfolio. If you go in that direction, you'd be better off just buying index funds, because at least the management fees would be cheaper. But make sure you follow our style box approach so you won't have overlap in your portfolio. Overlap is owning too many funds of the same style that invest in the same individual stocks. Overlap reduces your diversification.

Although it sure is easy to put all your money into one mutual fund family, such as Fidelity, Vanguard, American Funds, or Janus, we suggest looking for the best in each fund family. You can open up separate accounts with each family, but many have some type of fund "supermarket" that allows you to buy funds from a wide variety of families, though there may be a small transaction fee. Working through a supermarket will put all your records and funds on one single statement, so it will be easier to keep tabs on them. Every brokerage house and most financial planners can help you select funds from a variety of fund families and combine the reports on one statement, too.

The final point to understand is that a six-pack should not be divided equally among the six funds. The key to making money is finding the right mix for this six-pack to fit your financial objectives and risk profile. As you go about managing your new all-star portfolio, developing such an allocation should be the start of a long and prosperous investing career.

When to Sell a Fund

The No. 1 reason to sell is when your goals or objectives change. That usually means your time frame for investing shortens or lengthens. A complete review of your financial plan at those times might indicate your portfolio also needs a change to match your new plan.

If you're about to retire, need dollars for school, or got laid off and are going to need money from your investments, you'll need to figure out what to sell. On the other hand, if you find you really aren't going to need money for five years or more, then it may be time to rev up the portfolio. Another reason to sell is when a time horizon becomes shorter. This is why we recommended that you shift some investments to cash when your time horizon becomes shorter than five years.

> *The patient man realizes a profit on his investment whereas the only thing the impatient man realizes is his mistake.*

When else might it be a good time to consider selling? When there's a change in the management of any of your funds. An alarm should go off when a fund manager leaves. That doesn't mean that you want to sell the fund immediately, but just that it's wise to keep a close watch on the fund over the next several quarters. When you notice a management change, call the fund company and ask for information on the new manager. Get the track record on the new manager if possible. How long was he or she with the previous fund? What was his or her performance? Morningstar reports will also help here: the next update on the fund will list the manager's education and experience. You want the person managing your fund money to have a fair amount of experience. With over 11,500 funds available, why take a chance with a rookie manager?

Check to see if the new manager's style is very different from the style of his or her predecessor. If the fund changes style over the next year, it may no longer fit in your portfolio. A new manager coming in can also make a lot of stock changes, which can cause some real capital gain tax problems by the end of the year. Of course, if you sell a fund in a taxable account, you'll create your own tax liability. Balance out all the new information. Then, if the situation indicates that a change would be wise, make the change and pay the tax.

Every six or 12 months, and more often after a manager change, compare the performance figures for each of your funds with the figures for funds that are similar based on the style boxes. See if any of your funds have trailed their peers for three to six quarters. This is a sign that the manager may be making some bad decisions. If things don't change after two to three years, then dump them. That may sound like a long time, but you need to allow a manager to go through a cycle for a bare minimum of two years so you can judge whether he or she is investing in good stuff.

Another major reason to sell a fund is when the manager changes stripes. If a manager starts out with a small-cap style and then switches to a mid-cap or a large-cap style, then he or she may be messing up your portfolio diversification. Managers may change styles because a bunch of new money comes into the fund. This happens with funds that get a good track record and a lot of publicity. A manager often can't operate in the same pure style under these conditions.

When Not to Sell a Fund

Let us now take an opposite stance and tell you when *not* to sell a fund. Many investors fall into these traps and they end up buying high and selling low. Do not sell a fund because:

✔ *The fund loses money*. A fund manager who sticks to his or her style isn't going to do well every quarter. The market rotates styles in and out of favor, and funds in styles temporarily out of favor may lose money. Hang in there for the long term. If you picked a good fund with a good manager, you'll be rewarded with good performance over longer periods of time.

✔ *The fund under-performs another style of investing*. We repeat: don't compare your funds with funds managed in different styles. You selected certain styles to fit your financial objectives and comfort level, so stick to your plan.

✔ *The market goes down*. The stock market historically has gone down 20% or more every six to seven years on average since the Great Depression. And it has always recovered and gone on to new highs, no matter what triggered the correction. Long-term investors win with a patient, long-term time horizon. Manage your emotions and you'll manage your portfolio a lot better.

Benchmarks and How to Find Them

Here are some of the common benchmarks for comparing funds.

✔ Standard & Poor's 500 Index for large U.S. companies

✔ Russell Mid-Cap Index for medium U.S. companies

✔ Russell 2000 Index for small U.S. companies

✔ Morgan Stanley EAFE (Europe, Australia, and Far East) Index for international companies

✔ Morgan Stanley Emerging Markets Index for companies in developing countries

✔ Lehman Brothers Long-Term Bond Index for bonds with 20 years to maturity

✔ Lehman Brothers Intermediate Government/Corporate Bond Index for 5- to 10-year maturity bonds

✔ Lehman Brothers Bond Buyer Municipal Index for long-term municipal bonds

Buy a copy of *The Wall Street Journal* at a newsstand at the end of a quarter to find the index numbers for the last quarter. Turn to the "Money & Investing" section. On the left of the front page you'll see Markets Diary. Here you can find the Dow Jones, S&P 500, Russell 2000, and Morgan Stanley EAFE indexes. Below these, you'll find the Lehman Brothers' bond indexes. In the last column you'll see the year-to-date percentage changes.

The index for all of section C is also on this page, in the lower left corner. Find the page for the Bond Market Data Bank, where you'll see indexes on intermediate and long-term Treasury notes and bonds, corporate and municipal bonds, and mortgage-backed securities. All show 12-month and year-to-date percentage changes.

Finally, look in the index again for Lipper Indexes. Here you'll find a summary list of 29 of the Lipper Fund Indexes through the previous market trading day, with year-to-date percentage changes. A more complete listing of over 60 stock and bond mutual fund indexes is available in "Market Week' section inside and find the Lipper Mutual Fund Performance indexes.

Some of the index categories you'll find are:

✔ Growth Fund Index

✔ Mid-Cap Fund Index

✔ Growth & Income Index

✔ S&P 500 Fund Index

✔ European Fund Index

✔ Emerging Market Fund Index

✔ General U.S. Treasury Fund Index

✔ Short-Intermediate Muni Debt Fund Index

So now that you know where you can find all the data, you can compare your investments against the various indexes and see how you did. Just remember this very important point: this is just a quick gauge of investment performance, not a complete checkup. It just tells you how you did for a period of time. If something looks out of line, make sure you have the correct benchmark. If so, make a note to keep an eye on that investment over the next several periods to make sure it returns to your expected performance level. If not, then you may need to consider selling.

At least once a year, you'll want to do a more thorough diagnosis as part of a total portfolio review. Then you look at the performance of each part of your portfolio against the benchmarks for periods of one, two, three, and five years. A couple of *quarters* of performance below the benchmark can be expected. A couple of *years* means you may need to make a change. The annual review of your portfolio should take place following an annual review of your financial plan or whenever your financial plan changes.

Chapter 17 | International Investing

Should You Invest Overseas?

n a word, yes. In today's financial markets, no country is an island.
We live in an interrelated global marketplace of nations that are
highly interdependent on trading goods and services. In addition,
huge amounts of investment money flow around the world, seeking
the highest return.

The global link is clearly apparent when we see constant signs of
worldwide economic ripple effects. If Japan has a banking crisis, all of
Asia comes to a halt. When Mexico has political turmoil, Central
America and Canada shudder. When the Russian ruble collapses, the
U.S. markets retreat. It's all a result of a much more sophisticated global technology and communication infrastructure, which is just going to
get more linked.

The global investing scene can be divided into the *developed* countries, such as the U.S., Canada, the nations of Western Europe, and
Japan, and the *developing* countries.

There are about 125 developing countries, with 80% of the world's population but only about 10% of the world stock market capitalization. About 25 of these countries have established markets with enough companies listed to provide a good selection of stocks for investors.

The people in these developing countries have seen how the rest of us live and they all want a middle-class lifestyle. Half of them are under age 20 and they're becoming literate, educated, and skilled thanks to technology, communications, and plants established by international companies throughout the world. The demand of these millions of consumers for products is growing fast and their desire to raise their standard of living is passionate.

We can participate in this growth through investing in markets other than the U.S. Consider these facts:

✔ Half of the people in the world have yet to snap their first photograph.

✔ More than 93% don't have a VISA card.

✔ The average person outside the U.S. drinks 35 Cokes a year, as opposed to the average person in the U.S. at 310.

The world is growing around us. In 1970, the U.S. accounted for 47% of the world's economy and had 66% of the world's stock value. Within 26 years that situation has almost flip-flopped, as we are now about 33% of the world's economy and 50% of world's stock value. That's a trend that will continue for many years, as markets are emerging and growing all over the world.

This change is reflected in the performance of stock markets around the world. If you look at the U.S. stock market performance each of the last 10 years compared with the performances of markets in the other developed countries and the best emerging markets, you know that money can be made outside the U.S. No one can pick the best market ahead of time, of course, but an investment in a diversified foreign fund allows you to participate in the growth of economies outside the U.S.

> For many industries, the growth opportunities are in markets abroad.

Over the 10 years from 1990 through 1999, the S&P 500 turned in one of its best 10-year performances ever, with an average annual return of 19.4%. The best non-U.S. major market return for each of those years averaged 66.4%. And the average of the top emerging market in each of those years was a whopping 187.6%!

Some financial experts say that because we're the leader in the world market we shouldn't buy international stocks, especially when we look at the international earnings from our big players, such as Coke, GE, IBM, and Intel. That premise is correct—except when the

U.S. Market		Best Major Market		Best Emerging Market	
2000	-11%	Canada	5%	Israel	14%
1999	21%	Finland	153%	Korea	111%
1998	29%	Finland	119%	Korea	138%
1997	34%	Switzerland	45%	Turkey	118%
1996	24%	Spain	41%	Venezuela	131%
1995	38%	Switzerland	45%	Israel	24%
1994	2%	Finland	52%	Brazil	66%
1993	10%	Hong Kong	117%	Poland	754%
1992	7%	Hong Kong	32%	Jordan	40%
1991	31%	Hong Kong	50%	Argentina	405%

FIGURE 17-1. TOTAL RETURNS AROUND THE WORLD (Source: Morgan Stanley Dean Witter Capital International market indexes in U.S. dollars with dividends reinvested)

U.S. stock market goes down 20% to 30%. Even though these U.S. companies get most of their earnings from outside the country, they will still tank when the market drops. So buying stock in companies outside the U.S. may help you weather the storm a bit when our markets are down.

Think of it another way. If you buy their goods, why not their stock? Trade works both ways. Have you ever bought any of these brands—Alpo, Burger King, Dannon, Lipton, Nestlé, Michelin, Pond's, Q-tips, Shell, or Vaseline? If so, then you've bought something from a foreign company. Also, consider that the 10 largest banks are non-U.S., 8 of the 10 largest electrical and electronics firms are non-U.S., and 5 of the 10 largest broadcasting and publishing firms are non-U.S.

Risks and Returns

By late 1998, it seemed like almost anything that could go wrong in many foreign economies did. This uncertainty about the future affected the U.S. markets, too, because we're part of the global economy. By now, we hope you have realized that world of investing revolves around balancing risks and returns. (We'll cover investment risks more fully in Chapter 21.)

There are five additional types of risk involved in investing in foreign companies.

- ✔ **Political:** Changes in a country's political environment, such as major policy shifts, instability, changes in leadership, and government intervention in the economy.
- ✔ **Financial:** Currency changes and devaluation, controls on capital movement, local inflation, and recession.
- ✔ **Investment:** Different or inadequate audit standards, resulting in a lack of good information about a company's operations, management, finances, and product development.
- ✔ **Transactional:** Inefficient markets, causing security registration, delivery, and safekeeping of stocks and trade settlements to be delayed or lost.
- ✔ **Systemic:** Lack of regulation and enforcement, leading to fraud and manipulation of the stock; special interests, government

intervention in the markets, and discrimination against foreign investors; and a lack of a system of laws and enforcement of laws to protect property rights.

These are five reasons why we believe that experienced, professional management of your international investments is essential.

Here's just one example of what can happen. If you bought 100 shares in a Mexican stock fund for 454.5 pesos on Nov. 1, 1994, when the peso was trading at 3.44 pesos for one U.S. dollar, your investment cost 45,450 pesos or $13,212. In late December, the Mexican government devalued the peso. One year later, the Mexican stock fund had risen 10.38% to 471.6 pesos, but the peso was now trading at 7.33 per dollar. You sell your investment, but you receive only $6,434! You lost $6,778, or 51.3% of your investment, because of the currency devaluation—even though your stock rose more than 10%.

> *If it's such a small world, why does it take so much money to run it?*

If you just look at international investing by itself, you see a higher level of volatility. The Morningstar risk ratings show that international funds as a group have been about 25% more volatile than U.S. stock funds over the past 10 years. Despite the risks that affect investing in all foreign markets to a greater or lesser degree, the principle of diversification for the purpose of balancing a portfolio's risks says that international investing benefits your portfolio.

Diversification across many regions of the world is less risky than investing in any one country, including the U.S. All markets in the world don't rise and fall together over long periods. In the short run, fear and panic can become a global phenomenon, as we have recently seen. But the discipline of the long-term investor is based on an understanding that time reduces risk and increases returns with a diversified allocation of investments.

To put it simply, no one knows what any of the markets will do in any given year, so participation in more than one country helps to balance your overall risks and returns.

It will take many years, decades in some cases, for emerging countries to find a version of capitalism that provides an environment for stable development. It took the U.S. 150 years and we're still tinkering with our system. Some developing countries have built capitalistic economies in only 20-30 years since 1950 and others are well on their way. Other developed countries are rapidly changing how their economies work to meet the demands of the changing world economy.

We believe that putting 10% to 20% of your long-term investments into non-U.S. markets gives you the opportunity to participate in the greater growth of the global economy. We'll look at how in the next section.

Taxes on Foreign Investments

There's one other wrinkle that's important to understand regarding taxes on your mutual fund returns from investing in foreign countries. Usually the dividend and capital gain income is subject to taxes in the country of origin. A mutual fund normally pays these taxes before declaring any dividend to shareholders. But then the U.S. government expects to collect taxes on this money, too, if you're a citizen. To reduce this double taxation, the IRS allows you to claim either a foreign tax credit (deductible from your total tax) or a foreign tax deduction for the tax paid.

The fund company will report the full amount of income on your 1099-DIV, which will be more than the actual dividend paid to you (because of the foreign tax), and show how much money you're allowed to deduct or how much you can take as a tax credit on your 1040. (Check Chapter 24 to learn more about income taxes.)

This tax situation can get confusing rather quickly, so it will pay to get help from your tax advisor on how you should handle this. Just don't ignore it.

How to Get into the Game

Once you've decided to be a player in the international markets, what do you do? Your decisions on how much and what way to get in are based, once again, on your financial plan.

International investing requires a long-term time horizon, at least five years, and 10 to 20 years is even better. Investing 10% of your long-term equity allocation is enough to get some benefit and, using dollar cost averaging, you can slowly increase your commitment over several years.

Patience is a virtue here as much as in any area of investing. Some countries will be making progress while others will be taking a step backward to consolidate the progress they've made.

Diversification is also important, as we mentioned earlier, to smooth out the volatility in individual markets. Many small markets can rise or fall as much as 25% in a single day. An experienced manager will be able to make knowledgeable decisions about companies, sectors, and countries to invest in or to avoid at any given time.

If you go with mutual funds, as we would recommend, look closely at the length of time both the manager and the fund company have been investing internationally. The longer the track record, the more experienced the manager. A lot of international funds started up in the mid-'90s, but there was a shortage of managers and analysts with that kind of experience. In addition, since fund managers depend on information, organizations with experienced people stationed in foreign countries enjoy an advantage because of the quality of information the managers receive.

We have listed below the different types of mutual funds you can purchase to get into the international market.

Global/World funds allow the manager to invest in both U.S. and foreign companies to get the greatest diversification and take advantage of markets anywhere in the world.

International funds invest only in companies outside the U.S. This increases currency risk, but it also increases your diversification because there's little or no overlap with your domestic funds, though some domestic funds can invest up to 25% in foreign companies.

Regional funds focus on a single geographic area, such as Europe, Asia, South America, or the Pacific Rim countries. They can be more volatile, because geographic areas tend to rise and fall together economically. When a region is really doing well, these funds shine.

Country funds invest in securities of only one country. If you know something about a country's economy and the prospects of companies there, then this is a good way to invest. But these funds are very volatile, so they work best as part of a portfolio of country funds in various parts of the world.

Emerging Market funds select from the developing countries, skipping most of Europe, Japan, and other mature economies. This is the best way to participate in the huge potential of these young economies, but all the risks we looked at in the last section are heavily involved here. This is an aggressive style of investing, and you want your fund manager and fund company to be long-time players in these markets.

Sector funds invest in a single industry, but buy the companies with the most potential in the business anywhere in the world. Again, if you know something about the industry, especially if it's one in which you work, it will increase the comfort level in these funds.

Closed-end funds have long been involved in international investing. They focus primarily on a single country, region, or sector.

WEBS (World Equity Benchmark Shares) are index funds that track the performance of a specific country's major equity market index. There are currently 17 WEBS that trade on the American Stock Exchange (AMEX) where they are listed as WEBS, by country. As with single-country funds, they are volatile.

ADRs (American Depositary Receipts) are receipts for shares of foreign companies. The actual shares are held in deposit by a U.S. bank. The ADRs trade on the NYSE, AMEX, or NASDAQ markets just like shares of stocks. There are over 500 ADRs available for major foreign companies and they trade at U.S. dollar prices. The companies are required to meet U.S. accounting and reporting standards, but it isn't as easy to get timely information on many foreign companies as it is for most U.S. companies. The prices of ADRs reflect the values of the underlying stocks on their native exchanges, with the fluctuations in the currency exchange rates factored in daily by the market.

So, you have a lot of choices here. What do we recommend? Our preference from among all of these choices is a good, open-end international mutual fund that will give you diversification and an exposure to the rest of the world's economies. You can buy or sell them with a phone call every market business day. And you've got a world of choices. According to Morningstar, there are over 1,300 non-U.S. mutual funds available to the investor.

The expenses for foreign mutual funds are usually higher than for domestic stock funds, due to the higher costs of research, trading, and other operational expenses. Expense ratios (not including 12b-1 fees) average 1.85% annually. Both load funds and no-load funds are available.

Our six-pack of funds in Chapter 16 included one foreign fund. For larger portfolios, we would suggest a maximum of three funds, unless you decide to focus on specific countries and regions. Find three funds that should provide diversification: one that invests in large companies in developed markets, one that invests in small companies in developed markets, and one that invests in emerging markets—if your stomach can take the volatility.

Chapter 18 | Real Estate

Real Estate as an Investment

We aren't talking real estate as your primary residence or vacation property here. This is about owning it as a means to an end. It's a way to make money to improve your lifestyle, not to be part of it, like your home. It gives you a chance for investment growth, cash coming in as rent, and an investment you can really see and touch. Real estate ownership means *risk*, but it also means *opportunity*.

We're only going to brush the surface here. If you decide to invest in real estate do your homework. In order to figure out if it's right for you, we'll explore the seven questions on whether real estate is for you.

✔ How much time do you have?

✔ Where do you want to own it?

✔ How much money do you need?

✔ How much leverage should you use?

✔ What type of real estate do you want?

✔ How much liquidity do you need?

✔ How much money can you make?

The most important question is how much time do you want to put into it. Is it going to be a part-time hobby or is it going to be your own career? We ask this because, to use an old adage, "Time is money." If you're going to be doing this, then you have to figure out how much time it's taking up and what's the "opportunity cost." Are you giving up money you could earn elsewhere? Is it taking time away from your personal life?

> *More money has been made in real estate than in all industrial investments combined.*
> *—Andrew Carnegie*

Where do you want to own this real estate? Don't commit the first mistake of real estate, which is to buy property that's not close by. Long distance ownership means you can't keep an eye on it, so if there's a problem you've got to take a ton of time to rush somewhere to fix the toilet. Keep it local!

How much money you need is a big deal. Forget the "No Money Down" real estate games. If you want to buy investment property, you're usually going to have to put more money down than you did for your home so the bank will finance it. You'll probably have to pay higher interest as well. So assume that 20% down is going to be the entrance fee.

Leverage is key when it comes to doing very well or very poorly with your real estate portfolio. Leverage is just using OPM or other people's money, usually a bank's. Buying real estate with 20% down immediately makes the bank your 80% partner. You get the cash flow after you make the mortgage payment to your partner and all the appreciation over the years. In good times there's nothing better than maxing out on the leverage. The problem comes in tough times when you can't rent the properties and you can't pay the mortgage. So when you're using the bank's money, then put a financial cushion in your planning to help you ride out the tough times.

The type of real estate is also important to figure out and it determines the kinds of people you're going to be dealing with. First of all, realize that every tenant by definition is going to be a pain. Basically you've got residential single family, apartment buildings, office space, industrial space, and retail properties to choose from.

Liquidity is pretty important if you need to get your money out in a hurry for any reason. The best way is to just take out a loan against the property to take care of your liquidity needs, but that assumes you have enough equity in it. If you don't have much built up in the property, then you're going to end up in a pickle. Liquidity is a big obstacle in real estate, so don't even think about these kinds of investments if that's a concern. In good times this is no problem, but in bad times, it's a disaster.

Last but by no means least is how much money you can make. There are two ways to make money in real estate: from rental income and through property appreciation. You need to do a lot of calculating before you fork over the cash. If you're looking at just the cash flow, then compare the real estate investment's cash flow to bonds or REITs on the stock market. If the property isn't competitive with these, then why bother? Also, if you don't think you can beat the return of stocks over the last 50 years, about a 12% annual return, why bother with the headaches?

To get a handle on this comparison, figure out your return on equity (ROE) very much like you would on a company whose stock you were considering. Just take the equity you have which is your down payment if you're just buying it and do a guess of the property appreciation and the net cash flow after all expenses and mortgage payment. Don't forget to tack on the upkeep, repairs, taxes, and loss of rent if you're repairing it or can't rent it. Historically, real estate in general has appreciated over long periods of time at around the level of inflation or better. But it depends on the type of property, where it is and whether the purchase price was reasonable or not.

If you put down $20,000 on a $100,000 property, your equity would be $20,000. If the property appreciates at 4% a year that's $4,000. If you just break even on the income and expenses with not a dime left over for cash flow, you would still be earning 20% a year ROE ($4,000 divided by $20,000). Twenty percent per year is not a bad investment return by any standards. Just be sure to guess low on your appreciation and high on maintenance, repairs and unexpected expenses. Then factor the tax benefits back in, even though you have to pay taxes on your depreciation later. Take a look at Figure 18-1 to see how it's done.

Purchase price of property	$100,000	
Less down payment	20,000	
Mortgage loan	80,000	@ 8% interest for 20 years

Rental income @ $1,000/month		$12,000
Less:		
Expenses:		
Mortgage @ $669.15/mo.	$8,029.80	
Real estate tax	1,400.00	
Maintenance and repairs	1,000.00	
Insurance	650.00	
Professional fees	500.00	
1 month vacancy	1,000.00	
Total expenses:		$12,579.80
Net cash flow:		($579.80)
Negative flow		

Depreciation for 29 years on building only ($58,000)		$2,000.00
Plus:		
Negative cash flow as a loss for the year:		$579.80
Tax deduction:		$2,579.80

In a 28% tax bracket, you save $722.34 in federal taxes on other income, which creates after-tax cash flow of **+$142.54** .

FIGURE 18-1. SIMPLIFIED CASH FLOW ANALYSIS FOR A REAL ESTATE INVESTMENT

Depreciation is a critical factor in real estate investing. While you own the property, you are allowed to deduct depreciation on your tax return based on a schedule the IRS provides. But when you sell the property, the full amount of depreciation you took over the years is deducted from your tax basis, the cost of the property plus any improvements. The difference is your capital gain, and it can be quite a bit more than you think after many years of depreciation. That's the figure you owe taxes on, and the tax rate may be 25% or more on some of the gain.

There are a couple of good books that can help you crunch the numbers, *Investment Analysis for Real Estate Decisions* by Gaylon Greer and *Real Numbers: Analyzing Income Properties for a Profitable Investment* by Joseph Sinclair. Two other books for the beginner are

Getting Started in Real Estate Investing by Michael Thomsett and Jean Thomsett and *Keys to Investing Real Estate* by Jack Friedman. Check out **www.miningco.com** for help also.

Real Estate as a Business

In theory, real estate looks like a pretty simple business. All you have to do is buy a good property cheap, don't borrow too much, get and keep good tenants, charge fair rents, keep the place in good repair, and let the appreciation of the property just keep chugging 'til you cash in. Really, how tough is it to make money with the cruising down Main Street strategy? The answer is, "real tough," if you don't have what it takes. What it takes is a good team of professionals to help, an understanding of the long-term nature of real estate economic cycles, a discipline to study the numbers, and the ability to sniff out good and bad tenants. Above all, it's a business, not just an investment. If you can handle all that then let the games begin.

The best way to figure out if real estate investing is for you is to go out and find at least five people who have done it. Try to find some that are successful and some who tanked. Like anything else in the world, the more you like what you're doing, the better you'll be at it. So when you talk to people, ask them to paint a profile of the people who are successful and see if it sounds like your personality. Talk to at least five people before you plunk a nickel down to start anything.

One of the best ways to start is to be there all the time to watch over things and buy a duplex. This way you'll have your tenants constantly in sight and you can get a taste of the paperwork and tax info that's necessary to own an investment property.

Real estate investing doesn't usually produce a positive cash flow in the early years. You're building up equity while saving taxes on the depreciation deduction each year. Your depreciation deduction will reduce your tax basis in the property when you sell it. Meanwhile, you're compounding your gain from appreciation in the value of the property on a tax-deferred basis. The trick is the same as with investing-buy low, sell high, and think long term.

A good rule of thumb is not to pay more than five to seven times gross annual cash flow for the property, depending on whether interest rates are relatively high or low. If you can't make the numbers work, then don't buy that property. These numbers, your cash flow, are the lifeblood of the business, any business. Run them out for five years into the future (a pro forma cash flow projection which the bank may want, too) and let your accountant or a knowledgeable real estate pro-

fessional look them over for you. If you have to keep dipping into other money each year to cover negative cash flow, you might wish you had kept your money in the bank.

Don't buy in a hot market when the economy is strong and rents and prices are climbing monthly. Wait until times are a little tougher. And make sure you don't have to sell when the market is slow. Too many amateur real estate investors get financially ruined every real estate cycle because they bought when the market was hot and "could only go up." When it went down, they were forced to sell at the bottom or they lost the property to the bank.

You've got to put a team together to get this thing off the ground as well. You need to get a good banker or mortgage broker to get the financing when you need it. Next, find a good accountant to get you through the minefields of tax implications and to help you with all the records you need to keep tabs on. A good attorney is essential to try and insulate yourself from potential liabilities and to help get rid of nasty tenants who can make this whole real estate stuff too frustrating to deal with regardless of the rewards. You also need an insurance agent to make sure you cover all the potential losses and liabilities that can pop up.

Finally, and maybe most importantly, you need to be real handy yourself or have a team of contractors that can get things done when it comes to taking care of the property itself. Without them, you lose precious rental income as you wait for repairs. You also want to keep things in decent shape so you won't have all those big expenses for massive renovations. Remember what Ben Franklin said, "A stitch in time saves nine." A contractor who's also a certified property inspector can be a valuable addition to your team right from the beginning. At any rate, you need a thorough inspection before you commit to any property.

All these people on your team expect to be paid so make sure you factor their expenses into your number crunching early on. Most will be recurring expenses, not just one-time fees like closing costs. We suggest that you don't cut corners with any of these; they're all in that "pay me now or pay me later category."

The Risks and Rewards

Real estate is the best example of a two-edged sword. If done with a little caution, it's a marvelous vehicle for wealth building. When done to excess, it'll kill you. The excess is called leverage. Leverage is the money you're borrowing on the value of your properties. If you can balance the borrowing game and be able to withstand some economic turbulence, then real estate may do the trick for you.

If you borrow too much, too fast and it's late in an economic expansion, then you're committing financial suicide. It's not at all uncommon and quite frankly, it's easy to do. It's done in virtually every economic cycle. You start small, and a good economy allows you to make more and more money. But as you make more, you need to borrow more to expand. If you're doing well, the bankers will line up to lend you the money. Then, when the economic tide turns, your credit can get shut off because the banks get scared, and you're saddled with debts without the expanding revenue to pay for things and … pooooof! You're busted. So the simple answer to leverage is to do it gradually and with a lot of care.

Over-leveraging brings on the most common symptom, which is declining cash flow. When you're paying so much money in interest payments it's tough to generate cash to expand into more properties or to try and pay yourself to make ends meet. That means that you need to have a cash stash somewhere. This stash will get you through the unexpected repairs, the months when you can't rent the place, or the lack of income if you get a tenant who can't pay the rent. So try to get to a point where you can have a stash of three to six months of expenses or 1% to 2% of the market value of the properties. If you're just getting going, then get used to feeling poor when it comes to real estate, because it takes a while to build up the cash flow.

Figure 18-2 illustrates the effect of leverage at two levels on your cash flow and return on investment, depending upon how much leverage you use. You can see the tradeoff clearly with the ROI. With only 10% down, you get a great ROI but a negative cash flow as long as everything goes well. If not, you get into trouble quickly. On the other hand, with 50% down you have a positive cash flow but your ROI is about the same as the stock market over the last 40 years but a lot more trouble for you as a landlord. Both examples assume you really get a 2% per year appreciation in the value of the property, which may not be the case for your property.

These figures are hypothetical and don't necessarily represent a realistic picture. You'll need to run numbers like these based on all the variables before you invest in a property to see how the results come out at different levels of borrowing. Your tax bracket also affects the numbers, bot for deductions and any gains in the future.

In the example shown in Figure 18-2, you would get a bigger return on investment (ROI) with the higher leverage, but a negative cash flow and a higher risk if something were to go wrong. The projected appreciation of 2% annually in line 9 is included in your annual ROI. But if you don't realize that kind of value when you sell the property many years in the future, your ROI will suffer. These are some of the reasons why you need to consult with professionals familiar with real estate cash flows and taxation before you buy anything.

And if you decide to invest in real estate, always buy quality stuff. If it's run-down in a lousy part of town it may do OK in a good market but get really trashed when times get tough. This strategy is sometimes what you hear when people talk about the "No Money Down" schemes. The odds aren't good that you'll be able to get a nice proper-

Using expenses and other figures from Figure 18-1	Option A: Borrow $50,000 @ 8% for 20 yrs	Option B: Borrow $90,000 @ 8% for 20 yrs
1. **Mortgage payment per year** (12 payments)	$5,022.00	9,039.60
2. **Net pre-tax cash flow**	2,428.00	−1,589.00
3. **Less annual depreciation**	− 2,000.00	−2,000.00
4. **Taxable gain or loss** (2 − 3)	428.00	−3,589.60
5. **Tax effect at 28% - tax savings is** + (.28 × 4)	−120.00	+1,005.09
6. **Net after-tax gain or loss** (4 − 5)	308.00	− 2,584.51
7. **Add back depreciation** (non-cash charge)	2,000.00	2,000.00
8. **Net cash flow** (6 + 7)	2,308.00	−584.51
9. **Add first-year projected appreciation** (2%)	2,000.00	2,000.00
10. **Total net return year 1** (8 + 9)	4,308.00	1415.49
11. **Original investment** (down payment)	50,000.00	10,000.00
12. **Return on investment (ROI)** (10 ÷ 11)	**8.6%**	**14.2%**

FIGURE 18-2. EFFECT OF LEVERAGE ON A REAL ESTATE INVESTMENT

ty without a nickel of your own funds. Also keep in mind that a "No Money Down" strategy means 100% leverage! You just have a longer rope to hang yourself with. Quality properties bought at a reasonable price will hold their value better when times get tough.

A different kind of problem for real estate investors is that it's really hard for them to take advantage of their years of hard work. Many of the people we talk to feel poor because they don't have a lot of cash to do what they want. Yet if you look at their net worth they're doing terrific and may even be millionaires. The problem is that you can't spend real estate equity. Long-time real estate investors often

> No money down doesn't mean free. It just means you owe 100% of the selling price to someone else.

have extremely undiversified portfolios. They know real estate, they like real estate, and real estate has done well for them. But this is a lopsided, unhealthy portfolio.

Another thing that can throw real estate investors for a loop are tax law changes that upset the rules of the game enough to cause a real estate market recession. We saw how devastating a tax law can be when the real estate laws changed in 1986 making it impossible for many investors to get the tax breaks that were factored into their calculations. The real estate market took it on the chin and it was years before it came back. Congress loves tinkering with the tax laws, so there's no telling what they'll do in the future.

A slowing economy can certainly make it harder because, if you bought real estate at the top, it will take years to get your money back. Real estate cycles are even longer than the three- to five-year cycles that we see in stocks. That means that unless you want to sell and take a loss, you've got to hold on to the properties. If things get so bad that people have to move out of the area to find jobs, then it becomes tougher to rent your property. Personal bankruptcy can be the only way out for over-leveraged real estate investors when the economy is down for a few years.

The bottom line is that real estate can be a decent investment when done properly. You don't have to be a rocket scientist to make money here if you're disciplined, patient, and don't borrow more than you or the property can handle safely. But it definitely is not for everybody!

The Easy Way: REITs

Real Estate Investment Trusts (REITs) are the way to invest in real estate without getting your hands dirty or asking the bank for a loan. They are publicly traded businesses that invest in commercial real estate either directly or indirectly. Since 1990, many private real estate partnerships have become public REITs. They invest in a portfolio of one of the following: Shopping malls, office buildings, hotel chains, apartment buildings, industrial parks and fast food outlets, golf courses and even prisons. While each REIT focuses on one part of the real estate market, they are usually diversified geographically across the country.

Over time, commercial real estate has shown total returns competitive with the S&P 500. REIT shares track the real estate market, not the stock market, so they're a good way to diversify a portfolio away from stocks without giving up a chance to grow your money. In the last fifteen years the volatility has actually been much less than the S&P 500 (a beta of 0.60 where 1.0 is the same volatility as the market) and their returns have correlated most closely to small-cap stocks.

Equity REITs own and operate income-producing properties and earn rents plus appreciation. Mortgage REITs invest in the mortgages for commercial real estate and they provide the leverage much like a bank does and earn interest. Both pay shareowners dividends that range from about 5% to as much as 9%. REITs are required to pay out 95% of their earnings as dividends so they aren't taxed on them.

Operating profit isn't the main way to keep score in REITs. The yardstick used here is "Funds From Operations," known as FFO. This is net income plus depreciation less the gains from the sale of property or securities. You want to invest in conservative REITs with a price-to-FFO of under 14 (the lower the better). Look for a 6% to 8% annual dividend and a debt ratio of less than 50% ($5.00 of debt to $10.00 of market cap) to keep the leverage in a reasonable range. Another way to view the opportunities is to compare the dividend returns or yield to the current Treasury bond rates. Historically REITs have paid 110% of Treasuries. So if a Treasury is paying 7% then a REIT should be paying 7.7%. If this spread widens then REITs are a good deal. If the spread narrows then stick to the Treasuries.

Although there are several hundred REITs available, it's easier to invest in a wide variety of REITs through a mutual fund that invests primarily in these types of companies. Let the fund manager do the number crunching on the specific REITs and their real estate or mortgage portfolios. Either way, putting 5% to 10% of your equity allocation in REITs is a healthy way to diversify and invest in real estate without all the headaches. For more help on REITs check out *Real Estate Investment Trusts: Structure, Analysis and Strategy* by Richard Garrigan and John Parsons or check out **www.realtystocks.com**.

Chapter 19 | Retirement Plans

What Are Retirement Plans?

Retirement plans are various systematic savings and investment opportunities set up by the government to help you accumulate enough money to have a financially secure retirement. Some of them are set up for those who work for a company and others are for those who want to do it themselves or are self-employed.

401(k) Retirement Plans

So what exactly is a 401(k) plan? Well, for starters, the name comes from the IRS code. If you go to section 401 and then look for paragraph (k), you'll find the regulations governing this retirement plan.

But the code will not tell you the most important thing to know about 401(k) plans. They are not created equal. Sure, they're basically the same in format, but that's where the similarity ends. There are good plans and there are mediocre plans. But even a mediocre plan is better than none at all.

In a nutshell, a 401(k) plan is a defined contribution plan set up by the employer that permits an employee to contribute to a self-directed pension plan and allows the money contributed to compound tax-deferred until funds are withdrawn. Let's examine that nutshell. At the heart of it is a pension plan. But we need to make a distinction here.

> *The man who saves money nowadays isn't a miser, he's a wizard.*

Traditionally, companies have provided pension plans that promise an end result, such as guaranteeing you a percentage of your base salary for your lifetime upon 30 years of service to the company. That type of pension plan is called a *defined benefit* plan, because it specifies the benefit that employees would get out of the plan.

Now, however, many employers are forgoing defined benefit plans. Instead, they're setting up 401(k) plans because, in the long run, it's cheaper for them. A 401(k) plan, as we mentioned in our nutshell, is a *defined contribution* plan. A defined contribution plan is one that defines only what's going into the plan and does not promise any benefits. With a defined contribution plan, you, not your employer, are responsible for making the contributions to your retirement plan. Your employer may or may not match your contributions.

How It Works

The contribution rate is simply the amount of money you're allowed to contribute in a calendar year. For 2001 it is usually 15% or $10,500, whichever is less. That's what the rules state, but your company may not allow you to contribute the full 15%. You may be limited to 10% or 12% of your salary or they could allow you to contribute more like 16, 17 or 18%. The tax law changes in 2001 has increased the amount you will be able to contribute to your 401(k). Starting in 2002 you will be able to contribute $11,000, and the amount will increase each year till it reaches $15,000 in 2006 and then it will indexed to inflation.

A good thing about 401(k) plans is that the Department of Labor and the IRS oversee them. Congress mandated special non-discrimination regulations for 401(k) plans, out of a concern that workers earning less might not contribute to these plans. It set up a line of differentiation—$85,000. If you're earning more than $85,000, Congress considers you to be a "highly compensated employee" (HCE). If you're earning less than that figure, you're in the other category, a "non-highly compensated employee" (NHCE). To encourage NHCEs to participate in 401(k) plans, Congress created formulas to limit contributions to 401(k) plans by HCEs if participation by NHCEs is below a certain level.

The formulas that are used to figure out whether a company is in compliance with the non-discrimination rules are complicated and a pain in the butt for employers. But they serve as an incentive for employers to encourage non-highly compensated employees to participate in the 401(k) plans, which is what Congress intended. And employers have devised ways to stimulate participation.

Now, we said you would normally be able to contribute no more than 15% of your salary or $10,500. But the law sets a higher limit on contributions by you and your employer combined—$35,000 or 25% of your salary, whichever is less (in 2002 this number will increase to $40,000). That allows room for your employer to match your contribution, which is a great incentive to get more NHCEs to participate. It's also an excellent way to reward employees: a good 401(k) plan will attract and keep employees.

But that's up to your employer to decide. The typical match is between 3% and 6%, usually from 50 cents on the dollar to a dollar-for-dollar match up to 6%.

As of 1999, if an employer guarantees to contribute at a 3% contribution rate, this allows the employer to get around the non-discrimination rules, which means no more testing, and all employees are able to take full advantage of the 401(k) plan.

Your employer is responsible for setting up and maintaining the 401(k) plan. It typically is in the form of a salary reduction agreement, with you contributing pre-tax money to your individual account. Your employer will choose the plan provider. It may be a large mutual fund company with many choices and features, such as daily telephone exchanges or on-line access to your account. Each of these features increases the cost of the plan, so some employers may be a bit tighter with their money and offer something very basic, the plain vanilla variety.

More Rules and Regulations

Let's review some of the other standard regulations. Companies can make you wait up to one year before you can join the plan. This keeps the administrative costs down, but you lose the ability to accumulate retirement assets during that period. One year out of a retirement plan at age 30 for an employee earning $30,000 and contributing 10% with a 3% company match could mean $110,000 less in her nest egg at age 65.

You can't access your account until you reach age 59½ or you pay a 10% penalty. There are special rules if you retire between ages 55 and 59½ that allow you to get at your money without a penalty. However, you can borrow from your account—if the individual plan agreement allows loans. You can borrow one-half of the amount in your account, up to $50,000, and you must repay the loan within five years. If you use the loan to purchase a home, your plan may allow longer than five years to pay it back. If you separate from your employment for some reason (you quit or get terminated), the full amount left on the loan may be due and payable within 60 days or less. If you cannot pay it back, it is then considered a distribution, so you owe taxes and a 10% penalty. So if you're planning to borrow, be sure you have the ability to pay it back. Upon termination of employment, you have to decide what you want to do with you account. You have four choices:

✔ Leave it with your ex-employer. If you have more than $5,000 in your account, the employer must allow you to leave it.

✔ Roll over the amount in the account into a rollover IRA.

✔ Transfer the account directly to a 401(k) account with your new employer, if the new plan allows transfers. When making transfers, be sure that you do not take possession of the money, for the IRS may construe this as a distribution and you will owe taxes and possibly the 10% penalty. The transfers should be made from trustee to trustee (the people who administer the plans).

✔ Take the money, pay the taxes and penalty.

As of 2002 there will be two more alternatives available. You will be allowed to transfer your 401(k) money into a 403(b) plan or a 457 plan when changing jobs if your new employer offers one of these plans. If your employer had a policy of mandatory cash out for accounts under $5,000 they will be required to directly transfer the money into an IRA for you. The reason for this new regulation is that too many employees were taking the funds out of the 401(k) upon leaving their jobs, paying the 10% penalty and taxes and spending the money.

All good things must come to an end. The law requires that you start taking the money out of your 401(k) when you reach age 70½. And you've got to take out at least a certain amount every year: minimum required distributions are based on life expectancy using IRS tables. The distributions are taxed as ordinary income.

You can take a lump sum distribution. If you were born before January 1, 1936, you may be eligible to use the 10-year forward averaging method for calculating taxes on the lump sum. This method can only be used once. Your employer is required to withhold 20% of the amount for taxes unless you do a direct rollover transfer.

Your employer is supposed to make available to you the Summary Plan Description (SPD), a document that describes all of the ins and outs of your particular plan. So ask for a copy if you didn't get one when you signed up.

For more information on 401(k) plans, pick up a copy of *The Complete Idiot's Guide to 401(k) Plans* co-authored by Dee Lee.

Our advice is to make good use of your 401(k). If you can maximize your contributions, go for it. A defined contribution plan is the best tool available for saving for retirement.

Another major change the new tax law made for 401(k) plans is that it added a catch-up provision. If you have not put away the maximum amount over the years into your 401(k) pan and are 50 years old, you may increase your maximum contribution for 2002 by $1,000. This amount will increase $1,000 each year until it is $5,000 in the year 2006. Catch-up amounts then will be indexed for inflation in $500 increments. If you can afford to take advantage of this new provision do so. A good website for help is **www.mpower.com**.

403(b) Retirement Plans

The most common type of tax-deferred investment available to teachers and employees who work for nonprofit organizations such as hospitals is the 403(b) plan. This investment is sometimes referred to as a TSA (tax-sheltered annuity) or a TDA (tax-deferred annuity). The name of the plan comes (you guessed it) from section 403 of the IRS code, paragraph (b).

Employees can contribute pre-tax salary dollars to save for retirement. The 403(b) contribution limit for the employee is 20% or $10,500, whichever is less. Employee and employer cannot contribute together more than 25% or $30,000, whichever is less. Now in 2002 this will change also and will follow the 401(k) contribution levels.

But here's a difference between the 401(k) and 403(b): the employer does not set up the 403(b) plan for the employee. It's an arrangement between the employee and the 403(b) provider, usually an insurance company: the employer agrees to withhold the contributions for the employee and forward them to the provider. There's no one minding the store here, for there's not much government regulation in the 403(b) arena.

Employees often believe they have only the one or two choices that are on the employer's preferred list. Participants do have choices, but school districts or hospitals often make it very difficult or even impossible for them to use another source. If you're working for an organization with 403(b) arrangements, petition your employer to make available mutual funds through a fund family such as T Rowe Price or Fidelity.

The money in the plan compounds tax-deferred. The price you pay for this benefit is that you can't get at the money until you reach age 59½ or you pay a 10% penalty. If you leave your job, you should be able to roll your 403(b) into an IRA. And as of 2002 you will have the ability to roll the your account into a 401(k) or 457 plan if that is what your new employer offers. You've got to start withdrawing money from the plan when you reach the magical age 70½.

There has always been a catch-up provision that allows people who have not taken full advantage of their 403(b) plan to actually put more money pre-tax into their account as. they got close to retirement. These IRS rules are very complicated, so we suggest you get some help figuring them out. A good place to begin is the IRS. Call 800-829-3676 and request publication 571, "Tax-Sheltered Annuity Programs for Employees of Public Schools and Certain Tax-Exempt Organizations." Or check it out online at **www.irs.ustreas.gov**. Starting in 2002 there will be an additional catch-up provision available for 403(b) participants over 50. The first year you will be able to increase your maximum contribution by $1,000 and it will increase each year $1,000 until it is $5,000 in 2006. Then the annual increases will then be indexed to inflation.

As we mentioned, you can invest your 403(b) account money almost anywhere. Thanks to an IRS ruling in 1990, participants in a 403(b) can transfer out of their plan into mutual funds or insurance company annuities of their choice. The choices do not have to be on your employer's list of preferred providers and you don't have to change jobs to be able to transfer account money. You can transfer only accumulated savings, and you may be liable for surrender charges if you want to transfer everything out of an annuity you currently hold. (Typically surrender charges start at 7% and could last 7 years, maybe even longer.)

Just transfer your funds to a 403(b)(7) custodial account at a mutual fund or brokerage firm. Call the firm of your choice and ask for the forms you need to fill out; the firm will handle the transfer for you. You may have to educate the plan administrator that you have a legal right to transfer your funds, but it's worth the effort if you're unhappy with your current choices. Also, most annuities have a "penalty-free withdrawal" clause that allows you to move 10% of the balance each year without incurring surrender charges. But beware: we have found some annuities in 403(b) plans that forbid transfers and others that make getting your money out extremely difficult. Two good websites for help are: **www.403bwise.com** and **www.mpower.com**.

457 Retirement Plans

457 plans are non-qualified, deferred compensation plans established by state, county, or town governments for employees. For most employees, the program is voluntary. The rules governing 457 plans were developed based on non-qualified plan concepts. These plans are subject to different and less stringent regulations than are qualified plans.

An employee may elect to defer annually $8,500 or 25% of gross compensation in 2001, whichever is less except as permitted under a limited "catch-up" provision. The plan may allow a participant who is within three taxable years of normal retirement age to defer, for one or more years, $15,000 or the sum of the regular eligible plan limitations for the year (again, whichever is less) and so much of the maximum deferrals for prior years as the participant has not yet used. Got all that? This is complicated stuff. And the regulations are all changing. The tax law of 2001 leveled the playing field among retirement plans and in 2002 the amount an employee can contribute to a 457 plan is $11,000 and it will increase to $15,000 by 2006 and yes there will be an additional catch-up provision allowed such as those in the 401(k) plans.

Usually there's just one provider for state employees in 457 plans. And these plans can look very different from state to state. Money in the plan compounds tax-deferred until the participant retires. For anyone retiring in 2001, the assets in their account can be paid out or made available to a participant at any age, if he or she separates from service or experiences an unforeseeable emergency that is a severe financial hardship.

Upon termination of service or retirement, the participant must decide either to begin to receive benefits or to defer the start of payments to a fixed future date. If a participant takes a job with another employer that maintains an eligible 457 deferred compensation plan that accepts transfers, he or she may transfer the account directly to that employer's plan. Here we go again. The new tax law is changing the very fabric of 457 plans. Starting in 2002, you will be allowed to roll your money into an IRA, or if your new employer has a 401(k) or 403(b) you will be allowed transfer into it. But in doing so you will lose the ability to pull the money out of your 457 before age 59 ½ without a penalty. Many of the tax law changes are not yet clarified so stay tuned for an update and get some professional help before making an irrevocable decision on your retirement plan. To find out more about 457 plans, check out **www.mpower.com**. These are complicated plans, so you may need some professional help when trying to figure how to begin withdrawals.

The IRA Family

IRAs are Individual Retirement Accounts allowing you to contribute up to $2,000 annually to an account that you direct yourself. Congress made IRAs available because legislators recognized the need to help individuals increase their personal retirement savings. And for over 20 years that was all you were allowed to contribute. Changes within the tax law will allow you to contribute $3,000 annually for the years 2002-2004, $4,000 for 2005-2007 and $5,000 for 2008-2009 and then indexed for inflation. Also beginning in 2002 if you are 50 years old or older you can make catch-up contributions to your IRA. For the years 2002-2005 you can add an additional $500 to your IRA and after 2006 you can add an additional $1,000.

There are four types of IRAs now available, which we'll outline here: traditional, spousal, Roth, and nondeductible. IRAs are deductible only if they meet certain conditions.

All IRAs allow for tax-deferred compounding of your money. And with all of them you will be assessed a 10% penalty if you take the money out before age 59½, unless you either meet some hardship rules, become disabled, die, or receive distributions from your IRA that are part of a series of substantially equal payments made over your life time. Withdrawals from most IRAs must start by April 1 of the calendar year in which you reach 70½. The only exception to this rule is the Roth IRAs.

IRAs may be your only retirement savings tool or they may be a way to enhance your plans at work. Call the IRS at 800-829-3767 and ask for publication 590, which is all about IRAs, or visit the IRS Web site, **www.irs.ustreas.gov**.

Traditional IRAs

Let's talk about traditional IRAs first. If you or your spouse are not an active participant in an employer-sponsored retirement plan and you have earned income of at least $2,000, you can make a tax-deductible contribution of $2,000 to your IRA (remember this will increase to $3,000 in 2002). You also can't be older than age 70½ during the year.

For 2001, if you or your spouse are an active participant in an employer-sponsored retirement plan and you want to contribute more to your retirement savings, you can use a deductible IRA. But there's a limit for the maximum deduction of $2,000, based on adjusted gross income (AGI): for married taxpayers filing jointly it's $53,000 and for single taxpayers it's $33,000. But that limit is not black-and-white; there's a phaseout range. For married taxpayers filing jointly, the limit is phased out between $53,000 and $63,000 of AGI; for single taxpayers the limit is phased out between $33,000 and $43,000 of AGI. The limits and phaseout ranges are scheduled to increase each year until 2007. If you want to plan ahead, we can tell you that for the year 2007 the ranges will be $52,000 to $62,000 (single) and $80,000 to $100,000 (married filing jointly).

An individual is not considered an active participant in an employer-sponsored plan merely because he or she is married to someone who is an active participant. It used to be that spouses were penalized. If one was an active participant, the other was also considered a participant and could not contribute to an IRA. So now if you're covered but not your spouse, he or she may make a deductible contribution to an IRA. The deductible amount is phased out for married couples with an AGI between $150,000 and $160,000.

It is now easier to get at your IRA money and not have to pay the 10% penalty in case of hardship, although you would still owe taxes on this money. There's no penalty if you become disabled or have very large medical expenses or are unemployed and use the IRA distribution to pay premiums for health insurance. The medical and dental expenses must be higher than the 7.5% floor for your deductible medical expenses. The health insurance premium exception is allowed only if you have received at least 12 weeks of unemployment compensation. We did say *hardship* rules, didn't we?

There are two other situations where an individual under age 59½ can tap his or her IRA account without paying the early withdrawal penalty. This is if the money is used to pay for post-secondary education expenses for the taxpayer, the taxpayer's spouse, or children or grand-children. And there's no penalty if the money is used to buy a first home. The lifetime limit is $10,000 to build or buy a first home that will be the principal residence of the individual, his or her spouse, or any child, grandchild, or ancestor of the individual or spouse.

Spousal IRA

A working married individual may contribute to an IRA for his or her non-working spouse. The maximum is $2,000 for 2001 and will increase to $3,000 in 2002. Their combined compensation must be at least equal to the amount contributed. The couple must file a joint tax return for the year in which they take the deduction. However, this privilege is phased out at income limits of $150,000 to $160,000.

This part of the tax code is relatively easy to understand—except for that word "non-working." Why would Congress assume that all at-home spouses are "non-working"? We wonder if our legislators could have chosen better wording, but that's our Congress.

If you are a spouse who is only working at home to take care of the hearth and children, you may want to consider a non-deductible Roth IRA instead of the deductible IRA. Read on and we explain more.

Roth IRA

The Roth IRA is the newest addition to the IRA family becoming available in 1998. Contributions to Roth IRAs are not tax-deductible. You must have earned income to contribute to a Roth and the annual maximum contribution is $2,000. As with the traditional IRA, there are income limits and phaseout ranges. The maximum contribution is phased out for single taxpayers with an AGI between $95,000 and $110,000 and for joint filers with an AGI between $150,000 and $160,000.

If you hold a Roth IRA for at least five years, your withdrawals from the account will be free of income taxes if you're at least 59½ years old or you use the money for the first-time purchase of a home ($10,000 lifetime limit) or you become disabled.

Unlike the traditional IRA, the Roth IRA allows you to continue to contribute past age 70½. Also, the distribution rules that apply to traditional IRAs do not apply to the Roth IRA. You can leave your money in the account until you die and then your heirs will be able to withdraw the proceeds over their lifetimes and not be subject to income taxes. The Roth IRA may be subject to estate taxes if your estate is very large.

Congress always needs tax revenue to support its programs, so it will allow you to convert some or all of the money you have in your current IRAs to Roth IRAs. There will be no 10% penalty, but the conversion is taxable: you will owe income taxes on the amount converted.

Here you are faced with a different income limitation. If your AGI, whether you are filing jointly or are single, not including the conversion amount, is under $100,000 you will be allowed to convert the IRA. If you are a high roller, you are out of luck.

The younger you are, the smarter it is to convert. The taxes you pay now will be small price to pay for tax-free withdrawals in the future. But if you must use proceeds from the IRA to pay the taxes on the conversion, rethink the conversion. A conversion works to your advantage if you can leave all of the IRA money intact.

The older you are, the more complicated the decision. It may not be a good idea to pay the taxes now. But if you're not going to need this money and want to leave it for your heirs, then it may make sense to convert.

There are many mutual fund companies that will be more than happy to help you figure out if a conversion is the right tax move. In fact, many of them have on-line calculators to help you make a decision on the conversion. Check out **www.troweprice.com**, **www.fidelity. com**, or **www.vanguard.com** for some help.

Nondeductible IRAs

These are the stepchildren in the IRA family. But listen up, you high rollers—we have a great idea for you.

If you don't qualify for the traditional deductible IRA or the Roth IRA because you're making too much money, you may still contribute up to $2,000 to a nondeductible IRA and that will increase to $3,000 in 2002. The earnings still compound tax-deferred and, when withdrawn from the account, only the earnings are taxed as ordinary income. Withdrawals before age 59½ are allowed without penalty if the money is used for first-time home purchases or for higher education expenses.

So why bother with this IRA? Because nondeductible IRAs can be converted to Roth IRAs! If you have an income that fluctuates, there may be years when it's under the $100,000 current limitation for Roth conversions and then you'll be able to convert to a Roth IRA. Also Congress is thinking about changing the $100,000 limitation.

So why bother with the conversion? Because with a Roth IRA there are no mandatory withdrawals at any age and if you want to leave an

Age	50	55	60	65	70	75
25	$185,000	$300,000	$470,000	$740,000	$1,100,000	$1,700,000
35	$64,000	$111,000	$185,000	$300,000	$470,000	$740,000
45	$13,000	$33,000	$64,000	$111,000	$185,000	$300,000
55			$13,000	$33,000	$64,000	$111,000

asset to your kids that keeps on giving, a Roth IRA is it. So a nondeductible IRA may be the back door to getting your Roth IRA.

In the chart below, we've given you some idea as to what you can expect if you contribute to an IRA on a regular basis—$2,000 a year. We've assumed a 9% return on your investments. The earlier you start, the easier it will be, but even if you start at age 45 you can save considerable sums.

SEP-IRAs

A simplified employee pension plan (SEP) is an easy-to-administer plan for the small business owner or self-employed individuals and their employees. It has the format of an IRA and there is no IRS reporting required, which makes it a favorite among small business owners. A SEP allows you to contribute more than the $2,000 traditional IRA limit as well.

You can contribute 15% of net income or $25,500, whichever is less. The maximum amount of compensation that can be used in determining contributions is $170,000, and this limit increases to $200,000 in 2002 and then will be indexed for inflation in $5,000 increments.

SEPs are easy to set up; most mutual fund families as well as banks and brokerage houses have standard applications for you and your employees. We keep saying "employees" here because they must be included if they are least 21 years old and have received at least $450 in compensation from you. This amount too is indexed, in increments of $50.

This is probably the only drawback to a SEP, that the plan must include everyone. But for a small business, this retirement plan may be a great incentive for employees to stay.

With a SEP-IRA, the employer makes all of the contributions, usually at the end of the year when you have a handle on your profit. If you're having a down year, you can make a smaller contribution or choose not to contribute anything that year. Whatever percentage you put away for yourself, you must match for your employees based on their W-2 income. You contribute directly to the individual accounts, and the investing choices and decisions are the responsibility of each employee, and the employees are vested immediately. All of the contributions are deductible, another great plus for a small business. The only records required are to keep track of the contributions and report the deduction on your tax return.

The SEP-IRA, as we mentioned, has an IRA format. All earnings grow tax-deferred until withdrawn. Distributions are subject to income tax and, if the participant is under age 59½, there may also be a 10% penalty. Minimum distributions must start at age 70½. Unlike some employer-sponsored plans, there are no loans allowed and no provisions for hardship withdrawals. If a participant dies, the surviving spouse may roll over the SEP-IRA into his or her own IRA.

SIMPLEs

The Savings Incentive Match Plan for Employees (SIMPLE) was created in 1996 to enable small businesses to offer retirement plans for their employees without all of the hassle, paperwork, and costs of a 401(k) plan. In order to be eligible, an employer must have no more than 100 employees who have compensation of at least $5,000 and offer no other qualified retirement plan. There is no discrimination testing with SIMPLEs, so the contributions of the highly compensated employees are not limited by the contributions of the non-highly compensated employees. SIMPLEs come in two flavors, SIMPLE IRAs or SIMPLE 401(k)s.

A SIMPLE IRA allows an employee to make elective contribution of up to $6,500 annually for 2001. This amount will increase to $7,000 in 2002, $8,000 in 2003, $9,000 in 2004 and $10,000 in 2005. This amount will be indexed in future years after 2005 in $500 increments. SIMPLE IRAs require the employer to contribute to the plan on behalf of any employee who makes an elective contribution. The employer can either match the employee's contribution dollar for dollar up to 3% or use an alternate method of a flat 2% of employee compensation. If the employer is having a tough year, he or she can lower that contribution level to 1% two out of every five years, but must notify employees of the change before the end of the fiscal year.

Loans and hardship withdrawals are not allowed with SIMPLEs and there is immediate vesting of the employer's contributions. SIMPLEs must be set up October 1 of the tax year for which you're making the contributions. So you need to plan if you want to set one up.

As with all qualified plans, there's a penalty if you withdraw the funds before reaching age 59½. But with SIMPLEs, Congress aimed below the belt. Here's the kicker! The 10% penalty is increased to 25% if you make any withdrawals during the first two years you are in the plan. Congress really wants to discourage you from using your retirement money for anything other than your golden years. And you know, we don't think that's so bad.

You can also use a SIMPLE IRA if you're self-employed with no employees. A SIMPLE allows $6,500 for 2001 of salary deferral and there's no percentage limitation as there is with a SEP-IRA. So conceivably you could contribute up to $6,500 pre-tax and there could be another 3% in a company match. Although intended for businesses with employees, a SIMPLE may be a way for the self-employed to put away more than they could with an IRA or a SEP-IRA.

The other Savings Incentive Match Plan for Employees, the SIMPLE 401(k), is very similar to the SIMPLE IRA, but with a few more bells and whistles. It requires the employer to match 3%; there's no option for going below that. There's more record keeping involved and an annual report to the IRS.

Most mutual fund companies are not offering SIMPLE 401(k)s because it would duplicate the regular 401(k) plans they offer to small businesses. Also the cost of establishing a regular 401(k) has come down, so there's no real advantage in offering a SIMPLE 401(k).

Keogh Plans

A Keogh plan is another retirement plan for the self-employed, sometimes called an HR 10 plan. At one time this was the only retirement plan available for the self-employed.

Keogh plans allow the self-employed individual to contribute up to $35,000 for 2001. But there are some restrictions. These plans have reporting requirements: you must file Form 5500 with the IRS annually.

What are those restrictions? Well, to fully utilize the 25% limit, you need to set up two different plans within your Keogh plan.

The first would be a *profit-sharing* plan. Here your maximum contribution is 15% of compensation or $25,500, whichever is less. With a profit-sharing plan, you have some flexibility in the amount that you contribute each year. It will be a percentage of your profits, up to 15%. The incomes of most self-employed people fluctuate from year to year, so this is a nice feature.

The second part would be a *money-purchase* plan. Here you would designate a fixed percentage of your income to be contributed to your Keogh each year. There's no flexibility here. If you designate 10%, then 10% it will be.

You can set up either of the plans, profit-sharing or money-purchase. But to get the advantage of the 25%, you'll need both. These plans are not hard to set up and most mutual fund companies will help you set one up and help with the annual reporting.

Keogh plans require you to include employees. You may put in some restrictions, but the most you can require is that they be 21 years of age and have worked for you for one year. After that you must contribute on their behalf in the percentages that you use for your own contributions.

Contributions go into the plan pre-tax and are allowed tax-deferred compounding until you make withdrawals. The money must stay in your account until you reach age 59½ or you face a 10% early withdrawal penalty. Employees can borrow from a Keogh, but the owner/employer can not. Keogh plan distributions can be rolled into an IRA if an employee leaves or if you close your business. In case of death, a surviving spouse can roll over the proceeds into her or his IRA; this privilege is allowed only between spouses. It's mandatory that you begin taking withdrawals at age 70½, but if you continue to work and have self-employed income, you can continue to contribute to your Keogh after age 70½.

Social Security

Yes, Social Security does belong in a chapter about retirement plans. The idea behind Social Security is sound. You get workers to pay into a system during their working years and then when they retire you pay them a benefit. If they should become disabled, they'll receive benefits. If they die, benefits will be paid out to their survivors. It's a pension system at its very best. So what has gone wrong?

Congress passed the Social Security Act (SSA) in 1935. It was designed to start paying benefits at age 65. But back then, in 1935, most workers died before that age. Today people retire and then live well into their 80s—which really messes up the actuarial tables.

The Future

Social Security is a pay-as-you-go system: the dollars coming from workers supplement the reserves and are used to pay benefits to the retirees and survivors. You've read the headlines—"Social Security is going to go bankrupt." Well, not quite! By the year 2031, it will be in trouble big time. It won't be out of money; it just won't have enough to pay all of its obligations.

Why not? One of the reasons is that we have fewer workers coming into the job market; that means less money coming into the system. The other problem is the baby boomers. There are a lot of them who will be coming through the system and they will be living longer and putting greater demands on the system. There will be 76 million boomers who will turn 65 between 2011 and 2029.

The government is trying to solve this problem. There has been talk of privatizing Social Security, requiring participants to pay more into the system, making retirees wait longer to collect full Social Security benefits, and taxing all of the benefits. All we can do is wait for changes. In our opinion, Social Security will be around, but probably looking much different. Social Security and Medicare make up the largest part of our national budget, 34%. So it can't go away very easily.

There are 46 million people waiting for their checks each month from Social Security. Any way you cut it, that's a lot of people. Social Security was never intended to be the sole source of income in retirement. It was set up to be a supplemental program and a program that would not let the very poor slip through the cracks. Yet, according to the AARP, over 66% of retirees now rely on Social Security for half or more of their income.

The Present

Let's start with the basics. You get a Social Security number. That number is important, since it matches you with your account at the Social Security Administration. But there are more uses for your number. You can't take an exemption for your newborn unless she has a number. You need it to open a brokerage account, the IRS wants it all over your tax return, and so forth. A word of caution: do not give out your number just because someone asks you for it. If it's on your driver's license, request a change. Thieves can use your number to get credit cards, take out loans in your name, and play havoc with your finances.

As you work and pay taxes, you earn Social Security "credits" that count toward eligibility for Social Security benefits. You can earn a maximum of four credits each year. In 2001, you earn one credit for each $830 in earnings you have. The amount of money needed to earn one credit goes up every year. Most people need 40 credits (10 years of work) to qualify for benefits.

Social Security taxes are deducted right from your paycheck. You never get a choice in whether you want to pay or not. (It's right there, perhaps labeled as FICA—Federal Insurance Contributions Act, the law that authorized Social Security.) Social Security is broken up into two parts—Old Age, Survivors, and Dependents Insurance (OASDI) and Medicare.

Your share is 6.2% of your gross salary; your employer matches this amount. There's a salary cap for the OASDI, which for 2001 is $80,400. (This salary cap is raised each year.) For the Medicare portion of the contribution, there's no limit.

Let's take an example. If you're making $85,000, you pay $4,984.80 in Social Security taxes. (That ceiling helps a little here.) You and your employer will each pay 1.45% on your income into Medicare; since there's no income ceiling here, you would be paying Medicare taxes on the full $85,000 or $1,232.50. If you're self-employed, you must pay both the employee and employer percentages. But there's a deduction allowed for one-half the amount that's paid.

Your benefit is figured as a percentage of your earnings averaged over most of your working years. It's a complicated formula, but if you want to give it a try the SSA will send you a worksheet. However, unless you're crazy about math, we'd recommend that you just ask for a benefit estimate statement (800-772-1213 or **www.ssa.gov**). It's easier than doing it yourself. You fill out a form and return it to the SSA, which will then send you back an estimate of what your benefits will be, using today's dollars. The SSA wants to eventually have these benefit estimates available for all workers on an annual basis.

Full retirement benefits are currently payable at age 65. Reduced benefits are available as early as age 62 to anyone with enough Social Security credits.

Congress made some changes to Social Security benefits back in the '80s, in hopes of making the Social Security reserves last longer. They raised the age at which we can receive full retirement benefits, from 65 to 67, and scheduled to have this adjustment fully in place by the year 2027.

So as not to impact the planning of those close to age 65, Congress in its infinite wisdom set up a complicated phase in schedule. But let us try to explain it for you:

✔ If you were born between 1937 and 1942, you will need to add 2 months to the traditional retirement age of 65 for every year after 1937.

✔ If you were born between 1943 and 1954, you will be able to collect full Social Security benefits at age 66.

✔ If you were born between 1954 and 1960, you will need to add two months for every year after 1954 until 1960.

✔ If you were born in 1960 or later, your retirement age is 67.

Do those folks in Washington ever make anything simple? The chart at the top of next page should help.

A spouse is entitled to his or her own benefits or one-half of his or her spouse's benefits, whichever is greater. An ex-spouse is also entitled to spousal benefits, if the marriage lasted at least ten years.

Year of Birth	Age of Full Retirement Benefits
1937 or earlier	65
1938	65 and 2 months
1939	65 and 4 months
1940	65 and 6 months
1941	65 and 8 months
1942	65 and 10 months
1943 through 1954	66
1955	66 and 2 months
1956	66 and 4 months
1957	66 and 6 months
1958	66 and 8 months
1959	66 and 10 months
1960 or later	67

For 2001 the average monthly Social Security benefit is $845. For a married couple it's $1,410. Not a whole heck of a lot, is it?

So you need to be stashing the cash away for your retirement, because Social Security is not going to provide that wonderful retirement you've been daydreaming about. And we can guarantee you that if you don't start saving you'll be working forever.

A caveat: if you begin collecting benefits before your full retirement age and continue to work, you will lose some benefits if you earn more than a specific amount a year, depending on your age. For 2001, if you're under your full retirement age, you'll lose $1 for every $2 in earnings over $10,680. Ouch!

The moral of the story here is to start early in building your retirement fund, to use the retirement plans available to you, and then to consider anything you receive from Social Security as the frosting on the cake.

Chapter 20 | **Annuities**

What Are Annuities?

Annuities are packaged financial products sold by life insurance companies that offer an investment that grows tax-deferred and an insurance component that covers replacing the dollar amount you've invested. Taxes are deferred because these investments are all offered by insurance companies, which are allowed under the current tax laws to shelter the earnings of these investments.

The word "annuity" evokes a lot of things for investors in today's financial markets. For teachers and hospital workers, it's their tax-sheltered annuity contributions in their 403(b) retirement plan. (Check out Chapter 19 for more info on 403(b)s.) For some, it's a pension check every month. And some of you may have purchased or are considering purchasing an annuity as a supplemental retirement plan. In addition, some employers are now providing annuities for their employees in lieu of paying them a pension for life. So if you have an annuity or are considering purchasing an annuity, take the time to read this chapter.

An annuity is a contract with the insurance company to provide certain services, depending on the specific language in the contract. That contract involves several players:

✔ The *contract owner* is the person who makes the contract with the insurance company and puts in the money.

✔ The *annuitant* is the person who receives an income benefit from an annuity for life or for a specified period.

✔ The *beneficiary* is any person named by the contract owner to receive benefits from the annuity in case the annuitant dies during the build-up. The owner also names *contingent beneficiaries* in the event that the beneficiary dies during the build-up.

Annuities are offered by over 240 life insurance companies, although the top 50 companies control about 98% of the market. They are sold by insurance agents, stockbrokers, financial advisors, banks, and mutual fund companies, so it's easy to get information on a variety of plans to compare them. Because each plan is a little different, you have to do some research and ask questions to sort it all out before you make any commitment.

> *No amount of cash is ever petty.*

There are two basic categories—*immediate or payout* and *accumulation*. Choose between these two types according to your needs. If you need income right away, then an *immediate* or *payout* annuity fits the bill. This is the type of annuity that employers often buy for retiring employees. If you want to have the annuity grow in a tax-sheltered account until you retire, then you want an accumulation annuity.

An *immediate* or *payout* annuity is set up to make monthly payments to a person over his or her lifetime. In some cases it also covers the life of a spouse as well. You hand over a lump sum of money to the company and the annuity starts paying out immediately, as the name suggests. It's designed for someone who wants to be absolutely sure that a check is going to be in the mail for the exact same dollar amount for

> It's not making money first that's important; it's making it last.

life. So by "annuitizing" or setting up this immediate annuity, you shift the burden of investing your money to an insurance company. It's up to the company to figure out how to invest the money so it can send you your check every month. But you have given up total control of your money and have no inflation protection for those monthly checks.

An *accumulation* annuity is a deferred annuity. You don't receive payments until later. The general purpose of a deferred annuity is as an investment to accumulate money on a tax-deferred basis to supplement your income in retirement.

Your biggest choice here is what you invest in. Do you want the guaranteed option, which is called a *fixed* annuity? Or do you want to choose among mutual funds, which is the *variable* annuity? If you want an absolutely guaranteed rate, then choose a *fixed* annuity. If you want investment choices that you control, then choose a *variable* annuity.

The Fixed Annuity

When shopping for a fixed-rate annuity, there are some things you should consider. Getting the answers to these questions will make comparing contracts much easier. And *always* compare contracts.

✔ What's the rate? For how long is it locked in?

✔ What happens if the rate ever falls below the present rate?

✔ What's the rating on the company offering the annuity?

✔ What does the insurance company's portfolio invest in?

✔ Who services the contract?

✔ What's the penalty to get out if you want to move to another insurance company?

✔ What's the renewal history?

Asking these questions will put you way ahead of most consumers and the answers will tell you a lot about where your money is going and how it's coming back to you.

The rate question is the big one: you want to know what you're getting paid. Beware of enticing initial rates that impress you—until the following year. You may get a "trust me rate," which means that the insurance company will pay you whatever it wants.

Also be careful of good three- or five-year rate projections. That's because returns could be high for a few years, but then you'll have to take the "trust me rate." That's also why you want to ask the renewal history question. You'll want to see what the company has done in the past if you have to accept a rate change somewhere down the road. Most important, be very conscious of all penalties that the insurance company may impose on you.

In terms of the insurance company's portfolio, you want to make sure that it's full of "good stuff." That means keeping an eye on portfolios with a lot of junk bonds (over 20%), real estate or mortgages (over 20%), high amounts of a single security (5%), or ownership of affiliate insurance companies. In this area, you've got help. There are rating services that watch insurance companies closely. We'll look at them in a following section.

Asking about who services the contract is a big deal, too. You definitely want to know where and how to contact the complaint department when you find out things aren't turning out the way you expected them to.

Annuities are a roll of the dice for you and the insurance company. For fixed-rate annuities, the insurance company is betting that it can earn more on the premium you paid than it's going to have to pay you. And you are betting that you'll live a long life and screw up the actuarial tables so that the company has to pay out more than you paid in plus what it's earned on your premium.

The Variable Annuity

A variable annuity is a different animal altogether, totally unlike its fixed-rate sibling. You select mutual fund sub-accounts to invest your money in from a selection offered by the insurance company and managed either by the company or by one or more outside mutual fund managers.

You want a wide variety of selections in all styles and kinds, preferably from more than one company, because you're allowed to make exchanges between funds without paying taxes. Your needs may change, your time horizons become shorter, and a fund's performance may deteriorate, so you want to be able to make changes over time.

The value of a variable annuity rises and falls with the mutual funds in the sub-accounts. That's why this annuity is called *variable*. There's no guarantee that your annuity won't be worth less than you've invested in it. But a variable annuity has a thin layer of life insurance wrapped around it, sometimes referred to as the "nervous spouse clause." If the annuitant dies during the accumulation period, the beneficiary (often a spouse) is guaranteed the greater of the current market value or the total amount invested, if the market value is below this figure.

When it comes to the variable annuity choices, you have to look at the insurance company as well as the investment options it provides. You don't have to look quite as hard at the insurance company, because the assets in the mutual funds are kept absolutely separate from the insurance company itself. Be careful, though, because even variable annuities have "fixed choices" that are part of the general claims of the insurance company. So stick to the mutual fund options, which may offer bond funds and even money market funds.

When choosing the fund options, you have either multiple funds from various fund companies or a single fund family. For example, some insurance companies do none of the investing but simply put the package together. They may work with 10 or 20 mutual fund companies and offer 30 to 40 investment choices. Others allow you to invest with only one organization.

Be careful here. Usually the "brand name" fund listed in the annuity brochure is not run by the same manager as the regular mutual fund of the same name. That great mutual fund may actually be "the stepchild of the great mutual fund." The funds are probably very similar, but there will be differences. Also it's important to realize that the actual fund within the variable annuity will differ from the regular mutual fund in performance and fees. That's because the variable annuity must be held separately to keep its tax-deferred status. So it's smart to look to see if there's a big performance difference between the actual mutual fund and the fund with the same name within the variable annuity.

> *There are two ways to get rich—spend less than you make and make more than you spend.*

When choosing funds, use exactly the same discipline we spoke about in Chapter 15 on Mutual Funds. You've got to know the style of the funds, who's running them, what the long-term performance has been, and whether they fit your needs and time horizon.

Variable annuities have three layers of fees:

✔ The annual contract fee, $25 to $50.

✔ The various fees and expenses charged by the individual mutual funds, which are approximately equivalent to fees and expenses for traditional funds, depending on the type and style of the fund.

✔ The annual fee charged by the insurance company to cover the mortality benefit in case you die when the value of the account is underwater and to pay its expenses, including compensation, to the person who sold you the policy.

These insurance company expenses average 1.4% of the annuity value per year, so the total annual costs may run from around 2% to 3% or so each year. There are no-load annuities, with lower mortality and administrative expenses. The annual expenses are about 1% less a year and there are usually no penalties for withdrawing. So if you know what you want and don't need an advisor to help, then look for a no-load annuity and do your homework.

As with regular investments, you need to pay close attention to all fees and expenses because they reduce the net investment return on your money. Decide what you need in the way of benefits and advice and shop carefully so you don't overpay. If you feel you need assistance and advice, it's always worth paying something for it so you make the right choices.

Morningstar, a mutual fund rating service in Chicago, evaluates variable annuities. You can find the service online at **www.morningstar.com** or call 800-735-0700. Prices and performance figures for some are published in *Barron's*, a Dow Jones weekly financial publication, and in some Sunday newspaper financial sections. Or you can call the insurance company periodically to get the net asset value (NAV), usually with an automated 800 number.

Getting Your Money Out

The main reason investors put money into annuities is for the tax-deferral on their investment. Then they realize that it may be difficult to get their money out.

So how do you get your money out? This will depend on how much you want and how long you think you will need the money to last you. To figure out what you need for cash flow, you have to do some serious number crunching. Once you decide what you need, you can tap into an annuity in several ways.

✔ Take a lump sum and use the money any way you want.
✔ Take money out of the accumulation annuity as you need it and let the rest continue to grow tax-deferred.
✔ Start to "annuitize" it. That will provide you with an income stream of equal payments from the insurance company.

Whichever option you choose, you'll be liable for income taxes. If you choose options one or two and you're under age 59½, there's a possible 10% penalty.

Option 3, annuitization, is an alternative for those who are willing to give up control of their money to an insurance company for the promise of a regular payout. So make sure you've got a high-quality insurance company that's going to be around for as long as you are. This may mean not taking the highest dollar payment. You also have to decide if it's just going to be on a single life or, if the annuitant is married, on the joint lives of a husband and wife (co-annuitants).

The basic payout choices:

✔ *Straight life annuity* option: a fixed income stream for as long as you live.

✔ *Life annuity term certain* option: the insurance company guarantees a certain number of payments to the annuitant or, if the annuitant should die before receiving all of the payments, to the beneficiary.

✔ *Joint and survivor* option (several variations): a guaranteed income stream for two individuals.

The payment amount will vary, according to the age(s) of the annuitant(s) or the number of years selected for the payout. You may elect monthly, quarterly, semiannual, or annual payments. Each insurance company sets the amounts, based on mortality charts and its expected return on the money you've paid in as of that date. The company expects to make a profit on the deal; otherwise there wouldn't be any insurance company to guarantee the payments.

Taxes on the payout are based on a formula so that part of each payment represents your original investment and isn't taxable. The numbers here are a little tricky. For example, let's assume you're 65 years old and you annuitize $100,000 as a 20-year term certain annuity. At today's rates, you'd receive a monthly check for about $645, of which about 53% would be tax-free. The best way to figure this out is to have an insurance company run an illustration to show you the actual dollar amounts. Let them do the work for you.

We mentioned *penalties*. Here's what to expect if you buy these contracts. The owner of an annuity can usually take partial withdrawals of 10% of the original investment each year without a penalty. There will usually be back-end surrender charges for taking out more than 10% a year. That could run 5% to 10% the first year and decline by 1% a year thereafter for up to 15 years. The contract with the insurance company will spell this out and identify the penalties and time periods. Read the small print in your contract before you sign it.

For tax purposes, such a withdrawal is considered a withdrawal of earnings and is taxed at ordinary tax rates until there's nothing left except the original amount invested. Then there is a tax-free withdrawal of your original principal. That seems simple enough. But there's an exception to this: an annuity issued before August 13, 1982, where you're allowed to take your principal out first. In either case, however, you never pay taxes on the principal. Just remember that if you take the money out before you're 59½, there's that extra 10% penalty on your earnings. But, if you *annuitize* it, so you receive equal amounts each year, there's no tax penalty before age 59½.

If you have not started annuity payouts, you can move to another insurance company if you're dissatisfied. The problem is that dissatisfaction usually costs money, because the insurance companies almost always have some type of penalty if you leave before a certain period of time has passed. This exchange is covered under section 1035 of the tax code, so it's called a 1035 exchange. Carefully pick a company that better fits your needs and request forms for a *1035 exchange*. Fill them out and return them to the new company, which will contact the first company and take care of the transaction. Whatever you do, don't take the money yourself or have control of it at any time or you'll be responsible for income taxes and you may get whacked with an IRS 10% penalty if you're under age 59½.

> A gentleman farmer is one who has more stock in the bank than in the barn.

When the annuitant dies, the annuity (whatever the type) bypasses probate, but it's subject to income and estate taxes. When an accumulation annuity passes to a beneficiary other than a spouse, the income tax can be postponed for up to five years, depending on the choices available to the beneficiary. If an accumulation annuity has been deferred for many years, it can become an income tax time bomb if it passes to a non-spousal beneficiary.

How Safe Is Your Annuity?

The protection you have for your investment and your payout depends on the kind of annuity you have, whether it's fixed or variable.

The *variable* annuity is invested in mutual funds. The value fluctuates with the market values of the securities in the funds. Your mutual fund sub-accounts are protected just like regular mutual funds, because the money is not part of the insurance company's general investment money. Mutual funds are regulated by the Securities and Exchange Commission (SEC), the National Association of Securities

Dealers (NASD), and your state's security regulatory commission. You are also protected by Securities Investor Protection Corporation (SIPC) insurance against fraud and theft.

Fixed annuities are different. These are contractual obligations between you and the insurance company. Except with a few companies, your money now belongs to the company, to invest with other dollars as it chooses. The guarantee that you will receive what the company is contractually obligated to pay is based first and foremost on its financial strength and ability to pay claims. Insurance companies are required to set aside reserves to pay annuity owners, but the money is not otherwise secured. The states, not the federal government, are in charge of regulating insurance companies.

Between 1974 and 1989, 154 life insurance companies failed. They were unable to fulfill their obligations to policyholders, annuity owners, and annuitants. As it turned out, no one lost any principal, but interest wasn't paid in some cases or it was reduced and there were delays. Therefore, you want to be careful about the company you choose. Research its ratings before you sign anything and annually thereafter.

A.M. Best rates the financial soundness of insurance companies on a familiar A+ to C- scale. For a fixed-rate annuity, stick to companies rated A- or better in the most recent copy of *Best's Agents Guide to Life Insurance Companies.* Check your library or ask the person trying to sell you the policy for a copy of the rating page.

Moody's Investors Services and Standard & Poor's Corporation rate most insurance companies on their financial health and ability to pay claims. They use more letters than A.M. Best, but you want to see a Moody's rating of Aa3 or better or an S&P rating of A to AAA for assurance of current safety. Check one of these rating services each year in addition to the A.M. Best rating to keep on top of any changes. For an objective rating that you will have to pay for, contact Weiss Research at 800-289-9222 or online at **www.weissratings.com**. Weiss has a reputation for being very tough on companies that are not top quality.

Your next line of defense is the guaranty laws. Guaranty laws generally protect investors, annuitants, beneficiaries, and policyholders for up to $100,000 per contract. The money comes from a pool contributed to by the insurance companies doing business in the state.

Check with your state insurance commissioner or the National Association of Insurance Commissioners (NAIC):

National Association of Insurance Commissioners
120 W. 12th Street, Suite 1100
Kansas City, MO 64105
Phone: 816-842-3600
Web: **www.naic.org**

These laws have never been tested on a large scale, but so far they've worked reasonably well. Either your company is taken over by a healthy company (with possible adjustments to your interest rate) or you get paid from the guaranty pool. There may be some delay while everything gets worked out, even as much as five years. Some state insurance commissions and regulatory activities are better than others. If the company is licensed to do business in New York and has agreed to follow New York regulations in other states, you're in good shape. New York has the toughest regulations, but for that reason many companies refuse to do business there.

When you convert to a payout annuity or purchase an immediate annuity, you're relying on the insurance company backed by the state guaranty laws to make those payments for the entire contractual period. There's no other guarantor or federal regulations behind the promise to pay, so you've got to put your faith in the ratings. Make sure that you pick a healthy insurance company and that it stays healthy. Stick with companies that do a lot of annuity business and have been around for many years. *Big* isn't necessarily *strong*, so check out any company before you commit.

When to Use Annuities

Annuities aren't a realistic option for most individuals, even those with lots of money. We'll work through this process by elimination, identifying characteristics that make an annuity a questionable option.

Depending on age, some individuals are unable to buy an annuity. So if you're between 75 and 90 you may be out of the market. For most people under 50, an annuity isn't a good choice because there are too many things that could happen before you retire. The 10% federal penalty for taking the money out before age 59½ plus the insurance company penalty in the first five to ten years or so put too much of a financial burden on the money to make this a good investment for people under 50.

When you're over 50, what do you need to look at? First on the agenda is your tax bracket. If you're in the 15% federal tax bracket, you really don't need tax deferral. Invest all you can in tax-sheltered retirement plans such as 401(k)s and IRAs, then invest the rest in taxable accounts. You won't be in a lower tax bracket in retirement, so the costs outweigh any benefits in most cases.

If you're in the 36% or 39.6% tax brackets (the top brackets currently), the tax deferral may look great. But unless you know that you'll be in only the 15% tax bracket in retirement (and that's not very likely if you've been saving and investing some of that income for years), you could actually lose money in an annuity. That's because you can buy stocks and regular stock mutual funds and pay only a 20% federal tax on your capital gains today. Annuity income is taxed as ordinary income, plus you pay the extra fees along the way.

What if you're in the 28% or 31% brackets? Your tax rate may go down in retirement, and you end up in the 15% bracket. And you pay only 20% capital gains taxes today, so you're in the gray area where you have to look closely at your current situation and project it out 10 to 30 years into the future. Here's where financial planning pays off. You or your planner will need to project your income stream under several realistic assumptions, to see if a tax-deferred annuity fits into your plan.

Before you even consider purchasing an annuity, you should have taken full advantage of any tax-sheltered retirement plans available to you at work, as well as the new Roth IRAs. Then check to see if you have enough money invested to meet expected objectives, such as buying a new car, plus a healthy cash stash set aside for the unexpected things that happen to us. Then ask yourself this question: What proportion of the rest of my money do I want to tie up in an annuity until some point after I retire?

Part Five

How to Recognize Obstacles Along the Way

There are four major obstacles you will encounter along the way to financial success—risk, the economy, inflation, and taxes.

How much risk are you willing to take when making an investment? How much can you handle? Hopefully we'll have the answers for you as you read through this section. We'll discuss here the ups and downs that you can expect to face when investing. We point out that *volatility* and *risk* are absolutely not the same thing.

When investing, you need to understand the basic principles of our economy. Well, here's where you'll find the essentials. The world we live in is getting smaller and smaller and we'll show you why that's important to an investor. The global economy is causing things to happen much faster today than ever before, because of technology and instant communications.

Inflation over the years has had a profound effect on our economy, but what's happening now may be deflation. What's the difference? And how do inflation and *deflation* affect your investments and your buying power?

Of course, we can't write an investment book without talking about those guys in Washington who want a piece of your investing success. Uncle Sam gets involved wherever there is money, so we have some tips on what it takes to survive the mammoth IRS tax code.

Chapter 21 | Risks and Investing

What Risks Are Out There?

When it comes to risk, you have got to start with the premise that there are more risks than you'll ever be able to imagine. It could paralyze us if we imagined all the things that could hurt us right in our own homes. But we learn to live with the risks that surround us in life.

The same is true for investing. There are a lot of risks. But if we want to enjoy the rewards we've got to accept at least some of those risks. Although there are over 20 distinct investing risks we can identify, the six biggies are:

- ✔ Market
- ✔ Economic
- ✔ Company
- ✔ Inflation
- ✔ Fraud
- ✔ Emotions

Let's take a few moments to examine these six risks so you can better understand what causes them, how they can affect us, and who can help us deal with them.

Market risk is volatility in the short term. We refer to it as a "tornado warning." It tends to happen quickly and usually leaves a narrow path of destruction. Sometimes it just looks ugly for a short while but never really touches down. It results not only from economic news, but also from the flow of information, the flow of money in or out of the markets, investor psychology, earnings expectations, and reports. There are also changes in interest rates, which affect investors' earnings calculations for companies as well as the growth rate of the economy.

These factors all work together in unpredictable and often unfathomable ways to drive the market up and down over the short term. No one really knows why the market did what it did today, but that doesn't stop people from trying to guess. Over the long term, stocks tend to follow the market up.

Economic risk is when we listen to the news and read the paper and decide that the world is about to come to an end. We call it "the sky is falling" risk. Economic risk is about our budget deficit, our Gross Domestic Product (GDP), our trade balances, interest rates, industry competitiveness, and business profits. It's the vast amount of information that is so readily available today.

It's darn near impossible for most of us to ever be able to comprehend all of this stuff, not to mention how to use it to make money even if you could understand it all. We might even tuck in *political risk* in this category, because dumb political moves can disturb economies in a big way. The people who try to figure this stuff out are economists or investment strategists.

Company risk is a little easier to understand, because it deals with the issues of a specific company or industry. Perhaps the company's or industry's sales are dropping, or the top management of the company is cooking the books. When this becomes known, the stock price goes down until the problems are fixed and the earnings improve.

To get through this risk, it's best to try to understand how a business works. It takes a little research here, so you can try and figure out how cars are sold, how computers are marketed, or even how a software company is able to maintain its edge in a competitive marketplace. Fundamental analysis of the company and its products, industry, markets, financials, and management can reduce the risk of making bad investments. The industry and company stock analysts keep an eye on the specifics here.

Inflation risk is the "silent risk." That's because every day it just nibbles away at our money until we look back 20 years and remember what the cost of a car, a stamp, or a meal in a restaurant used to be.

Most people never even consider inflation in their investment decisions, but it's the most critical factor in the cost of their future lifestyles. The Consumer Price Index (CPI), which has averaged a little over 3% for this century, is a measure of inflation. If the total return of your portfolio doesn't increase fast enough to stay ahead of inflation over time, then you lose purchasing power.

Fraud risk is always lurking around the corner. It's the "There's a sucker born every minute" risk. The problem, though, is that you really don't have to be a novice investor to get taken. Some of the most creative minds and best salespeople in the world are crooks. The more money you have, the smarter they are.

It's estimated that investors lose $4 billion a year to investment fraud. Being skeptical is essential. That means checking up on companies, regulatory agencies, and advisors. If you don't know who you're doing business with, find out before investing your money. Be particularly aware of the "You've got to do it now" pitch. If it's really a good deal, it'll still be there tomorrow.

Emotional risk is one of the biggest risk investors must learn to deal with. Fear and greed are what you hear about the most. Many people, when confronted with a problem or a decision, become paralyzed. It's the "deer in the headlights" risk. They do nothing because they don't have enough information or lack the conviction to stick to a plan. At other times, they make the wrong decision based primarily on emotions. About the only guarantee we can give you when it comes to investing is this: without a plan and without the ability to keep your emotions balanced with your ability to be rational, you're setting yourself up for failure.

How Much Risk Can You Handle?

Numerous studies have shown that we are generally not averse to risks; it's just that most of us *hate losing* money more than we *like making* it. For most people, fear is generally more powerful than greed. If you can see that you're not likely to lose money over time, then you're much more likely to accept greater volatility, because your returns will also increase. The fear of losing money can be a healthy emotion. Don't ignore that fear. Just keep it under control.

As financial advisors, it's still hard for us at times to figure out how much volatility a client can deal with, especially when he or she has had no experience with the markets. We try and show a bunch of charts about markets going up and down and say that it's going to continue to happen. Most clients intellectually understand this and say, "OK, I can deal with that." Then with the first 10% correction (market downturn), amnesia and fear kick in at the same time.

> *Behold the turtle: He only makes progress when he sticks his neck out.*
> —James Bryant Conant

Ultimately, through experience, you'll discover how much volatility you can accept. The more you understand it, the easier it will be to manage your emotional responses.

A way of dealing with a downturn is to face it straight on. Avoid the sanitizing effect of percentages and instead use dollars, something real. *Percentages* are for someone else's portfolio; *dollars* are yours. (That reminds us of the story that it's a *recession* when your neighbor loses *her* job but a *depression* when you lose *yours*.)

Face the facts. Tell yourself that with a $100,000 portfolio you could lose $10,000 very quickly: in this century, 10% declines have happened about once a year. If you can handle this fire drill, then try thinking about losing $15,000 or $20,000 or even $42,000. (The market was down over 42% in 1973-1974, the worst time since WWII.) This fire drill can be a little painful, but it's good preparation. If you do well with this practice, you'll be better prepared when the markets decline.

How much volatility can you handle? The answer is a little like riding on a roller coaster. From the ground it looks fun. Even though all the people on the ride are screaming, they're still smiling. Then you get

on and your stomach gets tied up in knots. Some people like the ride and thrive on it; others wouldn't get back on if their life depended on it.

For those of you who choose to sit out the ride, you may be confusing *risk* with *volatility*. Ups and downs are a necessary part of the investing world and that's certainly not going to change. The real risk is never being able to achieve your goals in life. Stocks are the only things that are able to give you a return on your money that keeps pace with inflation over the years, even after you pay Uncle Sam.

Figure 21-1 represents the last 72 years of the stock market and shows a positive correlation between volatility (horizontal axis) and returns (vertical axis). In other words, the more volatile a type of investment relative to investments in general, the greater the returns. The wildest ride has been small company stocks, which have also yielded the highest returns. At the other end of the spectrum, the lowest volatility was with U.S. Treasury Bills, which also produced the lowest returns— only about one-fourth the rate of return as small company stocks.

The Expected Ups and Downs

When it comes to the stock market, you have to come to terms with expecting the unexpected. It's nearly impossible to figure out what the market is going to do over any span of time. It never seems to be the obvious problems; it's the things that come out of nowhere that whack the markets the hardest.

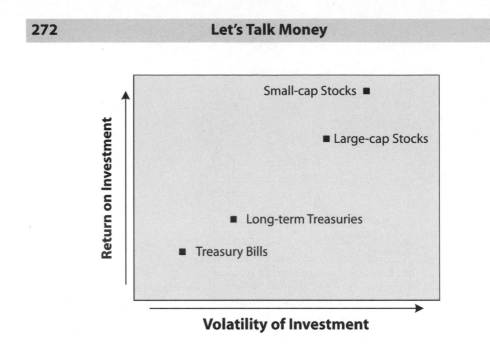

FIGURE 21-1. THE RELATION BETWEEN RETURN AND VOLATILITY

We can only try to prepare you for the "average" corrections or rates of returns. We're going to throw a bunch of numbers and charts at you in this section to give you a sense of what to expect over time from investing in the markets.

At times the market has gone down and stayed there for a long time. At other times it has just dipped and flipped back up again. In the '90s, the market has tended to have very sharp, quick drops and then to start moving up again. This might be because the flow of information is much faster with our worldwide communications systems. It may also be that we're in a great fundamental position. The U.S. is extremely competitive, our inflation rate is down, we're balancing the budget, our political system is stable, and corporations are generating steady profits.

Stocks have averaged a total return of over 10% per year this century and have outpaced fixed-income investments by better than a 2-to-1 margin. These figures tell you that if you can deal with the volatility, then the rewards are obvious. Since WWII there have been 43 years with positive market returns and only 12 with negative returns. During that time:

✔ The best year was 45.0% in 1954

✔ The worst was minus 29.7% in 1974

✔ The median was +16.5%

✔ The market went down two years in a row only once (1973-1974)

✔ The market dropped by more than 15% in any calendar year only twice

The good times in the market have far outweighed the down periods. When the markets are on a roll and the economy is healthy, stock prices can rise for years. During the last 52 years the stock market has seen four major bull markets with moves over 100% without a 20% correction. These figures represent large-cap stocks and include reinvestment of dividends to allow the return to compound.

Bull Markets

Period	Duration	% Increase	Compound Annual %
3/48 - 7/56	8 years, 5 months	478.0%	23.2%
1/58 - 12/61	4 years	104.6%	19.6%
8/82 - 5/90	7 years, 10 months	351.9%	21.5%
11/90 - 1/00	9 years, 3 months	503.3%	21.4%

Whatever the situation, it is guaranteed to change sooner or later, but as an investor you never know when and for how long. So by taking a look at the corrections of the market we can realize that volatility is the norm. Here's what you should expect when wondering how often the market is going to take it on the chin:

In the Dow Jones Industrial Average for the twentieth century:

✔ 5% corrections took place 3 times every year and lasted 40 days

✔ 10% corrections occurred about 1 every year and lasted for 109 days

✔ 15% corrections took place about once every 2 years and lasted 217 days

✔ 20% or more happened every 3 years, on average, and lasted 364 days

If we just look at the nine bear markets since WWII that were 20% or more, the worst was from January 1973 through September 1974.

> Fortune is not the side of the faint-hearted.
> —Sophocles

Large-cap stocks fell about 48% and didn't regain their previous high for about eight more years. This long period of recovery coincided with the extreme rates of inflation which kept the economy and companies struggling to cope.

By contrast, the last three big declines were just 20%. The first two lasted only three months (mid-July through mid-October 1990) and one and one-half months (mid-July through the end of August 1998). The last one, which began on the Dow when it hit a high on January 14, 2000, may have neded in mid-March 2001. In the first case, new highs were seen again in less than a year. In 1998, the market only took three months to recover.

No one knows when the next decline will hit, how far down the averages may go, or how long it will take to recover. But the market has always recovered and made new highs. The price for being in the market for the great bull runs we've had is sticking out the shorter declines.

Chapter 22 | The Economy

The Economics You Need to Know

Stock and bond markets don't operate in a vacuum. The economic environment and the markets are closely connected. When the rate of inflation is low, unemployment is falling, and people and companies are freely spending money, the economy is good. Company earnings are usually growing and that catches attention in the stock market. So, when it comes to investing, it's very useful to know where we are in the economic cycle.

The stock market tries to predict what the economy will be in six to twelve months. The common joke on Wall Street is that the market has predicted *ten* of the last *six* recessions.

The market usually leads the economy out of a recession, because investors eventually come to believe that the worst is behind and things will start getting better soon. In anticipation of better corporate earnings, investors start buying more stocks. As a result, market prices begin to rise. At some point, the economy is again growing fast, more people are employed, and money is flowing freely. If it gets really good, it's called a *boom*. Companies start raising their prices and employees want raises, too. When this gets out of control, inflation starts creeping up.

At some point in the boom, the Federal Reserve Bank (the "Fed") begins to raise interest rates to slow the growth of the money supply, thereby slowing the economy. If the Fed waits too long, short-term rates get increased substantially over a period of months and the economy gets choked off as money becomes expensive. Business slows down and the economy stops growing. This is the *bust*.

The market may have figured it out earlier when the Fed kept raising interest rates. Investors who try to time the markets start selling stocks in their portfolio before the bust. Sometimes they're right; sometimes they're wrong.

Figure 22-1 illustrates the classic economic cycle of boom and bust and how the market ideally tries to anticipate the next turn in the cycle. It shows how the stock market is always a little behind the economic cycle.

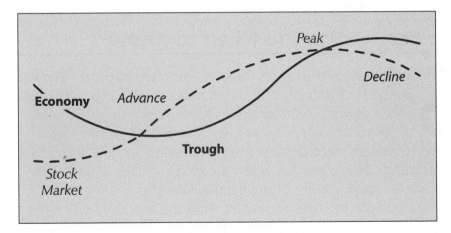

FIGURE 22-1. THE CYCLES OF THE ECONOMY AND STOCK MARKET

You'll notice something missing from this figure—measurements. This figure doesn't say how long a cycle lasts or how high and how low it will go. Each cycle is different from the last, because the economic environment is always changing. There are so many factors involved that most economists have given up trying to build huge computer models to predict the economy. The models just didn't work. With the steady decline in the rate of inflation since 1982, despite a strengthening economy, the old cycle models can't predict what will happen next or when.

Measuring the Flows of Money

For our investment decisions, it's critical to pay attention to the broad scope of events in the world around us. We can't change the economy to suit ourselves, but we can prepare for the inevitable ups and downs and try to keep them in a long-term perspective. A healthy cash flow into savings and investments and a realistic set of goals and financial objectives are paramount. Your financial plan is your anchor and your basis for making investment decisions as the events in the world and your life unfold.

When you invest, pay attention to the economic fundamentals that make up the companies you invest in, the industries they operate in, and the economies they buy from and sell into. Companies have little control over most of these forces; they, too, need sound financials, a solid strategic plan, and effective execution. The more you can understand about

> *Economics is a subject that does not greatly respect one's wishes.*
> *—Nikita Khrushchev*

these factors, the more successful you will be at investing. This knowledge may not tell you what to do with your investments, but it will help prevent fear and panic from urging you to do something you shouldn't do.

The markets react to government reports on the economy if the numbers are not what was expected. To traders, every report suggests a trend. For long-term investors, it takes a lot of monthly reports to spot a possible real trend. Therefore, you don't need to react to the constant flow of data, but it makes sense to follow it over a longer period of time, one to two years, to look for trends.

We'll look at what makes up the economy and how we measure it. The U.S. economy is kind of like an engine, running on the fuel of money or the cost of money (interest rates). The four cylinders are the four components of the Gross Domestic Product (GDP):

✔ Consumption—Consumer spending, divided into three categories: durable goods (items expected to last more than three years), non-durable goods (food and clothing), and service

✔ Investment—Expenditures, divided into three categories: nonresidential (spending on plants and equipment), residential (single-family and multi-family homes), and the change in business inventories

✔ Government Spending—Expenditures for defense, roads, schools, etc.

✔ Imports/Exports—Plus or minus net merchandise trade (a negative number if we import more than we export, as is the situation currently

These four components are assigned percentage weightings. Consumption accounts for about two-thirds, while Investment and Government are about equally weighted for the rest, except for a small percentage for Imports/Exports. This system of relative weightings, which is adjusted from time to time, provides a balanced measurement of growth in the national economy. This, in turn, may affect the interest rates, the dollar, currencies, the bond market, and ultimately the stock market. It's important to see the correlation between the economy and the markets.

Economic Reports

The following reports try to measure various kinds of recent economic activity. Taken together over a period of months, they may indicate a change in direction or a trend in the domestic economy. But each of them is often crude and inaccurate as an indicator. Nevertheless, when the reports are announced throughout the month, they can alarm the financial world, because the markets don't like surprises and often react when the numbers are not as expected.

Consumer Price Index (CPI). How much more or how much less are things costing? The CPI is made up of price changes at the consumer level for a "basket" of products and services. This is the popular measure of the rate of inflation. It is usually reported in two ways: as the full amount of the monthly percent change and as the percent change in the "core" rate—with food and energy price changes separated from the rest, because food and energy prices fluctuate much more than other prices.

Producer Price Index (PPI). What's the cost of making stuff? The PPI measures prices charged at the producer level for finished goods from the factory, intermediate goods from suppliers, and raw materials sold to factories. The report does not include services. This index should be viewed only in a long-term context to see if any real price pressures are beginning to work their way through the economy.

Housing Starts. Are people buying and building houses? This index is based on the commencement of building activity for single- and multi-family housing units. A number of factors influence this index, including weather, and it changes from month to month through the seasons. Housing starts indicate not only the demand for construction materials and labor but also future expenditures to furnish the homes.

The Index of Leading Economic Indicators. Where are we going? This index is compiled by The Conference Board, a private organization. It brings together a wide variety of 10 reports, with the information massaged and weighted to provide some insights into possible future business conditions in the country over the next six to twelve months. Three negative readings traditionally indicate a recession is at hand—but of course there are exceptions to that rule too.

Employment Report. Do you have a job? The Bureau of Labor Statistics reports from household and business surveys to determine the change in the number of people employed and unemployed but looking for work. The numbers are adjusted for seasonal variations based on past years. What's important is the longer-term trend based on later revisions, not the rough initial numbers.

Retail Sales. What are we buying at the malls? This indicator measures about 70% of the GDP, based on a survey of retailers of all kinds, from grocers to car dealers. The reports can fluctuate from month to month, based on regional weather effects, and they're also subject to major revisions as more data comes in.

Industrial Production Report. How much stuff are we making? The Federal Reserve Board produces this report, which measures the output from factories, mines, and utilities for the month, about 30% of the GDP. The rate of change over time is important, but the Fed and economists look at the output in terms of the estimated practical production capacity of the country, to see if pricing pressure is building due to demand versus supply.

Merchandise Trade Balances. Are we bringing more stuff in or sending more stuff out? This measures the difference in dollars between U.S. exports and imports, based on U.S. Customs valuation reports. Since the mid-1970s we've imported more goods than we've exported, but the numbers don't measure the value of services, including computer software exported, so it doesn't give an accurate total picture of real dollar trade figures.

National Association of Purchasing Management Report (NAPM). How much stuff do we think we're going to make? This report is based on a monthly survey of 250 purchasing managers by their national association, which reports any changes in new orders, production levels, prices, inventories, vendor performance, and employment. It's a manufacturing index and a consistent number over 50% suggests an expanding economy.

It's a Small World

When life is good, we spend more, perhaps take on more debt, and never think the good times will end. The same holds true everywhere else. Companies expand, borrow more money, and expand more. Countries, in turn, do the same, and then issue more government bonds to spend on social programs, roads, bridges and dams, etc.

Lenders are happy to lend, because that's how they make more money. The lenders borrow from us (our bank deposits and the bonds we own are loans), from other banks, and from private investors. Governments borrow from us through government bonds, from the World Bank, and from other governments. Everyone is borrowing from everyone else and lending it out again. This flow of debt is the source

of the liquidity in the world economy, the fuel that drives growth and development and makes the global economy go up and down.

What happens throughout the world is a lot like what happens in your own little world. When your personal debt is too high, you eventually try to cut back on expenses and pay it down. Your alternative is to allow it to continue increasing. Then, you find that you don't have enough cash coming in to pay all your current bills and the interest. This is called a *liquidity crisis*. If you can't resolve it, you head toward bankruptcy and the court reduces, restructures, or eliminates your debt. This is a *fiscal crisis* for you.

It works exactly the same way for companies and countries, except that the numbers get much larger. When you have these problems, your creditors can handle it. When lots of people have this problem, things get tough for local businesses and banks, which makes it worse for more people, which makes it worse … and so on.

At higher levels, a liquidity crisis means that companies and countries can't pay the interest and principal on their debts, either. They get shut off by banks and other lenders and head toward a fiscal crisis. A country, a region, and even the international banking and financial infrastructure of the world may be negatively impacted as the crisis snowballs. Each party in the chain is often both a borrower and a lender, thus spreading the crisis in all directions.

The markets, especially the bond market (because bonds are debt), try to anticipate economic events. The economic reports we noted earlier track the flows of money within our borders as well as the flows in and out of the country. Do foreigners want to buy our goods? Do they want to invest their money in our stocks or bonds? How much are we buying from other countries and how much did they buy from us? Who's borrowing how much and at what rate?

These factors and others like them affect not only the economy, but also the psychology of borrowers, lenders, and investors. Their mood, based on what they think is happening, determines how they manage their financial assets. However, fear and greed are contagious in the markets, often causing extreme volatility as the psychology shifts direction. Instant communication and money movement creates a herd effect. As with stampeding cattle, the momentum in one direction can change abruptly either when lightning strikes somewhere else or members of the herd start tiring and stop running.

Central banks such as our Federal Reserve Bank, the International Monetary Fund (the IMF so much in the news since 1997), and major governments try to inject cash and the means to spread the effects of the extra cash through lowering interest rates. They create liquidity to try and help keep the system from collapsing under the weight of the debt. It's a fairly clumsy method that doesn't always work well, but it's all they have to work with today.

A financial crisis somewhere in the world is often triggered when loans get called. Many of these big loans are short-term notes or even demand notes with a floating rate of interest and due without notice. Or major central banks see that the growth party is getting too wild and they take away the punch bowl. In the U.S., when growth increases too fast and for too long, the Fed raises short-term interest rates, usually several times in a short period, to make borrowing more expensive.

This means that the price of money, interest rates, rises quickly across the spectrum and the demand for borrowed money goes down, slowing the rate of growth in the economy. Businesses decide that new projects don't look so promising, so they cut back borrowing. Lending for new construction gets too expensive. Mortgage and car loan rates go up. Workers get laid off and plants may close as business slows down.

The Fed raises interest rates to prevent growth from becoming dangerous for the economy. When growth increases too fast and for too long, the demand for goods exceeds supply as more and more borrowed money gets spent and inflation creeps up and up. The party is in full swing, and there's only one way to slow it down. But, again, it's a slow and clumsy way to do things.

One of the reasons it's so clumsy is because of the economic data the Fed uses. It's a month or two old, since it takes that long to obtain and compile it, and then it's often highly inaccurate. Federal Reserve Bank Chairman Alan Greenspan has admitted as much in recent years. The Fed gets economic data by the truckload. The government and private organizations that collect the data and try to make sense of it know it's not accurate, because they have to revise it several times, often extensively, months later when more information comes in. Yet, the markets react to the initial reports as if they were gospel, then usually ignore the corrected reports later.

> *A study of economics usually shows that the best time to buy anything is last year.*
> —Marty Allen

The second reason the tools are so clumsy is that, once the data indicates a clear trend, the fiscal and monetary actions by the government take six to eighteen months to have an effect. The psychological effect of rate changes may be instantaneous, but that effect has just a limited impact on the economy. Historically, when the Fed and Congress react to the delayed confirmation of a recession, their actions often don't take effect until the recession has run its course in a year or two. The Fed's interest rate cuts and Congress's tax cuts kick growth off at a higher rate of acceleration—which leads to the next cycle of boom and bust.

What Will Change the World?

History, as many have observed, is cyclical. Themes repeat, but in new and different social, political, and economic contexts that create new events, crises, and trends. In order to get some insight to our present and future, you need to continually try to understand how themes or trends spiral through time.

Our insight is too dim to recognize the moments and events that mark the change in direction when an old theme is recycled in a new age. We can learn to perceive a change as it unfolds, yet still not know where it will take us over 10 or 20 years.

Since we can't predict the future by peering into the past, what key factors are known to us now that we can use to help us? What major trends and forces rise above the noise and tumult of the events of the day that usually capture our attention and distract us from the long-term view? We'll look at two of them in this section to give you some idea of the kind of things you should be looking at.

Government

The single most important factor in the *domestic* economy today or even, some may argue, in the *world* economy, is the U.S. government. Its activities, determined or accidental, can greatly affect the economy and the markets here and around the world in the following areas:

- ✔ Fiscal policy—the budget, the deficit, and the national debt
- ✔ Monetary policy—the amount of money in circulation and the cost and availability of credit
- ✔ Economic regulation and tax policy
- ✔ Foreign policy

The effects of governments in other countries with less free-market orientation are even more profound, because those governments try to manage their economies at many levels. We need to pay attention to critical world events, their economic and political effects, and the reactions to them on the state, national, and international stages to better understand where we may be going next. It's difficult to separate the truly important factors from the noise—and a lot of it is just noise, big news today that won't matter in a week. But persistence and practice pay off as you learn to see patterns and trends developing and can draw your own conclusions.

The complexity of the new world economic system, the rate of change, and the sheer size of the information flow are overwhelming. You should consider with skepticism the views of economists and market watchers and commentators, for two reasons. First, they're really guessing about the present and especially about the future. Second, they all have a bias of some sort or another, noble or less noble, that leads them to see things and interpret them a certain way. Listen to all sides of the public debates and try to draw your own conclusions as to how you may be affected, how to respond and act in your personal and financial life, and how to allocate your investments for the long term to achieve your objectives.

Finally, you'll notice that the opinions and predictions tend to conflict most of the time. Obviously, then, they can't all be correct. You must sort through the conflicting views with an awareness of your biases in order to come to a rational understanding of your own. Without such a position, one that will evolve with time, you're at the mercy of forces and people you don't understand and that may not have your best interests in mind. You'll lack a compass and a map, so you'll get more and more confused about what you should do with your money.

> *To have* national *prosperity, we need to* spend, *but to have* individual *prosperity, we must* save.

Demographics

A major trend, really a pair of trends, that will have many critical, long-term effects on our national economy and the global economy and politics can be found by looking at the demographic trends. We know the effect of the huge boomer generation as it has grown and aged from 1945 to the present. It has greatly changed the economic profile of the country at every stage. Developing countries, on the other hand, not only have many more people, but their median age is significantly lower than populations in developed countries.

In this country, the boomer generation will begin retiring around 2005-2010. Today, there are about 34 million people in the U.S. over the age of 65. There are 76 million boomers. Where and how much will they spend as they now begin entering their peak earning years? Where and when will they retire? How will they spend their time and money in retirement? We don't know the answers to these questions—but we know that they will drive the domestic economy to a considerable degree in the next 25 years.

Other developed countries—especially Japan, Germany, France, Italy, the United Kingdom, and Canada—are facing this issue even earlier than the U.S. They have fast-growing aging populations today but no huge boomer generation hard at work supporting them now. Their government pension systems are close to collapse already. Most of those countries have very low birth rates and little immigration compared with the U.S. Their populations are becoming extremely top-heavy while decreasing. What will this trend mean over the next 50 years to those national economies and to the world economy?

Finally, the average age in emerging-market countries is around 20, rather than the mid-30s and climbing as in the developed countries. Youth in the billions, wanting what we already have and with the skills and energy to try and get it—you can't keep them down on the farm after they've seen American TV. How will this affect the world economy and your life?

Chapter 23

Inflation and Deflation

I nflation, deflation—what's the difference? Understanding about inflation and deflation is fundamental to understanding our economy and to making smart financial decisions.

Let's start our discussion with what we've had the most experience with in recent history—inflation and disinflation. We all know about the effects of inflation: the price of bread and orange juice goes up every year. Inflation is actually the measure of the rate of increase in prices in general.

Inflation

The Federal Reserve Bank measures inflation monthly by checking the prices of a grocery basket of goods that's supposed to represent our spending habits. This basket of goods, as we mentioned in Chapter 22, is called the Consumer Price Index (CPI). The annual CPI figure gives us our inflation figure for the year; many things are tied to this number, such as the increase in Social Security benefits. The wholesale pricing the government uses is called the Producer Price Index (PPI).

Inflation is normally a natural occurrence. There are many theories as to what causes it. Workers demand higher wages, which can cause the prices of goods to increase, which then causes other workers to demand an increase in their income to compensate for the increase of goods they need to purchase. You get the picture. It's just a cycle that just keeps on going .... Another theory is that there is too much money chasing too few goods and services. Either approach serves as a basic way to understand inflation without getting into the economic debates.

A Little History

During the 20th century, the rate of inflation has averaged 3.2% per year. But prices fell for many years in the 1920s and 1930s, then rose rapidly during WWII and again during the Korean Conflict. After settling down for about 10 years, inflation began a 17-year run in 1965 that saw rates over 12% in 1979 and again in 1980. Since then, the rate of inflation has steadily decreased, averaging 2.3% per year from 1997 through 2000.

> *Inflation is when the buck doesn't stop anywhere.*

We were racked with high inflation in the '70s and '80s. Part of the reason for this was that borrowed money can be spent just as easily as money earned or money saved. So, the more people and companies borrow, the more they'll spend. When money is easy to borrow, that contributes to the demand for goods and services and may help drive up prices. Borrowers know they will be paying back the debt with cheaper dollars and prices will keep going up as long as the rate of inflation continues increasing.

Then, things cooled off a little later in the '80s and into the '90s where disinflation took over. Disinflation is a steady decrease in the rate of inflation. The rate of inflation is still going up, but at a steadily slower pace year after year.

What does this inflation mean to us? The effect of persistent inflation over time affects us in our daily lives. There are two ways to look at it.

We've mentioned that inflation erodes the buying power of your dollars. At the end of 2000, a dollar would only buy 28¢ worth of goods and services compared with a dollar's worth in 1974. Figure 23-1 shows this steady decline in the purchasing power of a dollar.

Another way to look at inflation is in terms of earnings. During this period from 1974 to 1998, the median family income went up 400%, from $12,500 to $50,100. This increase was ahead of the rate of inflation, but it was partly a result of a large increase in two-income families.

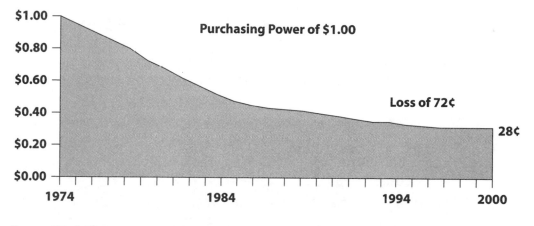

FIGURE 23-1. THE EFFECT OF 26 YEARS OF INFLATION ON $1.00
Data: Ibbotson Associates Yearbook, Chart: Flewelling Associates

Deflation

Now as we look toward the 21st century, we're hearing about the real possibility of deflation, which is prices going down. That's an economic phenomenon that we haven't experienced in over 60 years.

Deflation means just the opposite of inflation. Most of us have learned to live with inflation and to expect it at some level. Many have learned to fear its destructive effects at high levels, while others have learned to benefit from it. What we're not prepared for, because we haven't experienced it and have difficulty imagining it, is deflation.

How would we recognize it? The CPI and PPI would start recording month-to-month and year-to-year drops in the general level of prices. The PPI began doing just that at a moderate rate in 1998. Deflation CPI numbers would record the rate at which retail prices in general are declining.

If we enter a period of mild deflation, between 1% and 2% per year, your dollars will buy a bit more each year or you can save a little more as the things you buy become less expensive. But there can be too much of a good thing.

Accelerating deflation, like inflation, causes severe waves of dislocation throughout the economy. Some of the effects may harm you more than inflation. For instance:

- ✔ Company profit margins could decline or disappear because companies must lower prices faster than their costs are going down.
- ✔ Debt, both corporate and personal, becomes increasingly more expensive to pay off because dollars are worth more and may be harder to get.
- ✔ Your paycheck stops growing and may get smaller as companies cut costs.
- ✔ More companies layoff employees and close plants in an effort to reduce costs.
- ✔ Companies can't pay off their debts and go out of business or file for bankruptcy.
- ✔ More employees lose their jobs, can't pay their debts, and file for bankruptcy.

This is what happened from 1930 through 1932, triggering the Great Depression that lasted until the outbreak of World War II. Prices fell 23.7% in three years and unemployment rose to at least 25%. Economists still argue about the causes of the depression, but the effects were burned into the memories of generations of people who lived through it.

Economists assure us that this kind of deflation can't happen here again. The Federal Reserve and the governments learned their lessons, they tell us. The Feds have proved it can stop inflation in its tracks by driving up short-term interest rates until the economy cries "Uncle Sam!" and collapses into a recession. We saw how that worked from December 1980 through November 1981, as Treasury bill rates exceeded 16% briefly.

If deflation should rear its ugly head again, the Fed would probably drop short-term interest rates way down and flood the economy

> *I got all the money I need if I die by four o'clock.*
> *—Henny Youngman*

with money. This strategy would be aimed at stimulating demand by making money so cheap and easy to borrow that people and companies would eagerly borrow it and spend it. As long as the economy is humming along and people have jobs and are buying things, there won't be a depression.

How Will Inflation and Deflation Affect Your Investments?

Bonds

The bond market is like a magnet that hovers over the rate of inflation within a few percentage points. The Federal Reserve Bank keeps its finger on the overnight rates that banks charge each other as well as the rate at which banks may borrow from the Fed. The Fed also manipulates the supply of money through buying and selling Treasury securities, which affects the interest rates through supply and demand. The bond market takes its cue from the Fed's position and the market determines interest rates for T-Bills, notes, and bonds of all issuers.

There are periods when the Federal Reserve responds sharply to certain economic conditions. For example, in the early '90s current Chairman Alan Greenspan dropped rates to 3% for several years. This allowed the banking system to recover from the effects of its bad lending practices and the savings and loan crisis in the late '80s and '90s, even though inflation was over 3% during those years. Banks could borrow from the Fed at 3% and lend it at 7% by buying U.S. Treasuries. The 4% spread they earned allowed them to rebuild their capital at no risk.

As we showed in the chapter on bonds, when interest rates go up, the price of bonds goes down and vice versa. But, even if you hold a bond to maturity and get the face value amount back, you could actually lose on your investment because of inflation. How? If the rate of inflation rose while you held your bonds, the value of your principal plus the stream of income you received in interest may have less buying power than the money you lent. The true measure of your return on investment (ROI) is the total return on the bond after inflation. Remember: it's not what you get back in dollars that counts; it's what those dollars will buy.

Stocks

Next let's look at stocks. Stocks react to inflation and the strength of the economy even more strongly than bonds. They react to inflation and interest rates based not only on their own amounts of debt, but to the debt levels of their customers.

Most people buy *bonds* for income, stability, and the knowledge that the money will be returned at maturity. In contrast, most people today buy *stocks* for the expected appreciation in prices over time. Therefore, expectations and psychology play a greater role in the stock market. The bond market spends at least as much time looking backward as forward, but the stock market couldn't care less about yesterday. It reacts swiftly and sometimes strongly to a shift in expectations.

> *Inflation is when your nest egg is no longer anything to crow about.*

Those expectations are often totally wrong, because the future is unpredictable. As we mentioned earlier, the stock market actually "predicted" ten of the last six recessions. When enough investors believe that a recession is coming soon, they try to time the market and sell their stock. But they're wrong so often that successful long-term investors learn to shrug off market volatility and to buy when the prices of good companies fall off the cliff.

All stocks performed very well when inflation averaged 1.3% a year between 1952 and 1965. Real returns, subtracting the effect of inflation, were 13.1% per year—despite four losing years. It was a different story from 1973 through 1981, as the annual rate of inflation moved above 5% and stayed there, averaging 9.2% over the nine-year period. Stocks averaged only a 2.7% real total return after inflation and large-cap stocks lost 3.71% a year on average after inflation.

Since 1981, the rate of inflation has steadily decreased. This disinflation has help fuel the remarkable rise in the stock market through 1999. Stocks averaged a real return of 12.2% after adjusting for an average annual rate of inflation of 3.3%. Figure 23-2 graphically shows this performance.

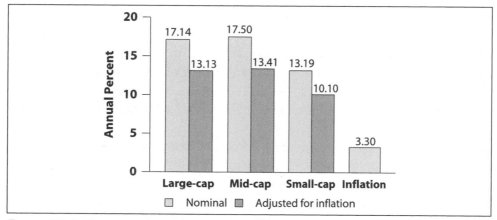

FIGURE 23-2. STOCK TOTAL RETURNS 1982-2000

These stock returns were not solely due to disinflation, but this greatly helped to create a healthier economic environment for companies to grow sales and earnings as well as for workers to finally see their incomes move ahead after inflation. Investors hope that the rate of inflation remains low for a long time.

Lessons from the Past for the Future?

Bonds had respectable real returns during this period, but stocks as a group outperformed an equal-weighted portfolio of the fixed-income securities we profiled by almost 70% each year on average. Within each period, there were years when bonds beat stocks, but not by nearly enough to abandon stocks for their long-term growth potential.

The only thing we can often predict with some success is how the markets will react in the very short term to changes in expectations about inflation, interest rates, and the economy. These reactions are often too fast for most investors to make any major portfolio moves. What you need to know is that expectations are frequently incorrect in the direction of the change or in the degree of change. In fact, predictions are often wrong on both. We know the markets are going to go up and down; we just can't predict when.

Managing in a Changing Economy

Financial planners have to play the guessing game on where the future of inflation rates are going and usually throw out a 3% to 4% number to help clients developing financial plans and investment allocations to meet their goals. No one knows what the rate of inflation will be over the next 50 years, so it's wise to pick a number that makes sense in terms of history and to aim even a little higher to provide a margin of safety.

It's clear that all investments perform better when the rate of inflation is falling or is low and relatively stable. Between 0% and 4% inflation, a diversified portfolio should perform relatively well. The pattern also fits with the message that we've conveyed throughout the book, that stocks and stock funds will grow your money faster than inflation and taxes. On the other hand, bonds not only provide income, but also can be a stabilizing force that makes the ride a little less bumpy.

> *Careful consideration is the best known defense against change.*
> —*John C. Burton*

Because it's impossible to predict inflation and inflationary expectations, a bond investor should diversify across the range of maturities. Just like investing in different styles of stocks, different bond maturities and styles may react in separate ways to what's happening in the economic world. Bonds should be bought to hold to maturity. The bond ladders we suggested in Chapter 14 serve to protect you against rising interest rates as well as anything and ensure strong returns in periods of falling rates.

Investments in a diversified stock portfolio or in a selection of mutual funds in several different styles will, over time, give you the best opportunity to come out ahead of inflation. Companies can change and adapt to the rate of inflation or deflation and eventually get their earnings back on track. Underlying all companies are real assets, not only land and buildings, but also patents and other intellectual property, and the abilities of their managers and employees. When you buy stock, this is what you're investing in. Together, these assets may be managed to generate earnings that will eventually push up the price of the stocks.

The best preparation you can make in order to profit, or just to survive, in whatever economic and investment climate the future delivers is to follow the major themes in this book:

- ✔ Put together a thoughtful financial plan.
- ✔ Maintain an adequate emergency fund.
- ✔ Save regularly and invest continuously in a well-diversified portfolio of stocks, bonds, or mutual funds appropriate for your plan.
- ✔ Review your portfolio's performance at least annually.
- ✔ Review your financial plan and portfolio allocation every two or three years to make sure they're still appropriate for you.
- ✔ Don't make hasty changes in your investments. Don't let your emotions, particularly fear and greed, drive your decisions.

It takes a while to begin to see solid results from following this course, but once your money begins compounding, the growth accelerates. The market will have setbacks, but patience is the most valuable tool a long-term investor can have. Getting rich slowly works when you do the right things and then let it happen.

Chapter 24 | Income Taxes

Let's start with an interesting set of facts. Here are several documents and the number of words in each of them:

Document	Number of Words
Gettysburg Address	269 words
Declaration of Independence	1,337 words
The Bible	773,000 words
Tax Code	7 million words and growing

The toll that we pay on the highway to success is taxes. We work hard all week to earn a few bucks, then we get a check that's a fraction of what we earned, primarily because of paycheck withholdings like FICA, Medicare, state taxes, federal taxes, and a whole host of company benefit plan withdrawals. Some 174 million of us spend an average of 21 hours a year just filling out our tax forms for the IRS. Then many of us end up having to find some cash to pay our tax bill.

Then there's a bunch of other taxes: sales tax, property tax, room tax, excise tax, and your last tax—estate tax. The average family in America pays 38% of its total income for all taxes every year, which is more than for food, shelter, and clothing combined. We pay a lot of taxes, but when we talk taxes, we're usually talking *income taxes*.

Income Taxes

Almost 80% of all Americans are taxed in the lowest bracket (15%), according to government figures for 1998. Only 6.7% of tax returns in 1998 reported adjusted groos income over $100,000, and they paid 57.5% of all the individual federal income tax for that year. The median two-couple family total income in 1998 was $54,180, and the total federal income tax paid was about $5,150, only 9.5% of total income. But let's put that percentage into perspective: when we started paying income taxes back in 1913, the *maximum* bracket was 6%! Since then, it's gone as high as 90% and currently is a hair under 40%.

Tax brackets, as well as personal exemptions, standard deductions, and many other tax figures are indexed for inflation. This means the bracket limits and other numbers increase each year based on the Consumer Price Index for the previous year. But keep in mind that the

only things that change more than tax brackets are the deductions. There are 40,500 pages of tax code, and it's constantly growing, so we have to keep an eye on what Uncle Sam giveth and taketh away. Tax brackets alone are just the beginning in understanding how to find your way through the tax maze.

> *Taxes, after all, are the dues that we pay for the privilege of membership in an organized society.*
> —*Franklin D. Roosevelt*

In the rest of this chapter, we're not going to get into the subject of whether we're getting what we pay for or whether a particular tax law is fair or not. We'll cover some of the basics of the tax law primarily as it relates to investing, but also in terms of where you can look for tax breaks and deductions if you do some tax planning each year. Our suggestion is get a tax advisor to help you with this stuff, because it changes too fast and too frequently.

Tax Planning

Your federal *tax bracket* refers to the percent of your last dollar of ordinary income (not capital gains) that you will owe a tax on to Uncle Sam. Check the Taxable Income line on your last 1040 tax form (line 39 on your 2000 taxes) and then take a look at Figure 24-1 on the next page so you can see exactly how much money Uncle Sam is actually taking from your last dollar earnings in 2001.

In May 2001 congress passed a $1.35 trillion tax cut package. These cuts phase in over as many as 10 years. Not all the details of the cuts and their timimg have been worked out as this edition of *Let's Talk Money* is being prepared. Therefore, the figures used in this chapter are the ones for 2001 released earlier in the year by the IRS, except as noted.

For 2001, the tax rates technically changed your tax on the first $6,000 of taxable income for singles, $10,000 for head of household filers, and $12,000 for married couples filing jointly to 10% from 15%. You should have received a rebate by the fall of 2001 of up to $300, $500, or $600 depending on your tax filing status for the year 2000.

Your 2001 Form 1040 will be calculated at the old 15% rate. The higher rates for 2001 will be 27.5%, 30.5%, 35.5% and 39.2% reflecting this decrease for half the year. Automatic withholding rates from paychecks changed after mid-2001 to reflect these rates.

Schedule X – Filing Single

If taxable income is			Of the
Over	But not over	The tax is	amount over
$ 0	$ 25,050	15%	$ 0
25,050	65,550	$4,057.50 + 27.5%	27,050
65,550	136,750	14,837.50 + 30.5%	65,550
136,750	297,350	36,909.50 + 35.5%	136,750
297,350		94,725.50 + 39.1%	297,350

Schedule Y-1 – Married, filing jointly

If taxable income is			Of the
Over	But not over	The tax is	amount over
$ 0	$ 45,200	15%	$ 0
45,200	109,250	6,780.00+27.5%	45,200
109,250	166,500	24,714.00+30.5%	109,250
166,500	297.350	42,461.50+35.5%	166,500
297,350		89,567.50+39.1%	297,350

Schedule Y-2 – Married, filing separately

If taxable income is			Of the
Over	But not over	The tax is	amount over
$ 0	$ 22,600	15%	$ 0
22,600	54,625	3,390.00 + 27.5%	22,600
54,625	83,250	12,357.00+30.5%	54,625
83,250	148,675	21,230.75+35.5%	83,250
148,675		44,783.75+39.1%	148,675

Schedule Z – Head of Household

If taxable income is			Of the
Over	But not over	The tax is	amount over
$ 0	$ 36,250	15%	$ 0
36,250	93,650	5,437.50+27.5%	36,250
93,650	151,650	21,509.50+30.5%	93,650
151,650	297,350	39,489.50+35.5%	151,650
297,350		91,941.00+39.1%	297,350

FIGURE 24-1. 2001 FEDERAL INCOME TAX RATE SCHEDULES

The rates that take effect on July 1, 2001 are scheduled to last through 2003, followed by another reduction of one percentage point decrease for 2004 and 2005. We suggest you take your tax planning one year at a time and stay alert for more changes that may affect you.

Now, here are some key tax terms to understand when we're talking about your income tax:

Adjusted Gross Income (AGI)—Total earned and unearned income from taxable accounts, including net business income or losses, capital gain or loss, retirement plan distributions, taxable pensions, rental income, and possibly some Social Security benefits, minus IRA, SEP, or Keogh contributions, self-employment health benefits (partially deductible so far), half your self-employment tax, and alimony paid. The AGI is the last line on the front of the Form 1040.

Taxable Income—The AGI minus personal exemptions and itemized or standard deduction. This is the figure on which you calculate your tax.

Capital Gain or Loss—This is the difference between what an investment sells for and its tax cost basis and any commissions and fees for buying and/or selling. A mutual fund or real-estate investment trust (REIT) may declare capital gain dividends to shareholders on the same basis.

Alternative Minimum Tax (AMT)—The AMT was created to make sure that wealthy people with a lot of fancy deductions and credits paid a reasonable minimum tax. But now it may affect single filers with taxable income of $35,740 and married taxpayers over $49,000 under temporary increase in exemptions set to expire after 2004. It's really a set of entirely different tax rules that affect millions of middle-class taxpayers who have high deductions or tax credits in certain areas. There's no simple way to figure out if it applies to you unless you do the calculations. If you don't calculate it, the IRS will. And if it applies to you, look out!

> *Why does a small tax increase cost you two hundred dollars and a substantial tax cut save you thirty cents?*
> —Peg Bracken

We mentioned that the government taxes us in three basic ways: income taxes (on the money coming in), miscellaneous sales and excise taxes (on the money going out), and estate taxes (on what we can't take with us when we go). You need to recognize that there are three things you can do to reduce taxes:

1. Reduce your taxable income by using tax-advantaged investments.

2. Know what deductions you can take and use them whenever they fit.
3. Use or give your assets away before you die so the government doesn't take a big bite.

Unfortunately, for most people, tax planning means getting around to scheduling time in April to "do their taxes" before April 15—and that's way too late to do any planning. But even if all you have is a W-2 wage statement from your employer and a 1099-INT statement showing some interest paid by your bank, you may find that it pays to look ahead and do some planning for next April. There are steps you can take in January each year that can affect not only your return but also your income in retirement. As with investing, it's the little things you do in tax planning that make a big difference over time.

Some suggestions:

✔ Contribute the maximum to a company retirement account.
✔ Decide to itemize if there are more deductions than the standard amount.
✔ Pre-pay your real estate taxes to take the deduction.
✔ Make maximum use of any capital losses you incurred (include mutual funds).
✔ Consider taking a loss if you have securities at low prices relative to what you paid for them.
✔ Adjust your W-4 form if you are getting large refunds so the government doesn't take as much out of your paycheck each time.
✔ Check out the new tax credits available.

As much as you hate working on your taxes, you don't know if you're overpaying until you get organized and do some planning regularly. If you don't want to spend much time reading up on tax law and figuring out what you can and can't do, we don't blame you. A professional tax preparer is paid to do these things for you with a little help from you with the necessary record keeping. Most people who file a regular 1040 use professionals and find that the service often pays for itself in tax savings, not to mention time, anxiety, and Maalox.

Tax Deductions

You pay taxes on what the IRS calls "taxable income." Anything that you can legally subtract from your gross income before you get to this point isn't taxed. For many people, *deductions* and *exemptions* can cut their total income by quite a bit.

A tax exemption is a deduction for each dependent you have, including yourself. In 2001 that was worth $2,900 per person. There are all kinds of other qualifications and tests to determine who is a dependent. In 2001, the IRS starts taking away the value of these exemptions for singles earning $132,950, married filing jointly earning $199,450, and heads of households at $166,200. It disappears in chunks of 2% per each $2,500 of AGI over these limits, which are indexed for inflation each year.

Deductions are determined by the total of allowable expenses you can legitimately put on Schedule A of Form 1040, Itemized Deductions. If your total is less than the standard deduction allowed, then you can take this instead and come out ahead. For 2001 the standard deduction is:

Single	$4,550
Married filing jointly or widow(er) with child under 17	$7,600
Married filing separately	$3,800
Head of Household	$6,650

These standard deduction figures are indexed upward every year for inflation, too. You also get an additional benefit for each dependent including yourself who is age 65 or older or legally blind. These deductions are not indexed.

> The hardest thing in the world to understand is the income tax.
> —Albert Einstein

If the total of your itemized deductions on Schedule A exceeds the standard deduction you're allowed, then it usually pays to use this higher amount. But in rare cases, the effect of the AMT may make it desirable to take the standard deduction. Allowable deductions:

✔ Medical and dental expenses over the 7.5% of AGI

✔ State, local, real estate, and other taxes

✔ Charitable gifts and donations

✔ Casualty and theft losses over 10% of AGI plus $100

✔ Job expenses and miscellaneous expenses over the 2% of AGI

The qualifications, limits, and exclusions for all of these categories are numerous and require close, careful reading. It's essential to maintain good records to keep track of your deductions and to be able to back them up in case of an audit. How long do you need to keep all those records? Well, the IRS can audit you up to three years after you file the return—and even longer if you underreported your income or filed a fraudulent return.

If you do your own return or tax planning, get one of the massive annual tax guides from J.K. Lasser or Ernst & Young to get the details and good advice. Your library should have a copy of at least one of these guides and they're available in bookstores for around $15. (The cost is deductible if you itemize.) New issues come out toward the end of the year. Many accounting firms also offer good information on their Web sites: Ernst & Young at **www.ey.com**, Deloitte Touche at **www.dttus.com**, Arthur Andersen at **www.arthurandersen.com**, and PriceWaterhouseCoopers at **www.pwcglobal.com**.

Tax Credits

After you calculate the tax on your taxable income, there are a few deductions allowed from this tax. These are called tax credits. Unlike deductions, which only reduce taxable income, credits reduce any tax owed, dollar for dollar. Unfortunately, there aren't very many and most of them phase out at various income levels. The table on the next shows some that may affect you.

The child tax credit is scheduled to increase from $600 in 2001 to $700 in 2005, $800 in 2009, and $1,000 in 2010. There are a few other credits for things such as rehabbing a home in certain qualified districts of your city or state if you get the proper paperwork, buying a qualified electric vehicle, earned income credit, etc. Like the credits above, there are a bunch of rules, regulations, and special forms to fill

Type of Tax Credit	Maximum/Yr.	Phase out at AGI Over
Child and dependent care expenses	$1,440	30% of expenses up to $10,000 income down to 20% over $28,000
Child tax credit for dependents under 17	$500 each	$75,000 single $110,000 joint filers $55,000 filing separate
Elderly or disabled	$1,125	Depends on type of income and age of you and spouse
Adoption	$10,000	$150,000
Hope Scholarship Credit, first two years of school	First $1,000 and 50% of next $1,000	$40,000 single $80,000 joint filers
Lifetime Learning Credit, can't be used with Hope	20% of qualifying expenses up to $1,000/year	$40,000 single $80,000 joint filers

out. Most credits are phased out above certain income levels, reducing or eliminating the credit. Don't look a gift horse in the mouth, though. Tax credits are worth their weight in dollar bills.

The foreign tax credit is one with which you may be familiar if you've invested in foreign and global mutual funds or American Depositary Receipts (ADRs). Most countries tax the earnings from dividends paid by their companies and withhold a portion of the dividend. You have a choice: you can take the tax withheld as an itemized deduction on Schedule A or as a tax credit. You should be aware that tax withheld is added to your dividend income on your 1099-DIVs, so the income reported will be higher than what you actually received from your fund or company. There's a formula used to determine the amount of credit you can use that's based on your foreign income relative to your U.S. income.

There's one other credit you may qualify for if you changed jobs during the year or held more than one job. Each employer is required to start from scratch when withholding Social Security taxes (FICA). So if your total Social Security withholdings for the year exceed the annual limit of $4,984.80 in 2001, you paid too much and can take a tax credit for the excess against any income tax you owe that year.

Taxes on Unearned Income

Once you become a saver and investor, you will have unearned income. Unearned? Well, yes, in that you didn't earn it by working, but rather by getting your money to work for you. And Uncle Sam usually wants his share.

The IRS and the states have made sure that almost all of your unearned income gets reported to you early in the following year on various 1099 forms. They don't do this to help you remember what you made; they do it so they can find out what you earned. This means that they will cross check to see that you reported it all. And if you have more than $400 of interest income, you must file either a Form 1040A or Form 1040.

A 1099-INT reports any interest income from banks, savings and loans, savings banks, and credit unions. You also get a 1099-INT or a comprehensive 1099-B from your broker for any interest you received from U.S. Treasury bills, notes, or bonds, from corporate bonds, and from foreign bonds. Most interest received from state and local municipal bonds is exempt from federal tax. Money market funds and bond funds earn interest on the securities they hold, but they pay dividends to shareholders. Don't include this as interest.

Although you don't pay taxes on them, you still have to report municipal bond interest and ordinary dividends from municipal bond funds on your 1040. The feds just want to keep track of this income for various reasons, including the AMT. Also, you are not allowed to borrow money and deduct the interest as an investment interest expense on Schedule A if you used the money to buy tax-exempt municipal bonds. You have to prove there's no connection between the two transactions, even indirectly, to be allowed to deduct the interest. This may not be easy.

One trick with interest on bonds is often overlooked. When you buy a bond, it almost always has earned some interest that hasn't been paid yet. You'll get the full amount of the next payment, but the previous owner wants what was earned before you bought it. Therefore, the price you pay includes "accrued interest" and will be noted on your confirmation slip. You deduct that amount on the next line on Schedule 1 or Schedule B and write in "less accrued interest."

Zero-coupon bonds accrue interest annually, even though you don't collect the money until the bond matures or you sell it. Your broker will include the accrued amount each year in the 1099-B; you owe taxes on this amount, unless it's a municipal bond. There's a similar situation with Treasury Inflation Indexed bonds. You receive a guaranteed rate of interest each year and the face value of the bond is adjusted for inflation each year. You owe federal tax annually on the amount of the adjustment, as this is considered interest.

The final bond interest subject can be even trickier—U.S. Savings Bonds, either Series EE or I. The interest accrues each year, but you don't collect it until you redeem the bonds. You can elect to pay the interest each year but most people pay when they redeem them. You can exchange them for Series HH Bonds and postpone paying the tax on the accrued interest until the HH Bond matures. You receive interest on the HH Bond and owe the tax on that each year.

Any interest as well as dividends and capital gains earned in a qualified tax-sheltered retirement plan such as a 401(k) or IRA or in a tax-deferred annuity are not reported to the government. You don't report any income from these accounts to the feds or to the states in most cases. Only upon withdrawal do you report this money and pay the taxes. Speaking of states, every state has a different approach to taxing unearned income. Don't make any assumptions that your state tax code looks the same way on unearned income as the feds do.

Rental income you receive for the use or occupation of property is also unearned income, but it is tied in to your ownership and expenses and has lots of twists and turns as we pointed out in Chapter 18 on Real Estate. You will want to get IRS publications 527, 535, 925, and 946 to guide you or use a qualified tax professional who is familiar with real estate rental income tax law

Dividends Are Not of Interest

Dividends are different than interest from the bank. Dividend income is paid to stockholders, mutual fund shareowners and Real Estate Investment Trust (REIT) stockholders. The amounts are reported to you in various boxes on Form 1099-DIV or as part of your broker or mutual fund company's 1099-B. In turn, they are reported by you to the IRS if your 1040 tax return totals exceed $400. Insurance companies also pay "dividends," but this type of dividend is really a non-taxable return of your premium. Don't confuse this payment with dividends from the sources listed below.

1a	1b	1c	1d	2	3	4
Gross dividends and other distributions	Ordinary dividends	Capital gain distributions (from mutual funds)	Non-taxable distributions (a return of capital)	Federal income tax withheld	Foreign tax paid	Foreign country or U.S. possession

If you have a number of stocks or funds reported on a comprehensive 1099-B, you don't need to list each one individually. Just list the name of the brokerage or fund company and break out the amount by type, interest, dividends, capital gain dividends, etc. and report the amounts in the proper places.

The first thing to do upon receiving a 1099 of any kind is to check to see that it agrees with your records. Go over your statements and add up the dividends and interest. If you find a disagreement, contact your broker, fund company, bank or whoever sent the 1099 and ask questions until you find out who made a mistake. If they did, request that a Corrected 1099 be issued so the IRS won't come looking for you.

Ordinary dividends (box 1b) are what companies and mutual funds pay to shareowners. The mutual fund will include any short-term capital gain dividends it declared and paid to you as ordinary dividends. There is no tax advantage to short-term gains, so they're lumped in here for simplicity and are reported on Schedule B.

The capital gains distributions in box 1c are long-term capital gain dividends declared by the mutual fund or REIT. It doesn't matter how long you owned the shares; they're still long-term gains. If, however, you hold the mutual fund or REIT for less than six months and sell the shares at a loss, special rules apply. Get IRS Publication 550 (800-829-3676) to find out how to report both these transactions.

Box 1d amounts, if any, represent a return of your original investment, for one reason or another, as part of a dividend. These are non-taxable, but they reduce your tax cost basis in the investment. You have nothing here to report to the IRS until you sell the security. File copies of your annual 1099s with your mutual funds. You'll be able to accurately calculate your capital gain or loss when you sell it.

Tax-exempt dividend income is noted elsewhere on your mutual fund's or broker's 1099-B. There's usually no federal tax due on this unless it is labeled an AMT preference income item, but the IRS requires this amount to be reported on your 1040. You may also need this information to prepare your state tax returns. You should receive a chart that allows you to determine if any of the dividend amount is also exempt from taxation in your state.

> *The United States is the only country where it takes more brains to figure out your tax than to earn the money to pay it.*
> —Edward J. Gurney

Box 2 indicates whether you had any federal tax withheld under backup withholding tax laws. Normally, you filed a form with the mutual fund company or broker certifying that you were not subject to backup withholding. If, however, any tax is withheld, make a copy of the 1099, attach it to your tax return, and include the amount withheld with other federal tax withheld from your paycheck.

The Foreign Tax paid, box 3, is the amount withheld by the country where the foreign dividend originated. You may either deduct this as an itemized deduction as "Other taxes paid" on Schedule A or take it as a tax credit, as explained in the previous section.

The Foreign Source Income box represents the amount that was earned on which the foreign taxes have already been paid. You use this information in the formula to calculate any limit to the tax credit.

You can find more detailed information on investment income in IRS Publication 550 by calling 800-829-3676. You can also download forms, instructions, and publications from the IRS Web site, **www.irs.ustreas.gov**.

Taxes on Capital Gains

When you buy or sell something you must remember that for every action there is a reaction. For tax purposes it's all a matter of time and how much money you make. The shorter the time period and the more money you have in taxable income, the higher the taxes you'll probably pay. For years now the government has been playing around with the time frames of capital gains. So for our purposes let's just look at short-term capital gains and losses (sale of securities, including mutual funds, held less than a year) and long-term gains or losses (longer than one year).

If you're in the 15% federal tax bracket, any capital gain is taxed at 8% starting in 2001 if you've held the asset for at least five years. For any period less than five years but greater than one year, the rate remains 10%.

A 25% tax rate applies in two areas of gains: (1) If you take a gain that is due to depreciation when you sell real property, such as rental property (also known as Section 1250 property). The rules are very complex, so get IRS Publication 544 if you sold rental property. (2) If you take a gain when you sell your residence and if you rented out or used a portion of it for an office or a business after May 6, 1997 and took depreciation deductions for this portion on any return since that date. The percentage of your house you allocated for business will be the percentage of your capital gain that is subject to the 25% tax, unless you've used the house exclusively as a personal residence in at least two out of the last five years.

Now, let's look at gains from the sale of stocks and bonds. Your tax cost basis is the price you paid plus the commission and fees, if any, charged to you on the confirmation slip. Your selling price is the total amount received from the sale less any commission and fee. The difference is your capital gain or loss. Note that this is where you get to deduct the commissions you paid.

If your losses exceed your gains, including any declared long-term capital gain dividends from mutual funds, you are allowed to deduct up to $3,000 ($1,500 if married filing separately) against ordinary income. Any loss exceeding this limit is carried over to the following year.

Gains on the sale of mutual fund shares in a taxable account can be more complex. You need to keep good records of each purchase of shares, including reinvestment of dividends to purchase additional shares, in order to determine your tax cost basis and holding period. Many of the major mutual fund companies are now keeping track of your cost basis for you, which makes it easier for you when you do sell shares.

There are four methods you can use to determine the cost basis:

✔ The specific shares identification method

✔ First in-first out method (FIFO)

✔ Single-category using average cost

✔ Double-category using average cost

Check out IRS Publication 564, "Mutual Fund Distributions," for details on all four methods. (Call the IRS to order this booklet at 800-829-3676.) Whichever method you pick to determine the cost basis, you must continue to use it whenever you sell shares from that fund in the future. You may use a different method for another fund if you want. It all balances out when you finally sell all the shares, so don't worry too much about which method you use.

Finally, there's the capital gain on your collectibles—antiques, art, coins, guns, gemstones, stamps, and rugs—at a 28% maximum tax rate. If you're in the 15% tax bracket, your tax is 15% here, too. This presumes that you held the articles for longer than a year and have a cost basis you can defend. You can get IRS Publications 550, 551, and 564 to learn more than you want to know about this and other investment-related tax topics.

Capital gains and losses may result in your tax bill being reduced in those years when they were incurred. Toward the end of the year, look at your capital gains picture, including what your mutual funds might surprise you with in December. Now, perhaps you have an investment that's under water and looks likely to stay there, at least for a while. Sell it in December and apply the capital loss to your gains to reduce your tax bill for this year.

Taxes in Retirement

By now you can see that figuring your taxes in retirement may be more confusing than when you were working. This is true because now you have a variety of potential sources of income: pensions and tax-sheltered retirement plans, annuities, regular savings, investments, and Social Security. Each source has its own sets of tax laws and regulations to wrestle with.

That may be bad news, but there's good news as well. If you have to concern yourself with taxes on income from three or four sources, you're in healthy financial shape in retirement. But that financial health comes at a price—not only are your taxes complicated, but also you're likely to be in the same or even higher tax bracket than when you worked! Don't plan on being in a lower bracket unless you've done accurate projections that indicate this. But that's the price for successful financial planning—and it sure beats the alternatives.

Now that you'll no longer have taxes withheld from a paycheck, you'll have to take more responsibility for ensuring that your taxes are paid up during the year. The IRS requires that the tax due with your 1040 be less than $1,000. However, if by the end of the year you've paid at least 90% of your total tax or 100% of the total tax you paid the previous year, there's no penalty, except if you have an AGI of $150,000 (married filing jointly) or $75,000 (married filing separately). If so, a 1999 change in the tax law states that to escape the penalty for tax year 2001, the estimated tax safe harbor is 110% of the tax shown on your previous year's return.

To escape the penalty, you'll need to file estimated taxes and pay quarterly installments. Retirees need to pay quarterly to escape the penalty, even if they subsequently are due a refund when they file their 1040.

The IRS will kindly figure your penalty for you, unless you are using the annualized income installment method because your receipt of income is unevenly distributed during the year. Then, you must file Form 2210 and follow the instructions. IRS Publication 505 has all the ugly details on estimated taxes, and you'll use 1040-ES to file quarterly, in addition to your usual 1040 once a year.

Estimated taxes are normally due in four equal installments—by April 15, June 15, and September 15 of the current tax year, and by the following January 15. If you filed estimated taxes the previous year, the IRS will automatically send you the booklet and forms. Otherwise, call 800-829-3676 to request a 1040-ES package.

How to Protect Your Assets

The earlier parts of our book introduced concepts such as figuring out what you've got and how to use it to achieve your goals. This section will introduce protecting those assets so that they'll be around for you and your heirs.

We all purchase insurance, but we usually don't really give it much thought. We want you to look at insurance as a financial product that you use to protect yourself and your family. Insurance is not meant to be an investment; it's simply an agreement by which you pay a premium to the big insurance company and in return the company promises to pay you if you have a loss. A simple transaction, but it can get complicated when bells and whistles are added to that basic insurance policy.

Protecting your assets doesn't end with buying proper insurance. Now that you've accumulated stuff and increased your net worth substantially, how do you plan to save it for your heirs so Uncle Sam doesn't get his hands on it? We'll show you how to protect it from estate taxes and tell you when it's a grand idea to give it away to heirs or to a charity.

The last part of our book puts it all together for you, so you can get what you really want from life. And if you don't want to take on the job of being your own financial planner and doing it yourself, we researched the resources available to help. Here we point out what is safe to tackle yourself and what you should not be doing on your own. If you want professional help, we'll show you where to find that help.

Chapter 25 | Insurance: Protecting Your Stuff

Life Insurance

Life insurance should be viewed as a financial product that you buy to help you protect your family or your business if you're not around. No more, no less! Life insurance should be used to protect the loss of an income stream for dependents. If you don't have dependents, you probably don't need life insurance. Life insurance also has some sophisticated purposes, such as providing an estate for your heirs, protection of a business partnership, and liquidity in an estate, allowing your heirs to use the proceeds to pay taxes on assets they may not want to sell, such as your business.

Here we are going to discuss life insurance a way to protect your assets. Your greatest asset is your ability to earn a living. Think about how much money you will earn over your lifetime. It can be mind-boggling. With life insurance, you protect the loss of that income stream if someone is relying on you for support. We'll help you figure out who needs life insurance, how much you'll need, and what kind to purchase.

A gentle reminder: you should buy life insurance with your head and not your heart. So often we have seen people buy policies that they really don't need. Treat life insurance as protection and not as an investment. There are other very good investments to use for saving for retirement or college funding.

So who needs life insurance? Well, if you're single with no dependents, you probably can save money by investing instead. Most individuals have some coverage where they work, so that may be adequate. If you're married with no dependents, here also you probably don't need life insurance, unless you want to leave your spouse an inheritance. If you're married and you have children, whether one spouse or both are working, you need life insurance; the more children you have, the more life insurance you need. Finally, older married couples with grown children may need life insurance if they have not accumulated enough assets for either spouse to survive if the other dies.

Life insurance is available in many formats—too many—the consumer is confused. But there are really only two categories—term and cash value.

Term Insurance

Term provides a benefit if the insured person dies within a specified period of time. It is pure protection; all you are buying here is insurance. No bells or whistles. And because of that, it's much less expensive. But the premiums increase with the age of the policyholder. Today there are many types of term insurance available. You can even buy it using your computer.

- ✔ *Yearly Renewable Term*: Provides protection for one year and must be renewed annually. Premium increases annually.
- ✔ *Level Term*: Provides protection for specified number of years, usually 5 to 20 years. Premiums remain stable throughout that period.
- ✔ *Decreasing Term*: Provides protection each year for a fixed premium, but the amount of insurance decreases annually. Mortgage insurance is an example.
- ✔ *Convertible Term*: Allows conversion to a cash value policy.

Cash Value Insurance

A cash value insurance policy offers both protection and a savings or investment component. It's more expensive than term protection, because you're paying for insurance and the added savings plus more administrative charges from the insurance company. The savings grow tax-deferred; this sum is referred to as the cash value.

In the cash value category, we have several basic variations:

✔ Whole Life

✔ Universal Life

✔ Variable Life

We'll describe each of these briefly.

Whole life insurance is life insurance with a savings component. At the time of purchase, the insurance company determines the cost of the premium according to the age and health of the person being insured. The premium then stays the same for as long as the policy is owned. During the first few years, the insurance company credits very little to the "cash value" (savings portion) of the policy. Most whole life policies allow the owner to borrow from the cash value. The cash value accumulates tax-deferred and the insurance company determines the interest each year. To accumulate large sums in the cash value portion, you need to hold this policy for at least 20 years and then you can expect an average return of 4% to 5%.

Universal life insurance is supposedly more flexible than whole life. Premiums are flexible. Protection (the amount of coverage) is adjustable and may be increased or decreased without the insured showing proof of insurability. After the first premium is made, additional premiums may be made, increasing the savings portion. Savings accumulate tax-deferred, borrowing is permitted, and the interest paid is usually determined by the money market rates, which makes universal life a bit more competitive than whole life.

Variable life insurance allows the policyholder to decide how the savings portion should be invested, whether in stocks, bonds, mutual funds, and/or zero-coupon bonds. There's a guaranteed minimum death benefit and amounts earned above the face value are credited to the policyholder. There is a preconception that this type of policy will produce the best investment return, but a policyholder who's unfamiliar

> *The protected man doesn't need luck.*
> *—Alan Harrington*

with investing may do less well with variable life than with whole life. The cash value of a variable life policy can decrease if the value of the investments chosen decrease. Savings accumulate tax-deferred and borrowing is permitted. Borrowing sounds good, but if you have a $50,000 life insurance policy and borrow $10,000 from the cash value and then die with the loan outstanding, your beneficiary gets only $40,000.

The insurance industry is fraught with unethical salespeople and they try to police their own. But don't be taken in by churning. Some agents "churn" contracts, meaning they'll have you replace your existing cash value policy with a new one—not because you need different coverage, but because they earn a large commission from selling you a new policy. The commission can be as low as 10% for term insurance or as high as 100% of the first year's premium for a cash value policy. Most agents place their customers' needs first, but not all do so. If you have a problem with an agent or company, contact your state Division of Insurance to see what your rights are.

If you're looking for help to purchase term insurance, look to the quote services that are available:

Direct Quote	800-845-3853 or **www.directquote.com**
InstantQuote	800-223-2220 or **www.instant.quote.com**
QuickQuote	800-867-2404 or **www.quickquote.com**
Quotesmith	800-431-1147 or **www.quotesmith.com**

To find more help on the Internet, check out these sites:

✔ **www.insure.com** allows you to research the strength of an insurance company.

✔ **www.quicken.com** and **www.moneycentral.msn.com** have good insurance sections and both have worksheets that you can use to determine how much insurance you need, as well as links to sites where you can purchase term insurance directly.

On the next page, we've included a Life Insurance Needs Worksheet here for you to figure just how much insurance you really need. Insurance professionals have come up with a rule of thumb of 5 to 8 times your present salary. We've also heard $100,000 per child and spouse. Before you can figure out how much insurance you'll need, you should determine what your living expenses are and what you have in assets that will be available to support your dependents. If you're using an insurance agent, he or she should have already done a needs analysis for you, but you should also do one yourself. If you have a computer, it's easy to find an insurance calculator on any of the above sites, and it will do the adding and multiplying for you. If you use our worksheet get out your calculator.

For our worksheet we assumed a family of four, major wage earner was the father, and the mother worked part-time. They want to send their kids to college and pay off the mortgage if something should happen to one of them. You will need to do the calculations for each parent. To be accurate in your calculations, you'll need to find out from Social Security what your survivor benefits will be (800-772-1213).

Property and Casualty: Protecting the Stuff

Property and casualty insurance covers those perils (insurance talk meaning exposure to dangers) that involve owning property such as a home, an auto, and stuff in general. The casualty insurance covers the liability or loss resulting from an accident. So this type of insurance covers your hard assets and resulting liabilities.

Homeowner's Insurance

The single largest hard asset most of us will probably ever own is our home. It's critical to protect it with insurance. In fact, you may not have a choice. You cannot get a mortgage today without proof of homeowner's insurance. If something should happen to your home, the mortgage holder wants to be paid.

When you purchase homeowner's insurance, you usually get coverage for lots more than the structure of the house. A quick review of the

Expenses	Example	You
Immediate		
Funeral	$6,000	_____
Final Expenses	2,000	_____
Subtotal	8,000	_____
1-9 Months		
Probate Expenses	2,000	_____
Estate Taxes	4,000	_____
Mortgage Payoff	50,000	_____
Subtotal	56,000	_____
Beyond 9 months		
Emergency Fund	10,000	_____
College Funding	100,000	_____
Subtotal	110,000	_____
Lifetime Living Expenses		
Annual Living Expenses (from Cash Flow Worksheet, Chapter 2)	60,000	_____
Less Mortgage Payments (if you pay it off)		
Less Spouse's Take-Home	-12,000	_____
Pay	-20,000	_____
Less Social Security	-6,000	_____
Benefits	22,000	
Subtotal		_____
Multiply by Years Needed	x 18	x _____
Subtotal	396,000	_____
Total Expenses	**$570,000**	_____
Assets (available for support of dependents)		
Cash	10,000	_____
Investments	50,000	_____
Retirement Plans	50,000	_____
Life Insurance Already Owned	150,000	_____
Mortgage Insurance	50,000	_____
Total Assets	**$310,00**	_____
Insurance Needs		
Total Expenses	$570,000	_____
Less Total Assets	-310,000	_____
Total	**$260,000**	_____

FIGURE 25-1. LIFE INSURANCE NEEDS WORKSHEET

different basic types of policies will help you sort out the forms of coverage available:

- ✔ HO1: Very limited coverage, it specifies the perils it will cover.
- ✔ HO2: Less limiting, yet it also specifies the perils it will cover.
- ✔ HO3: The most widely purchased coverage, it covers all of the risks on buildings and specified risks on personal property. However, it excludes floods, earthquakes, wars, and nuclear accidents.
- ✔ HO4: Policy for renters, it covers personal property only and not the residence.
- ✔ HO5: Policy for condominium owners, it covers personal property and loss of use.

Most of us own an HO3 policy. This covers you against fire, lightning, wind, storms, hail, explosions, riots, aircraft wrecks, vehicle wrecks, smoke, vandalism, theft, breaking glass, falling objects, weight of snow or sleet, collapsing buildings, freezing of plumbing fixtures, electrical and water damage from plumbing or heating and air conditioning systems to the basic structure of the home, outbuildings such as a detached garage or shed, and the contents of the home usually up to an amount equal to 50% of the value of the home. It will cover those personal items even if something happens to them when you have removed them from the home, such as having your skis and luggage stolen from your car. It also covers personal items that may have gone off to college with your kid. Most of us have a deductible of anywhere from $250 to $5,000. If the items stolen fall below the deductible amount, the insurance company will not reimburse you for the loss.

This coverage will also provide some limited liability insurance. If someone is injured on your property or harmed by something you own, like a dog or a snowmobile, you can be held liable for those injuries. This coverage will provide some relief and also will cover the medical expenses of the injured party, usually up to $1,000. This is the minimum amount required and you may want to increase this coverage. Also covered are living expenses, if you should need to seek shelter elsewhere after a loss to your home. These expenses are limited to 20% of the replacement costs of your home.

You want to be sure that your home is insured for its replacement cost and not what you paid for it. The value of your home increases over time—as you know from rising property tax assessments! So you want to be sure your insurance keeps up with that increase. You need to be covered for at least 80% of the replacement costs. If you fall below that percentage, the insurance company can refuse to reimburse you in full for a total loss. Be sure the contents are covered for replacement costs as well.

If you own Beanie babies and you are sure they're worth a fortune, you better be sure to properly insure them. Collectibles such as antiques, oriental rungs, coins, and stamp collections are not normally covered. There's often an internal limit to how much an insurance company will pay for such things as jewelry and furs, so you will need to purchase extra insurance in the form of a rider to your policy for anything of value not covered.

> *The types and amount of insurance available are measures of how much we have to protect.*

Do you remember when you figured out back in Chapter 1 what you own and what it's worth? Well, you may need to go one step further here and get it appraised to prove to the insurance company that your collectibles and jewelry are valuable and worth insuring.

If you work at home, as so many of us do these days, you want to be sure you have coverage for your equipment and any liabilities that might arise due to your home office. This usually requires purchasing additional coverage in the form of an endorsement. By not letting the insurance company know you're working at home, you're risking much more than the extra premium you may be saving. The company can refuse to pay a claim.

What if you don't own a home? What if you rent? Then you need renter's or tenant's insurance. It will cover your personal property whether it's in the apartment or strapped to the top of your car. It will also provide some liability coverage, in case someone is injured while in your apartment. Suppose, for example, that you throw a party and a guest is dancing on your kitchen table and falls. Unlikely? Maybe. But it's possible, so you want liability coverage just in case.

To save on your premiums may require a bit of work on your part, but it's worth the effort. Here are some ideas that can help:

✔ Raise your deductible. The higher the deductible, the larger the discount. But be sure you have an emergency fund available to cover any losses you may incur.

✔ Install a home security system, including a burglar alarm, smoke detectors, carbon monoxide detectors, and dead bolt locks. You may feel more secure owning a large dog, but Fido doesn't count here.

✔ Check around for lower rates if you own a newer home. They're less expensive to insure than older homes.

✔ Request a senior discount, if you're old enough. (Be sure to ask, since the "age of seniority" can vary.)

✔ Consider group policies through a business or alumni association.

✔ Purchase all of your property and casualty insurance from one company.

✔ Shop around and get quotes from several companies.

Auto Insurance

If you own a car, in most states you can't register it unless you have auto insurance. And if you drive, even just a few miles from time to time, you definitely want auto insurance. If you're involved in an accident, you'll be financially responsible for damages. Nobody needs to remind you how expensive medical costs can be—or how expensive an accident can become if someone decides to sue you.

Auto insurance is used to protect your assets. It's a smart investment. And you may not have any choice. In some states there is compulsory/standard coverage that specifies the least you should have. The insurance company may then add optional coverage—the extra stuff you can buy. When you purchase auto insurance, be sure to ask lots of questions until you understand fully what protection you're purchasing and what's required of you. If you use your car for business, tell the insurance company about it. If you're in an accident you want to be sure they will not deny you coverage.

> *A primitive form of auto insurance from a bumper sticker: "You toucha my car, I breaka your face."*

When you shop around for auto insurance, ask lots of questions about the policies. Make sure you understand the coverages. Then, when you purchase a policy, be sure to ask lots of questions again, to make sure you understand fully what you're getting and what's required of you.

Below is a breakdown of the various coverages that are available.

- ✔ **Collision:** Covers the damage to your car if you collide with another vehicle or object. Coverage may extend to car rentals.
- ✔ **Comprehensive:** Pays for losses resulting from perils such as theft, fire, flood, vandalism, and glass breakage, but not collisions.
- ✔ **Liability:** Protects you or someone driving your car if you or that driver are at fault in an accident. It will pay for injuries and damages to the other party. It will also protect your assets if you are held liable for the damages.
- ✔ **Medical:** Covers you and your passengers for medical costs resulting from an accident.
- ✔ **Personal Injury Protection** (PIP or no-fault coverage): Pays for medical expenses, loss of wages, and death benefits no matter who causes the accident.
- ✔ **Rental Car/Substitute Transportation:** Pays for a rental car if your car is disabled up to certain stated limits (usually low) and may include taxi, bus, and train fare.
- ✔ **Supplemental Death Benefit:** Pays a death benefit if the insured dies as a result of an accident while wearing a seat belt. All passengers in the auto at that time must have been wearing seat belts. (How do you think they determine that?)
- ✔ **Towing and Labor:** Covers towing and on-site labor charges if your car breaks down, up to certain stated limits. Check the limits for they are usually very low.
- ✔ **Uninsured and Underinsured:** Protects the driver and passengers in an accident for medical expenses and loss of wages when caused by an uninsured, underinsured, or unidentified driver (translation: hit and run).

How much does all of this coverage cost? Well, that depends on several factors, particularly location, driving record, age, and type of vehicle. Where do you live? If you live in Boston, you may pay twice as much for insurance as a driver living in the suburbs 30 miles to the west. How do you drive? Many insurance companies have good driver rates, so your driving record is important. How old are you? Younger drivers tend to have more accidents and speeding tickets, so insurance companies make younger drivers pay more. What kind of car do you drive? A Volvo costs less to insure than a similarly priced BMW. Cars that are frequently stolen are also more expensive to insure. The most popular targets for car thefts are as follows:

- ✔ Honda Accord
- ✔ Toyota Camry
- ✔ Oldsmobile Cutlass
- ✔ Chevrolet Full-Size Pickup
- ✔ Honda Civic
- ✔ Toyota Corolla
- ✔ Jeep Cherokee
- ✔ Chevrolet Caprice
- ✔ Ford Taurus
- ✔ Chevrolet Cavalier

To save on your auto insurance, look for the discounts for which you may qualify, such as low-mileage driving, senior citizen, driver training, airbags, anti-theft devices, and automatic seat belts. Joining an automobile club such as AAA gets you a discount, as does belonging to some fraternal groups. You might consider raising the deductible. If you drive an older vehicle, you may want to drop the collision or comprehensive coverage.

With auto insurance you're not only insuring your auto; you're also insuring against a loss if you're at fault in an accident. Without proper insurance, you could lose everything you've worked so hard to get. In some cases, you could even find your future wages garnished. So think of your car or truck not just as property, but as a legal liability on wheels. Make sure that you insure it at least adequately.

Umbrella Liability Coverage

There is liability coverage provided by your homeowner's policy and your auto insurance. If you have purchased the maximum amount, the coverage will be $300,000 for each. This is important coverage, because if you or yours damage another's property or injure someone, you are liable. Then the liability portions of your policies kick in.

But what if someone sues for you $1 million for the pain and suffering he or she has endured due to an automobile accident you caused? You won't have enough coverage with your auto policy, so the legal action could force the sale of your personal assets to satisfy the judgment and even garnishee future wages.

How likely is that? Well, we live in a very litigious society, where people are sued for missing a prom date and a woman who spills hot coffee on herself can collect $8 million from McDonald's for her pain and suffering. So you're not Ronald McDonald, you're saying. No, maybe you don't have what's known in legal circles as "deep pockets." But we're here to warn you about the evils that lurk out there. When it comes to dollars, even family members sue each other.

An umbrella policy behaves just as you think it might. It covers you where the other liability coverage ends. Umbrella insurance is typically available in $1 million increments and costs about $100 to $200 for each million of coverage. To use our example above, if you were sued for $1 million, your auto insurance would kick in at $300,000 and the umbrella policy would provide the next $700,000.

Do you need the extra coverage? That's an assessment you should make. If you own a big dog that bites and you like to zip through the woods on your snowmobile or your kid builds model rockets, you just may want to consider this extra insurance. A little money can buy a lot of peace of mind.

Medical Insurance

Medical insurance today is not an option but a must. Nobody can afford to go without this basic protection today. Medical costs are outrageous. An illness with a hospital stay could easily bankrupt even the best of savers. Medical insurance can mean a big difference in treatment. When you enter a hospital emergency room, the first thing the staff asks you is what kind of insurance you have.

Most individuals today have medical insurance through their employers. That's a very important benefit. The government provides medical insurance for some people, through Medicare for those who are 65 and older and Medicaid for the poor. But a number of people who are self-employed or who retired early have had to find health insurance on their own.

There are three kinds of coverage that are offered today. There are the traditional indemnity plans, health maintenance organizations (HMOs), and preferred provider organizations (PPOs). If you're lucky, your employer may offer more than one type of plan.

Indemnity plans allow you the most choices. They generally include reimbursement for hospitalization and other medical expenses. There's usually a deductible, an amount you pay out of your pocket before the insurance company will start paying. After you've met the deductible and incurred a specified amount of coinsurance payouts, you may reach the out-of-pocket limit. The out-of-pocket limit is set so you do not exhaust your savings during a major illness. Indemnity plans can be individually purchased or purchased by a company as a group benefit.

Health maintenance organizations (HMOs) offer an alternative to the traditional health care delivery system. An HMO is an organization of health care personnel and facilities that provide a broad range of benefits on a prepaid basis. There are many variations of HMOs. The two most common types are:

- ✔ Group practice model: The HMO hires or contracts with physicians and other health care professionals to provide medical treatment at a central facility.
- ✔ Individual practice association: The HMO contracts with individual physicians who treat HMO members in their own neighborhood offices.

Preferred provider organizations (PPOs) appear at first glance to be a compromise between an indemnity plan and an HMO. PPOs generally administer health care benefits through a predetermined network. A network is a group of doctors, hospitals, and other health care providers that have agreed to provide services at specially negotiated rates under contract with an insurance company administrator.

People who enroll in a PPO choose a network based on the hospitals and health care providers in the network as well as on their geographic location of residence. Under most PPOs, benefits are reduced if an out-of-network health care provider or facility is used.

Disability Insurance

Between the ages of 25 and 55, you're more than twice as likely to become disabled as to die. Life insurance protects your dependents if you should die. But what if you are unable to work? Disability insurance will protect you and provide an income stream for you and your dependents.

All of the rules here that we used to determine who needs life insurance go out the window. If you are single, you need disability insurance. Who will support you if you can no longer work? If you're married and both you and your spouse are earning money, each of you needs disability insurance. If you have children, you need disability insurance. Basically, anybody who's earning money probably needs disability insurance. Think of it as protecting your future income.

So how much do you need and where can you buy it? Insurance companies will not normally insure a worker for more than 60% of his or her current income. The insurance companies want you to have some incentive to return to work. If they guaranteed you 100% of your income, they fear that more workers would find ways to work the system and become disabled. So you cannot get complete income coverage.

Disability insurance is becoming more expensive. Look to your employer first, since that's where it will probably be the cheapest. Unfortunately, because of the abuses and the rising costs, fewer employers are offering disability insurance. If it's not being offered as a group benefit, ask why. Sometimes all it takes is for the employees to ask. If nothing is available, then you may need to seek outside resources.

Check with your insurance agent and see what he or she can find for you. Prices can vary dramatically, so check more than one source. It may not be easy to find or very affordable, especially for those who may need it the most, such as a self-employed construction worker. So do some research here. Visit Quicken's insurance site, **www.insure-market.com**, to get more information and even some quotes.

Disability insurance is complicated and so are the contracts. When reviewing a contract, look at how the policy defines "disability." The best definition would read that a disability would be your inability to perform the duties required by your specific occupation. This is a very narrow definition, which benefits the worker but certainly not the insurance company. Most policies will define "disability" is an inability to work in any job at all. The price of the policy will depend, of course, on the definition of disability.

Next you want to settle on a waiting period: how long must you be disabled before the policy benefits kick in? Usually you have some flexibility here. Of course, the longer you're able to wait, the lower the price. Waiting periods vary from 30 days to 18 months and the real savings begin after a 90-day waiting period. So look at that emergency fund you've accumulated. How long could it carry you if you became disabled? The more personal savings you have, the longer the waiting period you can afford to accept.

Then you need to decide how long you want the benefits to last. Benefits that last a lifetime will be expensive. You can get them to last for six months, for five years, or until you reach age 65 and become eligible for Social Security retirement benefits.

There are other sources of disability insurance available. Social Security provides disability benefits as well as retirement benefits. But it's extremely difficult to qualify for a Social Security disability. Most individuals who apply for disability benefits from Social Security fail; the failure rate for first-time applicants is over 80%. The average disability benefit for 2001 for a single worker is $786 and for a married disabled worker with one child the benefit is $1,310.

You also may be eligible for worker's compensation that is provided by your employer and pays a disability benefit if the disability is job-related. Payments here are low also and don't last very long, because again they want the worker back to work as soon as possible.

If you're now thinking, "This will never happen to me," hear us out. The chances that you'll experience a disability that will last three months or longer before you reach age 65 are up around 50%. So if you don't have disability insurance, be sure you have an adequate emergency fund stashed away. If your employer allows you to accumulate sick days and you've accumulated 90 days or more, you're probably covered adequately for a short-term disability. If not, then start setting aside a little something for a rainy day.

Long-Term Care Insurance

Long-term care is simply defined as the care needed for individuals with chronic disabilities. This care may be in the individual's home or it may mean custodial care in a nursing home. It isn't restricted just to the elderly. Christopher Reeve, for example, is receiving long-term care. We normally associate long-term care with growing old and none of us want to end up in a nursing home. But some of us just may.

Planning for long-term care is difficult. Why? Because we don't know if we'll ever need it during our lifetimes. Studies have indicated that 40% of Americans over age 65 will eventually need some kind of long-term care. But the key here is for how long. At age 65 if you have a hip replacement the hospital will discharge you in a week. You certainly are not capable of taking care yourself, so what does happen? You are admitted to a nursing home for rehabilitation. Now that stay may be 2 to 8 weeks depending how quickly you recuperate and then once you are home there may be more care needed. So you are thrown into the 40% statistic.

According to the National Center for Health Statistics in 1995 only 4% of the 65+ population lived in nursing home. That's about 1.4 million individuals. That breaks down to 1% of persons between the ages of 65 and 74, 5% for persons 75-84, and it goes up dramatically to 15% for individuals 85+. The good news is we're all living longer; the bad news is we're all living longer. Modern medicine works its miracles and a 79-year-old has bypass surgery and lives another 10 years. But as we age we become more frail and very well may need some sort of long-term care. So you need to look at your family history and your own health to decide if long-term care insurance is right for you. And from experience it is usually women who need long-term care insurance. Women live longer than men, and usually are the caregivers and may care for a spouse at home. Currently over 72% of nursing home residents are women.

> *Long-term care looks more sensible when you realize that without it, the short-term is all there is for you.*

There are other factors that should be taken into account before purchasing LTC insurance. Does it make sense financially for you? This is definitely middle class insurance. If you have assets over $150,000 excluding your home that you may want to protect you may want to purchase insurance. But if your major asset is your home and you have a retirement income from Social Security and your pension you probably don't need to buy insurance. And if you have enough assets that will produce an income to pay for long-term care you probably don't need to purchase insurance either.

The government would like us all to purchase long-term care insurance. Why? Because they don't like being in the business of providing nursing home care. If you cannot pay for your nursing home stay, the government provides payments to cover your stay through Medicaid. Medicaid is a jointly funded cooperative venture between the federal government and state government. It is designed to help those with low income or no income and very little resources. Each state has its own rules about who can apply for Medicaid, so you will need to understand what is available where you live.

So how much is this going to cost you if you do want to purchase insurance? It depends on how old you are when you purchase the insurance. The younger you are the less expensive it will be. How long do you want the policy to pay benefits on your behalf? And of course, how much do you want? The greater the daily benefit the more expensive the policy. It's like buying a pizza, the more toppings you want the more it costs. Work backwards here, the average annual cost of a nursing home stay is $45,000. Now on either coast it goes up to $60,000 very quickly. But let's work with the $45,000. That's about $125 a day. If your income from your pensions and Social Security is about $30,000 a year you will need insurance to provide you with a daily benefit of $50 a day.

But when you're figuring how much you need, remember that nasty threat to your well-being, inflation. That $45,000 number is good for 2000. In ten years, assuming a 4% inflation rate, you'll need $67,000. When reviewing policies be sure you consider an inflation rider so your policy keeps up with reality. So how much? A 65-year-old in good health (You don't think they want to insure the sick here, do you?) can purchase a good long-term care insurance policy with a 90-day waiting period, a 3-year benefit period, $100-a-day benefit for either home care or nursing home care for under $2,000 a year. For a 60-year-old that figure drops to $1,500. Even if you can afford it, be sure you need it. And do some comparison shopping. Get quotes from reputable insurance companies and compare the policies. Long-term care insurance is a fairly new product for the insurance industry and because of that standardization of policies and language doesn't exist across the board just yet.

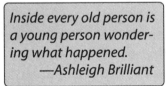
Inside every old person is a young person wondering what happened.
—Ashleigh Brilliant

Whatever policy you purchase, be sure it provides benefits for home care. Our elders want to stay in their own homes. According to the Department of Health and Human Services, the number of nursing home residents was up only 4% between 1985 and 1995 despite an 18% increase in population aged 65 and older. So home care is important.

Now we mentioned that the government has been the primary source for funding long-term care for our elders and it is expensive. It is costing all of us billions of tax dollars each year to support our elders in nursing homes. And some citizens don't think they should use the money they saved during their lifetime to pay for nursing home care costs. So they try to do an end run around the government and make themselves very poor so that they will be eligible to receive

Medicaid if they need nursing home care. This is probably not a wise decision because to make yourself poor you'll need to give up control of your money or give it all away. Buy insurance and if you have assets you want the kids to have and you can't afford the insurance, the kids should pay for the long-term care insurance. If the kids will benefit then let them pay for the insurance.

The government uses laws and taxes to help change social behavior. As incentive to purchase long-term care insurance you may now deduct the premiums if you itemize. All qualifying premiums are treated as medical expenses subject to the overall 7.5% of AGI limit. For the year 2001, for ages 40 or less, the maximum amount is $230. For ages 40-49, it's $430, for ages 51 to 60 it's $860, for ages 61 to 70 it's $2,290, and for those over 70 it is $2,860. These numbers will be indexed annually.

Chapter 26 | Estate Planning

You Can't Take It with You

You can't take it with you, but you can control who gets it. Too often, successful people devote their working lives to accumulating stuff and never give any thought as to how they might want to give it away, either upon their death or during their lifetime. The ideal scenario would be to use up all of your assets during your lifetime. Then there would be nothing to be concerned about. We once met a woman who said she wanted some help with her estate planning. When she died, she told us, she wanted the check to the undertaker to bounce so her children would have to sell her jewelry to pay for the funeral. As good as we are, we can't help you plan that accurately. Our goal for you as a retiree is to make sure you don't outlive your money so you won't have to live with one of your kids.

Estate planning is more than just having a will. It's about accumulating wealth, preserving and protecting that wealth, and passing on that wealth to your heirs. It's also about using that wealth to protect you if you should become incapacitated.

And by the way, we know that 70% of you reading this chapter don't have a will and have put off your estate planning. Estate planning allows you to put in place the mechanisms to protect your family, heirs, and assets when you die. Yes, this chapter is about mortality and that's why we put it at the end of the book. The one thing we are all sure of is that we are going to die; we just don't know when. So it just makes sense to be prepared. Estate planning not only helps you plan for the inevitable, but also helps you plan for the uncertainty as to when.

> *When it comes to dividing an estate, the politest men quarrel.*
> *—Emerson*

Inventory

Your first step in the estate planning process is something you've already done, we hope. Taking inventory consists of figuring out what you are worth and, if you're married, how your assets are owned.

It's basically simple. Your estate would include anything that you own. If it's owned jointly, then only half the value goes into your estate. Also include the proceeds from your life insurance policies here. That's right, you need to include the proceeds from your life insurance! If you own your life insurance policy, the proceeds will pass to your beneficiaries, but you include them in your estate when you go to figure out what taxes will be owed. (To keep the proceeds out of your estate, someone else should own the life insurance policy, such as a spouse or a trust.)

This figure should represent the sum value of what you own the day you die. The larger your estate, the more complicated your estate planning will need to be—you don't want to unconsciously make Uncle Sam one of your heirs. Estate planning is also more complicated if your life is more complicated. If you've had several marriages with kids from each and a business, well, you're going to need some sophisticated planning.

Essentials of Good Estate Planning

As we said, you can't take it with you, but if you do some planning it will go where you want it to go. What if you don't decide, at least in writing? If you die without a will (intestate), the state where you reside has laws that dictate how your assets will be distributed. If you have minor children, who will be their guardians? And each state has a different set of estate laws, some of them very archaic.

Good estate planning should accomplish the following:

✔ Name an executor to carry out your directions in the will.

✔ Name a guardian, if you have dependent children.

✔ Distribute your assets according to your wishes.

✔ Transfer assets smoothly.

✔ Reduce or eliminate estate taxes.

✔ Protect you, should you become mentally or physically incapacitated.

✔ Provide direction, if you are incapable of making medical decisions.

Let's start with the documents you will need to consider for your estate plan—a will, trusts, a durable power of attorney, an advance directive, and a letter of instruction. We'll discuss wills and trusts first, then cover the last three in the following section.

Wills

A will is a document that tells the world how you would like to have your worldly assets distributed and to whom. It is here where you designate a guardian for any dependent children and name an executor to carry out your wishes.

Your will won't work for assets that you own jointly with another person or for assets for which you name a beneficiary, such as your retirement plans or life insurance. Those assets will pass automatically upon your death.

> *A will can be a complicated legal document, but for your heirs it's not as complicated as not having one.*

To be valid, your will must be witnessed. In most states, you can meet that requirement by having two people witness your signature and then having both of them in turn sign the will. Your will should be notarized and the notary seal stamped on the will is further proof that you and your witnesses signed freely. It's not a good idea to have one of your heirs be a witness. That looks a bit like coercion.

What if you draw up your will, then change your mind? You can change your will accordingly, at any time; it becomes final only when you die. You can make changes in two ways. For significant changes, you create a new will, stating that this is the current will, and revoke the old will. The later date will be adequate proof, but you should destroy all old wills so there's no confusion. If the changes are simple, you can easily add a codicil (an amendment) to your current will and it will update effective the day you sign it.

Not only is it possible to change a will, it's generally a good idea, at least to keep it current. You should review your will periodically about every five years and after any major life change. What qualifies as a major life change? Here are the usual major life changes:

✔ You move to another state.

✔ Your family situation changes (marriage, children, divorce).

✔ Your estate increases or decreases.

✔ You change your mind about a beneficiary or his or her needs change.

✔ The federal or state estate tax laws change.

A will is subject to probate. This term comes from the Latin word, *probare*, meaning "to prove." Probate is the official proving of a will as authentic and valid. This is a public process that has costs associated with it. Your executor will file your will with the probate court and the court will oversee the process of the distribution of your assets and the payment of taxes due. Interested parties are notified and have a stated period of time in which to challenge the will.

> You may believe in free will, but in the case of wills, they are decidedly not free.

Trusts

Trusts aren't just for the Rockefellers any more. You and your heirs may benefit from using the various trusts available.

Think of a trust as a special account inside a box. You can put things into this box and maybe you can take them out. We say "maybe" because there are two basic types of trusts. If you make your trust *irrev-*

ocable, you can't get your stuff back out of the box. A *revocable* trust, on the other hand, allows you to make changes. Upon your death, your revocable trusts become irrevocable, since you won't be around to make any changes. A trust is a legal document, and if it is funded, it is responsible for paying taxes on earnings from its investments.

The most common trust is a *living* trust, which is used while you're still alive. You put everything you own into this trust and you name a trustee. You could name yourself or you could name a professional, such as a bank. If you are the trustee, you'll need to name a successor trustee to take over if you become incapacitated or when you die. If you are the beneficiary of your trust, you'll need to name a successor beneficiary for your trust and describe when and how that next beneficiary should receive the assets from the trust. The trust holds and manages your assets for your benefit or for the beneficiaries while you are alive. If the trust is revocable, you can take things out of it and you can put things into it. So the stuff in the box is accessible to you. And as the trustee you'll be responsible for filing an income tax return for your trust.

Here's the No. 1 reason people cite for using a living trust: it is not subject to probate. A person who wants to keep his or her affairs out of the public eye can use a living trust. When the person dies, the assets in the trust are transferred to the beneficiaries easily.

There's usually one big mistake people make with these types of trusts. They have their estate planning attorney draw up a wonderful trust—then they don't fund it properly. You see, the trust must now own all of your stuff. The title on your home needs to read "The John Rockefeller trust" and not "John Rockefeller." Upon your death, any of your assets that are titled in your name must pass through the probate process and your will. So if you're contemplating a living trust, make sure that it owns all of your stuff and that it's a revocable trust, so you can change it.

One final point on living trusts: they do not avoid estate taxes. If the assets in the trust exceed the unified gift and estate tax exemption ($675,000 for 2001), your estate will owe taxes.

A testamentary trust is created by your will and becomes effective upon your death. You can change it as you like, until you die. Your will pours assets into this trust and the assets will be managed for the beneficiary.

For example, you may leave your money to a minor child by arranging for a testamentary trust in your will. Upon your death, a trust is set up to manage the money for the child until he or she reaches an age specified in the trust. If you have a special needs child who is physically or mentally handicapped, you'll need to consider using a "special needs" trust. This trust would provide payments to the child rather than a lump sum payout that could cause him or her to be disqualified for government-provided benefits such as a group home.

> *A trust may be worth putting your trust in.*

We need to tell you that estate planning needs to be done by a competent estate planning attorney. Don't mess with this! This doesn't mean you shouldn't read books or hit the Web for research. But you should hire an attorney to draft the documents you'll need. You have too much at stake here to risk it by trying to do it yourself. The tax law changes made in 2001 will greatly affect estate planning through 2010 and you will need a competent attorney who understands all of the tax ramifications.

The Powers That Be

Wills and trusts are essential to estate planning. There are two basic ways of taking action to carry out your plans for the future. Now we need to discuss three more—durable power of attorney, an advance directive, and a letter of instruction.

Power of Attorney

Estate planning is more than passing assets to the next generation. It provides the mechanisms for you, while you are hale and hearty and (of course) of sound mind, to appoint representatives to act on your behalf, legally, financially, and medically should you become incapacitated.

A durable power of attorney is a legal document in which you designate someone to act on your behalf legally and financially. This person becomes your attorney-in-fact. You may limit this power or make it all-encompassing.

But what makes this document different is the word "durable." Not all powers of attorney are durable. Many of the powers created in the

'80s did not have the wording necessary to make them durable. A sentence in the document such as "This power of attorney shall not be affected by the subsequent disability or incapacity of the principal" makes it durable. If the power is not durable, it will automatically be revoked if you become disabled or incapacitated. In other words, just when you most need the assurance that another can act on your behalf, the person whom you trusted with this power will no longer be able to exercise it.

If you have not given someone a durable power of attorney to act on your behalf, the probate court must appoint someone to be your conservator or the guardian of your property. This applies to a spouse even if you own property jointly. The healthy spouse cannot sell, mortgage, or transfer the other spouse's interest in that property. Once a guardian is appointed, he or she will be subject to the jurisdiction of the probate court and have to make annual reports to the court.

A less expensive alternative is having a durable power of attorney in place. This power is omnipotent: it gives the legal right to enter your financial world and write checks from your account, sell your property, file your income taxes, pay your bills, gift your property away, sell your investments, etc. It's probably not necessary to mention this, but chose a person you trust. If you're married, your spouse is a logical choice, with an adult son or daughter as an alternate. Do not give two individuals joint power. That only leads to problems, especially if you choose two of your children. If they didn't get along together growing up, we guarantee you that things probably haven't changed much. And small problems tend to grow when there's a lot riding on the decisions involved.

There are several types of powers of attorney:

✔ *Limited power of attorney* grants authority to act on your behalf in specific situations or for limited time periods.

✔ *Springing power of the attorney* grants authority that "springs" into being only if and when you become disabled.

✔ *General power of attorney* grants authority to conduct all affairs on your behalf, but ceases if you should become incapacitated if it does not have a "durable" provision.

✔ *Durable power of attorney* grants authority that remains effective even if you should become disabled or incapacitated and provides assurance that you have assistance when you most need it.

Advance Directives

By law, every individual has control over his or her health care. Except in emergencies, medical providers must obtain a patient's approval for any form of treatment. In the case of a minor, approval is sought from the child's parents or guardian.

Advance directives are documents through which an individual can direct or delegate medical decisions in the event that he or she becomes incapacitated. The state where you reside dictates what type of advance directive is available to you. By federal law, hospitals and other health care institutions that accept Medicare payments must make known to their patients what advance directives are available to them. So if you have recently been admitted to the hospital, you may have been asked if you have an advance directive and, if you do not, if you would like to execute one prior to admission.

Advance directives fall into two categories: a health care proxy or a medical directive.

A *health care proxy* allows you to delegate someone to make health care decisions for you. It's sometimes called a health care power of attorney. It gives you an "agent" to make decisions for you if you cannot make them yourself. It gives your health care providers one person to consult, which makes it much easier if there are decisions to be made quickly.

A *medical directive* is a document that states your wishes if you should become incapacitated. The most common form of a medical directive is a living will, which allows you to determine the life-sustaining medical care you want to receive in the event of a terminal condition, a coma, or a vegetative state. In some states, living wills are not recognized as legal documents, but rather as guidelines for your agent and the health care professionals caring for you.

Choosing an agent is often the most difficult part of this process. The ideal agent should be someone who knows you well, understands your values and beliefs, and can make your wishes known and respected. Preparing an advance directive will force you to deal with the possibility of not always being able to make your own health care decisions. That thought may be uncomfortable for you.

Before naming an agent, discuss with him or her your feelings about the following:

✔ Terminal illness

✔ Mental incapacity

✔ Your sense of dignity

✔ Self-worth

✔ Personal values

✔ Religious beliefs

The ideal agent should be your philosophical "soul mate" and someone who can be a strong advocate for you. An agent should be willing and able to carry out your wishes regarding health care decisions. The decisions made should represent your wishes and desires.

Here's our advice. Do not name more than one agent to act on your behalf. Always have an alternate if your first choice can not serve, but naming several of your children or a child and spouse can lead to family squabbles just when your loved ones need to be supportive of you and each other. To find out what options are available in your state, contact Partnership For Caring by phone at 800-989-9455 or through their Web site at **www.partnershipforcaring.com**.

Letter of Instruction

A letter of instruction is a catchall document. It's a letter you write to your heirs, those you leave behind. It's not legally binding. In fact, a few states don't even consider it valid. In it you can state your wishes, such as how you may wish your executor to distribute your household and personal items. For example, you may want that new granddaughter to receive your pearl earrings or your grandson to receive your father's pocket watch. These are details that you might not include in a will, but that can be very important.

A letter of instruction is a convenient vehicle. You can change it periodically to suit the current situation, in case your luggage gets stolen and one of the bags contained the family heirloom pearls. (We hope that you had gotten a rider on your homeowner's policy so at least you were able to replace the pearls, although nothing can compensate for the emotional loss.) Since you no longer have the family heirloom pearls to give away, you can easily execute a new letter in which you can give the intended beneficiary something else. And you can do this without going through the fuss, bother, and expense of changing your will.

If you wish to make a personal statement and say something to your heirs that you have not said while living, a letter of instruction gives you a great opportunity. When we called it a "catchall document," we meant just that. Put all of the unfinished business in here.

Have you given any thought about funeral arrangements? Many people think about what would be appropriate; generally the older we grow the more often we think about our demise. So if you want to plan your funeral, go ahead and do it. You can arrange it yourself by paying in advance for the goods and services, such as a funeral and a casket, or you can leave instructions for the children or your spouse in a letter of instruction. If you include funeral arrangements in your letter of instruction, be sure your survivors know where to find this letter, so they can read it immediately after your death. That way, they can plan everything according to your wishes, rather than finding it later, when they can no longer respect your wishes.

A friend of ours told us the story of his uncle's funeral in Florida. His uncle was a healthy confirmed bachelor in his 60s and died very suddenly. His closest relatives were his sister and her three sons, the oldest of whom is our friend. All of the relatives lived in the north, so the oldest nephew made all of the funeral arrangements by phone, after conferring with his mother about what she thought her brother might like for a service. The service was to be on a Monday, and the family planned to convene on Sunday evening in time for the wake. The service was very simple, and the uncle was buried next to his mother on Monday morning. The brothers convened again, this time in the uncle's apartment, to begin to sort through the inevitable stuff one must go through after a death. There they found their uncle's will and his letter of instruction, which stated that he wished to be cremated and have his ashes thrown out to sea as he had spent so much of his adult life as a merchant marine. If you want your wishes carried out, make sure someone knows what those wishes are.

If you plan your funeral, be sure your loved ones know what you want and where to find your instructions. Computers are playing an every larger role in our lives, and we have seen funeral planning software(!) that is available to help you.

It's also a good idea to keep a contact list with your letter, a list of all the relatives and friends who should be notified, with phone numbers. (And check the list regularly to keep it current.) Here's another recommendation: if you've chosen to be an organ donor, make sure your family knows your wishes about this. It's not morbid; it's just common sense to be prepared. When death comes, time is suddenly very valuable.

Nothing Is Certain but Death and Taxes

Benjamin Franklin noted that "nothing is certain but death and taxes" over 200 years ago. Nothing has changed. The government still has its hand in your pocket right up until the end, and if you think you're taking it with you, think again. And if you've accumulated a lot, Uncle Sam will definitely stake a claim on it.

Before we begin this section, we must admit that we agree with you—estate taxes are not fair. They constitute double taxation in some instances, and they are very complicated. You can go to **www.amazon.com** or **www.barnesandnoble.com** and find over 600 books on estate planning. When researching a book be sure it has been updated to include the tax law changes of 2001. These new changes will keep lawyers employed for a long time to come. And worse not all of the changes have been made for we will need some correctiosn to the new law to fix some existing problems.

So, read up on the last taxes you'll ever pay—and find ways to leave a little more to your loved ones and a little less to your Uncle Sam.

Estate and Gift Tax

The federal estate and gift tax is a transfer tax assessed on property you give away either during your lifetime or upon your death. The estate and gift taxes are called *unified* because the same tax rates, deductions, and rules apply to both.

During your lifetime or upon your death you can give away in 2001 $675,000 of assets without incurring a federal estate or gift tax. The $675,000 is your *unified credit exemption* and will eventually reach $3.5 million by the year 2009 and for the year 2010, the estate tax is repealed, and then in 2011 it will go back to the levels of 2001 unless Congress makes changes in the law again. Stupid we know! You voted for them, what can we say! If you have not given away assets while you were living, then the unified credit amount will be the amount you can leave to your heirs free of federal taxes upon your death. If your estate exceeds that amount, your estate is subject to marginal tax rates starting at 37% and reaching 60%. This too will change and as our exemption increases over through 2009, the tax rate will decline. The charts just below provides more specifics. The chart just below provides more specifics.

Year	Estate and GST Exemption	Top Estate and Gift Tax Rate
2002	$1 million	50%
2003	$1 million	49%
2004	$1.5 million	48%
2005	$1.5 million	47%
2006	$2 million	46%
2007	$2 million	45%
2008	$2 million	45%
2009	$3.5 million	45%
2010	N/ATaxes repealed, top individual rate, 35% (gift tax only	N/A

If you're married, the government hands you a bit of a bonus: you may leave everything to your spouse free of federal estate taxes. That's called the *unlimited marital deduction*. But if your combined estates are over $675,000, you may want to do some planning so that each of you can take advantage of your own $675,000 exemption. If you don't use your exemption at death, it vanishes—your surviving spouse can't use it.

Let's take an example. Suppose that you finally surrender to our not so subtle hints that you fill out a net worth statement. You discover that your family's net worth is $1.5 million. Many of your assets are owned jointly and each of you is named as beneficiaries on the retirement plans and the life insurance policies.

Upon the death of the first spouse, everything will go to the surviving spouse. There will be no federal estate taxes owed because of the marital deduction. But what happens when the surviving spouse dies? She now has an estate worth over $1.5 million, and if she does not deplete the assets before she dies, she'll be able to use her $1 million exemption in 2002 to shelter some of the taxes. But her estate will still owe taxes on $500,000. At the marginal rate of 43% that amounts to $215,000. With some planning, though, you can disinherit Uncle Sam and give the $500,000 to your heirs free of estate taxes.

Both spouses need to take advantage of their unified credit exemptions and you'll need to set up a trust. Rather than owning most of the assets jointly, you should try to equalize your estates. (That may not be easy if one spouse has a large retirement plan.)

For example, let's give the husband $900,000 and the wife $600,000. When the husband dies (wives usually outlive husbands), his will leaves his assets to a family trust (also called a *bypass* or a *credit shelter* trust) designed to take advantage of his unified credit exemption. What does not go into the trust the wife can receive free of federal estate taxes. His widow can receive all of the income from the family trust and will be able to control it. When she dies, the assets in the trust pass to their children free of estate taxes. Her assets will also pass to the children free of federal estate taxes, because of her unified credit exemption. That planning results in a savings of $215,000. Now if we could plan exactly when they would die and it would in the year 2010 we would have no need for planning at all would we?

The more complicated your life and finances, the more complicated your estate planning needs to be. If, for example, you are in a second marriage and want to be sure your assets get to your kids from the first marriage, you may want to use a qualified terminable interest property (QTIP) trust. Only a spouse can be the beneficiary of the trust, which qualifies for the marital deduction. In your will, you authorize your executor or trustee to create a QTIP trust upon your death. Then your surviving spouse, as beneficiary, will receive income from the trust annually as long as he or she lives. You can arrange for this income to be all income from the trust, 5% or $5,000 (whichever is greater), or any amounts needed for the spouse's health, education, maintenance, and support. A QTIP trust does not allow the surviving spouse any control over the trust. Then, when he or she dies, the trust property will be distributed to the children.

50 States, 50 Sets of Laws

We pointed out to you earlier that every state has different estate tax laws and they all have different tax structures as well. It's impossible to cover them all here, so we'll be referring only to federal estate taxes.

Many states accept the state death tax credit from the federal estate tax return on estates over the exemption amount. Florida may claim not to have any estate taxes, but it still manages to get a piece of the action by "sponging" from the federal estate taxes your estate may pay if you're residing in Florida when you die. If you're a snowbird spending six months up north and six months someplace warm, carefully choose which state you want to legally reside in. Part of that thought process should include how the estate tax laws will affect you as well as the income tax laws.

Oops! One more thing we need to tell you, if you're married. All bets are off if you reside or have resided in one of the community property states—Arizona, California, Idaho, Louisiana, New Mexico, Nevada, Texas, Washington, and Wisconsin. All assets acquired during a marriage in a community property state are owned equally by each spouse, no matter whose earnings were used to acquire the asset. So check in with your attorney if you're married and a resident of one of these states.

Spouses Who Are Not U.S. Citizens

Married couples have an unlimited marital deduction, meaning that you can leave everything to a spouse when you die and there will be no taxes due. Well, there's an exception to that rule. If the spouse receiving the estate is not a U.S. citizen, the transfer of assets upon death will not qualify for the unlimited deduction.

Any gifts in excess of $100,000 to a spouse who's not a U.S. citizen will be subject to federal gift/death tax unless it passes to a qualified domestic trust (QDOT). A QDOT must have at least one trustee who is a U.S. citizen. No distributions other than income may be made from this trust unless the trustee has the right to withhold any additional estate tax imposed on the trust.

Now this may appear to be downright nasty on the part of the government. But there's a reason why the feds are so strict about this. They don't want a surviving spouse who's not a U.S. citizen leaving the country with the inherited assets. They would have no way of taxing those assets when the spouse dies as they do with U.S. citizens. If you fall into this category, you need to get some professional help here to figure it all out.

Gifting

"'Tis better to give than to receive." And certainly if you want to save on estate taxes, giving away assets will help reduce your estate and thus reduce your taxes. There are, of course, other reasons to give, but we're in the estate planning section so we'll focus on tax savings here.

There's a gift tax annual exclusion that each of you may take advantage of. You can give away $10,000 annually in money or property to as many individuals as you want to without incurring a gift tax or using your unified credit exemption. (This $10,000 exclusion will be indexed for inflation, in increments of $1,000.) The recipient of your gift does not pay a tax upon receiving the gift, and you do not get a tax deduction for the gift. The recipient will owe taxes on any income the gift produces. If you give property such as shares of stock, the recipient will take on your cost basis; if he or she sells the stock, there may be a capital gains tax to pay.

If you're married and your spouse consents to the gift, you can increase the gift amount to $20,000. For example, we know a couple in their late 70s with a current estate of $3.5 million. They have income from Social Security, pensions, and their portfolio, and they don't consume all of the income produced. They have four children, all married, and nine grandchildren, one married, and one great grandbaby.

To pare down their taxable estate, they begin a gifting program. The first year of the program, they can together gift $20,000 to each recipient. They have 14 descendants; if they wish to include their in-laws, that brings the recipients up to 19. They can give away $380,000 and they can continue this for as long as they have assets and the inclination to give. But if they do it for 3 years, they can pare down their estate by $1,140,000 and the bonus is a tax savings of $513,000. As we said, 'tis better to give than to receive.

And you can take this one step further if you like. The law allows you to pay anyone's medical expenses or tuition without a dollar limit and pay no gift tax. You could pay one of your grandkid's tuition bills and still give her the $10,000 to pay for the rest of her college costs that year. This exclusion applies only to tuition and not to room and board. The only catch here is you must pay the institution of higher learning yourself and not give the grandkid the money to do so. Same rules apply for medical expenses. There is no dollar limit on these gifts, but you must pay the provider directly.

Here's your quiz. We said it was a *unified* credit exemption. The *unified* was for estate taxes and what else? Gifts! So, if you want to take advantage of your unified credit exemption while you're alive you might want to consider giving away an asset that is appreciating, just to get it out of your estate.

Charitable Trusts

Happily for charities giving is not just on the agendas of the very wealthy these days. If you truly have a charitable intent there are ways to lower your estate tax by giving some of it away and in return getting some of it back.

There are charitable trusts you can set up that will either produce an income for you and your beneficiaries or produce an income for a charity. Setting up a charitable trust will accomplish many things. It should make you feel good about doing something good for others, it should lower your income tax by providing a charitable deduction on your income tax return, it should reduce the size of your estate and estate tax, and it should be able to produce an income for you or the charity of your choice.

You will need professional help to set up a charitable trust because these are sophisticated mechanisms to help you lower your tax bite and you don't want them to backfire. Here we are making them appear simple for explanatory purposes. You transfer an asset to a charitable trust and you can name yourself, the charity, or even someone else to be the recipient of the trust's income stream. As the maker of the trust (grantor) you get to name who will ultimately get the assets in the trust. You can save on capital gains tax by donating an appreciated asset to the trust.

Choosing yourself or someone else to receive the income from the trust you create a "charitable remainder trust" (CRT). The asset in the trust eventually becomes the property of the charity but the income is yours for your lifetime or a fixed period of up to 20 years. You get a tax deduction for the year you fund the trust and the deduction is based on the future value of the charity's interest. If you choose to keep the asset, you direct that the income from the trust go to the charity for a period of time and then ownership reverts back to you or a beneficiary of your choosing. This is referred to as a "charitable lead trust" (CLT).

You can also give to a charity of your choice without setting up a fancy trust. You can give them cash or, better still, give them appreciated assets that you have held longer than a year. Gifting such assets will get you a tax deduction based on the appreciated value of the asset and not on your cost basis. For example, if you give a charity $25,000 of Intel stock that you paid $5,000 for, you get a $25,000 deduction.

Mutual fund companies have discovered there is a market for charitable giving. Fidelity has set up the Charitable Gift Fund: for as little as a $10,000 donation deductible the year you make the contribution you can invest the money with Fidelity and have them make distributions of as little as $250 to the charities of your choice. The money grows tax-free within the account and you can take years to give it all away. Vanguard also has a charitable gifting program but the minimum investment is $25,000.

Chapter 27 | Putting It All Together

What Financial Planning Can Do for You

Congratulations! If you've gotten this far in the book, without even realizing it you've just completed Financial Planning 101. Now comes your final exam, known as your practical. Take what you have learned in the preceding 26 chapters and create for yourself and your family a financial plan and implement it.

Does that sound a bit overwhelming? Some of you are ready to go with the program, while others are wringing their hands saying, "Not me!" If doing it yourself is not for you, that's OK. At least you now know what a planner should be doing for you. And the rest of this chapter is all about finding a planner who can help you get started.

Financial planning is an ongoing process. This is not something you do once and then forget about it. You'll need to spend some time at it now, and then allocate time to monitor the process. Financial planning allows you to achieve your goals. It will give you the tools you need to

be financially successful. And being financially successful may help you achieve your non-financial goals and objectives as well.

This is the part of the book where we will tell you what we told you, tell you how to put it all together, and ask you what you really want to know. Still with us? In the past 26 chapters, we've walked you through the process just as if you were one of our clients. We tried to make this process user-friendly:

✔ *What have you got?*
> You did a net worth statement.
> You figured out where your paycheck goes each week.
> You realized that credit card debt was messing up your life.

✔ *What do you want from life?*
> What are your life goals—home, car, education, retirement?

✔ *How do you invest to achieve your goals?*
> You learned what it takes to be an intelligent investor.

✔ *What are the right investments for your goals?*
> You figured out which investment vehicle fit your needs and goals.

✔ *What obstacles will you encounter along the way?*
> You learned that you'd better not cheat on your taxes.
> You learned that inflation and risk are inherent in every investment.

✔ *How do you protect your assets?*

You figured out that you need insurance and how to buy it. You learned that estate planning is not just for the very old. You learned where to find professional help to navigate the financial labyrinth.

In the beginning, we strongly suggested that you spend some time figuring out how much stuff you own—your net worth. We told you to break it down to see what you had that could be invested. These investable assets are the basis of your portfolio.

Next we hounded you to spend the time to work on your cash flow, a fancy term for your budget. Set up a spending plan, we told you. Get it right, because here is the place where you're going to find the money you needed to invest. Unless your name is Rockefeller or Dupont, most of us need to save and invest to achieve our goals.

We even showed you how to cut corners on everyday things so you could save more. And then, if you found yourself in debt, well, we beat you up a little bit but offered real help on getting out of debt. You are now a born-again saver.

> *Getting started is always the hardest part of any enterprise. Once you're going, your momentum helps keep you going.*

Then you got yourself organized. You put all of that stuff you've accumulated where it belongs and even threw out stuff you didn't need anymore. That made you feel good, didn't it?

What do you want? we asked. What are your goals? A house? A car? An education for yourself or the kids? That perfect retirement? We showed you how to buy a house and put a car in the garage. We told you where to get the good deals. We want you to educate yourself and the kids and we threw in ideas on how to teach those kids about the value of a buck.

Then came the big shock. We showed you how much you were going to need to save and invest to get your dream retirement. We know we made a big impression on you then.

So now that you'd figured out exactly what was important to you, we helped you get started on investing so you could afford your dreams. You got the basics here. Your understanding of Wall Street has certainly broadened. You're not quite ready to host a CNBC special just yet, but you now know about asset allocation and the eighth wonder of the world, compounding. Then you went on to find the right investments for your goals—CDs, stocks, bonds, mutual funds, 401(k)s, and IRAs. Which is best for you? You were able to figure it out.

Oops! You discovered that something could get in your way and slow you down on the journey toward your goals. Investments have risks, you learned, and that can hurt in a down market. And your understanding of how the economy works now certainly will get you a place in Economics 102. Inflation is bad, we told you, but a fact of life and taxes are an everyday reality. The tax laws change annually and no ones sends you a notice in the mail. You now know it's your responsibility to keep up to date on tax changes.

Last on the agenda, we showed you how to protect what you've worked so hard to get. Insurance helps you manage the risks you face that otherwise would cause a financial disaster. Then we learned that Ben Franklin was a soothsayer when he said, "There is nothing certain but death and taxes," and we showed you how to disinherit Uncle Sam.

We've covered a lot of territory, haven't we? And if you followed our lead, you may actually have your plan in place.

If you don't, go back and start over. Go through the steps one at a time or repeat those that need repeating. Financial planning is a process and you will need to review your plan on a regular basis. Things in life happen: marriages, divorces, new jobs, new houses, births, and deaths. Each of these will affect your plan, so take the time to see where you are and what you need to do to keep on track.

Many individuals don't want to do this themselves. They want help. So read on and we'll show you how to get the help that you need. You don't have to treat this book as a Do-It-Yourself book. It can be a Show-It-to-Me book, a book you use to learn about what the professionals in your life should be doing for you.

When You Need Help

Going it alone is not for most people. Why? Most of you don't have the time or the inclination to go it alone. You want someone there to help you make decisions. Most of us are what we refer to as ChPs,

Chartered Procrastinators. You put off doing what needs to be done. We firmly believe that procrastination is a genetic defect in the human character and it affects most people. As proof of this theory, answer these two questions truthfully. How early do you get your taxes done? When do you send out your holiday cards? See what we mean?

It usually takes a life event to push people into doing something about their finances. That life event could be a new job, marriage, buying a house, an impending birth, a divorce, or a death. Something pushes you into thinking about and taking action regarding your finances.

We're grateful that your first step was to read our book and begin the financial planning process by learning about it. If you don't want to go it alone, we need to help you find the right person so you can get help, whether you're in Nebraska, California, Massachusetts, or elsewhere. In this process, the most important decision you will make is to choose your financial advisor.

We must admit to a certain bias here. We think you should start your search by looking for a Certified Financial Planner (CFP). In order

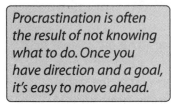

Procrastination is often the result of not knowing what to do. Once you have direction and a goal, it's easy to move ahead.

to be licensed as a CFP, a person must have passed a comprehensive exam that covers the key aspects of financial planning. He or she must have three to five years of experience (depending on educational background) in the financial planning field prior to receiving the right to use the CFP designation after his or her name. Every two years a CFP must earn 30 hours of continuing education. All CFPs must also sign a code of ethics. Now, will this guarantee you the very best financial advisor in the world? Not necessarily! But you will at least have somewhat equalized the playing field in your search.

Where do you start? Begin by asking your friends, family, and the people you work with if they use a financial advisor. If you're already using other professional advisors, such as a lawyer or a tax preparer, ask whom they would recommend.

In the next section we list three organizations that will also help you find an advisor. You want to find a planner who will understand your particular situation. If you're a school teacher, you'll want an advisor who is up to date on your state retirement systems as well as 403(b) plans. You don't want to be the oddball in a planner's practice.

Someone who might be perfect for your widowed grandmother might not be the right advisor for you.

Gather up a list of planners. Then interview at least three. Most planners (most professionals, for that matter) will not charge for an informational interview. This is an interview, so don't go in expecting to get free financial advice. This is an opportunity to see if there's a fit between you and the planner. The advisor will be doing the same thing you'll be doing, evaluating the relationship. Ask questions about the planner and his or her firm. Don't be afraid to ask tough questions. Remember: it's your money.

What kind of questions should you be asking? We offer some suggestions here that you'll want to cover during your interview. Just slide these questions casually into the conversation. (You'll get better at it after the first interview.) You want to know about a planner's background, experience, and the services that he or she offers. Many planners will provide you with a brochure outlining their services if you call and request it before the interview.

Questions you want to get answered during an interview:

✔ What is your educational background?

✔ What credentials have you earned?

✔ What is your business background?

✔ What kind of clients do you normally service?

✔ How long have you been practicing financial planning?

✔ How do you prepare a plan?

✔ How often do you send out client reports?

✔ How often do you meet with clients?

✔ How are you compensated? (key question)

✔ Do you personally research the products you recommend?

✔ Do you review taxes as part of your service?

✔ Who will be handling my affairs, you or a subordinate?

The organizations listed below will send you names of planners in your geographical area. They all provide consumer pamphlets on financial planning and hiring a financial advisor. Each has a Web site where you'll be able to find a planner and contact that person directly via e-mail.

Financial Planning Association (FPA)
5775 Glenridge Drive, NE, Suite B-300
Atlanta, GA 30328
800-282-PLAN
www.fpanet.org

The Financial Planning Assocation is the professional organization for Certified Financial Planners. Membership: 30,000

National Association of Personal Financial Advisors (NAPFA)
355 West Dundee Road, Suite 200
Buffalo Grove, IL 60089
888-FEE-ONLY (888-433-6659)
www.napfa.org

NAPFA has a membership of fee-only planners. Membership: 600+

There Are No Free Lunches

Planners are compensated in different ways for the service they provide you. No one way is really better, although you'll hear the argument that a fee-only form of compensation is the best way, because it's the most objective. That may be true, but there are not a lot of fee-only planners available. Some who call themselves fee-only may actually be fee-offset planners or money managers.

The reality is that, if we look at just the dollars, a commission-only planner is probably the cheapest way to go—if you want nothing but some advice on a product that you're interested in purchasing. But most of you will want more from your planner; you'll want ongoing advice. So you'll need to base your decision on more than just a form of compensation.

Fee-only. These planners charge only for advice, usually an hourly fee or a fee that's project-based. They may be retained on an annual basis as well. They may provide you with a comprehensive financial plan or they may charge extra for it. These planners can give objective advice to the consumer, but they're a rare breed in the financial planning industry.

Commission-only. These planners will review your situation, offer advice, and perhaps even produce a financial plan for you. They receive their compensation from the sale of financial products such as mutual funds or insurance.

Fee-offset. Often referred to as a *fee-based* planner, they earn their compensation from both sales and fees. The planner will charge an hourly fee to meet with you and do a financial plan. He or she will earn a commission from any financial products you buy and the commissions earned will offset the charges for the financial plan.

Money manager. This type of advisor earns compensation on an annual basis from your portfolio. A planner manages your investments for you, usually using no-load mutual funds and charging a fee that's a percentage of the assets under management. The fee is usually around 1%, but if your portfolio is under $200,000 the fee may go as high as 2%. Exercise caution when choosing a money manager, especially if you're giving someone discretionary power over your money. This has become the most popular form of compensation for planners.

Salary. Planners are employed by financial institutions such as banks, credit unions, mutual fund families, and insurance companies. The financial products they offer are limited, since they have only in-house products to sell. Some of these planners may also receive bonuses or commissions.

Who's Who on the Playing Field

This section hopefully will help straighten out the confusion somewhat by giving you a scorecard so you can figure out who's who on the playing field. We did say "somewhat," for in doing our research we discovered there are many designations out there associated with the financial planning field, too many. We figured that, if we didn't know what some of the designations meant, how could we expect you to know or understand them? The designations that we selected are the more popular ones.

When you are interviewing a planner or an attorney, check the business card and ask about the initials after his or her name. What kind of classroom work was involved? Did he or she pass an exam? What organization awards the designation? You might also ask about recent education. All but the MBA and RIA designations require the individual holding the designation to earn continuing education credits annually.

Remember—it's your money and your financial future, so don't be intimidated. Ask questions! And question the answers to make sure you understand! (Note: The following designations are listed in order of the importance of their credentials for financial planning, in our opinion.)

CFP—Certified Financial Planner: Individuals who have met educational and experience requirements, agreed to abide by a code of ethics, and passed a national exam administrated by the CFP Board of Standards. The exam covers insurance, investments, taxation, employee benefits, retirement planning, and estate planning. The most recognized of the financial planning designations.

RIA—Registered Investment Advisor: Individuals who hold themselves out to be investment advisors must register with either the Securities and Exchange Commission (SEC) or their state securities division. A planner with less than $25 million under management must register with his or her state authority, while those with over $25 million will be registered with the SEC. This registration is required of anyone who, for compensation and as part of a business, gives advice, makes recommendations, issues reports, or furnishes analysis on securities, either directly or through publications. If a planner is an employee of an advisory firm, such as a brokerage house, the brokerage house will have a blanket registration for all employees.

Stockbroker: This is an individual who has passed an exam to determine her or his basic knowledge in securities and is registered with the SEC. A broker acts as an intermediary between a buyer and a seller. A broker may specialize in stocks, bonds, commodities, or options. Some brokerage firms refer to their stockbrokers as "registered representatives," "account executives," "financial counselors," or "financial consultants." Brokers earn commissions on sales or fees for assets under management.

CPA—Certified Public Accountant: This is an experienced accountant who has met educational, statutory, and licensing requirements of the state where he or she resides. CPAs do tax work and auditing.

CPA/PFS—Certified Public Accountant/Personal Financial Planning Specialist: Personal Financial Specialists are CPAs who have passed a financial planning exam, have practical experience in financial planning, and are members of the American Institute of Certified Public Accountants.

CFA—Chartered Financial Analysts: This designation is awarded by the Association for Investment Management and Research (AIMR) to experienced financial analysts who have passed exams in economics, financial accounting, portfolio management, security analysis, and standards of conduct.

ChFC—Chartered Financial Consultant: This designation awarded by the American College is the insurance industry's financial planning designation. Consultants must meet experience requirements and pass exams covering finance and investing.

CLU—Chartered Life Underwriter: This designation is awarded by the American College to a life insurance agent who has business experience in insurance planning and related areas and has passed exams in insurance and related subjects.

JD—Juris Doctor or Doctor of Jurisprudence: Holders of this designation have a law degree. A person can use a JD and not be a practicing lawyer, since passing the state bar exam is a requirement for practicing law. An LLM after a lawyer's name indicates a Masters of Law degree. An LLB is an older degree, a Bachelor of Law. (There was a time when you could enter law school right out of high school and receive an undergraduate degree in law.)

Esquire: This is a title of respect dating back to old English, for people with a law degree. In old English law, it was the title of dignity above a gentleman and below a knight. Once it was debated as to whether female lawyers could properly use this title after their names.

EA—Enrolled Agent: This designation is controlled by the Internal Revenue Service. The designation gives the holder the right to represent taxpayers before the IRS. Individuals must either pass an exam that tests for skills in corporate, partnership, trust, and estate taxation or have five years or more of service in a technical capacity with the IRS.

EA—Enrolled Actuary: Not to be confused with enrolled agents, enrolled actuaries are licensed by a federal agency, the Joint Board for the Enrollment of Actuaries, to perform tasks for qualified benefit pension plans. EAs specialize in retirement planning.

CIMC—Certified Investment Management Consultant: This designation is awarded by the Institute for Investment Management Consultants. It requires at least three years of investment experience. Individuals may apply for the CIMC designation after completing some courses or, if they are employed by an investment firm, they may be awarded the designation upon attestation by their supervisor.

CFS—Certified Financial Specialist: This designation is awarded by the Institute of Business & Finance to financial services representatives who have completed course work in the study of mutual funds.

MBA—Master's in Business Administration: This is a general business degree. The holder may not have majored in personal finance. There's a big difference between the financial needs of a business and the financial needs of a family.

Who's Keeping Score?

You've done all things we've suggested. You've interviewed several planners. You're satisfied with how they're compensated. You understand the alphabet soup after their names.

There's one more thing left to do before you hire that planner. You need to check the candidates out with score keepers. These are organizations that either license planners or keep track of violations. Again, it's your money, so you'll want to be sure that the individual to whom you'll be entrusting it is all that he or she claims to be.

> The Certified Financial Planner Board of Standards (CFP Board)
> 1700 Broadway, Suite 2100
> Denver, CO 80290-2101
> 888-CFPMARK
> **www.cfp-board.org**

Consumers can call the CFP Board to confirm if a financial planner is currently licensed to use the CFP marks, to determine if a CFP licensee has ever been publicly disciplined, or to lodge a complaint against a Certified Financial Planner practitioner.

National Association of Insurance Commissioners (NAlC)
120 West 12th Street, Suite 1100
Kansas City, MO 64105
816-842-3600
www.naic.org

Contact NAIC to be directed to your state insurance commissioner's office, to check whether a financial planer is licensed to sell insurance or has any insurance violations.

National Association of Securities Dealers (NASD)
1735 K Street, NW
Washington, DC 20006
800-289-9999
www.nasdr.com

Consumers can call the NASD to obtain the disciplinary history of registered representatives and broker dealers, which is compiled and kept in a central registration depository (CRD).

National Fraud Exchange (NAFEX)
12020 Sunrise Valley Drive, Suite 360
Reston, VA 20191
800-822-0416

NAFEX offers consumers a "one-stop" background check on securities brokers, financial planners, real estate agents, trust advisors, mortgage officers, and financial advisors for a fee of $39 for the first individual checked and $20 per person for further background checks. The background checks reveal if the subject has been the subject of a criminal, civil, enforcement, or administrative action in the securities or financial services industry.

North American Securities Administration Association (NASAA)
1 Massachusetts Avenue, Suite 310
Washington, DC 20001
202-737-0900

www.nasaa.org

Consumers can call NASAA to get the phone numbers of their state securities regulators, who oversee the state securities-licensed financial planners. These are planners with under $25 million under management. The NASAA also provides a free pamphlet, "How to Check Out a Broker."

Securities and Exchange Commission (SEC)
450 5th Street, NW
Washington, DC 20549
800-732-0330
www.sec.gov

Contact the SEC to check whether a financial planner is a registered investment advisor, for information and advice on a particular individual or firm providing securities and investment services, or to lodge a complaint against a financial advisor.

That's it. Now let's stop talking and see some action!

Glossary

The Language of Money

If you want to talk money, it's a good idea to know the language. Yes, it's English, but there are lots of semi-technical terms you might need to know. So here's our review of the language of money.

account executive The title given by some brokerage firms to their stockbrokers. Other variations on the title include registered representative, financial counselor, and financial consultant.

administrator The person appointed by a court to administer and settle the estate of a person dying without a will or the estate of a person whose will appoints an executor who cannot serve.

adjustable life A life insurance policy that can be changed from term to whole life or vice versa.

adjusted gross income (AGI) Total earned and unearned income from taxable accounts, including net business income or losses, capital gain or loss, retirement plan distributions, taxable pensions, rental income, and possibly some Social Security benefits, minus IRA, SEP, or Keogh contributions, self-employment health benefits (partially deductible so far), half your self-employment tax, and alimony paid. The AGI is the last line on the front of the Form 1040.

American Depositary Receipt (ADR) A negotiable certificate held in a U.S. bank representing a specific number of shares of a foreign stock that is traded on a stock exchange in the U.S. ADRs make it easier for Americans to invest in foreign companies.

American Stock Exchange (AMEX) A stock exchange that traditionally trades smaller stocks and bonds than the *New York Stock Exchange*. Founded in 1842 as an outdoor market, it moved inside in 1921. It was known as the New York Curb Exchange until 1953. It recently merged with *NASDAQ*.

AMEX *American Stock Exchange.*

annual report A formal statement issued yearly by a corporation or a mutual fund. It shows assets, liabilities, equity, revenues, expenses, and so forth. It reflects the condition of the corporation or mutual fund at the close of the business year and the results of operations for that year.

annuitant A person who is entitled to receive benefits from an annuity.

annuitize To begin to receive payments from an annuity.

annuity A contract sold by an insurance company that makes a series of regular payments guaranteed to continue for a specific time, usually the annuitant's lifetime, in exchange for a single payment or a series of payments to the company. With a *deferred* annuity, payments begin sometime in the future. With an immediate annuity, the payments begin right away. A fixed annuity pays a fixed income stream for the life of the contract. With a *variable* annuity, the payments may change according to the relative investment success of the insurance company. Deferred annuities offer the advantage of tax-deferred compounding.

arbitrage An attempt to profit from momentary price differences that can develop when a security or commodity is traded on two different exchanges. To take advantage of such differences, an arbitrageur would buy in the market where the price is lower and simultaneously sell in the market where the price is higher.

asset Something with a monetary value, e.g., stocks, real estate, accounts payable. Net assets are assets minus liabilities.

asset allocation A strategy for keeping investments diversified. *Fixed* asset allocation plans set specific amounts or percentages in different areas and adjust the portfolio to match them. *Active* asset allocation plans vary the allocation depending on market conditions.

ask-bid system A system used to place a market order, that is, an order the investor wants executed immediately at the best prevailing price. The market order to buy requires a purchase at the lowest offering (ask) price and a market order to sell requires a sale at the highest (bid) price. The bid price is what the dealer is willing to pay for the stock, while the ask price is the price at which the dealer will sell to individual investors. The difference between the bid and ask prices is the spread.

at-the-market When an investor buys or sells a security "at-the-market," the broker will execute the trade at the next available price.

average annual return The annual return that, when compounded over a number of years, equals the total return for the same period. This is the average amount per year you would have made on the investment.

average maturity The average maturity is the weighted average of the maturities of all of the fund's bond holdings. This is related to a bond fund's volatility. In general, the longer a fund's average maturity, the greater the price fluctuation when interest rates change. Shortening the average maturity is one way a fund manager can defend share value when he or she anticipates rises in interest rates.

back-end load A fee charged by mutual funds to investors who sell their shares before owning them for a specified time.

back office The support operations of a brokerage firm that doesn't deal directly with customers. "Back office problems" usually refers to slow paperwork or other bottlenecks in the execution of customers' orders.

balance sheet A financial statement issued by a company describing its current assets, liabilities, and owners' equity. It is a "snapshot" of what a company owns and is worth at a specified point in time. See *book value*.

balanced fund A mutual fund that includes both equities (stocks or convertibles) and fixed-income securities (bonds) in its portfolio, thereby attempting to gain both capital appreciation and income in varying degrees.

basis Your cost, used in figuring gain or loss when you sell a house or other property, such as stocks, bonds, or mutual funds. For real estate, basis includes the price you

paid plus the cost of improvements.

basis point One one-hundredth of a percent (.01%); often used when talking about interest rates or yields. When one bond pays 35 basis points more than another, its yield is 0.35% higher than the other's.

bear market A declining trend in stock markets.

bearer bond Also called a *coupon* bond, this security is not registered in anyone's name. Rather, whoever holds the bond (the "bearer") is entitled to collect interest payments merely by cutting off and mailing in the attached coupons at the proper time. Bearer bonds are no longer being issued.

bearish A bear thinks the market is going to go down. This makes bearish the opposite of bullish.

beneficiary (estate) Person or organization entitled to receive income and/or principal under the terms of a trust, a will, or a retirement account such as an IRA.

beneficiary (insurance) Person designated to receive the benefits of an insurance policy or an annuity.

bequest A gift of property by will. Same as *legacy*.

beta or beta coefficient A measure of how much a fund moves when the market moves. The beta of the S&P 500 is defined as 1.00. Funds with betas greater than 1.00 react more to market changes than does the S&P 500. For both growth and growth and income funds, betas are fairly good measures of a fund's volatility. But because beta measures only that part of a fund's volatility due to stock market movement, it is less meaningful for sector funds and bond funds, which have other sources of volatility.

Big Board A popular slang term for the New York Stock Exchange.

blue-chip stock There is no set definition of a blue-chip stock, but most people would agree it has at least three characteristics: It is issued by a well-known, respected company, it has a good record of earnings and dividend payments, and it is widely held by investors. Blue chips can go down but, since they are unlikely to go bankrupt, they are generally considered a more conservative investment than stock in small companies. The term "blue chip" comes from the game of poker, in which the blue chip holds the highest value.

boiler room A blanket term used to describe the place of origin of high-pressure telephone sales techniques, usually involving cold calls to unsuspecting customers who would be better off without whatever is being offered to them.

bond An interest-bearing security that obligates the issuer to pay a specified amount of interest for a specified time, usually several years, and then pay the bondholder the face amount of the bond. Bonds issued by corporations are backed by corporate assets; in case of default, the bondholders have a legal claim on those assets. Bonds issued by government agencies may or may not be collateralized. Interest from corporate bonds is taxable; interest from municipal bonds, which are issued by state and local governments, is free of federal income taxes and, usually, income taxes of the issuing jurisdiction. Interest from

Treasury bonds, issued by the federal government, is free of state and local income taxes but subject to federal taxes.

bond fund A mutual fund that invests primarily in bonds.

bond rating A judgment about the ability of the bond issuer to fulfill its obligation to pay interest and repay the principal when due. The best-known bond-rating companies are Standard & Poor's and Moody's. Their rating systems, although slightly different, both use a letter-grade system, with triple-A the highest rating and C and D the lowest.

book value For investing purposes, this is the net asset value of a company, determined by subtracting its liabilities from its assets. Dividing the result by the number of shares of common stock issued by the company yields the book value per share, which can be used as a relative gauge of the stock's value.

boom A period of rapid economic expansion.

brokered CD A large-denomination certificate of deposit sold by a bank to a brokerage, which then slices it up into smaller pieces and sells the pieces to its customers.

broker's markup The commission the broker charges the client that is built into the actual price of the transaction.

bull market A rising trend in stock prices.

bullish A bull is someone who thinks the market is going up, which makes bullish the opposite of bearish.

bust A period of economic decline, generally sudden.

bypass trust A flexible trust that takes advantage of the exemption equivalent under federal estate and gift tax laws by allowing you to pass an amount up to the exemption equivalent to your beneficiaries free of estate taxes. It is also known as a *family trust* and a *credit shelter trust*.

by right of representation A term used to define the division of property among the descendants of the decedent. For instance, a will might provide for a distribution upon the death of the donor to the donor's issue by right of representation. If there are two children living and one child deceased with two children of that deceased child living, the property would pass in three equal shares. One full share would be allocated to each living child and the share of the deceased child would be divided equally between the two grandchildren. (The grandchildren "represent" their parent.)

call The right to buy a security at a given price within a given time. Also, the right of the issuing corporation or agency to redeem a callable bond before its scheduled maturity.

call option A right to buy a fixed number of shares of stock at a specified price within a limited period of time. The purchaser hopes that the stock's price will go up by an amount sufficient to provide a profit when the option is sold. If the stock price remains the same or goes down, the investment in the call option is lost.

callable A bond or preferred stock that may be redeemed by the issuing corporation or agency under specified conditions before maturity.

cap *Capitalization.*

capital appreciation An investment objective adopted by some mutual funds. The aim is to buy stocks (or bonds) and sell them at a profit, without necessarily worrying about dividends.

capital gain The profit made on the sale of property or securities. A short-term capital gain is made on holdings held less than a year; a long-term capital gain on those held for more than a year.

capital gains distribution Payments to mutual fund shareholders of gains realized on the sale of the fund's portfolio securities. These amounts are usually paid once a year and should be added to the basis of your investment.

capital loss The loss taken on the sale of property or securities.

capitalization The totality of a corporation's long-term debt, stock, and retained earnings. Also called *invested capital*. Also, the market price of an entire company, calculated by multiplying the number of shares outstanding by the price per share; also called *market cap* or *market capitalization*.

cash A holding of a relatively stable asset denominated in currency terms. A mutual fund holding "cash" does not have a pile of dollar bills somewhere; the money is invested in interest-bearing short-term securities.

cash flow The amount of money a company generates. Cash flow is a factor used in valuing stocks or companies. The figure differs from income, because income calculations include relatively abstract accounting concepts, such as depreciation, which reduces taxable profits without affecting cash in hand. Speculators and takeover specialists value companies with high cash flow because they can use the cash to pay off incurred debt.

cash value The amount payable in cash upon voluntary termination of a life insurance contract (except term).

casualty insurance Insurance on property that covers losses or liabilities resulting from an accident.

Certificate of Deposit (CD) A short- to medium-term instrument (one month to five years) that is issued by a bank or savings and loan association to pay interest at a rate higher than that paid by a passbook account. CD rates move up and down with general market interest rates. There is usually a penalty for early withdrawal.

charitable deduction The deduction available against federal estate taxes for the full value of all gifts or bequests to public, religious, charitable, scientific, literary, and educational institutions that meet the specific requirements of the Internal Revenue Code.

charitable lead trust (CLT) An arrangement by which the income from a property or an investment is donated to a charity while the grantor is living, with the property or investment passing to other designated parties upon the grantor's death.

charitable remainder trust (CRT) An arrangement by which a property or an investment is donated to a charity, but the donor continues to use the property or investment and/or receive income from it while living. This may be an *annuity* trust, which pays a fixed amount each year, or a *unit* trust, which pays an amount based on the value of assets held by the charity.

churning Improper handling of a customer's account by a registered representative or broker: he or she trades securities excessively, in order to generate commissions, regardless of the customer's interests and objectives.

circuit breakers The safety mechanisms instituted by the major stock and commodities exchanges to halt trading temporarily when the market has fallen by a certain amount in a short period of time. Created in the wake of the Black Monday crash of 1987 and modified since, circuit breakers are designed to stop a market free fall by allowing a rebalancing of buy and sell orders. Current circuit breakers on the New York Stock Exchange will halt trading if the Dow Jones Industrial Average falls by 2% of the last month's average closing value. Also known as *trading curbs*.

closed fund An open-end mutual fund that has temporarily or permanently stopped selling shares to new customers, usually due to rapid asset growth. The fund continues to redeem outstanding shares.

closed-end investment company A company that sells a fixed number of shares in its portfolio of securities. The securities in the portfolio may be bought and sold (managed). When the initial offering of shares is sold out, the closed-end fund trades on the secondary market at a price determined by investor supply and demand. For contrast, see the definition of *mutual fund*. Shares in the investment company, also known as a closed-end fund, trade on an exchange or over-the-counter. Their market value is determined by supply and demand and may be higher or lower than the actual net asset value.

codicil An amendment to a will that must be signed and witnessed with the same formality as a will.

cold calling The practice of brokers making unsolicited calls to people they don't know in an attempt to generate business.

collectible An item purchased for its value or enjoyment. Investors may purchase a collectible with that expectation that its value will increase and thus yield a profit when it is sold. Items include jewelry, diamonds, rare books, paintings, other art works, stamps, antiques, Oriental rugs, and beanie babies.

commercial paper Unsecured notes issued by corporations to finance short-term needs. Maturities range from a few days to several months.

commission A broker's fee for handling transactions for a client in an agency capacity.

common stock A unit of equity ownership in a corporation. Owners of this kind of stock exercise control over corporate affairs and enjoy any capital appreciation. They are paid dividends only after the owners of preferred stock. Their interest in the assets, in the event of liquidation, is junior to all others.

compounding The process of earning interest on the interest already earned on an investment. When interest is left to accumulate, compound interest is earned.

Consumer Price Index (CPI) A measurement of changes in consumer prices (food, transportation, housing, entertainment, medical care, etc.). Published monthly by the U.S. Bureau of Labor, it is used as a gauge for measuring inflation. The CPI is also used as a cost of living index.

contrarian An investor who thinks and acts in opposition to the conventional wisdom. When the majority of investors are bearish, a contrarian is bullish, and vice versa.

convertible security Essentially a bond or preferred stock that can be converted at the holder's option to equity (common stock) in a company at a fixed rate. Companies issue convertible bonds because they need not pay as high a rate of interest on them to attract investors. Investors buy convertibles because they offer some of the safety of a bond with some of the appreciation potential of a stock.

correction A price drop after a price rise, for either a specific stock or the overall market.

coupon The interest rate paid on a bond when it is first offered or when it is trading at par value. A $1,000 par bond paying $100 per year has a 10% coupon.

CPI *Consumer Price Index.*

credit rating A measure of a bond's risk, often expressed using a letter system.

Standard & Poor's (S&P) and Moody's rate companies on their ability to pay back interest and principal on their bonds. Though the two companies may not agree on the ratings of individual companies, the letter systems they use are directly comparable. The highest rating is S&P's AAA (Moody's Aaa). Ratings of AAA (Aaa), AA (Aa), A (A), and BBB (Baa) are all seen as "investment grade." Ratings of BB (Ba) or lower denote higher risk; bonds with these ratings are often called "junk bonds." A rating of D is reserved for bonds in default.

credit shelter trust In a two-will/two-trust estate plan, the trust that is subject to federal and state estate taxes, but is sheltered by the federal estate tax exemption for the estate of the first spouse to die, and escapes estate tax entirely upon the death of the surviving spouse. The federal exemption (unified credit) will be gradually increased to $1,000,000 and phased in through 2006. This type of trust is sometimes called a *bypass trust* or a *family trust*.

custodial account An account set up for a minor, usually with a bank or brokerage firm. Children, by law, can not own securities directly. The account is registered in the minor's name, using his or her Social Security number, and managed by an adult (the custodian) until the child reaches the age of majority (18 to 21, depending on state law). For children under 14, unearned income over $1,200 in the account will be taxed at the parent's rate; after age 14, it will be taxed at the child's rate. The assets in the account become the child's once they reach the age of majority.

Sometimes referred to as an UTMA account, after the Uniform Transfer to Minors Act, a law adopted by most states that sets the rules for administration and distribution of these types of accounts.

custodian Organization responsible for the safekeeping of a mutual fund's assets (securities and cash). Usually a bank.

customer For the purposes of disclosure of financial condition under SEC Rule 17a-5, a customer is any person for whom, or with whom, the broker/dealer firm has executed a transaction or holds or owes monies or securities for that month or the month following for which the firm's financial report is to be prepared.

customer's agreement A document that explains the terms and conditions under which a brokerage firm consents to finance a customer's account and credit transaction. No margin account should be opened or maintained unless the customer signs such an agreement. Also known as margin agreement or hypothecation agreement.

cyclical stocks Stocks in companies whose profits are closely tied to the state of the economy. Steel companies are cyclical stocks; as the economy slows, orders for steel go down. *Non-cyclical*, or *defensive*, stocks are those whose performance stays relatively steady during economic downturns. Most food companies are non-cyclical stocks, because people eat about the same amount, even during a recession.

death taxes Taxes imposed on the property that is transferred to another upon the death of an individual. Death taxes include the federal estate tax and state inheritance and estate taxes.

debenture A corporate IOU that is not backed by the company's assets and is therefore somewhat riskier than a bond.

declaration of trust A trust under which the donor and the trustee are one and the same person.

deflation A decline in general price levels, often caused by a reduction in the supply of money or credit. This is the opposite of inflation.

disinflation A drop in the rate of inflation rate, a reduction in the rate at which prices rise.

disclaimer A renunciation or refusal to accept a bequest under a will or a distribution under a trust, usually for tax planning purposes. For instance, if a husband's will leaves all of his property to his wife outright or to his children if she fails to survive him, she may wish to disclaim the unified credit amount in order to prevent taxation of this amount in her estate upon her death. The disclaimed amount would pass as if the wife predeceased her husband: i.e. to the children in that example.

discount broker A broker/dealer whose commission rates for buying and selling securities are markedly lower than those of a full-service broker. These brokers usually provide execution-only services and little or no research.

discount rate The interest rate the Federal Reserve Board (the Fed) charges on overnight loans to member banks.

distribution A payment made to a shareholder. Except for income from municipal funds, distributions are taxable.

diversification A technique for reducing investment risk. An investor diversifies by investing in several different areas. Disaster in one area usually doesn't affect an investment in the others. To diversify effectively, the investor must be certain that the areas are genuinely independent. For example, a broad-based growth mutual fund is diversified in one sense, because it covers many different sectors, but not in another, because its performance depends on that of the overall stock market.

dividend A share of company earnings paid out to stockholders. Dividends are declared by the board of directors and paid quarterly. Most are paid as cash, but they are sometimes paid in the form of additional shares of stock.

dividend reinvestment plan (DRIP) A program under which the company automatically reinvests a shareholder's cash dividends in additional shares of common stock, often with no brokerage charge to the shareholder.

dollar cost averaging A disciplined investment strategy that revolves around investing the same amount of money on a regular basis. Many mutual fund companies will help set up a plan and automatically deduct the money from your checking account on a monthly basis.

donee A person to whom a gift is made.

donor A person who makes a gift or who establishes a trust, whether by declaration or indenture.

Dow Jones Industrial Average A simple stock market index. Despite its popularity, this index is not very reflective of the market as a whole, because it is calculated by adding up the prices of only 30 stocks, all very large companies.

Dow Theory A belief that a major trend in the stock market isn't signaled by one index alone but must be confirmed by two—specifically, a new high or low must be recorded by both the Dow Jones Industrial Average and the Dow Jones Transportation Average before it can safely be declared that the market is headed up or down.

due diligence The work performed by a broker or other representative in order to investigate and understand an investment thoroughly before recommending it to a customer.

duration A measure of a bond fund's sensitivity to interest rate changes. A fund with a duration of three will lose 3% if interest rates rise 1%. However, duration is not that meaningful over larger changes in interest rates, especially for callable bonds and mortgage securities.

earnings per share A company's profits after subtracting taxes, bond interest, and preferred stock payments and dividing by the number of shares of common stock outstanding.

equity fund A mutual fund investing primarily in common stock or securities convertible into common stock.

equity ownership Interest in a corporation, represented by shares of common stock. An equity is not a right to some nominal sum of money; it is a portion of the company's net worth. Contrasts with bond.

EE savings bond A security sold by the U.S. government that offers fixed income with minimum risk and minimum investment. The bonds are sold at a discount, in face amounts of $25 to $10,000, and the interest accumulates over a designated time period. Also known as a Series EE bond.

estate The assets you leave to your heirs.

estate planning The process of analyzing your assets and liabilities, managing them effectively during your lifetime, and disposing of them at your death through a will so as to best serve the needs of your beneficiaries.

estate tax An excise tax assessed against property transferred upon death by a decedent. It applies to property in the decedent's name alone, property jointly owned by the decedent and another, life insurance policies, annuities, pension and other retirement arrangements, and certain lifetime transfers. Federal estate taxes range from 37% to 55% and are subject to an exemption, which is set at $650,000 for 1999 and will increase to $1,000,000 by 2006.

ex-dividend date (for mutual funds) The date on which mutual funds deduct dividends or distributions from the funds' assets and set them aside for payment to shareholders. On this date the net asset value (NAV) per share is reduced by the per-share amount of the distribution.

exchange A transfer of money from one mutual fund to another within the same fund family.

executor or executrix A man or a woman nominated by the individual who writes a will (testator or testatrix) to carry out the directions and requests in a will.

exempt trust A trust to which the donor's $1 million generation-skipping transfer tax exemption has been allocated. It may be segregated and administered as a subtrust. All distributions from an exempt trust to a beneficiary who is more than one generation below the donor of the trust will be exempt from the generation-skipping transfer tax. A non-exempt trust is a trust to which none of the donor's generation-skipping transfer tax exemption has been allocated.

expense ratio The percentage of a fund's total assets expended for the operation and management of the fund during a year. Everything else being equal, a higher expense ratio reduces the fund's total return.

Fannie Mae The pronounced acronym (FNMA) for the Federal National Mortgage Association, which buys mortgages on the secondary market, repackages them, and sells off pieces to investors. The effect is to infuse the mortgage markets with fresh money.

face amount The amount of coverage provided by an insurance policy.

Fed *Federal Reserve System.*

Federal Deposit Insurance Corporation (FDIC) Agency that insures deposits up to $100,000 in commercial banks, savings banks, savings and loans, and mutual savings banks. These banks must be approved by the FDIC and meet certain standards of safety and use sound banking practices. All types of deposit accounts made at FDIC insured banks are covered—checking or NOW accounts, savings accounts, certificates of deposit, and money market deposit accounts—but not other products, such as mutual funds and annuities.

Federal Funds Excess reserves that banks lend to one another for brief periods of time. The Federal Funds Rate is the rate of interest charged to borrow these funds.

Federal Home Loan Bank Board The government agency that regulates federally chartered savings and loan associations.

Federal Insurance Contributions Act (FICA) Law that authorized Social Security and requires employers to withhold from employee wages and make payments into a trust fund for Old Age, Survivors, and Dependents Insurance (OASDI) and Medicare.

Federal Reserve Bank One of a system of 12 regional banks established to maintain reserves, issue bank notes, and lend money to member banks.

Federal Reserve Board The board of governors that oversees the Federal Reserve Banks, establishes monetary policy, and monitors the economic condition of the nation.

Federal Reserve System A banking system under the control of a central board of governors (*Federal Reserve Board*) with a central bank (*Federal Reserve Bank*) in each of 12 districts. The Fed (as it is often called) is responsible for regulating the monetary and banking system in the

United States and exercises broad powers to control credit and the flow of money.

FICA *Federal Insurance Contributions Act.*

fiduciary The individual to whom or institution to which you grant specific rights, duties, and powers to act for you or in your behalf to carry out the provisions stipulated in your will.

fixed income investment A catchall description for investments in bonds, certificates of deposit, and other debt-based instruments that pay a fixed amount of interest.

401(k) plan An employer-sponsored retirement plan that permits employees to divert part of their pay into the plan and avoid current income taxes on that income. Money directed to the plan may be partially matched by the employer. Investment earnings within the plan accumulate tax-deferred until they are withdrawn. The 401(k) is named for the section of the Internal Revenue Code that authorizes this plan.

403(b) plan Section 403(b) of the Internal Revenue Code permits employees of certain non-profit organizations, such as schools and hospitals, to set up tax-deferred retirement plans. The plans are designed to compensate for the absence of profit-sharing plans at these organizations. Many such plans permit investments in mutual funds or annuities.

457 plan Named after the Internal Revenue Code section 457, this plan is a tax-deferred supplemental retirement program that allows public employees to defer the lesser of $8,000 for 1999 or 25%

of their salary before taxes to a retirement account. The amount saved is tax-deferred until the participants' funds are distributed to them upon separation from service. There is no penalty for receiving a benefit before age 59½.

Freddie Mac The pronounced acronym (FHLMC) for the Federal Home Loan Mortgage Corporation; it operates similarly to Fannie Mae.

front-end load The sales commission charged at the time of purchase of a mutual fund, insurance policy, or other product.

full-service broker A brokerage firm that maintains a research department and other services to supply its individual and institutional customers with investment advice.

funds from operations (FFO) A performance measure for Real Estate Investment Trusts (REITs). This is net income plus depreciation less the gains from the sale of property or securities.

futures contract An agreement to buy or sell a certain amount of a commodity (such as wheat, soybeans, or gold) or a financial instrument (such as Treasury bills or deutsche marks) at a stipulated price in a specified future month, which may be as much as nine months away. As the actual price moves closer to or further away from the contract price, the price of the contract fluctuates up and down, thus creating profits and losses for its holders, who may never actually take or make delivery of the underlying commodity.

generation-skipping transfer tax A tax imposed upon transfers, whether direct or by trust distribution, to any person more than one generation below the generation of the person making the transfer. The tax is imposed at highest federal estate tax rate. Each transferor is entitled to transfer $1,000,000 exempt from the generation-skipping tax. Exemption must be carefully allocated between "exempt shares" and "non-exempt shares" in large trusts. The purpose of the tax is to ensure taxation of family wealth at the death of each generation.

gift A voluntary transfer of property from one person to another. Gifts can be given while you are still living or after your death through your will.

gift tax A tax on lifetime gift transfers designed to complement the federal estate tax system. Lifetime gifts are applied first against the $650,000 (for 1999) federal estate and gift tax exemption; gifts in excess of this amount begin to generate gift tax at the same rates as are applicable under the federal estate tax. An exclusion from gift tax exists for gifts of up to $10,000 per person to any one person during a single calendar year. A couple, giving a joint gift, can give a total of $20,000 to each individual per year. Amounts above these are subject to the gift tax.

Ginnie Mae The pronounced acronym (GNMA) for the Government National Mortgage Association, a government corporation that sells securities backed by GNMA. A Ginnie Mae fund is one that invests in these securities. Warning: with Ginnie Maes, the effective average maturity is uncertain, because people can pay off their mortgages early if they move or refinance at a lower rate.

good-till-canceled order An order to buy or sell a security at a specified price, which stays in effect until it is executed by the broker at that price or until it is canceled by the customer.

grace period The period of time between the premium due date and the policy lapse date.

Gross Domestic Product The total market value of all final goods and services produced in the U.S. in a given year. It is calculated as the total of consumer, investment, and government spending, plus the value of exports minus the value of imports.

group insurance A contract made with an employer or an association that covers a group of persons related to that association.

growth fund A mutual fund that seeks capital appreciation, that is, to make its shareholders' capital grow over time by investing primarily in stocks that increase in value. Dividends are a minor consideration.

growth and income fund A mutual fund that seeks to make its shareholders' capital grow and also to provide income. There can be wide variations in the relative emphasis on these two objectives.

guaranty laws Laws enacted by states to protect investors, annuitants, beneficiaries, and policyholders against financial losses due to insurance company insolvency.

guardian A person who has the responsibility to care for a minor or an incompetent adult or to control the property of such an individual, or both.

heir Person who inherits property.

HH savings bond A security offered by the U.S. government that can be purchased only by trading in Series EE bonds at maturity. This bond is sold in amounts from $500 to $10,000. It may be redeemed after only six months and the interest is exempt from state and local taxes. Also known as Series HH bonds.

income In mutual fund parlance, the money paid as stock dividends or bond interest. An income distribution is a return to shareholders of income paid on the underlying holdings of a fund. Income funds concentrate on earning interest or dividends, rather than increasing share prices.

indenture of trust A trust in which a person or organization other than the donor serves as trustee.

index A benchmark against which financial or economic performance is measured. **index fund** A passively managed mutual fund intended to produce the same returns as investors would get from investing in all the stocks in a specific index.

Index of Leading Economic Indicators An index compiled by The Conference Board (a private organization) composed of weighted reports from various sources and published monthly to provide some insights into possible future business conditions in the country over the next six to twelve months.

Individual Retirement Account (IRA) A tax-sheltered account ideal for retirement investing because it permits investment earnings to accumulate tax-deferred until they are withdrawn. Penalties usually apply for withdrawals before age 59½. The contribution limit is $2,000 per year.

inflation The rate at which prices in general are going up, usually quoted on an annualized basis. The consumer price index (CPI) tracks many consumer goods; the producer price index (PPI) tracks many industrial goods and materials. Inflation is a decrease in the value of money and is thought generally to result from an increase in the supply of money (both actual dollar bills in circulation and readily spendable money, such as checking accounts).

initial public offering (IPO) A corporation's first public offering of an issue of stock.

institutional investors Mutual funds, banks, insurance companies, pension plans, and others that buy and sell stocks and bonds in large volumes. Institutional investors account for 70% or more of market share volume on an average day.

intangible personal property Assets that document and represent an interest in assets of value. Examples of intangible personal property: currency, stock certificates, partnership interests, bonds, other securities, and certain trust instruments. Contrast with *tangible personal property*.

inter vivos trust A trust created while you are still living. (The Latin words "inter vivos" mean "among the living.")

interest The compensation that a borrower pays a lender for the use of the money borrowed.

interest rate The interest payable each year expressed as a percentage of the principal.

intestate The situation of a person who dies without leaving a valid will.

investment company An arrangement by which investors pool their assets into a corporation or trust that employs professional management to invest the assets according to a stated objective. Mutual funds are one form of investment company.

IRA *Individual Retirement Account*

irrevocable trust A trust over which the donor retains no rights to amend the trust, withdraw trust assets, or control the administration or distribution of trust assets. A trust that you cannot change or cancel. Irrevocable trusts are normally used for gift transactions and allow protective management of gifted assets for trust beneficiaries.

issue Any descendants of an individual by blood. Issue includes the individual's children, grandchildren, great-grandchildren, and so forth, but not the spouses of any of these descendants.

joint tenants in common Ownership of an asset shared by two or more people, with the interest of any owner, upon death, becoming part of that person's estate.

joint tenants with rights of survivorship (JTWROS) Ownership of an asset shared by two or more people, with the interest of any owner, upon death, passing to the surviving co-owners.

junk bond A high-risk, high-yield bond rated BB or lower by Standard & Poor's or Ba or lower by Moody's. Junk bonds are issued either by relatively unknown or financially weak companies or by reasonably solvent companies but with only limited backing.

Keogh plan A tax-sheltered retirement plan into which self-employed individuals can deposit up to 25% of earnings and deduct the contributions from current income. Investments within the Keogh grow tax deferred until they are withdrawn. Withdrawals from the plan are restricted before age 59½.

large-cap Term describing a corporation with over $5 to 10 billion in capitalization.

leading indicator An economic indicator that changes before the economy changes (as opposed to *coincident indicator* or *lagging indicator*). Examples of leading indicators: stock prices, money supply, unemployment insurance claims, inventory changes, and building permits.

legacy A gift of property by will. Same as *bequest*.

letter of instructions A memorandum of personal details that should be attached to your will, with a copy to your executor and one for you so that it may be kept up to date. The letter of instructions should include such information as location of the will, location of vital documents, location of assets, employment or business information, and funeral and burial instructions.

leveraging Investing with borrowed money in the hope of multiplying gains. If you buy stock for $100,000 and its price rises to $110,000, you've earned 10% on your investment. But if you leveraged the deal by putting up only $50,000 of your own money and borrowing the rest, the same $10,000 increase would represent a 20% return on your money, not counting interest on the loan. But if the price of the stock goes down by $5,000, your loss would be 10% of the money you put up and you'd still have to pay back the $50,000 loan and pay interest.

liability Something owed; any form of indebtedness for which an individual, family, or a business is legally liable. The opposite of an asset.

liability insurance Insurance on a home and/or motor vehicle that protects the owner in case of injuries caused by or on the insured property.

limited partnership A business arrangement put together and managed by a general partner (either a company or an individual) and financed by the investments of limited partners, so called because their liability is limited to the amount of money they invest in the venture. Limited partnerships can invest in virtually anything. They have often been characterized by high fees for the general partners, complicated tax reporting requirements, and elusive payouts for the limited partners.

limit order An order to buy or sell a security if it reaches a specified price. A stop-loss order is a common variation.

liquidity (financial) The flow of money that drives any economy, whether personal, regional, national, or global.

liquidity (investments) The ability to quickly convert an investment to cash.

Stocks and bonds of widely traded companies are considered highly liquid, while real estate and limited partnerships are illiquid.

liquidity crisis The situation of an economy when the amount of money coming in cannot cover current bills and interest.

living trust Trust created by an individual to be effective during his or her lifetime. The property is placed in the hands of a trustee to manage for the benefit of one or more individuals. May be *irrevocable* or *revocable*.

living will A document stating the maker's intention regarding extraordinary lifesaving measures that may or may not be taken to prolong the maker's existence.

load *Sales load* or *sales charge*.

load mutual fund An open-end investment company that charges a fee when an investor buys the fund shares.

long-term care insurance Insurance that provides coverage for the care needed for individuals with chronic disabilities.

marital deduction The amount of property that can be left to a spouse tax-free. The Economic Recovery Act of 1981 permits an unlimited marital deduction.

marital trust A trust qualifying as a bequest actually passing to the surviving spouse and therefore qualifying for the estate tax marital deduction. Examples of marital trusts are qualified terminable interest property (QTIP) trusts and general power of appointment trusts.

margin buying Financing the purchase of

securities partly with money borrowed from the brokerage firm. Regulations permit buying up to 50% "on margin," meaning that an investor can borrow up to half the purchase price of an investment. See *leveraging*.

market maker A brokerage or bank that maintains a firm bid and ask price in a particular security by being ready, willing, and able to buy or sell at publicly quoted prices. This is called *making a market*.

maturity date The date on which the principal of a note, draft, acceptance, bond, or other debt instrument becomes due and payable. Also, the termination or due date on which an installment loan must be paid in full. Also known as *maturity*.

micro-cap Term describing a corporation with under $250 million in capitalization.

mid-cap Term describing a corporation with $1 to 5 billion in capitalization.

money market The markets in which short-term obligations are traded. Short-term obligations are relatively stable assets, such as commercial paper; certificates of deposit (CDs), bankers' acceptances, and U.S. government and agency obligations.

money market fund A mutual fund that invests in short-term corporate and government debt and passes the interest payments on to shareholders. A key feature of money-market funds is that their market value doesn't change, which makes them an ideal place to earn current market interest with a high degree of liquidity.

municipal bond A debt issued by a state,

territory, or possession of the U.S. or by any municipality or other political subdivision. The interest earned is usually free of federal and state tax.

mutual fund An open-end investment company. Its portfolio is managed; that is, it buys or sells securities according to changing conditions. It sells new shares on a continuous basis and buys back (redeems) outstanding shares. Buy and sell prices are equal to the fund's net asset value (NAV) plus sales and redemption charges, if any. Contrasts with *closed-end investment company*.

NASDAQ The computerized National Association of Securities Dealers Automated Quotation System that provides price quotations of securities traded *over the counter*.

National Association of Purchasing Managment Report (NAPM Report) A report based on a monthly survey of 250 purchasing managers by their national association, which reports any changes in new orders, production levels, prices, inventories, vendor performance, and employment.

National Association of Securities Dealers (NASD) Association of brokers/dealers in over-the-counter securities organized on a nonprofit, non-stock-issuing basis. Its general aim is to protect investors in the OTC market. The NASD also registers stockbrokers as qualified to handle securities trades.

National Credit Union Administration (NCUA) Organization that insures accounts in federally chartered credit unions up to a maximum of $100,000.

Negotiable Order of Withdrawal Account (NOW Account) A checking account that earns interest or, viewed another way, a savings account on which checks can be written. Savings banks, savings and loan associations, commercial banks, and credit unions were permitted to offer NOW accounts starting in 1981.

net asset value (NAV) per share A fund's assets (securities and cash) less its liabilities, divided by the number of shares outstanding. Also called the "bid" price. The net asset value is the buying and selling price of shares in a no-load fund.

net worth What a person owns minus what he or she owes.

New York Stock Exchange (NYSE) The oldest and largest stock exchange in the U.S., located on Wall Street in New York City. The exchange provides the facilities for trading and is responsible for setting policy, listing securities, supervising member activities, overseeing the transfer of member seats, and evaluating applicants.

no-load mutual fund An open-end investment company that allows investors to buy and sell fund shares without paying a fee when the shares first are purchased.

non-exempt trust A trust to which none of the donor's generation-skipping transfer tax exemption has been allocated.

nonqualified retirement plan A retirement plan that does not meet the Internal Revenue Service requirements for favorable tax treatment.

NYSE *New York Stock Exchange.*

odd lot Any number of shares less than a round lot. (A round lot is usually 100 shares.)

Old Age, Survivors, and Dependents Insurance (OASDI) Half of Social Security, with Medicare.

open-end investment company A company that buys and sells shares according to changing conditions. See *mutual fund.*

opportunity cost The cost of passing up one investment in favor of another. For instance, if you pull money out of an investment that is earning 7% to invest it in a stock that has promise but yields just 4%, your opportunity cost while you're waiting for better times is 3%.

option The right to buy or sell a security at a given price within a given time. Investors who expect the price of the security to rise buy the right to buy (a *call* option). Investors who expect the price of the security to fall buy the right to sell (a *put* option). The specified price is called the *strike price.* Investors use puts and calls to bet on the direction of price movements without actually having to buy or sell the security. Options are used for stocks, commodities, currencies, indices, and debts. For stock, one option represents 100 shares and sells for a fraction of the price of the shares themselves. As the time approaches for the option to expire, its price will move up or down, depending on the movement of the stock price. Options can also be used to wring a little income out of a security you own without selling it. By writing (selling) a *covered call,* you collect the premium and, assuming the price stays under the call price, get to keep the stock. The risk, of course, is that the security will get called away and you will miss out on the price rise.

over the counter (OTC) The place where stocks and bonds that aren't listed on any exchange (such as the New York or American stock exchanges) are bought and sold. Despite the small-stock, small-town image conjured up by its name, in reality the OTC market is a high-speed computerized network called NASDAQ, which is run by the National Association of Securities Dealers.

par The stated or face value of a bond; the amount that will be paid when the bond matures.

par value In bonds, the face value. In stocks, an arbitrary value assigned primarily for bookkeeping purposes.

P/E ratio *Price/earnings ratio.*

penny stock Generally thought of as a recently issued stock selling for less than $5 a share and traded *over the counter*. Penny stocks are usually issued by small, relatively unknown companies and lightly traded, making them more prone to price manipulation than larger, better-established issues. They are, in short, a gamble.

point (bonds) Percentage change of the face value of a bond expressed as a point. For example, a change of 1% is a move of one point. Each point is worth $10 for a bond with a $1000 face value and $50 for a bond with a $5000 face value. Bond yields are quoted in basis points: 100 basis points make up 1% of yield.

point (real estate and other commercial lending) Up-front fee charged by the lender, separate from interest but designed to increase the overall yield to the lender. A point is 1% of the principal of the loan. For example, on a $100,000 mortgage loan, a charge of 3 points would mean $3000.

point (stocks) Change of $1 in the market price of a stock. If a stock rises 5 points, the price per share is up by $5.

point (stock market averages) Unit of movement for stock market averages, (such as the Dow Jones Industrial Average) which are composites of weighted dollar values.

policy loan A loan made by an insurance company to a policy owner, who uses the cash value of the insurance policy as collateral.

policy owner A person who owns an insurance contract.

power of appointment A right or power given to a person under a will or trust, specifically limited by its terms, to choose the recipients of property subject to the power. A general power of appointment allows the power holder to appoint the assets to any person or organization, including himself or herself, his or her estate, his or her creditors, or creditors of his or her estate.

power of attorney A legal document by which a person authorizes somebody to conduct his or her financial affairs.

PPI *Producer Price Index.*

preexisting condition A physical condition that existed prior to the effective date of the policy.

preferred stock Stock on which a company promises to pay fixed dividends. Because of this promise, preferred stock is really more like a bond than common stock. However, the promise is not absolute; preferred stockholders, unlike bondholders, cannot force a company into bankruptcy court to pay the dividends. The promise is backed only by the fact that a company cannot pay any dividend to the holders of its common stock until it has paid the fixed dividend to the holders of the preferred stock.

premium (bonds) The amount above the list price or face value of a bond.

premium (insurance) The price of insurance protection. In general, the net premium for life insurance equals the mortality expense *plus* the administrative and marketing expenses *minus* expected earnings from investments.

preservation of capital An investment objective for some funds and investors (usually paired with some income). The aim is not merely to keep the same nominal amount of capital, but to keep the capital growing at least at the rate of inflation.

price/earnings ratio (P/E) The price of a stock divided by either its latest annual earnings per share (a "trailing" P/E) or its predicted earnings (an "anticipated" P/E). Either way, the P/E is considered an important indicator of investor sentiment about a stock, because it indicates how much investors are willing to pay for a dollar of earnings.

primary beneficiary The first person who is entitled to receive benefits from an insurance policy or a retirement account.

prime rate The loan rate that banks advertise as their best rate, that is, available to their best customers.

principal The capital value of an investment, as opposed to the interest or dividends that it pays. Also, the amount of a debt, as opposed to the interest paid on the debt.

probate The process of proving the validity of the will in court and executing its provisions under the guidance of the court.

Producer Price Index (PPI) An index that measures changes in the cost of wholesale goods, published monthly by the U.S. Bureau of Labor. The PPI tends to forecast changes in the Consumer Price Index (CPI) before they occur, so it is a leading indicator that is watched carefully.

program trading A complex computerized system designed to take advantage of temporary differences between the actual value of the stocks composing a popular index and the value represented by futures contracts. Computer programs issue orders to sell stocks and buy futures contracts or to buy stocks and sell the futures, depending on which prices are lower. The result is virtually risk-free profits for the program traders and more volatility for the market because of the vast numbers of shares needed to make the system work.

property Anything owned of value, including cash, securities, real estate, and any other possessions.

prospectus The document that describes

a securities offering or the operations of a mutual fund, a limited partnership, or other investment. The prospectus divulges financial data about the company, the background of its officers, and other information needed by investors to make an informed decision. Required by the SEC.

proxy A document requesting shareholders of a stock or a mutual fund to vote on proposed changes to management, fees, or operations. The proxy card instructs management on how the represented shares should be voted on the proposals.

proxy statement Material information that the Securities and Exchange Commission requires a corporation to give to its stockholders as a prerequisite to solicitation of votes. It is required for any issuer subject to the provisions of the Securities Exchange Act of 1934.

publicly held Term applied to any corporation whose shares are traded according to the rules of either the Securities and Exchange Commission or the New York Stock Exchange.

qualified retirement plan A plan that meets the requirements of Internal Revenue Code Section 401(a) and is thus eligible for favorable tax treatment.

qualified domestic trust (QDOT) A type of trust very similar to a *qualified terminable interest property (QTIP)* trust except that it is used when the surviving spouse is not a U.S. citizen. A QDOT must have at least one trustee who is a U.S. citizen. No distributions other than income may be made from this trust unless the trustee has the right to withhold any additional estate tax imposed on the trust.

That is, the spouse cannot access any of the assets without the approval of the trustee, who is then personally liable for the tax imposed.

qualified terminable interest property (QTIP) trust A type of trust that will qualify either as a marital or as a credit shelter trust, depending on whether the decedent's executor elects to qualify the trust as a marital trust. By this arrangement, the surviving spouse has a right to the income from the principal for life, but no access to the principal. On the death of the surviving spouse, the property goes to such person(s) or organizations(s) as determined by the spouse who instructed the trust to be set up.

rating service A company that publishes credit ratings for investments or insurance companies, such as Morningstar, Standard & Poor's, or Moody's.

Real Estate Investment Trust (REIT) A publicly traded company, rather like a closed-end mutual fund, except that it invests directly in real estate properties, rather than stocks and bonds.

receipt A written acknowledgment that grants legal validation to a repayment of all or part of a debt.

redemption Sale of mutual fund shares by a shareholder back to the fund.

registered representative The formal name for a stockbroker, because he or she must be registered with the National Association of Securities Dealers as qualified to handle securities trades.

reinvestment plan Use of fund distributions to purchase additional shares rather than receive distributions in cash. Most fund companies do not charge sales loads on reinvestments, unless the distributions are redirected to a fund with a higher sales load.

REIT *Real Estate Investment Trust.*

residuary Property left in your estate after payment of your debts and distribution of specific bequests.

rest, residue and reminder Wording commonly used in wills for disposing of the balance of the estate after specific bequests have been made. If a prior bequest fails for lack of a beneficiary, the bequest is said to "fall into the residue of the estate" and passes to the beneficiaries under the "residuary clause" of the will.

return on equity (ROE) A measure of a company's use of reinvested earnings to generate additional earnings. ROE is fiscal year after-tax income (calculated after dividends on preferred stock but before dividends on common stock) divided by book value, expressed as a percentage.

return on investment (ROI) A measure of a corporation's profitability, equal to fiscal year income divided by common stock and preferred stock equity plus long-term debt.

reverse mortgage Transaction that enables retirees to cash in on the increased value of their homes by borrowing against the increased value. The concept of a reverse mortgage was approved in 1978 by the Federal Home Loan Bank Board, which regulates federally chartered savings and loan associations.

revocable trust A trust over which the

donor has retained the right to revoke the trust, withdraw any assets, or amend the trust at any time. Revocable trusts are funded while the donor is living, as a way to avoid probate costs after his or her death.

ROE *Return on equity.*

ROI *Return on investment.*

round lot 100 shares of a stock

rule of 72 A means of calculating the time needed to double an investment at a given rate of compounding or the rate needed to double an investment in a given time. To determine the number of years at a given rate, divide the rate into 72. For example, to double at 6% would take 12 years (72 ÷ 6 = 12). To determine the rate for a given number of years, divide the years into 72. For example, to double in 8 years would take 9% (72 ÷ 8 = 9).

S&P 500 Standard & Poor's benchmark indicator of 500 stocks, an index that is often used as a standard against which money managers measure their performance. Because the index is weighted by market capitalization, it is primarily composed of large capitalization companies.

sales load or sales charge The amount paid in order to purchase mutual fund shares. The charge is a percentage of the total amount invested. For example, if $1,000 is invested in a fund with a 3% sales charge, the load is $30 and the net amount invested is $970. Often simply called a load.

Sallie Mae The pronounced acronym (SLMA) for the Student Loan Marketing Association, which buys student loans from colleges, universities, and other lenders and packages them into units to be sold to investors. Sallie Mae thus infuses the student-loan market with new money in much the same way as Ginnie Mae infuses the mortgage market with new money.

savings bond A registered, non-callable, non-transferable bond issued by the U.S. Government and backed by its full faith and credit. The face values range from $50 to $10,000. Savings bonds come in two series, EE and HH.

SEC *Securities and Exchange Commission.*

secondary market The general name given to stock exchanges, the over-the-counter market, and other marketplaces in which stocks, bonds, mortgages, and other investments are bought and sold after they have been issued and sold initially. Original issues are sold in the primary market; subsequent sales take place in the secondary market. For example, the primary market for a new issue of stock is the team of underwriters; the secondary market is one of the stock exchanges or the over-the-counter market. The primary market for a mortgage is the lender, which may then sell it to Fannie Mae or Freddie Mae in the secondary market.

sector A distinct area of the economy or an industry, such as utilities or computers.

Securities and Exchange Commission (SEC) A government agency responsible for supervising and regulating the securities industry.

Securities Investor Protection Corporation (SIPC) Formed by the Securities Investor Protection Act of 1970, a government-sponsored, private, non-profit corporation that guarantees repayment of money and securities to customers in amounts up to $100,000 of cash or $500,000 of securities per customer in the event of broker/dealer bankruptcy.

security A certificate (or a book entry) used as evidence of debt or ownership of property, especially bond or stock certificates. More generally, the term "securities" means stocks or bonds.

settlement date The date on which money or securities are due once securities have been bought or sold.

share A unit of measurement of the equity ownership of a corporation or a mutual fund.

Sharpe Ratio A number measuring the reward-to-risk efficiency (volatility vs. return) of an investment. The ratio compares beta with return of the fund compared with the return of Treasury bills.

short selling A technique used to take advantage of an anticipated decline in the price of a stock or other security by reversing the usual order of buying and selling. In a short sale, the investor borrows stock from the broker and immediately sells it. Then, if the investor guessed right and the price of the stock declines, he or she can replace the borrowed shares by buying them at the lower price. The profit is the difference between the price at which the investor sells the shares and the price at which he or she later buys them. Of course, if the price of the shares rises, the investor will suffer a loss.

sinking fund Financial reserves set aside to be used exclusively to redeem a bond or preferred stock issue and thus reassure investors that the company will be able to meet that obligation.

small-cap Term describing a corporation with under $1 billion in capitalization.

specialist A member of the stock exchange who serves as a market maker for a number of different stock issues. A specialist maintains an inventory of certain stocks and buys and sells shares as necessary to maintain an orderly market for those stocks.

spray trust A trust held for the benefit of more than one beneficiary, with the trustee authorized to "spray" income and/or principal among the beneficiaries. Spray trusts allow shifting of income among family members to obtain the benefit of a lower marginal tax rate. Sometimes called a "sprinkle trust."

spread The difference between the bid and ask prices of a security. (Also called the broker's markup.) In options and futures trading, a spread is the practice of simultaneously buying a contract for the delivery of a commodity in one month and selling a contract for delivery of the same commodity in another month. The aim is to offset possible losses in one contract with possible gains in the other.

stock split An increase in a corporation's number of outstanding shares of stock without any change in the shareholders' equity. For example, if you own 100 shares of IBM valued at $50 each and IBM announces a 2-for-1 split, you will own 200 shares valued at $25 each.

stop-loss order Instructions to a broker to sell a particular stock if its price ever dips to a specified level. A common variation on a *limit order*.

street name The description given to securities held in the name of a brokerage firm but belonging to the firm's customers. Holding stocks in a street name facilitates trading because there is no need for the customer to pick up or deliver the certificates.

successor guardian An additional guardian listed in a will or trust, who can assume the responsibilities of guardian in case the first guardian dies or is otherwise unable to perform the duties of a guardian.

successor trustee An additional trustee listed in a will or trust, who can assume the responsibilities of trustee in case the first trustee dies or is otherwise unable to perform the duties of a trustee.

take a bath Slang, meaning to incur a large loss.

tangible personal property Wording commonly used in wills to refer to the personal effects and belongings of the testator. Examples of tangible personal property include furniture and furnishings, automobiles, clothing, jewelry, and other movable, tangible goods in general. Contrast with *intangible personal property*.

taxable income The adjusted gross income (AGI) minus personal exemptions and itemized or standard deduction. This is the figure on which you calculate your tax.

10-K A detailed financial report that must

be filed by a firm each year with the Securities and Exchange Commission. It has much more detail than an annual report.

tender offer An offer to shareholders to buy their shares of stock in a company. Tender offers are usually a key element of a strategy to take over or buy out a company and thus are usually made at a price higher than market to encourage shareholders to accept them.

term insurance Life insurance policy that does not build up cash value. It is written for a specified period of time and expires at the end of that period.

term insurance (convertible) Term life insurance policy that can be changed to a cash value policy.

term insurance (decreasing) Term life insurance policy whose face amount will decrease.

term insurance (group) Term life insurance policy providing protection for a number of people under a single policy.

term insurance (increasing) Term life insurance policy whose face amount periodically increases.

term insurance (level) Term life insurance policy whose face amount remains level for a stated amount of time.

term insurance (renewable) Term life insurance policy that can be renewed, before it expires, without a medical examination.

testate The state of having made and left a valid will.

testator or testatrix A man or a woman who makes out a will.

tip A suggestion as to what to buy or sell that is based on "inside" information. Buyer beware!

total return The most meaningful measure of investment performance, indicating how much an investment has grown. Total return is calculated by adding yield (dividends or interest) to capital appreciation.

Totten trust A bank account that is payable on death. Established without a written trust agreement, the Totten trust (also known as a "payable-on-death" or "POD" account) is technically not a trust, but rather a permitted asset or a beneficiary form of bank account ownership. The trustee deposits his or her own money into the account, then retains ownership of the account but holds it in a revocable trust for a named beneficiary. Upon the death of the trustee, the beneficiary may claim the balance in the account. Any beneficiary designated must be the owner's spouse, child, or grandchild, and must be designated by name in the account records of the depository institution. The title of the account must include a term such as "in trust for [beneficiary]" or "payable-on-death to [beneficiary]."

Treasury Any negotiable U.S. government debt obligation, backed by its full faith and credit. The obligations come in three types, which vary in maturity: bills, notes, and bonds. The interest is exempt from state and local taxes.

Triple Witching Hour The last hour of stock market trading on the third Friday of

March, June, September, and December. That's when options and futures contracts expire on market indexes used by program traders to hedge their positions in stocks. The simultaneous expirations often set off heavy buying and selling of options, futures, and the underlying stocks. This term was made popular by *program trading*.

trust Property held and managed by a person (trustee) for the benefit of another (the beneficiary). The terms of the trust are generally governed by a formal legal arrangement that the grantor prepared when establishing the trust.

trustee Person or organization entrusted to manage, administer, and distribute the trust for the benefit of the trust beneficiaries, in strict compliance with the terms of the document. Trustees are held to a high fiduciary duty to be loyal to the beneficiaries and reasonable in investing and making distributions to trust beneficiaries.

12b-1 fee An extra fee charged by some mutual funds to cover the costs of promotion and marketing. In practice, 12b-1 fees are often used to compensate brokers for selling low-load and no-load funds. The effect of the fee is reflected in the performance figures reported by the funds.

umbrella liability insurance Insurance that extends liability coverage on a home or a motor vehicle. Umbrella insurance is typically available in $1 million increments and costs about $100 to $200 for each million of coverage.

unified credit See *unified tax credit*.

unified credit exemption The amount of assets that a person can give away, either while living or through a will without incurring a federal estate or gift tax. The limit is $650,000 for 1999 and will rise incrementally to reach $1 million by the year 2006.

unified tax credit An estate tax credit that can be deducted from the federal estate or gift tax to offset the first $240,500 of federal estate or gift taxes incurred on any transfer or services of transfers. Up to $650,000 may be transferred at death or during your lifetime and the entire amount of the transfers will be sheltered from tax by the unified credit. Taxable gifts are gifts in excess of the annual $10,000 gift tax exclusion for gifts to any single beneficiary. (These figures are for 1999 and are scheduled to rise.)

Uniform Gifts to Minors Act (UGMA) account Account set up for a minor, with an adult designated as custodian of the property for the minor, who is the legal owner of the property, pays taxes on earnings generated by the property, and has an unrestricted right to use it upon reaching the age of majority (18 to 21, depending on the state).

U.S. Treasury Bill (T-bills) Security that matures in three, six, or 12 months and is backed by the full faith and credit of the U.S. government. The T-bill pays an attractive yield that is exempt from state and local income taxes but subject to federal income taxes. It is sold at a discount from its $10,000 face value.

U.S. Treasury Bond Security that matures in ten or more years and is backed by the full faith and credit of the U.S. government. The bond pays a fixed rate of interest twice a year throughout ownership. The interest is exempt from state and local income taxes but subject to federal income taxes. It is sold at face value.

U.S. Treasury Inflation-Indexed Bond 10-year Treasury bond that provides protection against inflation, because the principal amount of the bond changes according to inflation, while the interest rate remains constant. The first auction of 10-year notes took place in January 1997.

U.S. Treasury Note Security that matures in two to ten years and is backed by the full faith and credit of the U.S. government. The interest is exempt from state and local income taxes but subject to federal income taxes. The minimum investment is $5,000 for a two- to four-year note and $1,000 for a four- to ten-year note.

universal life A cash value life insurance policy that provides adjustable benefits and flexibility in premium payments.

unlimited marital deduction The amount of property that can be left to a spouse tax-free, as established by the Economic Recovery Act of 1981.

variable life A cash value life insurance policy that allows the owner to determine the investment selection.

volatility The degree of risk in an investment. A standard measurement of market volatility is the beta coefficient.

ward A person incapable of managing personal affairs and for whom a court has appointed a guardian.

warrant A certificate giving the holder the right to purchase securities at a predetermined price; warrants are written directly by the issuing company.

wash sale A sale of an investment to register a tax loss, followed within 31 days by a repurchase of the same investment. IRS will disallow tax loss.

whole life A life insurance policy with a savings component.

World Equity Benchmark Shares (WEBS) Index funds that track the performance of a specific country's major equity market index. These securities are traded on the American Stock Exchange, where they are listed as WEBS, by country. They offer fast and economical access to international equity markets but, as with single-country funds, they are volatile.

will A legal document, almost always in writing and properly executed, that describes how a person wants his or her property distributed after death and designates a person or an institution to be responsible for executing the terms of the will.

yield Income from an investment in the form of dividends or interest. It does not include capital appreciation or depreciation.

yield to maturity The yield of a bond, including the premium or discount of the bond amortized annually to maturity.

zero-coupon bonds Bonds bought at a discount to their face value that pay no interest until they mature. Although they make no cash distributions, the owner is liable for taxes on the income every year.

Index

About the Authors

Dee Lee CFP, heads up Harvard Financial Educators located in Harvard, Massachusetts. Her firm, which does financial workshops across the country, focuses on educating and motivating the financial consumer to take action regarding their finances. Dee has a passion for educating the financial consumer, and she is committed to helping them understand the nuts and bolts of financial planning.

Dee is a Certified Financial Planner, and a Registered Investment Advisor with the state of Massachusetts. She received her MBA from Simmons College. She dissolved her successful financial planning practice for individuals so that she could devote all of her energies to educating the financial consumer. Dee is a member of the Institute of Certified Financial Planners and serves on the national Board of Directors for the Institute.

She interacts with the readers of the *Sunday Boston Herald* through her weekly column, answering their personal finance questions. She contributes regularly to Brill.com, an interactive mutual fund site and for *Lamaze Family* magazine, where she helps young families solve their financial planning dilemmas. Dee also co-authored *The Complete Idiot's Guide to 401(k) Plans*, an essential resource book for 401(k) plan participants.

David Caruso is a Certified Financial Planner practicing in Manchester-By-The-Sea, Massachusetts. He has been in the investment business since 1980 and is currently a Senior Vice President of a major Wall Street Firm. With his almost two decades of experience Dave has spent his career trying to educate, motivate, and humor consumers and clients about the proper way to handle their money. He's done this through his news experience, television and radio shows, personal newsletter, seminars, and college course teachings. He has also commented or written many articles in publications like *The Boston Herald, The Boston Globe, The Boston Business Journal, Parenting, Medical Economics*, and *Banker & Tradesman*.

Currently managing over $100 Million for clients he separates fact from fiction when it comes to investing, saving, and spending. His mantra is to get a financial plan that works for each of his client's needs whether they are sophisticated investors or novices. Then he tries to be their "Money Coach" to keep them on track when the market whirlwinds stir up the dust.

Dave has been married to his wife Diane for 15 years and has two small children Alex and Laura. He lives on the North Shore of Boston.